CRIMINAL LAW

Second Edition

By

PETER W. LOW

Hardy Cross Dillard Professor of Law, University of Virginia

BLACK LETTER SERIES®

THOMSON

™

WEST

Mat # 18397978

Black Letter Series and Black Letter Series design appearing on the front cover are registered trademarks used herein under license.

COPYRIGHT © 1984, 1990 WEST PUBLISHING CO.

COPYRIGHT © 2002 By WEST GROUP
        610 Opperman Drive
        P.O. Box 64526
        St. Paul, MN 55164–0526
        1–800–328–9352

ISBN 0–314–25942–2

 TEXT IS PRINTED ON 10% POST CONSUMER RECYCLED PAPER

CRIMINAL LAW

p. 189-223

PUBLISHER'S PREFACE

This "Black Letter" is designed to help a law student recognize and understand the basic principles and issues of law covered in a law school course. It can be used both as a study aid when preparing for classes and as a review of the subject matter when studying for an examination.

Each "Black Letter" is written by experienced law school teachers who are recognized national authorities in the subject covered.

The law is succinctly stated by the authors of this "Black Letter." In addition, the exceptions to the rules are stated in the text. The rules and exceptions have purposely been condensed to facilitate quick and easy recollection. For an in-depth study of a point of law, citations to major student texts are given. In addition, a Text Correlation Chart provides a convenient means of relating material contained in the Black Letter to appropriate sections of the casebook the student is using in his or her law school course.

If the subject covered by this text is a code or code-related course, the code section or rule is set forth and discussed wherever applicable.

FORMAT

The format of this "Black Letter" is specially designed for review. (1) **Text.** First, it is recommended that the entire text be studied and, if deemed necessary, supplemented by the student texts cited. (2) **Capsule Summary.** The Capsule Summary is an abbreviated review of the subject matter which can be used both before and after studying the main body of the text. The headings in the Capsule Summary follow the main text of the "Black Letter." (3) **Table of Contents.** The Table of Contents is in outline form to help you organize the details of the subject and the Summary of Contents gives you a final overview of the materials. (4) **Practice Examination.** The Practice Examination in Appendix B gives you the opportunity of testing yourself with the type of questions asked on an exam and comparing your answer with a model answer.

In addition, a number of other features are included to help you understand the subject matter and prepare for examinations:

Short Questions and Answers: This feature is designed to help you spot and recognize issues in the examination. We feel that issue recognition is a major ingredient in successfully writing an examination.

Perspective: In this feature, the authors discuss their approach to the topic, the approach used in preparing the materials, and any tips on studying for and writing examinations.

Analysis: This feature, at the beginning of each section, is designed to give a quick summary of a particular section to help you recall the subject matter and to help you determine which areas need the most extensive review.

Examples: This feature is designed to illustrate, through fact situations, the law just stated. This, we believe, should help you analytically approach a question on the examination.

Glossary: This feature is designed to refamiliarize you with the meaning of a particular legal term. We believe that the recognition of words of art used in an examination helps you to better analyze the question. In addition, when writing an examination you should know the precise definition of a word of art you intend to use.

We believe that the materials in this "Black Letter" will facilitate your study of a law school course and assure success in writing examinations not only for the course but for the bar examination. We wish you success.

THE PUBLISHER

SUMMARY OF CONTENTS

TABLE OF CONTENTS

PART FOUR: COLLATERAL DEFENSES: JUSTIFICATIONS

CAPSULE SUMMARY OF CRIMINAL LAW

PART ONE: INTRODUCTION

I. GENERAL CONSIDERATIONS

American criminal law is derived from the English common law as received in this country shortly after the Revolution and as developed by American courts and legislatures since then. Perhaps the most important modern influence has been the Model Penal Code, which has inspired legislative reform in more than 30 States in the last 25 years. The criminal law today is a blend of the common law and the Model Penal Code, and hence they both must be studied.

PART TWO: THE DEFINITION OF CRIME

II. THE COMMON LAW

A. Starting the Analysis

Read the definition of the offense carefully.

B. The Actus Reus

Crime requires conduct. The conduct can be an act, an omission where there is a legal duty to act, or possession. Normally, the conduct must occur under prescribed circumstances and sometimes it must cause a prescribed result. The "actus reus" is all of the conduct, circumstances, and results required by the definition of the offense.

C. The Mens Rea

1. Elements of the Mens Rea

"Mens Rea" means the mental state required for crime. Crimes that require mens rea are crimes of specific or general intent. Crimes that do not require mens rea are crimes of strict liability.

a. Specific Intent

There are three kinds of specific intent crimes, all focusing on an actual subjective intent concerning something the defendant did or planned. The first kind requires that the defendant plan some conduct not yet undertaken. The second kind requires that the defendant hope conduct already engaged in will have some specified result. The third kind requires that the defendant know that specified conduct has occurred.

b. General Intent

"General Intent" means either recklessness or negligence. Recklessness focuses on actual awareness of risk that an element of a crime will occur. Negligence refers to situations where the defendant should have been aware of a risk that an element of a crime will occur.

There are many other mens rea terms, the meaning of which is not settled. The best approach is to read each case carefully, and see whether you can translate the court's mens rea talk into one of five concepts: purpose, knowledge, recklessness, negligence, or strict liability.

2. Strict Liability

There are three basic times when strict liability is imposed: public welfare offenses, elements of any crime that do not affect the criminality of the defendant's behavior, and elements of certain sex offenses in certain jurisdictions that do not affect the immorality of the defendant's behavior. There are also other crimes, like felony murder, that impose strict liability.

3. Concurrence of Actus Reus and Mens Rea

The defendant's conduct and mens rea must concur in time. Required results may occur later.

4. Transferred Intent

If the defendant's conduct is designed to harm a particular person, but in fact harms another person in exactly the same way, the defendant's intent will be "transferred" from the first person to the second and the crime will be regarded as having been committed against the second person.

5. The Relation of Motive to Mens Rea

"Motive" means the defendant's objective, goal, or purpose. Proof of motive is usually not essential, but often it is relevant *evidence* of mens rea and it is always relevant to sentencing. Good motives do not exonerate, but sometimes they can establish a defense, e.g., self defense. Sometimes motive can establish guilt, e.g., a specific intent.

D. Actus Reus, Mens Rea, and Proportionality

Two important aspects of the actus reus and mens rea of crimes should be noticed.

1. Corroborative Behavior

The actus reus of a criminal offense ought always to contain enough conduct so as, under the circumstances as they actually exist, to corroborate the mens rea required for the offense.

2. All Criminal Liability is Based Upon Both Subjective and Objective Ingredients

We blame based on a combination of subjective and objective ingredients of behavior. We blame for conduct when people knew enough about what they were doing (subjective) so they should have known better (objective). All levels of measuring mens rea—even strict liability—conform to this observation.

Four principles follow from this:

(1) Strict liability in whatever form is justified only if a criminal conviction can fairly be based on the rest of what the defendant knows.

(2) All criminal liability involves some combination of subjective and objective factors, some combination of subjective knowledge by the defendant and holding the defendant to an objective standard.

(3) It is ok to use negligence and strict liability in the criminal law.

(4) The trick is that the grade and sanction for the offense must be proportional to the combination used for the offense of conduct, subjective inquiry into what the defendant knew, and objective judgment about what the defendant ought to have known.

E. Causation

Result elements must be "caused" by the defendant's behavior. Determining causation requires two steps: cause in fact; and proximate cause.

1. Cause in Fact

The question here is whether the result would have occurred if the defendant had not acted. Where two independent causes operate simultaneously to produce the same result, both are causes in fact.

2. Proximate Cause

The question here is whether the result is a sufficiently direct or foreseeable product of the defendant's conduct such that it is fairly attributable to that conduct. A "dependent" intervening cause is one that is sufficiently foreseeable or sufficiently related to the defendant's conduct so as to make it fair to hold the defendant responsible for the result. An "independent" intervening cause is one that is *not* sufficiently foreseeable or sufficiently related to the defendant's conduct so as to make it fair to hold the defendant responsible for the result. The test takes two steps: (1) What is the difference between what actually happened and what the defendant intended or foresaw?; (2) Does this difference make it unfair or unjust to hold the defendant responsible for the result?

F. Proof of the Elements of Crime

1. Burden of Proof

The term "burden of proof" refers to two quite different ideas that should always be distinguished: having the "burden of production" means you must introduce the first evidence on an issue or lose if you do not; having the "burden of persuasion" means you must persuade the jury on an issue or lose if you do not. There are two standards of proof normally used by the criminal law: beyond a reasonable doubt, and by a preponderance of the evidence. The prosecutor must establish the essential elements of guilt beyond a reasonable doubt. Normally, when the burden of persuasion is placed upon the defendant the standard of proof the defendant must meet is a preponderance of the evidence. Sometimes, the standard is "clear and convincing evidence."

2. The Order of Trial

The prosecutor must first establish a "prima facie case" of guilt. The "prima facie case" is the actus reus, the mens rea, and any required causation. If the prosecutor proves these elements, the case will go to the jury. But the defendant will first have the opportunity to rebut elements of the prosecutor's case or to raise an independent defense.

3. Proof of the Actus Reus

The prosecutor must prove each element of the actus reus beyond a reasonable doubt.

4. Proof of the Mens Rea

The prosecutor must prove each element of the mens rea beyond a reasonable doubt. You should separate *what* must be proved from *how* it may be proved. Both specific and general intent will normally be proved by circumstantial evidence. The presumption of natural and probable consequences complicates matters. Normally it is used only in general intent crimes. It can be read to satisfy the burden of persuasion, to shift the burden of persuasion or the burden of production, or as the basis for a permissive inference.

5. Proof of Causation
The prosecutor must prove all causation elements beyond a reasonable doubt.

III. THE MODEL PENAL CODE

A. Starting the Analysis
Read the definition of the offense carefully.

B. The Actus Reus
All crime requires conduct.

1. Elements of the Actus Reus
Distinguish conduct, result, and circumstance elements.

a. Conduct
The conduct is the required physical activity. It can be an act, an omission where there is a legal duty to act, or possession.

b. Result
A result is any consequence caused by the defendant's conduct.

c. Circumstances
The circumstances are the external conditions that must exist at the time of the conduct.

2. Problems of Interpretation
Be sure to look for definitions of terms whenever you attempt to interpret a provision of the Model Penal Code or any other statute.

3. Problems of Categorization
Normally, it doesn't matter whether you get a Model Penal Code actus reus element into the right category—whether you are right that an element is "conduct," a "result," or a "circumstance." The important thing is be sure that each actus reus element of the offense is separately considered.

The one time under the Model Penal Code where it does matter whether an actus reus element is placed in the right category is in application of the law of attempt. See pages 34–35.

C. The Mens Rea
1. Elements of the Mens Rea
Each is carefully defined.

a. **Purpose**
"Purpose" means "conscious objective or desire" for conduct and result elements, "awareness, belief, or hope" for circumstances.

b. **Knowledge**
"Knowledge" means "awareness" for conduct and circumstances, "awareness of practical certainty" for results.

c. **Recklessness**
The distinctive characteristic of recklessness is that the defendant is actually aware of a risk that the element exists or will result. The jury will determine whether taking the risk was a gross deviation from what a law-abiding person would have done in the situation.

d. **Negligence**
The distinctive characteristic of negligence is that the defendant should be aware of a risk that the element exists or will result. The jury will determine whether failure to perceive the risk was a gross deviation from what a reasonable person would have observed in the situation.

2. **The Analytical Structure**
"Elements" include all conduct, results, and circumstances required by the definition of the offense, by its grading, *and* by any defense. An element is "material" when it is relevant to the harm or evil sought to be prevented by the law defining the offense. The culpability structure applies to all "material elements." Culpability must be separately considered for *each* actus reus element of every offense, grading component, and defense.

3. **Principles of Construction**
a. **No Culpability Provided**
Where the definition of the offense is silent as to culpability, recklessness is required for all material elements.

b. **Culpability Provided**
If there are culpability words in the definition of the offense, the case will be one of two types:

1) **Culpability Designated for One Actus Reus Element**
If a culpability term establishes the mens rea for at least one actus reus element, then that mens rea applies to all actus reus elements, *unless* the grammatical structure of the definition makes it clear that the term was meant to be applied only to a limited number of actus reus elements. In that case, the term applies only to those elements,

and the culpability for the remaining elements is determined by independent application of the rules of construction.

2) Culpability Required in Addition to Actus Reus Elements
If a culpability term establishes some special goal, purpose, or belief with which the defendant must commit the offense, and does *not* describe the mens rea for a particular actus reus element, then it should be temporarily ignored while you ascertain the mens rea for the actus reus elements of the offense. The mens rea for the actus reus elements will be determined by applying the principles of construction outlined above.

4. Additional Mens Rea Provisions
Proof of any *greater* culpability than is required is always sufficient. A purpose that is conditional in nature is still sufficient to establish the mens rea of "purpose," unless the condition negatives the harm or evil sought to be prevented by the definition of the offense. "Wilful" means "knowledge."

5. Strict Liability
The Model Penal Code imposes strict liability for only a very few crimes. Because of the provisions of § 2.02(3), the only way this can be done is by explicit provision in the definition of an offense. Public welfare offenses are treated as violations by the Model Penal Code. Violations are not crimes. The Model Penal Code imposes strict liability for all violations, unless the definition of the offense otherwise provides. Offenses defined outside the criminal code are violations if they impose strict liability. Misdemeanor sanctions can be imposed for violations if negligence is proved as to all elements.

6. Concurrence of Actus Reus and Mens Rea
The defendant's mens rea must concur in time with the conduct and circumstance elements of an offense. Required results may occur later.

7. Transferred Intent
The Model Penal Code does not use the concept of transferred intent. Such cases are treated as presenting problems of causation.

8. The Relevance of Motive
The discussion of motive under the common law is fully applicable to the Model Penal Code.

D. Actus Reus, Mens Rea, and Proportionality
The discussion of this topic on page 3 is fully applicable to the Model Penal Code.

E. Causation
Determining whether conduct has "caused" a result involves two questions: (1) whether the defendant's conduct was an antecedent "but for" which the result

would not have occurred. Concurrent causes qualify as a "but for" cause under this inquiry. (2) whether the following inquiries are satisfied:

1. **Comparison of Actual Result With Designed, Contemplated, or Risked Result**
   Compare the details of the actual result with the details of the result as to which the defendant was culpable. If the only difference is that a different person or different property is harmed, or that a lesser harm has occurred, then the defendant's conduct is the cause of the result. If unexpected factors intervene, but still lead to the same kind of injury or harm as to which the defendant is culpable, the question for the jury is whether the actual result is "too remote or accidental to have a [just] bearing on the actor's liability or on the gravity of his offense."

2. **Strict Liability**
   In strict liability offenses, causation is determined by asking whether the actual result was a probable consequence of the actor's conduct.

F. Proof of the Elements of Crime

The general structure of the trial discussed under this heading in the common law materials is applicable to the Model Penal Code. However, the *content* of what must be proved is quite different. And there are provisions of the Model Code related to proof that should be noted.

1. **Proof Beyond a Reasonable Doubt**
   Unless specific provision is made to the contrary, the prosecutor must prove *all* elements of a crime beyond a reasonable doubt. This includes the actus reus, the mens rea, causation, any grading elements, *and* the absence of any defense.

2. **The Prosecutor's Prima Facie Case**
   The prosecutor's prima facie case under the Model Penal Code is the same as at common law: the actus reus, the mens rea, and any causation requirement.

3. **Defenses and Affirmative Defenses**
   The Model Penal Code distinguishes between defenses and affirmative defenses, but there is no practical difference between them. The defendant bears the burden of production for all defenses and affirmative defenses, and the prosecutor bears the burden of persuasion. The only exception is where a particular provision explicitly shifts the burden of persuasion to the defendant.

4. **Presumptions**
   A "presumed fact" is an element of an offense the proof of which is aided by a presumption. If the prosecutor offers enough proof of the facts giving rise to a presumption to satisfy the beyond a reasonable doubt standard, the judge is

required to submit the presumed fact to the jury, unless satisfied that the evidence as a whole negates the existence of the presumed fact. The judge must then give two charges: (1) that the presumed fact must be proved beyond a reasonable doubt; and (2) that the law permits the jury to regard proof of the facts giving rise to the presumption as sufficient evidence of the existence of the presumed fact.

PART THREE: DERIVATIVE DEFENSES

IV. THE COMMON LAW

A. Introduction
A number of defenses are in effect an effort to rebut an element of the prosecutor's prima facie case.

B. Involuntary Acts
It is a defense if the defendant's conduct did not include an act which was the product of the defendant's choice or will. This defense is quite narrow in scope.

C. Mistake of Fact
1. Specific Intent
An honest mistake is a defense to a specific intent crime if it negates the specific intent.

2. General Intent
An honest and reasonable mistake is a defense to a general intent crime. This rule will apply to the actus reus elements of a specific intent crime if strict liability is not imposed.

3. Strict Liability
A mistake of fact is not a defense if it relates to an element for which strict liability is imposed.

a. Immoral Behavior
A mistake of fact is not a defense if the defendant's conduct would be immoral if the facts were as the defendant believed them to be *and* if the offense concerns sexual behavior.

b. Elements Not Central to the Criminality of Behavior
A mistake of fact is not a defense if the defendant's conduct would be a crime if the facts were as the defendant believed them to be.

D. Mistake of Criminal Law
1. The Paradigm Case
Ignorance or mistake as to whether given conduct is a crime is not a defense. And mistakes about the meaning or application of the words used in the definition of an offense are not a defense *if* the mistaken meaning is one controlled by the *criminal* law.

2. Exception: Interpretation of Mens Rea Terms
Mens rea words have on occasion been interpreted to permit a defense in the case of good faith mistakes about the meaning of the criminal law.

3. Exception: Misled by Official Authority
Some courts have acquitted on grounds of fairness in cases where the defendant made a mistake of criminal law in reliance upon an official statement.

4. Exception: Strict Liability Unfair
Application of the principle that ignorance of the criminal law is not a defense is unacceptable in situations where the context provides no warning signals to the reasonably socialized individual that give the individual a fair opportunity not to become a criminal.

5. Exception: Due Diligence Effort to Ascertain the Law
There is some support for the proposition that a defense should be provided to a person who diligently tries to avoid criminal conduct by learning about the law in advance. Not in very many places, however.

E. Mistake of Non-Criminal Law
A mistake of property law, family law, and the like, can sometimes be a defense.

1. Specific Intent
An honest mistake of non-criminal law is a defense if it negates a specific intent.

2. General Intent
A mistake of non-criminal law is often not a defense to a general intent crime, but the courts disagree. In places where it is not a defense, a premium is placed on being able to distinguish between mistakes of fact and non-criminal law. There is no magical formula for doing so.

F. Intoxication
1. Terminology
Intoxication includes alcohol and drugs. "Voluntary" intoxication is the voluntary introduction of artificial substances into the body which the defendant knows or should know are likely to have intoxicating effects.

2. Admissibility to Negate Actus Reus
Evidence of extreme intoxication would be admissible to show that the defendant did not physically perform the required conduct. Evidence of voluntary intoxication is *not* admissible to show that the defendant did not engage in a voluntary act.

3.   **Admissibility to Negate Specific Intent**
     There are essentially three views: (a) evidence of voluntary intoxication is not
     admissible to negate a specific intent; (b) it is admissible whenever relevant; or
     (c) it is admissible only to show that the defendant lacked *capacity* to form a
     specific intent. The burden of persuasion is on the defendant by a
     preponderance of the evidence in States which follow the latter view.

4.   **Admissibility to Negate General Intent**
     Evidence of voluntary intoxication is inadmissible to negate a general intent.

G.   **Evidence of Mental Disease**
     1.   **Diminished Responsibility Defined**
          The term has three quite different meanings: it refers to the admissibility of
          evidence of mental disease (a) to negate mens rea; (b) to mitigate the grade of
          an offense; or (c) to avoid a capital sentence.

     2.   **Admissibility to Negate Mens Rea**
          The original position was that evidence of mental disease was *not* admissible to
          negate mens rea. Current law spreads across the entire spectrum of
          possibilities. A few States do not admit such evidence on any mens rea
          issue. Some admit it only on mens rea issues in homicide cases. Others admit
          it only to negate a specific intent. Some States limit expert testimony to
          evidence of a recognized mental disease. Some States limit such evidence only
          to proof of lack of capacity to form mens rea.

V.   THE MODEL PENAL CODE

A.   **Introduction**
     You *must* understand the culpability structure to understand the following
     defenses.

B.   **Involuntary Acts**
     The Model Penal Code incorporates essentially the narrow common law notion of
     what constitutes a voluntary act.

C.   **Mistake of Fact**
     1.   **Mistakes That Negate Mens Rea**
          A mistake of fact is a defense if it negates any mens rea requirement of the
          offense.

     2.   **Mistakes That Establish a State of Mind Constituting a Defense**
          A mistake of fact is a defense if it establishes a state of mind that constitutes a
          defense.

3. Grading Elements

Since grading factors require mens rea, a mistake of fact as to a grading factor can be a defense if it negatives the mens rea. *But* if the defendant would be committing a lesser offense on the facts as they were believed to be (as will always be the case with grading factors), the defendant will be convicted of the lesser offense.

D. Mistake of Criminal Law
1. The Paradigm Case

Ignorance or mistake as to whether given conduct constitutes a crime is not a defense. And ignorance or mistake as to the existence, meaning, or application of the law determining the elements of an offense is not a defense.

2. Exception: Where the Definition of the Offense So Provides

If the definition of the offense specifically permits a defense based on ignorance or mistake of the criminal law, then it would be a defense.

3. Exception: Where the Code So Provides

Under § 2.04(3)(a) ignorance of the criminal law is a defense if the law is unknown to the defendant and has not been published or otherwise reasonably made available. Section 2.04(3)(b) contains a list of official sources. A mistake as to the meaning of the criminal law based on one of these sources is a defense if it is not negligently made. The defendant has the burden of persuasion by a preponderance of the evidence on the defenses authorized by § 2.04(3).

E. Mistake of Non-Criminal Law

A mistake of the non-criminal law is a defense if it negates mens rea.

F. Intoxication
1. Terminology

You need to know the meaning of three terms: "intoxication," "self-induced intoxication," and "pathological intoxication."

2. Admissibility

Intoxication is not in itself a defense to crime. But intoxication can be a defense if it disproves the existence of an element of the offense, *except* where intoxication that was not pathological and that was self-induced is offered to negate the awareness required for recklessness.

G. Evidence of Mental Disease

Evidence of mental disease or defect is admissible whenever relevant to establish or rebut a required mens rea element.

PART FOUR: COLLATERAL DEFENSES: JUSTIFICATIONS

VI. THE COMMON LAW

A. Introduction

A "justification" is a defense provided because behavior is affirmatively desirable, or at least ought not to be discouraged by the law. An "excuse" is a defense provided because the defendant is not blameworthy for having engaged in socially undesirable conduct. These terms are theoretically helpful, but have no modern legal significance.

B. Self Defense

A defendant is privileged to use force against another person in self defense when reasonably believed to be necessary to defend against immediate unlawful force employed against the defendant by the other person.

1. Elements of the Defense

If *D* attacks *V* and *V* responds in legitimate self defense, *V*'s force is not "unlawful" and *D* may not respond in self defense. But if *V* responds with excessive force, then *D* may respond in self defense. And if *D,* having attacked *V,* then communicates a withdrawal, *D* may respond in self defense if *V* does not quit. In most jurisdictions, a person may respond to an unlawful arrest with non-deadly force—and with deadly force if the person making the arrest uses deadly force. But the emerging view is that the defendant may not resist an arrest made by a known police officer—unless the police officer uses excessive force.

The defendant may respond only with proportionate force, enough to repel the attack and no more. Deadly force may be used in self defense only in response to deadly force. Retreat is required before deadly force is used in some jurisdictions, but only if the defendant knows that retreat can be accomplished with complete safety. Retreat is not required from the defendant's home and usually not from the defendant's place of work unless the attack is made by a person who also works there.

2. Effect of Mistake

A reasonable mistake of fact does not affect the defense. But if the mistake is unreasonable, the defense is lost. The defendant is then likely to be guilty of murder or assault, although some jurisdictions mitigate a homicide to manslaughter. This is called "imperfect self defense" or "imperfect justification." The ordinary rules governing mistakes of law are applicable.

C. Defense of Others
1. Elements of the Defense

Most jurisdictions permit a defendant to use force in defense of another when reasonably believed to be necessary to protect the other from immediate unlawful force. The rules of self defense are in general applicable to this defense. Some jurisdictions limit the right to defend another by statute to defense of listed persons.

2. Effect of Mistake

Where the rule is stated to require a "reasonable belief," the mistake rules are the same as for self defense. In some jurisdictions, however, liability is strict: the defendant is permitted to defend another only where the other is in fact privileged to act in self defense.

D. Defense of Property

Force may be used when reasonably believed to be necessary to protect real or personal property in the possession of the defendant from imminent and unlawful damage, trespass, or dispossession. The force may be used to prevent this harm before it occurs, or to re-enter real property or, immediately or in hot pursuit, to recapture personal property.

1. Elements of the Defense

Force may not be used if there is time to invoke law enforcement first; or if a request to desist, when practicable, is not first made. Most jurisdictions prohibit the use of deadly force to protect personal property. The old view was that deadly force could be used to protect the home after warning the intruder to stop and not to enter. Most States permit the use of deadly force to stop forcible entry only if the defendant believes that the intruder intends to commit a felony inside. Some States *also* permit the use of deadly force if the threat is to harm some person inside in any manner. Mechanical devices may be used if they are non-deadly, there are warnings, and they are reasonable under the circumstances. They may be deadly in some jurisdictions, but liability is strict.

2. Effect of Mistake

A reasonable mistake does not deny the defense; an unreasonable mistake does; and a mistake of criminal law is irrelevant.

E. Arrest, Escape, and Crime Prevention
1. Use of Force to Make Arrest

A police officer is permitted to use non-deadly force when reasonably believed to be necessary to make a lawful arrest. A private citizen called to help a police officer is equally privileged. A private citizen acting alone can probably use force only when reasonably believed to be necessary to make an arrest for a felony that was in fact committed.

Deadly force is permitted when in justified self defense. And in most jurisdictions when reasonably believed to be necessary to prevent a fleeing felon from escaping arrest, but not to prevent the escape of a fleeing misdemeanant. Some jurisdictions are more restrictive. They allow deadly force only in self defense and only to prevent escape of a person reasonably believed to be dangerous to life or limb.

Deadly force by private persons is probably ok if reasonably believed to be necessary to arrest a person who has committed a felony, and perhaps only a dangerous felony. But the privilege is lost if no felony was committed, no matter how reasonable the belief.

2. Use of Force to Prevent Escape
Force is permitted if and when it would be permitted to arrest the same person.

3. Use of Force to Prevent Crime
A person who reasonably believes a felony or a misdemeanor involving a breach of the peace is being committed or is imminent may use non-deadly force when reasonably believed to be necessary to stop or prevent the crime. The old but still prevailing view is that deadly force may be used to prevent the commission of any felony. The modern and gaining view is that deadly force may only be used to prevent a felony that is dangerous to life or limb.

F. Public Authority
A public officer may use force when reasonably believed to be necessary to enforce a valid law, court order, or process. The courts are divided on whether a mistake of law as to the validity of the law, court order, or process deprives the officer of the defense. But the emerging view is that such a mistake does not cost the officer the defense if it is reasonable under the circumstances.

G. Domestic Authority
Persons who have responsibility for the care, safety, or discipline of others may use non-deadly force when reasonably believed to be necessary to the discharge of their duties.

H. Consent or Condonation
Consent is a defense when it negates an element of the offense or when it precludes infliction of the harm at which the offense is aimed. Contributory negligence is not a defense, nor is the fact that the victim is also guilty of a crime. Condonation is not a defense, except where specifically permitted by statute.

I. Necessity; Choice of Evils
Whether the defense exists is disputed. But its elements are nonetheless clear: (a) there must be an emergency threatening the imminent occurrence of a harm that cannot reasonably be avoided without committing a crime; (b) the emergency must not have been caused by the fault of the defendant; and (c) the harm that is

avoided by committing the crime must be more serious than that caused by committing the crime. A reasonable mistake as to the nature of the emergency will probably not result in denial of the defense. But a mistake as to the balance of harms will result in rejection of the defense; this is a question of law for the courts.

VII. THE MODEL PENAL CODE

A. Introduction
The justification defenses are contained in Article 3. The approach to mistakes is particularly important.

B. Structure
Each provision of Article 3 is stated in terms of the defendant's belief in the existence of justifying factors. A correct belief is a defense. The defendant who makes a negligent mistake can be convicted only for an offense for which negligence is sufficient. The defendant who makes a reckless mistake can be convicted only for an offense for which recklessness or negligence is sufficient. A mistake that is neither reckless nor negligent is still a defense.

Mistakes of criminal law negate the defense. But a mistake of non-criminal law is treated like a mistake of fact. The defendant is liable for injury to an innocent party to the extent that the defendant is culpable for such injury.

C. Self Defense
The defendant must believe that force is immediately necessary for self protection against unlawful force on the present occasion. Force may not be used to resist an arrest known to be made by a peace officer, whether or not the arrest is lawful. Deadly force is permitted only if believed to be necessary to protect oneself from "death, serious bodily harm, kidnapping or sexual intercourse compelled by force or threat." And deadly force is prohibited if the defendant initiated the encounter with intent to kill or seriously injure or if the defendant does not retreat when required.

D. Defense of Others
Force can be used to protect any third person when the defendant believes that the other person would be entitled to use force in self defense. The retreat rules are modified to be applicable to defense of others.

E. Defense of Property
Force is permitted when the defendant believes it immediately necessary to protect land or personal property in the defendant's possession or in the possession of a person for whom the defendant acts. Force may also be used to re-enter or recapture land if certain conditions are met.

Section 3.06 contains a complicated set of limitations on the use of force in this context, the most important of which are: (a) a request to desist must when practicable be made before force is used; (b) deadly force is severely limited by § 3.06(3)(d), essentially to situations where the defendant's dwelling is being defended or a life endangering crime is threatened by the aggressor; and (c) use of mechanical devices is severely restricted, essentially to situations where they are reasonable under the circumstances and not life endangering.

F. Arrest, Escape, and Crime Prevention
1. Use of Force to Make Arrest

Force can be used when believed to be necessary to make a lawful arrest. Non-deadly force is justified only where, if practicable, the person being arrested is told why the arrest is being made and if, when a warrant is used, it is valid or believed to be valid. Four conditions must be met before deadly force can be used: (a) the arrest is for a felony; (b) the defendant is a peace officer or is helping a person believed to be a peace officer; (c) the defendant believes that no substantial risk of injury to innocent persons is created; and (d) the person to be arrested is dangerous, as manifested either by the use or threat to use deadly force in the crime for which the arrest is made or by a threat to cause death or serious bodily harm if the arrest is delayed.

If the arrest is unlawful, ignorance or mistake of the provisions of law governing the legality of an arrest or search will negate the defense. Otherwise, the normal approach to mistake is followed.

A citizen summoned to aid a peace officer has the same protections as if the arrest were lawful, unless the arrest is believed to be unlawful. In other cases of arrest by a private citizen, the defendant is not protected if the arrest would be unlawful were the facts as the defendant believes them to be.

2. Use of Force to Prevent Escape

In general, the use of force to prevent an escape is governed by the provisions that apply to an arrest of the person involved. But deadly force may be used by a guard or other peace officer if believed to be immediately necessary to prevent an escape from jail, prison, or other institution for the detention of persons charged with or convicted of a crime.

3. Use of Force to Prevent Crime

Force may be used if believed to be immediately necessary to prevent suicide, self-inflicted serious bodily harm, or the commission or consummation of a crime involving or threatening bodily harm, damage to or loss of property, or breach of the peace. But the fact that conduct is a crime does not displace any limitations on the use of force established by the other justification defenses in Article 3.

Deadly force is not permitted unless: (a) the defendant believes that there is a substantial risk that death or serious bodily harm will be caused by commission of the crime and that the defendant's use of force will not create a substantial risk of injury to innocent persons; or (b) the defendant believes that deadly force must be used to suppress a riot or mutiny and an order to disperse and a warning that deadly force will be used is first given.

G. Public Authority

Conduct is justifiable when required or authorized by the legal sources specified in § 3.03(1) or by any other provision of law imposing a public duty. But if the use of force is limited by some other provision of Article 3, that limitation applies. And deadly force is never permitted unless specifically authorized by some other provision of Article 3, except in war or when expressly authorized by law. There are also special mistake provisions in § 3.03(3) and a separate military orders provision in § 2.10.

H. Domestic Authority

The use of force by parents, guardians, schoolteachers, custodians, etc., is governed by § 3.08. In general, the force must be designed to accomplish objectives legitimately within the scope of authority of the person who uses it. Deadly force is prohibited for this purpose, as well as force that is degrading, causes extreme pain or emotional distress, or is disfiguring.

I. Consent or Condonation

Like the common law, the Model Code provides no defense for condonation or contributory negligence. And it is no defense that the defendant's victim was also guilty of a crime.

Consent is a defense if it negates an element of the offense or precludes infliction of the harm sought to be prevented by the law defining the offense. Consent to bodily harm is a defense if: (a) the harm is minor; (b) the defendant's conduct and the harm caused are "reasonably foreseeable hazards" of "joint participation" in competitive sports; or (c) Article 3 establishes a justification.

Consent is ineffective if the person is legally incompetent or incapable, if it is induced by force, duress, or deception, or if the offense is designed to guard against improvident consent by the victim.

J. Necessity; Choice of Evils

The defendant must believe it necessary to commit a crime to avoid a greater harm or evil. The legislature must not have struck the balance of harms differently.

If the defendant purposely or knowingly brought the situation about, there will be no defense. If the defendant recklessly brought it about, there is no defense to prosecution for an offense that requires recklessness. If the defendant negligently brought it about, there is no defense to prosecution for an offense that requires negligence.

A mistake as to whether the harm caused is less than the harm avoided negates the defense. This is a matter of law for the court. Other mistakes are treated in the customary fashion.

PART FIVE: COLLATERAL DEFENSES: EXCUSES

VIII. THE COMMON LAW

A. Introduction
"Excuses" are provided because the defendant is not blameworthy, even for socially undesirable conduct.

B. Infancy
A child under the age of 7 cannot commit a crime. A child between 7 and 14 is presumed incapable of committing a crime, but the presumption can be rebutted by proof of capacity. To prove capacity, the prosecutor must probably prove beyond a reasonable doubt that the child fully appreciated the nature and consequences of any behavior and what it means to say that it is wrong. Children over 14 are treated like adults. Age at the time of the offense is determinative. Many States have changed these ages by statute.

If a child is below a determined age, usually 14 or 15, trial for a "criminal offense" will occur in a Juvenile Court, where the defendant will be "adjudicated" a "delinquent" if found to have committed the offense. If between designated ages, usually 14 or 15 at one end and 18 at the other, the Juvenile Court is usually permitted to transfer jurisdiction to an adult court. If above the top age, a young person will be tried as an adult.

C. Insanity
1. The Traditional Formulations
All insanity tests require that the defendant have been suffering from a "mental disease or defect" at the time of the offense. Psychotic disorders are clearly included. Persons with an "anti-social personality disorder" are excluded in most places. In between these extremes, the concept is unclear, except that a physically observable defect is not required.

All insanity tests also require that the mental disease or defect be related to the offense in some particular manner. They differ in how this is described:

(1) The *M'Naghten* test has two branches. Either is a complete defense. The questions are whether the defendant at the time of the offense as a result of mental disease or defect was unable to know:

(a) the nature and quality of the act committed; or

    (b) whether the act was right or wrong.

Both branches state a "cognitive" inquiry, to be contrasted to the "volitional" or "control" inquiry of the irresistible impulse test. The words "unable to know" require a complete incapacity. There is disagreement about what "know" means, ranging from purely intellectual or cognitive knowledge to emotional appreciation and understanding (or "affective" knowledge). There is also disagreement about whether legal or moral wrongs are meant in the second branch.

(2) The "irresistible impulse" test is used as a supplement to *M'Naghten*. It focuses on whether the defendant at the time of the offense as a result of mental disease or defect had lost the "power to choose" between right and wrong.

(3) The "product" test asks whether the offense was the offspring or product of mental disease. It was adopted in New Hampshire for use instead of *M'Naghten,* and was used in the D.C. Circuit for 18 years. It is of little importance today.

(4) The Model Penal Code combines the second branch of *M'Naghten* with the "power to choose" aspect of the irresistible impulse formula. It asks whether at the time of the offense as a result of mental disease or defect the defendant lacked "substantial" capacity "to appreciate the criminality [wrongfulness] of his conduct" or "to conform his conduct to the requirements of law."

(5) The federal insanity defense is a rejection of the Model Penal Code and a return to a version of the *M'Naghten* rules. It requires a "severe" mental disease that makes the defendant "unable" to "appreciate" either of the two branches of the *M'Naghten* inquiry. The defendant must establish the defense by clear and convincing evidence.

2. Trial of the Insanity Defense

The burden of production is on the defendant, plus the defendant must give notice before trial in some jurisdictions. In some States, two trials are held, one on guilt and one on insanity. The States are divided on the burden of persuasion. In some the prosecutor has the burden to negate the defense beyond a reasonable doubt. In others, the defendant has the burden to establish the defense by a preponderance of the evidence. In federal courts, the defendant must establish the defense by clear and convincing evidence. Putting the burden on the defendant is constitutional. The traditional verdict options are: Guilty, Not Guilty, Not Guilty by Reason of Insanity. Some States permit a verdict of "Guilty but Mentally Ill" as a fourth possibility. All it does is convict the defendant, but recommend psychiatric treatment. Some think it is designed to undermine the insanity defense.

3. Effect of Insanity Acquittal

Traditionally an insanity acquittal meant automatic commitment until "cured." It still means this in some places, but in most an additional proceeding must be held before commitment. The defendant will be committed for evaluation. A hearing will then be held. The duration of any commitment is typically indefinite. Discharge can come by court order on application of the custodial authorities or the defendant, but the defendant who seeks discharge must prove grounds for release. Often the standards for civil commitment are applied both to commitment and discharge.

4. Efforts to Restrict or Abolish Insanity Defense

There are essentially four positions: evidence of insanity should be considered only at sentencing or only on mens rea issues, the verdict of "Guilty But Mentally Ill" should be added, and the "volitional" or "control" inquiry should be eliminated.

D. Involuntary Intoxication

Involuntary intoxication is a defense if it causes precisely the same symptoms as are required by the insanity defense in the jurisdiction in question.

E. Duress

The elements of the defense are: (a) coercion by another person; (b) the coercion must threaten imminent death or serious bodily harm to the defendant or another; (c) the coercion must be such that a reasonable person in the defendant's situation would have committed the crime; and (d) the defendant must not have willingly participated in creating a situation where coercion was likely. Duress is not a defense to an intentional killing. Originally, but probably no more, a wife was presumed coerced by her husband if she committed a crime in his presence. The elements of the defense are varied by statute in many States.

The person who coerced the defendant ought to be guilty of the crime as a principal in the first degree, as one who has caused an "innocent agent" to commit the offense.

F. Entrapment

There are two views of entrapment: (a) the "subjective" view, under which the idea of committing the crime must have originated with the police, and the defendant must be a person who was otherwise "innocent" and would not have committed the crime anyway—this view is used by the federal courts and most States; and (b) the "objective" view, under which the idea of committing the crime must have originated with the police, and the police behavior must have been likely to entice an average, innocent person to commit the offense. Some States follow this view. Under the subjective view, evidence of the defendant's prior criminal record and "predisposition" to commit the offense is admissible, and the entrapment issue is tried to the jury. Under the "objective" view, such evidence is not admissible, and entrapment is tried to the court.

Serious crimes are excluded from the defense. Both the burdens of production and persuasion are on the defendant. The defense is available only if the entrapment is perpetrated by a law enforcement officer or employee. The defense is not constitutionally required.

IX.   THE MODEL PENAL CODE

A.   Introduction
The Model Code contains excuses derived from the common law.

B.   Infancy
Sixteen is the minimum age for commission of a crime under the Model Penal Code. Persons under 16 are referred to Juvenile Court. Persons between 16 and 18 will be dealt with by Juvenile Court unless transferred to adult court. Persons 18 or over are adults.

C.   Insanity
Prior to 1984, the Model Penal Code insanity defense had been adopted by every federal Circuit and a majority of the States. Since then, however, Congress has adopted a new insanity defense for federal criminal prosecutions and the trend in the States has been away from the Model Code formulation.

1.   Elements of the Defense
The elements of the Model Penal Code insanity defense are considered in the context of the evolution from the common law *M'Naghten* formulation to the federal insanity defense. See page 20.

2.   Trial of the Insanity Defense
The burden of production is on the defendant, and prior notice to the prosecutor must be given. The burden of persuasion is on the prosecutor to negate the defense beyond a reasonable doubt. The verdict options are: Guilty, Not Guilty, and Not Guilty by Reason of Insanity. An insanity acquittal must specify insanity as the reason.

3.   Effect of Insanity Acquittal
Mandatory commitment. Procedures for discharge are detailed in § 4.08.

D.   Involuntary Intoxication
Section 2.08(4) provides that intoxication which is not self-induced or which is pathological is a defense if the standards of the insanity defense are met.

E.   Duress
The defense of duress does not affect a choice of evils defense that would otherwise be available. The Model Code duress defense is based on an "excuse" rationale. Its

elements are: (a) coercion by another person; (b) any "unlawful" threat of force against the defendant or another; (c) coercion which a person of reasonable firmness could not have resisted; and (d) the defendant must not have recklessly participated in creating a situation where coercion was likely (negligently if the offense charged requires negligence).

The person who coerced the defendant will be guilty of the offense under § 2.06(2)(a) (innocent agent).

F. Entrapment

The Model Code entrapment defense is based on the "objective" view. Trial is to the court and evidence of predisposition is inadmissible. The burdens of production and persuasion are on the defendant. Entrapment is a defense if a law enforcement official (or "person acting in cooperation with such an official") encourages another to commit an offense by (a) making a knowingly false representation designed to induce the belief that the conduct is lawful; or (b) creating by persuasion or inducement a substantial risk that the offense will be committed "by persons other than those who are ready to commit it."

PART SIX: PARTIES

X. THE COMMON LAW

A. Introduction

This section concerns the rules that govern the liability of one person for a crime committed by another.

B. Liability as an Accessory
1. The Terminology

The "principal in the first degree" is the person who commits the crime. A person who uses an "innocent agent" or an animal or robot is also a principal in the first degree. An "innocent agent" is a person coerced or duped into doing the act, or known to have a defense.

The "principal in the second degree" is a person who aids another to commit a crime, and who is either physically present or "constructively" present. "Constructive presence" means a lookout or driver who stays in the getaway car: a person not immediately present, but close enough to help if needed.

The "accessory before the fact" is a person who aids another to commit a crime, but is not present at the scene.

The "accessory after the fact" is a person who aids a criminal after the crime has been committed. At common law, a husband or a wife could not be an accessory after the fact; the exclusion applies today by statute to other relatives too.

All parties to treason were principals. All parties to a misdemeanor were principals. There could be no accessory after the fact to a misdemeanor.

2. Consequences of Classification
An accessory before the fact was tried where the aid was given. A principal in the second degree was tried where the crime was committed. A mistaken allegation that a principal was an accessory before the fact, or vice versa, was fatal. A mistake as to which category of principal was not. The principal in the first degree had to be tried and convicted prior to the accessory before the fact. If the principal in the first degree escaped punishment for any reason, the accessory before the fact went free. These rules did not apply to a principal in the second degree.

3. Current Law
Most States have merged the categories of principal in the first degree, principal in the second degree, and accessory before the fact, and have abolished the old procedural distinctions. But not all States have done so completely, and you therefore have to be careful. Accessories after the fact are treated differently everywhere.

4. Elements of Liability as an Accessory
a. The Actus Reus
Giving help or assistance; the hard question is "how much?" The law gives no systematic answer to this question. Physical aid, words, and standing by to help are enough *if* the principal knows that is why the accessory is there, as is an omission if there is a legal duty to act. An attempt to aid that is ineffective and of which the principal is unaware is probably insufficient, though there is no reason in principle why an attempt to aid should not be enough. In any event, it is enough if the defendant actually helps, even if the principal doesn't know it, or if the defendant communicates encouragement, even if no help is actually given.

Often a "victim" cannot be convicted as an accessory. If a crime requiring two participants is defined to impose punishment on only one, often courts will hold that the other party cannot be an accessory. But if a crime requires that the perpetrator have certain defined characteristics, the accessory need not have these characteristics, so long as the principal does.

b. The Mens Rea
The accomplice must have at least the mens rea for the object offense. It is *sufficient*—but may not be necessary—if the accessory has a purpose to promote or facilitate the occurrence of the object offense. Some courts require a purpose to promote or facilitate in all cases, but may be liberal in allowing cases to go to the jury—and purpose to be inferred—where knowledge is shown. Some courts will permit a conviction based on

knowledge that a crime will be promoted or facilitated. Most courts will convict if knowledge is shown and (a) the crime is especially serious or (b) a significant amount of aid is given or (c) the benefit to the accessory is significant. Some legislatures have created a separate offense, graded less severely than being an accessory, to punish one who knowingly renders a substantial amount of aid to the commission of a serious offense.

If the accessory aids in the commission of conduct, the accessory should be liable for any results caused by that conduct *if* the accessory has the mens rea required for the principal. The accessory is generally held liable for all offenses which are a "natural and probable consequence" of the offenses aided. This imposes liability for negligence, even though the principal must meet a higher standard of mens rea. Many criticize the rule for this reason.

c. The Principal's Behavior: Conduct or Guilt

Most jurisdictions still require that it be shown that the principal was guilty of a crime before any accessory to it can be convicted. The accessory can be convicted for aiding and abetting an attempt in cases where the principal is guilty of an attempt. Some cases, however, permit conviction of the accessory where (a) the accessory has committed the actus reus for accessorial liability with a sufficient mens rea but (b) the principal has committed only the actus reus of the object offense and lacks the mens rea or otherwise has a defense.

There is no reason in principle why one should not be convicted of attempting to aid and abet in cases where (a) the accessory has committed the actus reus for accessorial liability with a sufficient mens rea but (b) the principal has committed no crime and engaged in no conduct. But few courts will do so. In many such cases it won't matter as to guilt (though it may as to grading) because a conviction for solicitation or conspiracy will be possible.

d. Grading of Accessory's Crime

Traditionally, the accessory is convicted of the same crime as the principal. But at common law, the accessory could be convicted of a different grade of criminal homicide, depending on the accessory's mens rea as to death. And some modern cases and statutes permit the accessory and principal to be graded independently, each according to their own mens rea.

e. Withdrawal of Aid

Withdrawal is a defense if three conditions are met: (a) repudiation is communicated; (b) prior aid is rendered ineffective; and (c) the accessory acts in a timely manner.

5. Accessories After the Fact

Originally, the accessory after the fact was convicted of the same offense as the principal. The elements were direct aid to a person who in fact had committed a felony, with knowledge that the other person had committed a felony and a purpose to hinder detection, conviction, or punishment. A husband and wife, and today by statute often other relatives too, could not be accessories after the fact.

Today there are two approaches. One is to retain the common law terminology and definition of the offense, but punish it less severely than the object offense. The other is to abandon the traditional offense, and substitute an offense punishing obstruction of justice or hindering prosecution. Often these offenses encompass a broader range of prohibited conduct, e.g., they include helping misdemeanants and helping those merely charged with crime even if in fact they are not guilty.

C. Vicarious Liability

Liability based solely on a relationship that is itself legal. It is imposed only when a statute is construed specifically to impose it, generally in connection with public welfare offenses. Vicarious liability dispenses with the actus reus, whereas strict liability dispenses with the mens rea. Some offenses are both vicarious and strict, and the justifications for vicarious liability are close to those for strict liability. Some courts recognize a defense if the defendant has done all that could possibly have been done to prevent the offense; others, that the employer has issued specific instructions not to commit the offense. The requirement that punishment be proportioned to fault would prohibit vicarious liability in many contexts.

D. Enterprise Liability

Employees of a business organization who commit a criminal offense are liable under ordinary principles of criminal responsibility. Their bosses are liable under ordinary principles of accessorial liability. Vicarious liability can be imposed on the business enterprise itself based on acts of employees *if* the applicable statute is construed to permit such a conviction. In such a case, the person who commits the offense (a) must be an employee of the organization, (b) must commit the offense in order to benefit the organization, and (c) must act within the scope of granted authority or responsibility. Some jurisdictions require in addition that the employee be a high-ranking official, important enough in the hierarchy so that it is fair to assume that official policy is reflected in the commission of the offense.

XI. THE MODEL PENAL CODE

A. Introduction

The Model Code discards the common law terminology for accessorial liability. It deals with vicarious liability by implication, but does deal explicitly with enterprise liability.

B. Liability as an Accessory

1. The Terminology

A person who commits the offense or who is "legally accountable" for its commission can be convicted for the offense. A person is "legally accountable" who (a) with the mens rea required for the offense causes an "innocent or irresponsible person" (an "innocent agent") to commit an offense; or (b) fits some special provision of the law; or (c) is an "accomplice." The elements of "accomplice" liability are set forth below.

2. Consequences of Classification

Accomplices may be prosecuted anywhere aid was given or where the offense was committed. Misdescription of accessorial category has no consequences. What happened in a prior trial of the principal is inconsequential.

3. Elements of Liability as an Accessory

a. The Actus Reus

One is an "accomplice" who "solicits," "aids," "agrees to aid," and "attempts to aid." Physical aid, words of encouragement, participation in a conspiracy, or standing by to help (if the principal knows it) are sufficient. Failure to prevent a crime is sufficient only if the law imposes an affirmative duty to act. The defendant can be convicted as an accomplice for an "attempt to aid" in any case where the aid is ineffective, where the principal is unaware of the aid, or both.

A "victim" of an offense cannot be an accomplice. If a crime requiring two participants is defined to impose punishment on only one, the other party cannot be an accessory. If a crime requires that the perpetrator have certain defined characteristics, the accessory need not have these characteristics, so long as the principal does.

b. The Mens Rea

The accomplice must have at least the mens rea required by the object offense. The accomplice must have a purpose that all conduct elements of the object offense be committed and knowledge or belief that all circumstance elements exist. Remember that grading factors and defenses are elements. Knowledge that aid is promoting or facilitating an offense is insufficient.

Where the object offense contains a result element, a distinction must be made. In cases where the principal did *not* actually cause the result, the accomplice must have a purpose to cause the result. In cases where the principal *did* actually cause the result, the accomplice must have the same mens rea as is required for the object offense. The defendant is not liable for other offenses which are the "natural and probable consequences" of offenses aided unless the mens rea as described above is satisfied.

c. **The Principal's Behavior: Conduct or Guilt**

What the principal did is not central to conviction; but it may affect grading. Assuming the accomplice has committed an actus reus and mens rea sufficient for accomplice liability, (a) the accomplice is guilty of the object offense if the principal is guilty of the object offense; (b) the accessory is guilty of an attempt to commit the object offense if the principal is guilty of an attempt to commit the object offense; (c) the accomplice is guilty of the object offense if the principal engages in the conduct required for commission of the object offense; (d) the accomplice is guilty of an attempt to commit the object offense if the principal engages in the conduct required for commission of an attempt to commit the object offense; and (e) the accomplice is guilty of an attempt to commit the object offense if the principal does nothing or if the principal engages in some conduct but not enough to constitute an attempt.

d. **Grading of the Accessory's Crime**

The accomplice is graded on the basis of the offense that would be committed by one who engaged in the principal's conduct with the accomplice's mens rea. If the principal engages in no conduct or insufficient conduct to constitute an offense, the accomplice is guilty of an attempt.

e. **Withdrawal of Aid**

Withdrawal of aid is a defense. The defendant must "terminate" any complicity and (a) "wholly deprive" any aid of effectiveness; or (b) give timely warning to law enforcement authorities; or (c) otherwise make proper effort to prevent commission of the offense.

4. **Accessories After the Fact**

The Model Code has abolished this common law category. It has substituted the offense of "hindering prosecution," which is more broadly defined than the old common law to include misdemeanors and helping people who are not in fact guilty. There are also other offenses in Article 242 that apply to the former accessory after the fact.

C. **Vicarious Liability**

The Model Penal Code contemplates the imposition of vicarious liability on natural persons, but has no explicit provisions on the subject.

D. **Enterprise Liability**

The Model Code deals explicitly with vicarious liability on corporations, partnerships, and unincorporated associations.

Generally speaking, a corporation is liable for public welfare offenses, violations, situations where the legislature specifically intends liability, situations where affirmative duties are placed on the corporation itself, and cases where high officials commit the offense on behalf of the corporation.

Generally speaking, a partnership or other unincorporated association is liable for situations where the legislature specifically intends liability and situations where affirmative duties are placed on the entity itself.

A carefully circumscribed due diligence defense is sometimes available to the enterprise. The employee is personally liable under ordinary principles for offenses committed on behalf of the enterprise. A boss can be personally liable under ordinary principles as an accomplice. And a person who has the primary responsibility for discharging an affirmative duty placed upon an enterprise is personally liable for "recklessly omitting" to perform the duty, and can be sentenced to imprisonment.

PART SEVEN: INCHOATE CRIMES

XII. THE COMMON LAW

A. Introduction
The major inchoate crimes are attempt, conspiracy, and solicitation.

B. Attempt
An attempt is an act that falls short of completion of a specific criminal offense, committed with the intent to commit that offense.

1. The Mens Rea
Attempt at common law is a specific intent offense. The specific intent required is an intent to engage in all of the conduct, result, and circumstance elements that would constitute a completed criminal offense. It does not encompass the conclusion that completion of the conduct would constitute a crime. An attempt cannot be committed recklessly or negligently. An attempt to commit a strict liability offense also requires a specific intent.

2. The Actus Reus
One must distinguish between acts of preparation and the occurrence of the attempt. The common law has developed a number of tests for making this determination: (a) the "last proximate act," which focuses on whether the defendant has done the last act and is adequate as a test of *inclusion*, but inadequate as a test of *exclusion*; (b) the "physical proximity tests," which focus on the dangerousness of the defendant's conduct, on what remains to be done to complete the offense; and (c) the "probable desistance tests," which focus on the dangerousness of the defendant, on what the defendant has already done and the likelihood that a crime will be completed. How to determine how much conduct is enough is a hard problem with no easy answer.

3. Impossibility
"True legal impossibility" is where the defendant seeks to do something that is not a crime. Asking whether the defendant has the mens rea for attempting to commit a criminal offense will identify all such cases.

"Legal" impossibility occurs if the act as completed would not constitute a crime. "Factual" impossibility occurs if the crime cannot be completed because of some physical or factual condition unknown to the defendant. "Legal" impossibility is a defense. "Factual" impossibility is not a defense. The trouble is that any standard "impossibility" situation can be placed in either category.

Some analyze "impossibility" cases by distinguishing between primary and secondary intent. "Primary" intent is a fictional attribution of an intent to do what was actually done. "Secondary" intent is the defendant's actual intent, what the defendant thought was being done. "Primary" intent is then said to be the appropriate measure of attempt liability. The trouble is that those who use this distinction convict some defendants on the basis of their primary intent and some on the basis of their secondary intent, without telling you how to tell which is which.

What one should do is ask mens rea and actus reus questions in the normal manner. First ask the mens rea questions. This will eliminate cases of "true legal impossibility." Ask it in the normal manner, that is, by asking what the defendant actually intended to do. Then ask the actus reus question. If the "proximity" approach is taken, the question will be whether, based on what remains to be done, the defendant has completed enough conduct to constitute an attempt. If the "probable desistance" approach is taken, the question will be whether, based on what the defendant had already done, the defendant has completed enough conduct to constitute an attempt.

4. Abandonment
Once an attempt has been committed, abandonment is not a defense at common law.

5. Grading
Attempt was a misdemeanor at common law. Modern statutes vary widely in their grading schemes.

6. Assault With Intent
"Assault with intent" offenses emerged in order to upgrade the punishments for attempts to commit serious crimes that came very close to fruition. They are unnecessary in codes that punish attempts severely.

C. Conspiracy
A conspiracy is a combination between two or more persons for the purpose of accomplishing an unlawful act or a lawful act by unlawful means.

1. **The Actus Reus**

   The actus reus of conspiracy is an agreement between two or more persons to achieve an objective prohibited by the applicable law of conspiracy. Some statutes require an overt act in addition to the agreement, but any act will do. The common law did not require an overt act.

   A single agreement with multiple objectives is a single conspiracy. Multiple agreements can constitute multiple conspiracies. Some use the "wheel with spokes" and "chain" analogies to think about this problem, but these images are none too helpful since the issue is whether there is one agreement or several and either a "wheel" or a "chain" can consist of either arrangement. The key is who can be joined together in an agreement with a common objective.

   The common law required at least two guilty parties to the agreement. Under some modern statutes and decisions, however, it is enough if one party thinks there is an agreement.

   The common law also precluded a conviction of conspiracy where the object of the agreement was a crime that itself required concerted action (Wharton's Rule). This rule does not apply where the agreement involves more parties than it takes to commit the object offense. The Supreme Court has held that Wharton's Rule limits the federal conspiracy statute only as a matter of statutory construction, applicable for particular substantive offenses only when in accord with Congressional intent.

   Often a "victim" cannot be convicted of a conspiracy with the perpetrator of an offense. But a person who would alone be incapable of committing an offense can be guilty of conspiring with a person capable of committing the offense that the capable person will commit it. Co-conspirators need not actually know each other, so long as they know *of* each other. A husband and wife could not be guilty of conspiracy at common law. Many jurisdictions have changed this rule today.

2. **The Mens Rea**

   Conspiracy at common law requires a specific intent. There must be an intent to agree. There must be an intent to achieve a common objective or set of objectives that is within the prohibition of the crime of conspiracy as defined in the applicable jurisdiction. A purpose to promote the illegal venture should be required, but that purpose can be proved by inference from knowing participation in the venture. A "corrupt motive" (knowledge that the agreement is illegal) is required by some courts for conspiracies to commit regulatory or public welfare offenses (the *Powell* rule). Most commentators and courts believe today that this element is inappropriate.

3. **Impossibility**

   Impossibility problems rarely arise in conspiracy cases. It is not a punishable conspiracy for two persons to agree to do something not prohibited by the law of conspiracy, even though they think it is. The conspiracy is complete upon the making of the agreement (and commission of the overt act, where required). This will usually be *before* any impossibility problem could arise. But an impossibility problem can arise if the parties agree as to *how* a particular crime will be committed and it cannot be committed in that manner. In such cases, liability for conspiracy will be measured by the facts as the parties believed them to be.

4. Abandonment as a Defense

Once a conspiracy has been committed, abandonment is not a defense at common law.

5. Duration: Accomplishment, Abandonment, or Withdrawal

A criminal conspiracy is a continuing offense. Its duration matters for purposes of applying the statute of limitations, the co-conspirator's hearsay exception, for determining the venue for trial, and for determining liability for substantive offenses committed in furtherance of the conspiracy.

A conspiracy is over when all of the planned crimes have been committed. This time can be extended if the prosecutor can prove that an agreement to conceal was an express part of the original agreement (which is hard) or that the objective of the conspiracy was such that concealment was an integral part of its success (which is easier). The conspiracy is also over when the parties have abandoned its objectives. It is over as to a single party when an effective withdrawal is made. Withdrawal is effective when communicated to all conspirators in time for them to abandon the conspiracy, in a manner that would inform a reasonable person of an intent to withdraw. One court has also required a successful effort to persuade the others to abandon the conspiracy.

6. Liability for Substantive Offenses

Conspirators are liable for conspiracy *and* any offenses committed pursuant thereto, under the following rules: (a) all parties to the conspiracy are liable for any offense committed by a conspirator which was explicitly contemplated as part of the conspiracy; and (b) a co-conspirator is liable for all offenses committed by other conspirators in furtherance of the conspiracy that were "reasonably foreseeable" (the *Pinkerton* rule). Many are critical of *Pinkerton*. Not all jurisdictions follow it.

7. Grading

Conspiracy was a misdemeanor at common law. Modern statutes vary widely in their grading schemes.

8. Cumulative Punishment

The common law permits punishment for both the conspiracy and an offense that was its object. But many States now preclude punishment for both. Of course, if the conspiracy contemplates additional offenses then punishment for offenses committed and the continuing conspiracy remains appropriate.

D. Solicitation

Solicitation is encouraging another to commit a crime, with intent that it be committed by the other person.

1. The Actus Reus

Enticing, inciting, ordering, advising, counseling, inducing, or otherwise encouraging another to commit a crime. Actual communication is not essential, though the prosecution may have to be for attempting to solicit. The States vary in whether it is a crime to solicit any crime or only specified crimes. At common law, it was a crime to solicit any felony, or any misdemeanor that constituted a breach of the peace, an obstruction of justice, or some other injury to the public welfare.

If the defendant is for some reason immune from conviction for a particular crime, it will not be a crime to solicit the commission of that offense.

2. The Mens Rea

Solicitation is a specific intent offense. The defendant must intend that the person solicited commit an offense that, in the relevant jurisdiction, can be the object of a criminal solicitation.

3. Impossibility

Impossibility problems rarely arise in solicitation cases. It is not a punishable solicitation for the defendant to encourage conduct not prohibited by the law of solicitation, even though the defendant thinks it is. The solicitation is complete upon encouraging the commission of the offense. This will usually be *before* any impossibility problem could arise. But an impossibility problem can arise if the defendant solicits a particular crime to be committed in a particular manner and it cannot be committed in that manner. In such cases, liability for solicitation is likely to be measured by the facts as the defendant believes them to be. In addition, it is not a defense for the defendant to solicit another to commit a crime if the person solicited is (unknown to the defendant) incapable of committing the offense.

4. Abandonment as a Defense

Once a criminal solicitation has been committed, it is not likely that abandonment will be recognized by the common law as a defense.

5. Liability for Substantive Offenses

The solicitor is liable for any offenses committed by the person solicited under normal principles of accessorial liability.

6. Grading

Solicitation was a misdemeanor at common law. In most jurisdictions today, it is graded as a lesser offense than attempt or conspiracy.

7. Cumulative Punishment

The defendant cannot be convicted of the separate offenses of solicitation and aiding and abetting the solicited offense or an attempt by the person solicited to commit the solicited offense. Some courts hold that solicitation itself can amount to an attempt. Others disagree. It is clear in any event that the defendant cannot be convicted *both* of solicitation and attempt based on the same behavior. The defendant cannot be convicted for both solicitation and conspiracy if the person solicited agrees to commit the offense.

E. Other Inchoate Offenses

There are many other inchoate offenses. Crimes like larceny and burglary are inchoate in nature. But one can be convicted for attempting to commit, conspiring to commit, or soliciting those offenses. There are also many inchoate offenses—like "assault with intent" offenses, possession offenses, or vagrancy—which are designed to supplement the crime of attempt, either by increasing its punishment or allowing earlier intervention of law enforcement in incipient crime.

XIII. THE MODEL PENAL CODE

A. Introduction

The major inchoate crimes in the Model Penal Code are attempt, conspiracy, and solicitation, defined in Article 5.

B. Attempt

The text of § 5.01(1) is confusingly drafted. Note that it divides attempts into two categories: those where the defendant has completed all planned behavior; and those where the defendant falls short of completing all planned behavior.

1. The Mens Rea

The mens rea for attempt is a purpose to engage in the conduct actually engaged in by the defendant, plus the required mens rea towards the elements of the object offense (the offense the defendant is charged with attempting to commit). Divide the elements of the object offense into conduct, result, and circumstance elements and note any ambiguities: (a) the defendant must have a purpose to engage in all of the conduct elements of the object offense; (b) in cases where the defendant has completed all planned behavior, the defendant must have a purpose to cause all of the result elements of the object offense *or* must believe that all of the result elements of the object offense will occur without any further conduct by the defendant; (c) in cases where the defendant falls short of completing all planned behavior, the defendant must have a purpose to cause all of the result elements of the object offense; (d) the defendant must have the same mens rea for all circumstance elements as is required for those elements of the object offense; and (e) the defendant must also have *at least* the mens rea required by the object offense—thus any additional mens rea requirements of the object offense must also be satisfied.

Recklessness, negligence, or strict liability can apply to *circumstance* elements in an attempt under the Model Penal Code (in cases where the object offense does so). They cannot, however, apply to result elements.

2.   The Actus Reus

There are three important aspects of the Model Code approach to the preparation-attempt problem: (a) the defendant must take a "substantial step" toward the commission of the offense; (b) the substantial step must be "strongly corroborative" of the defendant's purpose to engage in the object offense; and (c) § 5.01(2) contains a non-exclusive list of conduct that normally the judge is expected to send to the jury for its determination whether it constitutes a substantial step.

3.   Impossibility

It is not punishable under the Model Penal Code to attempt to do something that is not a crime, even if the defendant believes that it is a crime ("true legal impossibility"). The "legal" and "factual" impossibility cases are handled by the following rule: the defendant is guilty of an attempt if the offense would have occurred had the facts been as the defendant believed them to be, except when the behavior is silly, as in shooting to kill with a water pistol. The Model Code permits the charge in such cases to be reduced or dismissed if the judge believes the defendant does not pose the danger sought to be prevented by the offense. Receiving stolen property is defined to include cases where the defendant "believes" the property probably has been stolen. This takes care of the *Jaffe* case.

The Model Code solution has been criticized. The "strong corroboration" requirement does not apply to cases where the defendant has completed all planned behavior. Some "impossibility" cases thus might pose an unacceptable risk of convicting the innocent based on entirely ambiguous behavior.

4.   Abandonment

The Model Penal Code contains an abandonment defense, which has three dimensions: (a) the defendant must abandon the effort or otherwise prevent commission of the offense (abandonment is not a defense to cases falling within § 5.01(1)(a)); (b) the abandonment must involve a renunciation of the criminal purpose that is "complete" ("complete" means not motivated by a decision to postpone the crime until later or to a different but similar objective or victim); and (c) the abandonment must involve a renunciation of the criminal purpose that is "voluntary" ("voluntary" means not motivated by an increase in the probability of detection or getting caught or by a change in circumstances that makes it more difficult to commit the crime).

5. Grading

An attempt is an offense of the same grade and degree as the offense attempted, except that an attempt to commit a capital felony or a felony of the first degree is a felony of the second degree.

6. Cumulative Punishment

It is not permissible to convict the defendant of both a completed offense and an attempt to commit that same offense. Nor can there be a conviction of more than one inchoate offense for conduct designed to culminate in commission of the same crime.

7. Assault With Intent

There are no "assault with intent" offenses in the Model Code.

C. Conspiracy

Conspiracy is limited in the Model Penal Code to agreements to achieve objectives that are themselves criminal.

1. The Actus Reus

An agreement that the defendant or another party to the conspiracy will commit an offense, attempt to commit it, or solicit its commission; or an agreement that the defendant will aid in the planning of the commission of a crime, an attempt to commit it, or its solicitation. Proof of an overt act is required, except for a conspiracy to commit a felony of the first or the second degree.

A single agreement with multiple criminal objectives is a single conspiracy. Multiple agreements that are part of a "continuous conspiratorial relationship" constitute a single conspiracy. Multiple agreements in other contexts constitute multiple conspiracies.

The Model Code permits conviction on the basis of a "unilateral" agreement, that is, an agreement which the defendant *thinks* has been made with another person.

The Model Code does not explicitly adopt Wharton's Rule. But it does preclude multiple convictions for a conspiracy and its object offense, and thus makes Wharton's Rule unnecessary at least in this respect.

A person who cannot be guilty of an offense as a perpetrator or an accomplice cannot be guilty of a conspiracy to commit that offense. A person who lacks a particular characteristic necessary for the commission of an offense may be guilty of a conspiracy to commit that offense, so long as the person believes that some member of the conspiracy has that characteristic. The parties to a conspiracy need not know each other, so long as they know of each other. There is no reason why a husband and wife cannot be convicted of conspiracy under the Model Penal Code.

2. The Mens Rea
The defendant must have a purpose to promote or facilitate each conduct and result element of the object offense, must know or believe that all circumstance elements of the object offense will exist, and must satisfy any additional mens rea elements contained in the object offense. Each party to the conspiracy must be shown to have had the mens rea for the same crime. An intent to agree is included by implication. The Model Code does not adopt the *Powell* "corrupt motive" doctrine.

3. Impossibility
Since impossibility problems rarely arise in conspiracy cases, the Model Code does not cover them explicitly. It is not punishable under the Model Penal Code to conspire to do something that is not a crime, even if the defendant believes that it is a crime. The defendant is guilty of conspiracy if the crime would occur on the facts as the defendant believes they will be.

4. Abandonment as a Defense
The Model Code contains an abandonment defense, which has two dimensions: (a) the defendant must have "thwarted the success of the conspiracy"—withdrawal from the conspiracy is *not* enough standing alone; and (b) the abandonment must constitute a "complete and voluntary" renunciation of the criminal purpose. The terms "complete" and "voluntary" have the same meaning as in the abandonment defense for attempt.

5. Duration: Accomplishment, Abandonment, or Withdrawal
A criminal conspiracy is a continuing offense. Its duration matters for essentially the same reasons as at common law.

A conspiracy is over when all planned crimes have been committed or when all parties have abandoned all planned crimes. Abandonment is presumed if no overt act is committed during the period of the statute of limitations. An individual may terminate participation in a conspiracy by withdrawing in one of two ways: (a) advising the other conspirators of the intent to withdraw; or (b) informing police of the conspiracy and one's own participation in it.

6. Liability for Substantive Offenses
Liability of conspirators for offenses committed in furtherance of the conspiracy is governed by general rules of complicity, covered in § 2.06. The traditional separate conspiracy rules have been discarded.

7. Grading

A conspiracy is an offense of the same grade and degree as the most serious planned offense, except that a conspiracy to commit a capital crime or a felony of the first degree is a felony of the second degree.

8. Cumulative Punishment

It is not permissible to convict the defendant of both a completed offense and a conspiracy to commit that same offense. Nor can there be a conviction of more than one inchoate offense for conduct designed to culminate in commission of the same crime. If the conspiracy has additional criminal objectives not yet accomplished or for which the defendant has not been prosecuted, however, conviction of the conspiracy in addition to those crimes already committed pursuant to it is permissible.

D. Solicitation

The solicitation of any criminal offense is punished by the Model Penal Code.

1. The Actus Reus

The defendant must command, encourage, or request another to (a) commit a crime; (b) attempt to commit a crime; or (c) become an accomplice in the commission of a crime. A person who cannot be guilty of an offense as a perpetrator or an accomplice cannot be guilty of a solicitation to commit that offense.

2. The Mens Rea

The defendant must have a purpose to promote or facilitate the commission of a crime, which includes a purpose to promote or facilitate all conduct and result elements of the object offense, knowledge or belief that all circumstance elements of the object offense will exist when the offense is committed, and any additional mens rea elements contained in the object offense.

3. Impossibility

Since impossibility problems rarely arise in solicitation cases, the Model Code does not cover them explicitly. It is not punishable under the Model Penal Code to solicit behavior that is not a crime, even if the defendant believes that it is a crime. The defendant is guilty of solicitation if the crime would occur on the facts as the defendant believes they will be.

4. Abandonment

The Model Code contains an abandonment defense, which has two dimensions: (a) the defendant must have persuaded the person solicited not to commit the offense or "otherwise prevented the commission of the crime"—a change of heart alone, even if communicated to the person solicited, is *not* enough; and (b) the abandonment must constitute a "complete and voluntary" renunciation of the criminal purpose. The terms "complete" and "voluntary" have the same meaning as in the abandonment defense for attempt.

5. Liability for Substantive Offenses
Liability of a person who solicits an offense for offenses committed pursuant to the solicitation is governed by general rules of complicity, covered in § 2.06.

6. Grading
A solicitation is an offense of the same grade and degree as the offense solicited, except that solicitation of a capital crime or a felony of the first degree is a felony of the second degree.

7. Cumulative Punishment
It is not permissible to convict the defendant of both a completed offense and a solicitation to commit that same offense. Nor can there be a conviction of more than one inchoate offense for conduct designed to culminate in commission of the same crime.

E. Other Inchoate Offenses
The Model Code continues the tradition of defining crimes like burglary and theft in inchoate terms. And the defendant can be convicted for attempting, conspiring to commit, or soliciting those offenses. Since inchoate crimes are so severely graded, there are no crimes in the Model Code (such as the traditional "assault with intent" offenses) designed to supplement the crime of attempt by increasing its punishment. But there are several other offenses designed to reach incipient criminality.

PART EIGHT: CRIMINAL HOMICIDE

XIV. THE COMMON LAW

A. Introduction
A criminal homicide occurs if the defendant causes the death of another person without justification or excuse. There were two grades of criminal homicide at common law: murder and manslaughter. The terms "justification" and "excuse" have no legal significance. They describe all defenses and a lack of minimum culpability. A baby must be born alive and capable of life independently of its mother in order to be a "person." Some States depart from this rule. The killing of a dying person can be a criminal homicide. When "death" occurs is uncertain. At common law, the death had to occur within a year and a day in order to be "caused" by the defendant. Most States no longer follow this rule.

B. Murder
Murder is causing the death of another "with malice aforethought." The quoted term has nothing to do with "malice" or "aforethought," but includes any one of four

conditions: (a) intent to kill or knowledge that death will result; (b) intent seriously to injure or knowledge that serious injury will result; (c) extreme recklessness; and (d) felony murder.

At one time, all criminal homicides were murder and were punished by death. Much of the subsequent history concerns more sophisticated grading of the offense. Manslaughter became all criminal homicides committed without malice aforethought. The degree structure further confined capital murder. The death penalty became discretionary for the highest category of murder in all States.

The felony murder rule is primarily characterized by a long series of limitations:

(1) Some States limit first degree murder to specified felonies, and second degree murder to "inherently dangerous" felonies. Some States without a degree structure limit all felony murder to "inherently dangerous" felonies.

(2) Some States limit it to deaths that are "reasonably foreseeable" from the manner in which the felony was committed.

(3) Lesser included offenses to murder cannot be the underlying felony.

(4) Some States have arbitrary limits on when the felony begins and when it ends, but in most it is from when an attempt occurs through immediate flight.

(5) There are two views when a person is killed by someone other than a felon: (a) the "proximate cause" theory, which holds all surviving felons for any "reasonably foreseeable" deaths; and (b) the "agency" theory, which holds all surviving felons *only* for killings actually committed by a felon. The "agency" theory prevails. The "proximate cause" theory is more consistent with the deterrent purposes of the felony murder rule. But the "agency" theory reduces the disparity between the defendant's culpability and the culpability otherwise required for murder. And note that even in States that use the "agency" theory a prosecution for murder without relying on the felony murder rule may still be possible.

(6) Delaware requires that some culpability towards death be shown before permitting a felony murder conviction (recklessness for first degree; negligence for second).

(7) Accomplices are also liable under the felony murder rule, but there are limits here too: (a) courts sometimes require that the death be a "natural and probable result" of the felony or that the killing be "in furtherance of" the felony; and (b) the New York statute, copied in other States, provides that it is an affirmative defense if the defendant didn't commit the act or encourage it, wasn't armed, had no reasonable ground to believe that others were armed, and had no reasonable ground to believe that others would be violent.

C. Manslaughter
Manslaughter is any criminal homicide committed without malice aforethought.

"Voluntary" manslaughter includes cases which would otherwise be murder, but which are reduced in grade because of extenuating circumstances. There are two types of extenuating circumstances:

(1) An intentional killing will be reduced to manslaughter if committed in the heat of passion caused by adequate provocation before a reasonable person would have cooled off. The defendant must have actually lost control, the loss of control must have been in response to "legally adequate provocation," and the defendant's reactions must have been reasonable or understandable. Moreover, the defendant must not have actually cooled down, the time between the provocation and the killing must not have been too long (as determined by the court), and it must have been reasonable for the defendant not to have cooled down given the actual passage of time. The prevailing view is probably that any mistake must have been honest and reasonable.

(2) Cases of "imperfect justification." See page 13.

Once an intentional killing is shown, malice aforethought is presumed in many jurisdictions. This probably shifts only the burden of production.

"Involuntary" manslaughter includes cases of recklessness or negligence, terms which at common law were not very precise. It also includes a concept of misdemeanor-manslaughter, which has been limited much like felony murder and in many jurisdictions has been abolished.

D. Diminished Responsibility
A "junior version" of the insanity defense has been used in England and in some American States to reduce the grade of a criminal homicide.

XV. THE MODEL PENAL CODE

A. Introduction
Criminal homicide is "purposely, knowingly, recklessly or negligently [causing] the death of another human being." The prosecutor must negate any justification or excuse defenses raised by the defendant. A "human being" is "a person who has been born and is alive." When "death" occurs is not addressed. The year and a day rule is abolished.

B. Murder
The term "malice aforethought" has been dropped. Murder is a criminal homicide committed purposely, knowingly, or "recklessly under circumstances manifesting extreme indifference to the value of human life." Both "recklessness" as defined in

§ 2.02(2)(c) and this standard must be satisfied. The felony murder rule is abolished, but there is a presumption of extreme recklessness in the case of listed felonies. The degree structure is abolished.

C. Manslaughter

The terms "voluntary" and "involuntary" manslaughter are dropped. Imperfect justification is handled by § 3.09(2). And reckless and negligent homicide are placed in different grading categories.

Conduct that would otherwise be murder is reduced to manslaughter if committed "under the influence of extreme mental or emotional disturbance for which there is reasonable explanation or excuse." The reasonableness is determined "from the viewpoint of a person in the actor's situation under the circumstances as he believes them to be." This standard has been widely adopted. It departs from the common law in five main ways: (a) it does not require a particular provoking event; (b) it eliminates any occasion for the courts to build a doctrine excluding certain kinds of provocation; (c) the defendant is measured against an objective standard, but the word "situation" permits the personalization of that standard (including acceptance of the theory of "diminished responsibility") where appropriate; (d) the separate "cooling time" limitation is eliminated; and (e) in case of mistake the defendant is judged from the facts as they are believed to be.

D. Capital Punishment

The Model Penal Code takes no position on whether capital punishment should be authorized for murder, but does prescribe how it should be imposed if authorized. There are two important aspects of the proceeding: (a) a separate post-conviction hearing must be held, usually before the same jury; and (b) there are criteria for decision—the judge may preclude capital punishment under stated criteria, and after the separate hearing capital punishment may be imposed only if at least one of a specified list of aggravating factors is found to exist *and* if the aggravating factors outweigh any mitigating circumstances.

Evidence of mental disease or defect short of insanity can be used for at least three purposes: (a) to preclude the separate hearing; (b) to show extreme mental or emotional disturbance as a basis for mitigation; or (c) to show cognitive or volitional impairment as a basis for mitigation.

PART NINE: OTHER CRIMES

XVI. OTHER CRIMES

A. Introduction

This section considers rape, theft, and RICO. It combines discussion of the common law and the Model Penal Code in its coverage of rape and theft. RICO is a modern federal statute dealing with organized crime. It has no common law or Model Penal Code counterpart.

B. Rape
The Model Penal Code is somewhat out of date when measured against many modern rape statutes. Although it differs in important ways from the common law, it also borrows significantly from the common law tradition.

1. The Common Law
The traditional definition of rape is "the carnal knowledge of a woman forcibly and against her will."

a. Theory of the Offense
There are two competing modern justifications for the offense. One is that rape is an offense against the person akin to assault. The other is that rape is an offense against sexual autonomy. The former rationale emphasizes the force component of a sexual attack. The latter emphasizes the victim's lack of consent.

It also helps to explain some of the doctrinal vestiges of the early law to understand that sex out of wedlock was itself the offense of fornication or adultery. Therefore a woman who was not raped but who engaged in consensual sex with a man who was not her husband was committing a crime. A claim of rape was therefore a way for her to escape from her own criminality, which may explain why, for example, there are analogies between the coercion that is required for rape and the duress that will serve as an excuse for crime.

b. Elements of the Offense
Rape was limited to penile-vaginal intercourse by a man with a woman who was not his wife. Force by the man and lack of consent by the woman, often evidenced by substantial resistance, were independent elements.

c. Mistakes of Fact
Mistakes of fact on consent were often not an excuse—perhaps because a crime (or at least a moral wrong) was being committed even on the facts as the defendant believed them to be. Often today a reasonable mistake of fact on consent is a defense. In England, recklessness is the standard.

2. The Model Penal Code
a. Force and Consent
The Model Penal Code emphasizes force by the man that "compels" the sexual act. Lack of consent by the woman is not a separate element.

b. Alternatives to Force
Various alternatives to force have always been recognized by the law. The Model Penal Code extends this notion to include:

(1) Threats of serious harm;

(2) Impairment by drugs or intoxicants administered by the defendant without the woman's knowledge for the purpose of preventing resistance;

(3) Where the woman was unconscious;

(4) The victim is less than 10.

Lesser offenses are committed when the victim's judgment is impaired in other ways, as where an older man preys on a young girl or where the victim is misled as to the nature of the act being performed.

c. Sexual Act
The common law was limited to penile-vaginal penetration. The Model Penal Code also covers "intercourse per os or per anum."

d. Spousal Exclusion
The Model Penal Code retains the common law limitation that a man cannot rape his own wife. Many modern statutes disagree.

e. Sex Neutrality
Many modern statutes include male-male and female-female encounters in the law of rape, as well as situations where the female is the aggressor against a male. It is also common to rename the offense without using the term "rape," e.g., "criminal sexual assault," "criminal sexual conduct," and the like. The Model Penal Code maintains the tradition of the common law on this point, although it does include a lesser offense drafted in sex neutral terms.

f. Procedural Provisions
The Model Penal Code contains a "prompt complaint" provision and requires that the victim's testimony must be corroborated. It also requires an instruction that the testimony of the complaining witnesses must be considered "with special care." These provisions are much criticized, and are not followed in many jurisdictions. Many jurisdictions also have adopted "rape shield" laws, which severely limit the extent to which the defendant can focus the trial on the sexual history of the victim.

C. Theft
Article 223 of the Model Penal Code consolidates into one theft offense the various theft offenses that were separate crimes at common law.

1. The Common Law
a. Larceny
Larceny was the taking and carrying away of the personal property of another with intent to effect a permanent deprivation. The taking had to

be a trespass against the rights of the person in possession of the property. The common law expanded the coverage of larceny significantly through the doctrine of "constructive possession."

b. False Pretenses
Parliament adopted the first false pretenses statute in 1757. It punished a person who obtained title to property by deception.

c. Embezzlement
Parliament expanded the law of theft more broadly in 1799 with the first embezzlement statute. Embezzlement covers the fraudulent conversion of property over which the thief has lawful custody.

Fine distinctions existed in the common law of theft. To express an example in modern terms, if a person who rented a car meant to keep it at the time of rental, this was called "larceny by trick" and was viewed as a trespassory taking from the possession of the car rental agency. But if the renter decided to keep the car after driving it for a while, it was embezzlement because at that stage the car was in the lawful custody of the renter. Variations of this sort between the charge and the facts as they emerged at trial could prevent conviction at common law.

2. The Model Penal Code
The Model Penal Code solved this problem by consolidating the law of theft into a single offense. This solution has been widely influential. Section 223.2(1) of the Model Code combines larceny and embezzlement into one offense. Section 223.3 covers obtaining property by false pretenses. The remainder of Article 223 deals with other forms of theft. All of these offenses can be charged as "theft" in a single count of an indictment. The particulars of how the defendant obtained the property and applications of the lines between theft and non-criminal uses of other people's property are left to evolution at trial, with proper protection against unfair surprise to the defense falling to the supervisory role of the judge.

The Model Penal Code also follows the common law by punishing, in separate Articles, robbery, burglary, and various forms of fraud. Robbery is essentially theft from the person accompanied by violence or the threat of violence. Burglary is essentially an attempt to commit theft (or any other crime) combined with a trespass to property. Burglary is especially serious when committed in the dwelling of another at night.

D. RICO
Congress passed RICO in 1970, but RICO didn't really get off the ground until the decision in United States v. Turkette, 452 U.S. 576, 101 S.Ct. 2524 (1981).

1. Structure of the Statute
The heart of the statute is in three provisions. The first punishes buying one's way into a legitimate business by using profits from organized crime. The

second punishes forcing one's way into a legitimate business by threats or violence. The third punishes operating a legitimate business by using threats, force, and other anti-competitive tactics of the sort engaged in by organized crime.

2. *United States v. Turkette*

That was the theory, but it didn't work that way. *Turkette* held, in effect, that it was a crime for organized crime to act like organized crime. That is, RICO covered persons who conducted the affairs of organized crime through a pattern of racketeering activity.

Turkette accomplished this by interpreting the word "enterprise." RICO punishes people who are associated with an enterprise who conduct the affairs of the enterprise through a pattern of racketeering activity. The original idea was that the "enterprise" would be a legitimate business infiltrated by organized crime—the effort was to get at penetration of the legitimate business world by organized criminality. But *Turkette* held that the "enterprise" could be an *illegal* entity as well as a legal entity. Thus, a person who operated an *illegal* entity (organized crime) through a pattern of racketeering activity (how else would organized crime operate?) violated RICO.

3. Definitions

There are three key definitions in the operation of RICO.

(1) The first is "enterprise," which covers lawful entities as well as unlawful entities. A unit of government can be a RICO enterprise. A corporation or a partnership can be a RICO enterprise. And, as *Turkette* held, organized crime itself can be a RICO enterprise. An enterprise is a group of people who have a common or shared purpose; that functions as a continuing unit over time; and that has an ascertainable structure different from the level of organization required to commit a series of crimes.

(2) The second is "racketeering activity," which encompasses just about any old crime. There is a long list of federal crimes in the statute, plus an array of state crimes. Think of a crime that organized crime might commit, and it's on the list. Also add mail fraud, securities fraud, and a host of other offenses. Finding a qualifying "racketeering activity" is not a serious limitation on the scope of RICO.

(3) The third is "pattern." A pattern is any series of two or more offenses on the list of "racketeering activities" that are continuous and that are related in terms of scope or purpose.

4. Relation to Conspiracy

It is not easy to tell the difference between a RICO violation and an ordinary conspiracy involving two or more crimes. The way to think about it is that

RICO is "conspiracy plus." The "plus" is the organizational characteristics that satisfy the definition of "enterprise" and the continuity and relationship that satisfies the definition of "pattern."

One can also be guilty of a conspiracy to violate RICO.

5. Sanctions

RICO is a serious offense. The maximum penalty is 20 years (or life if a racketeering act carries life). Plus there is a broad forfeiture provision and there are high fines.

6. Civil Sanctions

RICO can also be enforced by a civil suit, but civil RICO is more known for its abuses than its successes. The federal crimes of mail fraud and securities fraud are so broadly defined that they can be alleged as "racketeering acts" in many ordinary commercial, breach of contract suits. The fact that treble damages and attorneys fees are available in a RICO civil suit invites such allegations and frequently distorts what otherwise would be ordinary commercial litigation.

PART TEN: CONCLUSION

XVII. CONSTITUTIONAL LIMITS ON PUNISHMENT FOR CRIME

A. Introduction

The Supreme Court has addressed itself to general principles that limit the way crimes are defined and punished.

B. The Definition of Crime

The Constitutional limits on how crimes are defined are not involved in most cases.

1. Vagueness

A criminal law is unconstitutional if so vaguely drafted that its meaning cannot fairly be determined from the words used. This requirement has *never* been used to strike down a serious "core" crime involving seriously immoral behavior like murder, rape, or theft. Nor is it used to foreclose the legislature from accomplishing legitimate objectives. The doctrine is quite limited, usually to situations where the crime is aimed at no particular evil, where it may apply to perfectly innocuous conduct, where there is large opportunity for law enforcement officials to pick and choose whom they would like to arrest, and where the law is not really necessary to accomplish the legitimate law enforcement interests at stake.

2. An Act

The Supreme Court has held that crime cannot be based upon a status or a condition, but must be premised on an "act." An "act" in this sense can be affirmative conduct, an omission, or possession. This limitation is rarely at issue, since the common law and modern statutes require an "act" in this sense anyway.

3. A Voluntary Act
The Constitution has *not* been interpreted to require that the criminal's act be "voluntary."

4. Mens Rea
The Supreme Court has held that it is unconstitutional to convict a person of a crime for engaging in innocuous behavior in a context where the average person would have no idea that the criminal law might apply or where one's moral signals do not warn. This is very limited too, since most crimes—even those that impose strict liability—occur in a context where one knows enough to avoid criminal liability if careful.

5. Statutory Interpretation
The Supreme Court has held that the common law "presupposes a measure of evolution" and that rules of statutory interpretation adopted after an offense has been committed can fairly be applied to criminal defendants so long as they are not "unexpected and indefensible."

C. PROPORTIONALITY
1. Capital Punishment
The Supreme Court has held that mandatory capital punishment is unconstitutional for any criminal offense. The Court has also indicated that each State's procedures for imposing capital punishment will be examined on an individual basis, both in structure and in specific application. The decision to impose the death penalty must be discretionary, it must be limited to a genuinely narrowed class of persons, the defendant must have every opportunity to offer evidence in mitigation, and the conduct of both prosecutor and judge will be closely scrutinized for behavior that undermines the independence and reliability of the sentencing determination. Most States now use a bifurcated sentencing procedure, with instructions at the conclusion of the capital sentencing hearing on criteria for the imposition of the death penalty. Normally the same jury that heard the guilt phase of the case also determines the sentencing question.

The Court has held that the death penalty is not always constitutionally disproportionate for murder, but that it might be on given facts. It has held that the death penalty cannot be imposed for rape, nor for an accomplice to murder who did not intend death or anticipate the use of deadly force. Death is not always an unconstitutional punishment for a person who was a major participant in an underlying felony and was recklessly indifferent to the possibility of death.

2. Imprisonment

The Supreme Court has held a life sentence without the possibility of parole constitutionally disproportionate for a seventh non-violent felony. It looked to "objective" criteria in doing so: the gravity of the offense and the harshness of the penalty; the sentences imposed on other criminals in the same jurisdiction; and the sentences imposed for commission of the same crime in other jurisdictions.

D. Proof

The Supreme Court has held that elements of a crime—the actus reus, the mens rea, and causation—must be proved by the prosecutor beyond a reasonable doubt. This means that "[o]ther than the fact of a prior conviction, any fact that increases the penalty for a crime beyond the prescribed statutory maximum must be submitted to a jury, and proved beyond a reasonable doubt." This ruling does not affect the proposition that the burden of persuasion on defenses may be placed on either party.

The Court has also held the presumption of natural and probable consequences unconstitutional in a prosecution for "purposely or knowingly" causing a death. The rationale was that the presumption could have been interpreted by the jury to relieve the prosecutor of the burden of proving the mens rea elements "purpose or knowledge" beyond a reasonable doubt.

*

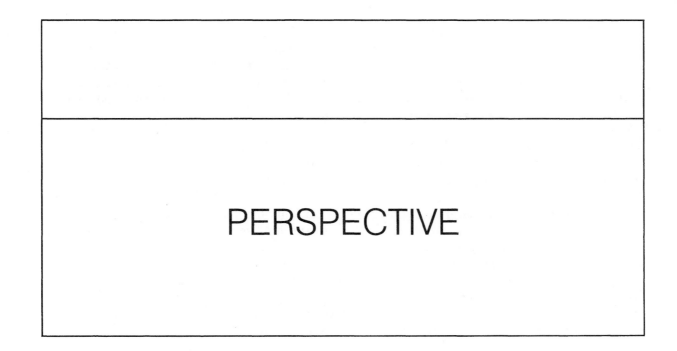

THE STUDY OF CRIMINAL LAW

Most criminal law courses these days are not a study of the specific content of various "crimes," but of the general structure of the criminal law. They are an effort to help you understand the principles upon which crime definition is based and defenses are grounded. This is the approach followed in this outline. If what you want is the definition of all of the crimes in the world, you won't find them here.

One of the interesting questions to play with at the beginning of a criminal law course is what it is that makes the criminal law unique. How is a "crime" different from a civil wrong for which a person may be required to pay damages? A variety of answers can be suggested. A crime is a lawsuit filed by the State. A person can be deprived of liberty if convicted of a crime. A fine can be imposed for a crime. Crimes involve public injuries, whereas private lawsuits are to recover for private or personal injuries.

All of this is true, but it is also true that each of these objectives can be accomplished in a private lawsuit. Plenty of non-criminal lawsuits are filed by the State, as in an effort to stop pollution or to break up AT&T or Microsoft. Ask a person who has been civilly committed but who would rather not be institutionalized whether anyone can be deprived of liberty in a non-criminal proceeding. Punitive damages can be imposed in a private lawsuit (sound like a fine?). Pollution and predatory pricing by corporate behemoths are hardly "private" wrongs. And so on.

How, then, is a crime different from a tort? The answer, in a few words, is punishment, stigma, "conviction," "guilt," "paying a debt to society." The unique feature of the criminal law is its moral content. It constitutes a public stamp of disapprobation, a scarlet letter. The criminal law is society's morality play. It is society's way of isolating and stigmatizing an individual who presents a serious danger to the public order. We make something a crime when we want to do our very best to keep it from happening, and when we want to convey our most emphatic message to those who would do it that we really would rather it not be done.

This last point deserves emphasis. The ultimate objective of the criminal law is prevention. Society wants crimes not to occur, and it punishes those who commit them in order to prevent their reoccurrence. This is often called "social control" by criminal lawyers, as in: "the objective of the criminal law is social control" or "this defense should be disallowed in order to achieve social control objectives." Obviously deterrence—both "general" and "special" (this would be a good time for you to use the glossary in Appendix D)—is another way of talking about the preventive goal of the criminal law. So is "rehabilitation," though you might not think so at first. We don't rehabilitate people simply to make them better, and indeed grave moral questions would be raised in American society if we deliberately set such a course. Rather we "rehabilitate" people (or try to) who have committed crimes, and our objective is to get them back on the streets to lead a normal, non-criminal life. The object of our "rehabilitation" is to prevent crime.

What about retribution? Retribution should be thought about from two perspectives. The first is as a *justification* for punishment. Lots of people think that retribution justifies punishment. A famous English historian and judge once wrote that it is "morally right to hate criminals," that society serves a noble end in itself when it punishes those who do bad things. Fair enough. Many people claim they don't believe this any more, and that they would trade a lot of retribution for a little crime prevention. But whatever the right view of the matter, the language in which we talk about the criminal law—"guilt," "punishment," "the offender should pay for a crime"—is heavy with retributive overtones, and there is great public outcry when a person is perceived to have put one over on the system by "escaping" from deserved punishment. When John Hinckley was acquitted by reason of insanity for attempting to assassinate President Reagan, there was great hue and cry because it was perceived that he should have been "punished" for his crime, even though the preventive goals of the criminal law were in some sense accomplished by the civil commitment that followed and that is as of this writing still being imposed.

The second and far more important perspective on retribution is how it functions as a *limitation* on punishment. Retribution implies blame and responsibility, and proportionate punishment when a person has chosen to do wrong. This in turn implies *no* punishment if a person is not in a position to make a voluntary and free choice. Perhaps you can see how we could derive an insanity defense from such an idea. Or perhaps you see why this notion supports the requirement of "criminal intent." If a person didn't mean to do it, or if a person really couldn't help it, our retributive instincts are quire different than they are for a person who derives pleasure or profit from a crime gladly committed. And perhaps you can see something of why penalties are proportioned to the crime, why sentences are "graded" in terms of the severity of the harm, why murder is punished more severely than theft. In fact, as you will see, the criminal law has built an entire superstructure of doctrine on the simple idea that the criminal law is based on blame for bad choices to which we give a proportionate response.

But now lets go back to where we started. If the principal objective of the criminal law is prevention, isn't it inconsistent with that objective to let somebody off who is dangerous and might do it again, even if the person is not somehow "at fault" or "to blame" for the conduct? Even if John Hinckley was a completely crazy—which in terms of the appropriate legal standard for the insanity defense he probably was not—why should he "get off" for something as dangerous as shooting the President? Doesn't that invite others to try the same sorts of things, hoping they might get off too? Herein lies the great tension of the criminal law—the tension between blame and social control, between retribution and deterrence, between a system based on fault and responsibility and a system based on prevention and social order. Virtually every criminal law doctrine must somehow strike a balance between these two inconsistent—and they are inconsistent—objectives. Virtually every controversial issue in the criminal law can be translated into these terms. Try it yourself based on what you already know about the insanity defense.

There are two more grand ideas that must be taken into account in thinking about the objectives of the criminal law. The first is individual liberty, personal autonomy, the right to be let alone. We live in a society where this value is important. And obviously whenever we put a criminal in jail, we are denying to that individual the very liberty which we hope to preserve for ourselves. We justify punishment for criminals, of course, on the utilitarian ground that it is necessary to protect the liberty of others, and perhaps a little bit (or a lot?) on the ground that one who has invaded the liberty of another "deserves" (here comes retribution again) to lose proportionate liberty in return. But the important point is what this idea of personal autonomy means to the doctrines of the criminal law. For it means more inconsistency with the purely preventive objective. My liberty can be maximized only if I am given a fair chance not to be arrested for crime; my liberty is seriously at risk if I can be arrested for a crime any time the police would like and I can't do anything to avoid it. This means, if you think about it, that the criminal law should punish conduct, not status. And it means that the criminal law should punish *voluntary* conduct, that is, conduct where the defendant exercised some choice. It means, in short, that the criminal law should concern itself with the minimum conditions under which it is justified for society to deprive a "free" citizen of liberty in the name of social control. And as soon as you develop doctrines designed to protect the liberty of the citizen, they are sure enough going to conflict with what you might want to do purely in the name of prevention. And so we are back where we were a moment ago, having to balance the goal of prevention against other concerns in order to decide what the doctrinal content of the criminal law should be.

Finally, another civil liberty which we take very seriously in this country is equal treatment—each person is equal before the law. This idea too has implications for how the criminal law should be defined. It suggests, for example, enough specificity so that those who must administer the law will be guided by adequate criteria to assure that the same standards will be applied to everyone. Police should make arrests not because *they* think something wrong has occurred, but because there is an apparent violation of a previously written rule. A jury should determine guilt based on standards that can be applied by the next jury in the same manner. There should, in short, be a *law* against which people are measured before they are put in jail, and that law should be written down so that it can be the same for everyone.

This, in a nutshell, is an overview of some of the great philosophical issues of the criminal law. Now to something more mundane.

APPROACH TO OUTLINES

Those of you who are using this outline as an aid in a criminal law course will be reading cases, perhaps for the first time. It is important at the outset for you to understand that neither this outline nor any other can be a substitute for reading and reading, and reading again, the cases you have been assigned. Your law school courses have two objectives, and the first is far more important than the second. The first is to teach you to think—to read and analyze a judicial opinion, to learn how to use the tools of the law. This you have to do on your own, and you have to do it over and over until you learn how to do it by yourself and for yourself. No one is going to do it for you after you graduate.

I often tell first year students on their first day about an experience my wife and I had, and you will have had too if you have been around young children, with one of our young daughters many years ago just before a new semester started. She had learned to sit up in a high chair and eat from a spoon, but only when held by someone else. All went reasonably well until one day she decided that it was time to feed herself. From that day forward no spoons were welcome when held by another; she was going to do it. And the results, at first, were a disaster—food in the hair, food on the floor, food in the ear, and every once in a while a bit of food in the mouth where it belonged. But soon she managed to hit her mouth most of the time, and eventually she got pretty good at it.

The analogy to a first-year law student is not inapt, nor is the moral. At first you will miss your mouth a whole lot, and the results may seem pretty messy. But I hope you realize, as our daughter did, that the only way to learn to do it is to do it yourself. No one can do it for you. And no outline or any other shortcut can substitute for reading your casebook over and over again until you learn to do it efficiently and learn to draw out for yourself the kinds of things your Professor will emphasize.

I said there was a second but less important objective of a law school course. It is substantive, to get you to learn something about the area of the law you are studying so that you can think through the difficult problems with which you as a practitioner will be faced and with which those who are policymakers—legislators and judges, and perhaps someday you—must deal. Here outside reading, even an outline if you use it right, can help you see the forest for the trees. It is important to be able to step back from your cases—to remove yourself from the details on which you will dwell each day in the classroom—and try to see how things fit together. You must try to understand the organizing principles on which the law is based. An outline or a hornbook can be helpful for this purpose, and it is for this purpose that this outline has been written.

APPROACH TO THIS OUTLINE

It may be helpful if a few words of explanation are added about how this outline is organized. Note first that it is impossible to describe with accuracy the law of 50 States and the various federal jurisdictions. What can be described is how the Anglo–American system approaches the criminal law, and the general doctrines that have commonly been used to analyze various situations. If you are interested in the law of a particular jurisdiction, there is no substitute but to examine its cases and statutes carefully.

The various parts of this outline have the following purposes:

(1) The "Capsule Summary" is a short "highlight film." It does not contain the detail of the main body of the book, but it should be helpful for review at the end to make sure you have covered all the bases and to remind you of what you have looked at in more detail.

(2) The "Perspective" section which you are now reading is a brief introduction to the purposes of the criminal law, as well as some hints about how to approach the subject. I have not dwelt at any length in the body of the outline on two great subjects: (a) the philosophical objectives of the criminal law (retribution, deterrence, rehabilitation, incapacitation, etc.); and (b) the factors that go into whether to make something a crime (the "criminalization" decision). Everyone has their own approach to these questions, and it seemed to me better in the limited space available to try to help you get a solid grounding in the technical structure of the law. Only when you have that grounding can you make any sense of the broad philosophical issues with which your Professor may try to challenge you.

(3) Part One is a brief introduction. It talks about why the common law and the Model Penal Code are studied and how the subject matter of the criminal law has been broken down in the main body of this outline.

(4) Parts Two through Eight are the main body of the book. Each of these parts is organized in the same manner: it first addresses the "common law" approach to the subject, and then the "Model Penal Code" approach. Two points should be made about why this organization was chosen.

First, it permits you to use the outline in any order. Each individual section is independently written so that you may read them in the order that corresponds with the way your course is taught. Thus, if your Professor covers "Inchoate Crimes" (Part Seven) with "The Definition of Crime" (Part Two), as I have sometimes done in my course, you may read the outline in that order.

Second, the "common law" and "Model Penal Code" approaches to each subject have been kept separate throughout the book so that you can study each as an integrated unit. As you go through your course, it is likely that your Professor will refer to both the common law and the Model Penal Code on each subject as it is taken up. When the law of attempts is studied, for example, it is likely that you will examine both approaches together for comparative purposes, and then treat conspiracies, etc., the same way. But it is important, I think, for you to try to understand both the common law and the Model Penal Code as integrated systems. The way this book is organized will permit you to spend a study session reading only about the common law or only about the Model Penal Code on several different topics in order to understand the common themes they bring to the solution of related problems. The book is designed for such flexibility of use, so that you can quickly see how both systems approach a single problem or study either system as an independent unit.

(5) Part Nine departs from the format of its predecessors to look at the law governing three of the substantive offenses you are likely to encounter in your criminal law course. The common law and the Model Penal Code are considered together on the first two—rape and theft. The third examines RICO, an important federal statute dealing with organized crime. The point is to give you an opportunity to review the general principles governing these three major offenses. Together with the law of criminal homicide covered in Part Eight, these offenses will give you a good overview of the kinds of major policies that inform the substantive reach of crimes you will be studying.

(6) Part Ten is a conclusion, devoted to constitutional limits on punishment for crimes. You are likely in your criminal law course not to study these doctrines as a single unit, but to examine each case with the material to which it is most relevant. For example, your Professor is likely to ask you to read the *Robinson* case (page 408) with material covering the act (page 73) or the voluntary act (page 143). Or your Professor may not assign *Robinson* at all, preferring not to confuse you with constitutional doctrines before you have studied Constitutional Law. You may easily use this outline to follow the organization of your own course, since the constitutional topics follow headings that can be quickly related to other parts of the outline. But all of the constitutional doctrines were put in one place so you could see them together to look for common threads.

(7) Finally, a word about several of the appendices. Appendix D contains a Glossary of Terms, a short dictionary of words commonly used in a criminal law course. Appendix D can also be used as an Index, since it contains page references to where in the body of the outline you can find a discussion of most major criminal law doctrines. Appendix E shows you where materials in this book fit into the various casebooks most commonly used in criminal law courses. Appendix G contains a Table of Cases. Not many cases are cited in this outline; the outline is not designed for legal research, and it is neither fun nor informative to read a bunch of meaningless case names after every sentence. But the few cases that are cited are collected in Appendix G. Appendix F should be more important to you. It

contains a Table of Model Penal Code references allowing you quickly to find the discussion of any particular section of the Model Penal Code that concerns you.

STUDY, REVIEW, AND EXAMINATION

Except for the Introduction, Part Nine, and the Conclusion, each section of the book is followed by review questions. Most are true/false and are designed to help you think through what you have just read. It is important as you answer these questions that you identify *why* they are false, if they are. I often include tricky, and sometimes ambiguous, true/false questions like some of these on my own examinations, but always give the student four or five lines following the question in which to explain the answer. You might find it useful to try that with these questions too. There are also essay questions after each section. Many of these are questions I have used on prior examinations. You should use them as an opportunity actually to write out a sample answer. If you are in a study group, and study groups are a particularly good idea in the first year, you should get other students to do so too, and then compare your answers. When you read a colleague's answer, you should really try to rip it apart—that's how both of you will learn from the experience. Answers to these review questions appear in Appendix A. In addition, there are three sample examination questions in Appendix B, and suggested lines of analysis to each of these questions in Appendix C.

Criminal law is a technical subject, and many find it difficult. One reason I like it is that it spreads the gamut from very tight technical statutory analysis to broad philosophical issues of great social and moral significance. If you are a typical student, you will like the broad stuff, and be pretty good at it. But you will be *awful* at the tight, technical analysis. For that reason, the technical stuff is where you ought to concentrate your energies. As you will learn, the ability carefully to analyze a legal situation, and particularly to read a statute and pull out its various ambiguities and difficulties, is what distinguishes good law students from not-so-good law students and, more importantly, good lawyers from not-so-good ones. I don't mean to say that this is all that law is about, or that it is even the part that is the most fun. What I do mean to say is that if you can't get the technical part right, then all the rest of what you have to say doesn't matter.

How should you study for an exam? My advice is to pay a lot of attention to your casebook and to what your Professor did with it. It would be a good idea to prepare your own outline of the course, perhaps in conjunction with a study group. Secondly, I would spend far more time *after* class on the topic for each day than you spent *before* class on that same topic. The time to figure out that you didn't understand something, and the time to do something about it—ask a fellow student, ask your Professor in class or after class the next day—is when the subject is fresh in your mind, not two months later when you are trying to cram everything into your head for the examination. Third, I would use this outline as a backup, in order to help get a perspective on how things fit together and to make sure I didn't forget anything important. Don't be surprised if your Professor tells you something different from what you read in these pages. Lawyers disagree with each other all the time, and the law is not certain enough so that there is no room for disagreement. And it is also possible that we're both right—or both wrong. What you ought to try to figure out is *why* we said what we did, and whether you can put it together in a form that makes sense.

How should you go about taking the examination? Carefully. The important thing is to *think*, and not just run off at the mouth, or pen, or computer as the case may be. Most law students take an examination like a search engine. Once they see a buzz word or two in a question—"intoxication" or "insanity" or "mistake"—they proceed to tell the Professor everything they know about that subject, and forget the most important part of the whole process: *answer the question that is asked*. This requires that you read the question, slowly and carefully. And it requires that you think before you write, and perhaps jot down a short outline of your proposed answer. Where you start your answer is important. The best answers will cut to the heart of the question quickly, laying aside unnecessary underbrush. One thing law students love to do is go on and on at preposterous length about all the easy stuff involved in a question, and often either don't save enough time to get to the hard part or save barely enough time to mention it. I always design my exams so that there are parts that any idiot ought to be able to get, and parts that no one can reasonably be expected to get—with most of it in between. The best answers will really struggle with the hard stuff, and dispose quickly of the part that's there for the picking.

PART ONE
INTRODUCTION

Analysis

I. *General Considerations*

*

I

GENERAL CONSIDERATIONS

Analysis

A. Why Study the Common Law?
B. Why Study the Model Penal Code?
C. The Organization of These Materials

A. WHY STUDY THE COMMON LAW?

Criminal law was originally judge-made in England, promulgated over time as problems came before courts for resolution. The "common law process" refers to the evolution of law from the decisions made in individual cases. The resulting body of "common law" was centuries in the making. As we might say today, it was "made" (invented?) by the judges. As they most likely would have said at the time, it was "discovered" by the judiciary based on immutable principles of natural law. The judges merely articulated the law that was there all the time waiting to be discovered.

Eventually, Parliament got into the act and, always against the background of the common law, enacted supplementary statutes. At the time of the American Revolution, English criminal law consisted of "common law" crimes (crimes resulting from judicial decisions) and "statutory" crimes (crimes resulting from enacted legislation). Most defenses to crime that existed at this time had also been developed by the judges, and hence were "common law" in origin. By and large, the vocabulary and structure of the criminal law was also of judicial origin.

The original 13 States, and most of the later ones as they were admitted to the Union, formally adopted the English "common law" as the basis for their legal systems. They did so as of a specific date, usually 1607, 1775, or 1776. The "common law" that was adopted included *both* the original common law made (or "discovered") by the judges up to that point *and* the supplementary English statutes then in force.

The new American judges inherited the common law tradition. They too evolved legal principles from the decision of individual cases and developed, over time, distinctive twists and turns to the inherited common law that were unique to each State. The federal courts resolved disputes that came before them in the same tradition. Both state and federal courts used the common law methodology to fill gaps in the law as required to resolve the litigation that came before them.

American state legislatures, and the federal Congress as well, soon did what Parliament had done, passing new statutes against the background of the now American "common law" as it was evolving in each particular jurisdiction. Today, American law consists of a complex interplay between statutes and common law, complicated by differences that exist among the States, by the coexistence of state and federal law within each State, by the coexistence of state and federal courts within each State, by the emergence of new law-making entities (such as administrative agencies), and by the overlay of constraints imposed by the state and federal constitutions.

The term "common law" is used in this book in a systemic sense, to describe a way of thinking about law rather than its particular origin in a statute or judicial decision. Today, the practice of judicial invention of new crimes has disappeared. But the criminal law in many States (as well as the federal criminal law) still consists of the original judge-made law, as supplemented and refined over the years by the judges and the legislatures. Importantly for present purposes, the common law evolved a distinctive vocabulary and a distinctive analytical approach to the criminal law that still prevails in many American jurisdictions. It is still the case that the criminal law remains heavily influenced by the ideas that originated in the English common law and that have been nurtured over two centuries of American experience. Study of the "common law" approach to a question is therefore not a study of history. It is a study of a current, mature system of law.

B. WHY STUDY THE MODEL PENAL CODE?

With a few exceptions, the American States did not systematically codify their criminal law until late in the 20th Century. Rather, criminal codes grew in a hodge-podge, catch-as-catch-can fashion. Whenever something bad happened, the legislature passed a law against it. The result in many places was incredible inconsistency, caused by the fact that the legislature that passed a new statute often paid no attention to what was already on the books. My favorite example is the law in California that authorized a 15–year maximum sentence for a person who broke into a car to steal something inside. Another statute on the books at the same time authorized a maximum of 10 years for stealing the entire car. The law in several other States punished a person who tried to get another to commit perjury by a 5-year maximum, while another provision in the same Codes established a 1-year maximum if the attempt was successful.

The American Law Institute is a private organization of lawyers, judges, and law professors that was formed in 1923. Beginning in 1952, after years of false starts, the Institute began to draft a "model" criminal code, designed to encourage States to revise their penal codes so as to eliminate inconsistency and redundancy. Tentative Drafts emerged for comment and criticism during the period between 1953 and 1962, and finally in 1962 the Proposed Official Draft was approved. Three volumes of commentary to Part II of the Model Penal Code (the specific crimes) were finally published in 1980, and the volumes on Part I (the general provisions) were published in 1985.

The Model Penal Code is studied by students of the criminal law for two reasons.

First, it was prepared over a 10-year period by the best minds that this country and others have to offer. As an academic document, it is a first-rate attempt to state what a modern criminal law ought to look like. As a general matter, it is principled, consistent, and much more transparent than is the common law. For complicated historical reasons, the common law developed a vocabulary that often bears little resemblance to the ordinary English meaning of the words used to state its doctrines. The Model Penal Code translates these concepts into ordinary English, and in the process exposes a different perspective on many issues central to the criminal law. Today, anyone who intends to give serious thought to the basic principles of the substantive criminal law must take the Model Penal Code into account.

Second, the Model Penal Code has been remarkably successful in accomplishing its primary objective. It was designed by its drafters, as its name suggests, to serve as a model against which States could revise their criminal codes. It has been so successful in this sense that in many respects the Model Penal Code *is* the law in many American jurisdictions. There is no State that has done nothing in response to the Model Penal Code. After nearly 200 years in which virtually no State at any time approached its criminal code systematically and sought to enact a coherent and consistent set of crimes and punishments, at least 30 States have passed substantial revisions of their criminal codes since 1962 based largely on the work of those who drafted the Model Penal Code. [Among the enacted codes, the one in New York has been the most influential in other States.]

But the Model Penal Code has not only been noticed in legislative halls. Judges have taken account of it too, and it has had a significant influence on both reasoning and results in criminal cases from the United States Supreme Court through the rest of the State and Federal court systems. The result is that an educated criminal lawyer today has to speak two languages, the language of the common law and the language of the Model Penal Code. In virtually all States the language of the common law is on the way out and the language of the Model Penal Code on the way in. As you will see, there is much in common between the two systems in terms of results, but they do indeed speak in a different tongue.

This is why this outline spends so much time on the Model Penal Code, and why it continually contrasts, as it is likely that your criminal law course will do, the "common law" and the "Model Penal Code" as though they were two different systems of thought—which they are. I have assumed, incidentally, that you will have access to a copy of the Model Code, probably as an appendix to your criminal law casebook. It would have added more than a hundred pages to this outline to reprint it here. It will be necessary that you carefully read the relevant sections as I talk about them in the material to follow. I have assumed that you will be doing so, and what I have to say will not make much sense unless you do.

It is appropriate to add a further word about federal criminal law. The job of combating the kinds of crime that are most visible to most people, in particular the general run of crimes against person and property, is primarily for the States in this country. There is, however, a substantial body of federal criminal law that exists independently of the criminal law of the States. It speaks to many of the same subjects, but also addresses distinctly federal interests as well as issues (terrorism, organized crime, corporate fraud) that transcend state lines and are difficult, if not impossible, for a single American State to prosecute. When Bonnie and Clyde reached the state line, the cops had to forego pursuit.

For present purposes, three points should be made.

First, all criminal cases in the federal system must be based on a specific statute enacted by Congress. There are no common law crimes. [As stated above, new crimes are not created to fill gaps by judges today the way they were centuries ago in England. In some States, however, crimes created by judges years ago remain on the books today, even though not specifically enacted by legislation. This is not true at the federal level, nor in most States. Note what the Model Penal Code has to say on this subject in § 1.05(1) ("No conduct constitutes an offense unless it is a crime or violation under this Code or another statute of this State.") Many modern State codes have a similar provision.]

Second, there was a substantial effort to prepare a new federal criminal code based on the Model Penal Code, but in the end it did not command sufficient political support to get enacted. There are a number of drafts of a new federal criminal code written in the 1970s floating around, and you may see references to them from time to time. [The same thing has happened in several States, by the way. California is one of them.]

Third, this means that the federal criminal law consists of statutory crimes enacted by the Congress over the years—a hodge-podge of specific enactments collected alphabetically in Title 18 of the United States Code, plus many others scattered throughout the Code. This statutory law uses the common law vocabulary and was enacted against the background of the common law. It is supplemented by common law gap-filling decisions by the federal courts fleshing out those aspects of the law not covered by statute. A good example for many years was the law of insanity, which was covered completely by common law decisions by the federal courts until Congress finally enacted a statute on the subject in 1984 in response to the acquittal by reason of insanity of John Hinckley in his trial for attempting to assassinate President Reagan.

But this does not mean that the Model Penal Code is irrelevant to federal practice. More and more federal judges, including some on the Supreme Court, are thinking and talking in the language of the Model Code. The vocabulary of the Model Penal Code and its approach to the analysis of crimes are slowly making their way into the federal law, as is happening in some States that remain oriented towards the common law in their basic approach. The federal criminal lawyer too, then, needs to know about the Model Penal Code, as do state lawyers who practice in common law jurisdictions.

C. THE ORGANIZATION OF THESE MATERIALS

Criminal law is a technical subject. It starts with the definition of the crime with which the defendant has been accused. That definition is precise, and virtually every word must be carefully analyzed and its function understood. The objective is to isolate the "elements" of the offense that the prosecutor must prove beyond a reasonable doubt in order to get a conviction.

This outline starts in Part Two with materials on "The Definition of Crime." These materials focus, first under the common law system and next under the Model Penal Code, on the various "elements" of a criminal offense, the components that go into the definition of a crime. You will come to know these elements as the "actus reus" (the conduct) and the "mens rea" (the mental state) of the offense. In some crimes, but not all, specific results must have been "caused" by the defendant's conduct, and for these the concept of "causation" must also be understood. Both the common law and Model Penal Code discussions conclude with a section on "Proof of the Elements of Crime," which deals with how the prosecutor goes about proving the various elements contained in the definition of the offense.

The next section, Part Three, takes up the subject of "Derivative Defenses." These are defenses the substance of which is derived from the elements of the offense discussed in

Part Two. In effect, Part Two deals with what the prosecutor must prove in order to obtain a conviction. Part Three deals with efforts by the defendant to dispute the existence of one of those things, and thereby to gain an acquittal. If Part Two requires in a given case that the prosecutor prove elements $A + B + C$ to gain a conviction, Part Three deals with an effort by the defendant to answer the prosecutor's case by showing not-A or not-B or not-C. The prosecutor will need, in other words, to prove *all* of the elements of the offense beyond a reasonable doubt in order to gain a conviction. The defendant can get off by creating a reasonable doubt as to any one of them.

The term "derivative defense," by the way, is mine and will be found nowhere in the law. I use it in order to signal that certain defenses are "derived from" elements of the offense in the sense that they are reciprocals of those elements. If one person needs to show A, it makes sense to me to say that the defense of "not-A" is "derived from" the obligation of the other party to show that A exists. The proof requirement and the defense are different sides of the same coin.

The next two sections, Parts Four and Five, deal with "Collateral Defenses" of two kinds, first "Justifications" and second "Excuses." This term too is mine. These are defenses, like self-defense or insanity, which do not rebut the elements of the prosecutor's case, but raise matters that the law chooses to recognize as a defense even though they do not show that an element of the offense is missing. They are, as it were, a confession and avoidance. In effect they say to the prosecutor: "Even though you may have proved $A + B + C$ and even though those elements normally amount to a crime, I am entitled to get off because D is true and D is a defense to this crime." It helps me to think of these defenses as "collateral" because they are not derived from an element of the offense but are a recognition that certain conditions permit exoneration even though all of the elements of the offense have been proved beyond a reasonable doubt.

Normally, an intentional killing of another person is going to be murder. In the vocabulary I have invented for this purpose, it would be a *derivative* defense to show that the killing was accidental and not intentional. The defense is *derivative* because it shows that one of the elements of the offense—an intent to kill—is not present. It would be a *collateral* defense to show that, yes the killing was intentional, but it was by a cop acting in self defense or an executioner obeying the duty to implement capital punishment ordered by a court. The defense is *collateral* in these cases because the defendant admits that all of the elements of the offense occurred but attempts to show that the killing should nonetheless be justified or excused.

The next two sections change the subject from the elements of a crime and its defenses. Part Six deals with "Parties to Crime," which concerns who in addition to the person who actually commits a crime can be liable for it. Obviously, if I help you commit a crime both of us should be punishable even though you were the one who actually did the deed. Part Seven covers "Inchoate Offenses." These are crimes, like attempt and conspiracy, that are concerned with efforts to plan or commit a crime. When, in other words, should we punish a person who has not yet committed a crime but who is trying hard to do so or has agreed with one or more persons that one of them will commit the offense?

Parts Eight and Nine are the sections of the outline that address specific criminal offenses.

Part Eight deals in some detail with the subject of "Criminal Homicide." There are several reasons for the detail. One is that there are many unique and interesting doctrines associated with these most serious of all crimes. This is one reason why most criminal law courses devote at least some attention to the subject. A second reason is that criminal homicide is a good example of the "grading" of criminal offenses, that is, the use of mens rea and other doctrines to define the severity of various levels of the offense as well as whether it should be a crime in the first place.

Part Nine departs from the format of the rest of the book by combining common law and Model Penal Code discussions of two other specific crimes, rape and theft, that are often studied in criminal law courses around the country. It also addresses the federal RICO statute, an organized crime provision that is often studied in connection with the law of conspiracy. There are a number of practical difficulties in dealing with particular substantive offenses in a book of this type. Any list of *all* of the crimes covered in *all* of the criminal codes of this country would be huge, and the detail required to cover *all* of their elements would extend this outline into multiple volumes, would require the discussion of endless minutiae, and would provide little aid to the objectives of most criminal law courses. Moreover, the definitions of the usual array of crimes in a criminal code (or in a criminal law course that gives particular attention to the law of a given State) vary significantly from jurisdiction to jurisdiction, as do the sentencing structures that govern the specific punishments provided for similarly defined offenses. In addition, the influence of the Model Penal Code has been far greater in the "general part" of the criminal law (those subjects covered in Parts Two through Seven of this book) than in the "special part" (the specific crimes). For that reason, as well as the simple bulk of the material, little would be gained by marching through all of the substantive offenses of the Model Code and comparing them to comparable offenses in jurisdictions that approach their crimes through the prism of the common law.

There is value, however, in consideration of the general principles governing several examples of a typical American substantive offenses. Even here, minute examination of all of the details of each offense would add more detail that would be useful or practical. Part Nine is therefore a compromise. It provides an overview of three offenses often studied in criminal law courses, but it resists the temptation to get lost in the details of any of them.

Finally, Part Ten addresses "Constitutional Limits on Punishment for Crimes." It collects in one place the various constitutional doctrines the Supreme Court has announced of relevance to the prior materials in the outline, and puts them at the end on the theory that you are more likely to understand constitutional "limits" once you know something about what it is that the Constitution is limiting.

It bears repeating that there is no magic to the order in which these materials have been presented. They have been designed so that you can read the various sections in whatever order fits your own course. I do not follow the order of this book in my own course, nor is this the order in which the Casebook which I have co-authored proceeds. The progression is logical, however, and it was chosen in part because it might help your review to examine the materials from a slightly different perspective than you may have followed in your course.

PART TWO

THE DEFINITION OF CRIME

Analysis

I.   *General Considerations*

*

II

THE COMMON LAW

Analysis

A. STARTING THE ANALYSIS

The first step in the analysis of any substantive criminal law problem is to find the definition of the offense in the statutes or the case law, and then to isolate from it the actus reus, the mens rea, and any required element of causation.

B. THE ACTUS REUS

Crime requires conduct. It cannot consist of propensities, desires, hopes, wishes, status, or personal condition. The defendant must do something. As will be seen immediately below, failing to do something when there is an obligation to act counts as "conduct" for this purpose. So does possession.

There are important moral and civil liberties reasons for requiring the all crime be based on conduct in this sense.

Morally, blame is justified for acting on bad choices, for engaging in *behavior* in contexts where we would be justified in saying: "You shouldn't have done that. You should have known better." If we blame people for what they "are" or "have become," as sometimes happens, it is because we condemn actions that produced the condition we condemn or the failure to take actions we think they are obligated to take. These principles are mirrored in the criminal law by precluding criminal punishment in the absence of provable behavior.

The requirement that criminal law be based on conduct provides an essential component of our civil liberties. It precludes conviction based on speculation about what *might* happen in the future, or about what a person might be "predisposed" to do. It establishes that the defendant firmly resolved to act against the interests of society. It gives each of us an important measure of control over the intrusion of police and other legal authorities into our lives by giving us "space" within which we can freely operate. As long as we refrain from *doing* certain things—from engaging in forms of conduct described in advance by the criminal law—we know that we will not be subject to arrest and prosecution for crime. Individual liberty, in other words, implies a right to be left alone in the absence of predefined *behavior* that intrudes on social order in a manner that justifies criminal sanctions. Each of us can preserve that liberty by refraining from punishable *conduct*.

The term "actus reus" refers generically to the specific behavior required by any given definition of a crime. The "actus reus" thus will change from crime to crime. The words in the definition of a particular offense tell us the kinds of behavior that will constitute the "actus reus" elements of that crime.

In modern usage, although the common law did not talk this way, the "actus reus" elements of an offense will consist of "conduct" committed under certain "circumstances" that may or may not have "caused" certain "results." The "actus reus" is all the conduct, circumstances, and results required by the definition of an offense.

Examples: The actus reus of burglary at common law was "breaking and entering the dwelling house of another in the nighttime." The actus reus of larceny was "taking and carrying away the personal property of another."

Obviously a person who has not done these things cannot be guilty of burglary or larceny.

1.   ELEMENTS OF THE ACTUS REUS

The behavior required for a crime *must* include an act, an omission, or possession. This is often called the "conduct" component of the offense. Usually the "conduct"—that is, the act, omission, or possession—must occur under defined circumstances, and sometimes it must cause a result.

a.   Act

The required behavior usually will include an affirmative act or series of acts described in the definition of the offense. These acts usually must occur in a specific context. Often the law refers to this context as stating the "circumstances" in which the acts must occur.

Examples: The "acts" required for burglary are that the defendant must "break and enter." The context is that the acts must occur to or in "the dwelling house of another" and in the "nighttime." The "dwelling house of another" and "in the nighttime" are the "circumstance" elements of the offense.

The "acts" required for larceny are "taking and carrying away." The context is that the items taken must be "the personal property of another." It is often said that phrase "personal property of another" describes the "circumstance" elements of the offense.

b.   Omission

The conduct can be an omission, in either of two circumstances:

(1)   where the definition of the crime explicitly punishes an omission; *or*

(2)   where the definition specifies a result that must occur, where it does not describe specific affirmative conduct that must cause the result, where there is a legal duty to act, *and* where it is possible for the defendant physically to perform the act.

Examples: Failure to register for the draft or failure to file an income tax return are cases where the definition of the offense explicitly punishes an omission. In effect, the criminal law establishes a duty to act in these situations and the failure to obey that duty is a crime.

The definition of murder requires that the defendant cause the death of another. Typically, it does not specify any particular conduct that must cause the death. In this situation, an omission that causes the death of another will suffice for murder *if* the defendant had a legal duty to act and *if* it was physically possible for the defendant to act. For example, a mother who allowed an infant child to starve when food was readily available would be guilty of murder.

1) Sources of a Legal Duty to Act

A legal duty to act can arise from any source of positive law—civil or criminal. The duty can arise from a relationship (e.g., parent and child, doctor and patient), a statute (e.g., the obligation of a driver to stop and render aid at the scene of an accident), a contract (e.g., a lifeguard or a practical nurse), the voluntary assumption of care (e.g., an elderly person becomes dependent upon the voluntary assistance of another person), and from other similar sources. A moral duty is *not* sufficient.

c. Possession

The conduct can be possession whenever the definition of the offense so specifies.

Example: The possession of burglar tools and the possession of controlled narcotic substances are frequently defined as crimes.

In effect, possession is an example of the punishment of conduct and/or an omission where there is a legal duty to act. Possession of something either is the result of an act of acquisition and/or it is the failure to divest something where there is a duty established by the criminal law not to possess. The punishment of possession is therefore consistent in theory with the punishment of acts and omissions.

2. PROBLEMS OF INTERPRETATION

Ascertaining whether the defendant has engaged in the required actus reus will frequently present difficult questions of interpretation.

Example: If burglary requires breaking and entering the dwelling house of another, is a defendant who reaches through an open window guilty of the "breaking" component of the offense (does this element require physical "breaking" or is it enough to "break" the plane of the window)? If murder requires the killing of another person, is it murder to kick a pregnant woman in the stomach and cause the "death" of a viable fetus? Is the partner who appropriates partnership property to personal use taking the property "of another"?

The answer to questions such as these will turn on a number of factors, among them: (1) the precise words in the definition of the offense; (2) the intent of the legislature; (3) the policies served by the offense; (4) the learning to be gathered from prior cases; (5) the coverage of related crimes; (6) the degree of creativity required to include the behavior in the definition of the offense; and (7) the political sensitivity of the issue and the extent to which inclusion of the behavior in the offense would be controversial as a matter of policy.

C. THE MENS REA

Crimes generally require that a prescribed mental element (the "mens rea") accompany each actus reus element of the offense. An element of a crime that does not require mens rea is said to impose "strict liability." Strict liability is relatively rare in the criminal law.

The term "mens rea" is used to refer specifically to the mental attitude required for a given element of an offense. It is also used generically to refer to the mental attitude required for a crime. In both cases, the mens rea required in a given context is determined by the definition of the offense and by applying the common law mens rea structure outlined below.

1. COMMON LAW MENS REA TERMS

Common law mens rea is usually described as falling into one of three categories: "specific intent," "general intent," or "strict liability."

It is often said that "this is a specific intent crime," that "this is a general intent crime," or that "this is a strict liability crime." As will be demonstrated, it is an overstatement to describe "the crime" in this manner because often one element of a crime will have a different mens rea from another element. It is therefore better practice to ask about the mens rea that applies to each element of the offense rather than to speak generically of the mens rea for the offense itself.

a. Specific Intent

A specific intent in a crime focuses on what the defendant was actually thinking, planning, or hoping at the time of the offense. Usually, a specific intent is stated explicitly in the definition of the offense. Examples fall into three types of situations:

1) Contemplated Conduct

The first requires that the defendant must, in the common sense usage of the word, *intend* to engage in certain additional conduct beyond what has already been done. Exactly what the defendant must intend to do will be determined by the definition of the offense.

Example: Burglary at common law required that the defendant break and enter the dwelling house of another in the nighttime "with the intent to commit a felony therein." In addition to an actus reus of breaking and entering the dwelling house of another in the nighttime, the defendant must have the specific intent to commit a felony (e.g., rape, murder, larceny) inside the dwelling.

The offense occurs at the moment of entry. The offense that the defendant intends to commit inside the dwelling *need not occur*. It is enough that the defendant intended to commit it at the time of the breaking and entering. The offense of burglary therefore consists of certain described behavior (breaking and entering) plus an intent to engage in additional conduct beyond what has already been done (an intent to commit a felony inside the dwelling).

2) Contemplated Impact

The second requires, in the common sense meaning of the words, that the defendant hope or intend that conduct will have some future impact or effect. What the impact or effect must be will be determined by the definition of the offense.

> ***Example:*** The crime of "hindering prosecution" might be defined as volunteering false information to a law enforcement officer "with the purpose of hindering the apprehension or prosecution of another person." The actus reus of the offense is "volunteering false information to a law enforcement officer." Whatever the immediate effects of that conduct (and whether the law enforcement officer believed the defendant or not!), the defendant must, in the common sense usage of the term, *intend* that the apprehension or prosecution of another person be hindered by the information provided. That impact need not in fact occur.
>
> As in the burglary example above, the crime occurs when the actus reus is completed if it is accompanied by the required intent. In this case, the intent consists of something the defendant hopes will happen rather than something the defendant intends to do.

3) Knowledge That One or More Elements of the Actus Reus Exists

The third requires that the defendant *know* that one or more elements of the actus reus exists or *believe* that a state of facts included in an actus reus exists whether or not it actually does. What the defendant must know or believe will be determined by the definition of the offense.

> ***Example:*** A crime defined as "knowingly receiving stolen property" requires as the actus reus that the defendant receive stolen property and as the mens rea that the defendant know that it was stolen.

Note that an entirely different analysis follows if the definition of the offense is changed. If receiving stolen property is defined as "receiving property *believing* it to have been stolen," the actus reus would be "receiving property" (it would not in fact have to be stolen) and the mens rea would be "*believing* it to have been stolen" (whatever the actual fact of the matter might be). The required mens rea would still be described as a "specific intent."

b. General Intent

"General intent" is difficult to define. It is a residual term, used to describe the default mens rea for elements that do not require a specific intent and that do not impose strict liability. The idea is that specific intent and strict liability are for exceptional situations where there are special reasons for having a high mens rea standard or having none at all. General intent is the default standard that applies to everything else—to all elements of a crime that do not fall into one of these special categories.

The tricky part is that the common law did not develop a clear default meaning of mens rea that would apply whenever it was said that "general intent" was the standard.

The best understanding you can have if asked the meaning of "general intent" is to say (a) it is a chameleon whose meaning will change with the context; (b) I don't know what it means until I understand the context and how the particular jurisdiction I am dealing with defines the term in that context; and (c) it states the default mens rea—whatever it turns out to mean in a specific context—that the jurisdiction is question applies to situations where there is no specific intent and where strict liability is not to be imposed.

Often "general intent" will mean ordinary negligence, as when a mistake of fact defense is asserted. See page 147. But often it requires more than ordinary negligence, as in the offense of involuntary manslaughter. See page 371. Sometimes it refers to recklessness or negligence, although most common law jurisdictions do not sharply distinguish between the two and neither term has a generally accepted meaning. Frequently the concepts of recklessness and negligence are defined with circularity or by epithet. There is, however, an emerging view, based on the Model Penal Code (see page 109), that these terms should be defined and distinguished as follows:

1) Recklessness

"Recklessness" means: (a) the defendant's conduct created an unacceptable risk that an element of a crime would occur (e.g., a risk that a person would be killed); (b) the defendant was aware of the risk; and (c) given what the defendant knew about the context and the situation, the defendant was seriously at fault for engaging in the conduct.

2) Negligence

"Negligence" means: (a) the defendant's conduct created an unacceptable risk that an element of a crime would occur; (b) given what the defendant knew about the context and the situation, the defendant *should have been aware* of the risk; and (c) given what the defendant knew about the context and the situation, the defendant was seriously at fault for engaging in the conduct.

c. Other Mens Rea Terms

The common law uses a variety of additional mens rea words, among them: maliciously, feloniously, corruptly, fraudulently, wantonly, wilfully, scienter, and wrongfully. Like recklessness and negligence, these words also lack commonly accepted meanings. Moreover, they are used singly or in combination to create endless possibilities. One crime, for example, might require that the defendant act "feloniously and wilfully," another "feloniously *or* wilfully," still a third "feloniously and corruptly," etc. It is beyond human imagination to think of independent meanings that each of the possible combinations might signify. What they are, in effect, is a license to courts to define an "appropriate" mens rea to fit the context.

In addition, the meaning of mens rea words tends to come up in cases where a particular defense is asserted and the question is whether that defense disproves the required mens rea. What often happens is that the court will define the mens rea in light of policies appropriate for controlling that particular defense to the crime involved. The difficulty arises in the next case, where perhaps the policies controlling a different defense to a different crime lead the court to a different definition of the same term. The definitions of common law mens rea words thus can vary from jurisdiction to jurisdiction, from offense to offense within a given jurisdiction, and even from defense to defense for the same crime within the same jurisdiction.

d. Foreign Language Analogy

One useful way to think about common law mens rea is to treat all common law mens rea words as though they were components of a foreign language that you do not speak, even though ordinary English words are used to fool you into thinking that you know what they mean. If you see a word like "malice," you should refrain from looking in an English dictionary or even a legal dictionary and assume, even if you think you know what "malice" means in ordinary discourse, that you have no idea what is meant. You should then examine all relevant legal materials applicable to the context in which you are working and attempt to derive from them—not from your general knowledge of the English language—what the word means for that court in that context in that jurisdiction.

To confound you even further, the next time you see the word "malice" in a different context, or perhaps in a different court or a different jurisdiction, it is as likely as not that it will have a different meaning. So don't be fooled into thinking that once you have translated a common law mens rea word into terms that are accessible to you that you have learned anything that can be transferred to a different context. As pointed out above, common law mens rea words are chameleons—they change color to suit the background.

So common law mens rea words are (a) a foreign language that you do not speak; and (b) it is a hard language to learn because the meanings of the words are likely to change every time you see them.

e. The Best Approach

The best approach is to read the applicable cases and try to translate the court's language into one of four ideas: (1) purpose, meaning a conscious desire or objective; (2) knowledge, meaning awareness or belief; (3) recklessness, as defined in the "general intent" discussion immediately above; and (4) negligence, also as defined in the same discussion. One of these four ideas should match what the court is trying to say on any occasion. This of course assumes that the court is requiring mens rea in the first place. A fifth alternative is that the court, though using the language of mens rea, actually means to impose strict liability.

This insight is based on the Model Penal Code. One of the major contributions of the Model Penal Code to modern thinking about the criminal law—perhaps its single most important contribution—is the idea that there are really only four substantive correlates to the variety of mens rea terms used by the common law. These four ideas—purpose, knowledge, recklessness, and negligence—are both necessary and sufficient to capture the variety of meanings that common law courts have assigned to mens rea over the years. Strict liability—that is, no mens rea for the element in question—is a fifth possibility, but if liability is not to be strict, one of these four ideas is likely to apply.

DO NOT make the mistake, however, of assuming that once you have translated a mens rea term in a given situation into one of these ideas that you will now know what that same common law mens rea term will mean the next time you see it. The smart thing to do is to retranslate the term into one of these ideas each time you see it, no matter what the context.

f. A Generalization

It is not a bad generalization to say the following. A common law specific intent can usually be translated into either "purpose" or "knowledge." A common law general intent can usually be translated into some form of "recklessness" or "negligence." Strict liability means that no mens rea is to be required. But, as with all generalizations, don't be fooled if you find that this one does not always work.

2.   STRICT LIABILITY
Crimes impose "strict liability" or "liability without fault" if no mens rea is required for some element. There are several contexts in which the law imposes strict liability.

a.   Public Welfare Offenses
There is a class of offenses, called "public welfare" or "regulatory" offenses, to which the normal common law requirement of mens rea does not apply. Public welfare offenses first emerged in the middle of the 19th century. They are a product of social changes brought about by the revolution in manufacturing, technology, and travel in the modern world. Many traffic offenses, for example, will fall into this category, as will laws designed to protect food and drug products from adulteration, impurities, or mislabeling. Serving alcohol to minors is also usually a public welfare offense.

1)   Characteristics of Public Welfare Offenses
These offenses usually share the following characteristics: (1) no harm need actually occur, although the conduct creates the potential for significant and widespread harm and the defendant is usually in a position to prevent the harm by the exercise of care; (2) the offense does not involve conduct designed to harm a particular individual, but conduct that may harm random members of the public at large; (3) the underlying conduct is not itself immoral, or not necessarily immoral, but is sought to be controlled for reasons of public health or safety; (4) public injury when it occurs will occur irrespective of good or bad intentions of the defendant; and (5) normally, the penalties and the stigma of conviction are relatively minor.

b.   Elements Not Central to the Criminality of Behavior
There are numerous elements of crime that are important for *grading* purposes but are not central to the *criminality* of the behavior. The common law does not require mens rea for elements that are important only for grading purposes.

1)   Grading vs. Criminality
Elements are important for grading purposes when they relate only to the severity of the crime. They are central to criminality when without them no crime would be committed.

> ***Example:***   Assume two crimes: breaking and entering the dwelling house of another; and breaking and entering the dwelling house of another in the nighttime with intent to commit a felony therein. The first offense is a minor felony; the second a major felony.
>
> In this example, the "nighttime" element of the major felony is not central to criminality, since even if it is missing the

defendant will still be guilty of the minor felony. The "nighttime" element is therefore of grading significance only and no mens rea will be required for this element by the common law.

c. Immoral Behavior

There is a class of offenses closely associated with private morality, and in particular with sexual behavior, that traditionally has not required mens rea for one critical element of the offense. For example, statutory rape is usually defined as sexual intercourse with an underage person, whether or not consensual. Traditionally, the defendant need have no mens rea as to the age of the victim. Adultery also was traditionally a strict liability offense, at least if, were the facts as the defendant believed them to be, the defendant would have been engaging in an immoral act. What these offenses seem to have in common is that the underlying conduct—sexual intercourse unsanctioned by marriage—was widely viewed as immoral at the time the offenses first emerged.

d. Miscellaneous Crimes

There are a number of other crimes of strict liability which are not so easily classified. The most important is felony murder, dealt with beginning at page 364.

3. CONCURRENCE OF ACTUS REUS AND MENS REA

The defendant's conduct and any required mens rea must concur in time. Any required *results* may occur later.

Examples: Larceny can be defined as "taking and carrying away the personal property of another with intent to deprive the owner of the property permanently." If the defendant borrows the property of another (with or without permission), and later decides to keep it, has larceny been committed? The answer is "no." Even if the taking is without permission, the intent to steal was not formed at the time of taking, and therefore larceny has not been committed. The defendant's conduct and intent were not concurrent in time. (Of course it may be possible that some *other* crime has been committed, but that does not affect whether the crime of larceny as defined above has been committed.)

    The defendant shoots another person with intent to kill. The victim dies two weeks later. Has the defendant committed murder? The answer is "yes." The defendant's conduct (shooting the victim) and mens rea (the intent to kill) were contemporaneous in time. It does not matter that the resulting death was delayed by two weeks (so long, of course, as it was "caused" by the defendant's conduct).

4. TRANSFERRED INTENT

Assume a murder prosecution where the defendant meant to kill *A*, but due to bad aim in fact killed *B*. The common law had a conceptual difficulty with this case, namely that the defendant committed the actus reus for one crime (killing *B*) but had the mens rea for another (killing *A*). The common law thus reasoned that there was not a concurrent actus reus and mens rea for a single offense.

The common law solved the problem through the fiction of "transferred intent." The intent to kill *A*, which is a sufficient mens rea for murder, is "transferred" to the killing of *B*. Now the crime of murdering *B* is a completed offense: the defendant committed the actus reus of killing *B* and the mens rea for killing *B* is supplied by the intent "transferred" from the defendant's attempt to kill *A*.

5.   THE RELATION OF MOTIVE TO MENS REA

It is often said that motive is not essential to proof of guilt, defining motive to mean the defendant's objective, goal, or reason for acting. This is usually true, but in fact the relevance of motive in a criminal case is far more slippery than such a statement reveals. As a general proposition, a good motive will not exonerate from otherwise criminal conduct. Nor will a bad motive turn otherwise innocent conduct into a crime.

> *Examples:*   The defendant shoots a victim and is indicted for murder. It is shown by contemporaneous statements heard by eyewitnesses at the time of the offense that the defendant meant to kill the victim, but there is no evidence as to *why* the defendant wanted to do so. In this case, the mens rea is established by showing the defendant's purpose to kill and a murder conviction could be obtained. The fact that the prosecutor cannot establish a motive for the killing does not prevent the conviction.
>
> The defendant shoots a victim and is indicted for murder. It is shown by the defendant's own statements that the defendant meant to kill the victim, but that the reason for the killing was to put a long-suffering loved one out of misery, a classic mercy killing. Here the defendant's *good* motive, if it is so regarded, will not exonerate. The defendant is still guilty of murder.
>
> The defendant shoots a victim and is indicted for murder. It is shown by conclusive evidence that the death was accidental and unavoidable. It is also shown, however, that the defendant hated the victim, stood to gain a large inheritance upon the victim's death, and is glad the victim is dead. The fact that the defendant had a motive to kill the victim does not, however, transform an otherwise innocent killing into a criminal act. The defendant is not guilty of murder, or any other crime, on these facts.

There are many situations, however, where motive is relevant to a criminal prosecution. Establishment of an evil motive—greed, bad feelings toward another—is always relevant *evidence* to help the prosecutor establish mens rea. And establishment of good or bad motives is always relevant to sentencing.

Examples: Reconsider the first example given above. The prosecutor established that the defendant meant to kill the victim. This is a sufficient mens rea for murder. If the prosecutor can show in addition to the other evidence of mens rea that the defendant stood to gain a large inheritance if the victim died and had always hated the victim anyway, the jury is much more likely to believe that the defendant meant to kill the victim. Here, evidence of motive is relevant evidence of the required mens rea, even though it has no independent significance, i.e., it in no sense is an independent element of the offense. The defendant's motive would also be relevant at sentencing, i.e., it might justify the imposition of a harsh sentence.

Now reconsider the mercy-killing example. Here the defendant's "good" motive would not prevent a conviction for murder. Indeed, it *helps* the prosecutor establish the necessary mens rea, the intent to kill the loved one. Probably, however, it would justify a lenient sentence.

There are, moreover, two situations where the defendant's motive is especially important:

a.   Establishing a Defense

A justification defense requires that the defendant have a particular motive for acting. Among the justification defenses are self-defense, protection of others, protection of property, and acting to enforce the law. There are carefully defined restrictions on each of these defenses, elaborated below. See page 187. For now, consider a case where the defendant intentionally killed another and asserts the defense of self-defense. Here the defendant will assert that the reason—or motive—for the killing was to save the defendant's life. The defendant's motive or goal for acting, in other words, is a necessary component of a valid defense. It is not a sufficient condition, as the materials on page 193–95 develop. There are additional elements of the defense that must be established. But it is a necessary condition that the defendant's motive be that of self-preservation.

b.   Establishing Specific Intent

Specific intent often is nothing more than a requirement that the defendant act with a particular goal or motive. Consider the traditional definition of burglary: "breaking and entering the dwelling house of another in the nighttime with the intent to commit a felony therein." In this case, it could be said that the defendant's goal or motive for breaking and entering the house of another at night must be to commit a felony inside. Of course the defendant might have other goals too, like getting rich. But it is a particular goal or motive for acting that is the distinctive mens rea differentiating burglary from a less serious form of criminal trespass.

D. ACTUS REUS, MENS REA, AND PROPORTIONALITY

Two important aspects of the actus reus and mens rea of crime should be noticed here. The first is a prescriptive principle that *ought* to obtain in the definition of crimes, and that usually does. The second is an observation about the nature of blaming that leads to several important principles about the actus reus, the mens rea, and proportionality.

1. CORROBORATIVE BEHAVIOR

The actus reus of a criminal offense ought always to contain enough conduct so as, under the circumstances as they actually exist, to corroborate the mens rea required for the offense.

Ascertaining the defendant's mens rea is *always* an inference from available evidence, even if the defendant confesses to having had the mens rea but particularly if the defendant does not. [The defendant who confesses to having had the mens rea will be giving evidence about a state of mind held in the past. The defendant could be lying for a variety of reasons, could simply be confused, or could be drawing an inference ("if I did *X*, I must have meant to do it"). If the defendant doesn't confess with absolute accuracy, any judgment about what the defendant was thinking or planning is an educated guess.]

Our guesses about mens rea are likely to be more accurate if corroborated by the defendant's behavior. We run less risk of error—less risk of convicting an innocent person—if the acts committed by the defendant provide strong evidence that the defendant had the required mens rea. Without corroborative behavior, conviction may be based on unwarranted speculation—or worse yet, on unacceptable stereotypes based on the defendant's race, sex, religion, or other unacceptable criterion. Actual conduct by the defendant, in other words, is the best evidence of a firm resolution to violate the norms of society that are enforced by the criminal law. Too much reliance on mens rea in the absence of conduct risks unwarranted interference with individual liberties.

This principle can be implemented in both of two ways. First, where possible, ambiguity in the meaning of words used in criminal statutes should be resolved by interpreting them to require conduct that is more rather than less corroborative of mens rea. Second, whatever the required actus reus, proof of mens rea should always be grounded in the defendant's behavior.

Example: Assume an offense worded as follows (compare § 221.2(1) of the Model Penal Code): "An offense is committed if, knowing that there is no license or privilege to do so, a person enters or remains in any building or occupied structure." Is the phrase "knowing that there is no license or privilege to do so" a mens rea element only? Or is "knowing" the mens rea for the actus reus element "no license or privilege to do so"?

To ask the same question another way, must the prosecutor prove that the defendant was *actually* not licensed or privileged to enter or remain (as would be required if it was an actus reus element)? Or is it enough to show that the defendant *believed* that there was no license or privilege to enter or remain (as would be sufficient if it were only a mens rea element)?

The language of the statute is ambiguous. It could mean either. It should be interpreted so that "no license or privilege to do so" is an actus reus element, because otherwise the actus reus will consist of "entering or remaining in a building," which is completely innocuous conduct—something we all do every day. Since entering a building is completely innocent behavior by itself, we run a lesser risk of error— not no risk but a lesser risk—if the offense is construed to punish entering a building when the defendant is not in fact licensed or privileged to do so. The effect of reducing the risk of error by requiring more conduct is a marginal increase in the protection of our civil liberties.

In this context, moreover, this construction of the statute does not come at high cost in terms of reducing the social control function of the law. We do not lose much by not being able to convict persons who are excluded from conviction by this interpretation. If we read the disputed language as establishing an actus reus element, we will not be able to convict of the offense itself persons who actually were licensed or privileged to be in the building, but who thought they were not. It may be, as will be seen when that topic is considered, that we could convict of an attempt in this situation. But, in principle at least, such a conviction should not be possible unless the mens rea conclusion was corroborated or confirmed by the actual behavior in which the defendant engaged. See pages 310–11, 334.

2. ALL CRIMINAL LIABILITY IS BASED ON BOTH SUBJECTIVE AND OBJECTIVE INGREDIENTS

At one level, the process of blaming is very simple. We hold people at fault, that is, we blame them for their behavior, when we think they knew enough about what they were doing so they should have known better. There is an element of subjective awareness in this criterion ("they knew enough about what they were doing") and an element of holding them to an objective standard ("they should have known better"). We blame, in other words, based on a combination of subjective and objective ingredients of the behavior involved.

These characteristics of this simple standard exist in every level by which criminal liability is measured. Consider each of the four substantive correlates of mens rea identified above, plus situations where strict liability is imposed.

a. Purpose and Knowledge

"Purpose" and "knowledge" are both subjective inquiries. They are based on what the defendant knew and intended. So where's the objective standard?

The answer is that we assume without proof that people who purposefully or knowingly engage in criminal conduct know they are not supposed to act that way.

Examples: Assume a person who, without justification, purposely kills another person. We will convict that person of murder. What result if the defense is "I didn't know that murder was wrong"?

The answer is that "ignorance of the law is no excuse." The defendant will be held to strict liability on the moral standard breached by intentional killings, that is, will be held to an objective standard of behavior without asking at the trial whether the defendant "knew" it was wrong intentionally to kill other people. We assume in our society that people are sufficiently socialized to know that committing crimes is wrong. Defendants who claim that they do not in fact understand moral standards are convicted nonetheless. Liability on this point is strict.

The same could be said of cases where the mens rea is "knowledge." Defendants who knowingly receive stolen property will not be heard to claim that they did not know that such conduct violated the law. They will be convicted if they knew the property was stolen, whatever they thought about the propriety of receiving stolen property. On that point, they are held to an objective standard.

b. Recklessness and Negligence

Examine the definitions of both "recklessness" and "negligence" provided on pages 78–79 above. In the end, both are based on the judgment that the defendants were seriously at fault for engaging in the conduct. Here the jury holds them to an objective standard of behavior—the defendants should have known not to do it even if they didn't. But in both cases, the jury's judgment is based on subjective findings about what the defendants actually knew about the context and the situation in which they acted. Both recklessness and negligence, in other words, involve the application of an objective standard to the context as the defendant subjectively understood it.

Examples: Consider a famous example from Oliver Wendell Holmes. A workman on a rooftop knows that there is a busy street 12 stories below, and tosses excess lumber over the side just to get rid of it. Is he reckless or negligent if someone is hit and killed? Sure. He knows enough so that he ought to know that there might be people on the busy street below, that heavy lumber that falls 12 stories is a dangerous instrument, and that someone might get hurt. He knows enough so that we are comfortable in holding that a standard of due care should be applied to him, whether or not he actually understands why people should act with due care for others and whether or not he actually thought about the potential consequences of what he was doing.

Consider another famous example from H.L.A. Hart. A switchman works for a railroad. His one job is to switch the tracks at midnight so that two oncoming trains don't collide. Knowing that this is his job, he accepts a poker game with his buddies and doesn't pay attention to the time. Midnight arrives, he does nothing, and the trains collide. Blameworthy behavior? You bet. Reckless or negligent? You bet. Do we care if he defends on the ground that he thought there was nothing wrong with ignoring the duty to act in such a situation? Not in the least. Again, the judgment of blame is based on a combination of subjective (what he knew about his job) and objective (his violation of an appropriate standard of care) factors.

c. Strict Liability

In order to understand that the same principle applies to strict liability, it is necessary to generalize about the kinds of situations when strict liability is imposed for serious crimes. No crime is based on strict liability as to all of its elements. Stated another way, strict liability is imposed in situations where, given what the defendant knows about the rest of what is going on, it seems appropriate to hold the defendant to strict liability for one or more aspects of the behavior. Strict liability, in other words, is appropriate only for defendants who are sufficiently aware of the context so that it is fair to hold them accountable even though they didn't know about—and may even have tried hard to avoid—one particular aspect of their behavior.

Examples: One example comes from the Model Penal Code. It provides in § 213.1(1)(d) that it is rape for a male to have sexual intercourse with a girl who is less than 10 years old. Liability is strict on the element "less than 10 years old." This means that it would not be a defense for the defendant to claim that he thought the girl was 11, no matter how non-negligent the defendant was in coming to that belief. The defendant might say: "I'm not the type who has sex with 10-year-olds, so I made sure she was 11." The law says: "Tough."

Is this fair? I always ask my students how many of them want to provide a defense for the defendant who thinks the girl is 11. So far in many years of asking the question, no takers. Why? Because given what the defendant believes about the situation—he thinks he is having sexual intercourse with an 11-year-old girl—he knows enough so that he ought to know not to do it. The strict liability is justified, in other words, because of what the defendant knows about the rest of the situation and about the context in which he is acting.

3. CONCLUSION

What lessons can be drawn from these principles? At least four:

a. Strict Liability Requires a Subjective Inquiry

One is that strict liability in whatever form is justified only if a criminal conviction can fairly be based on the rest of what the defendant knows. Strict liability should never be imposed unless it is fair to blame the defendant based on the defendant's awareness of the total context in which the behavior occurs. This principle applies in the rape example given above, but also applies in situations where we say that "ignorance of the law is no excuse," as in the murder example given above. We blame people every day for crimes without asking whether they actually knew or understood the criminal law. That is a form of strict liability, just as is refusing to admit the defense that the defendant thought the girl was 11.

b. Defining a Crime Involves Achieving the Proper Balance of Subjective and Objective Factors

As discussed above, all criminal liability involves some combination of subjective and objective factors, some combination of subjective knowledge by the defendant and holding the defendant to an objective standard. The goal in establishing the culpability requirements for a given offense is to get the right combination. Purpose obviously requires more subjective culpability than negligence, knowledge requires more than strict liability. The question for those who define crimes is how much of each is appropriate to the particular offense in question.

Another way to approach this latter point is to think of the tension described on page 53. It was pointed out there that the "great tension" of the criminal law lies between the conflicting principles of "blame and social control, between retribution and deterrence, between a system based on fault and responsibility and a system based on prevention and social order." The higher the *subjective* standard of liability, the more an offense is based on principles of retribution and blame—and the more it protects the civil liberties of potentially innocent defendants. Conversely, the more the offense relies on *objective* standards of liability—and strict liability is the ultimate objective standard—the more the offense is motivated by principles of prevention and social control. The trick is to get the right balance between these conflicting objectives in the definition of each crime.

A related point is who makes the objective judgment on the element of blame based on what the defendant should have known or done. Sometimes it is the law, as where the defense of ignorance of the criminal law is categorically denied. The murderer or the rapist is denied the defense "I didn't know such conduct was wrong" by the law as written by the legislature or the courts, not by jury consideration of the facts of the particular case. The concepts of recklessness or negligence, by contrast, depend on the facts and circumstances of each case. For that reason, we leave application of the objective standard to a judgment by the jury based on appropriate instructions from the judge.

c. **It Is OK to Use Negligence and Strict Liability in the Criminal Law**
The discussion above can be taken to reject an idea that is sometimes defended in the literature of the criminal law. Some have argued that it is always inappropriate for the criminal law to use objective standards of liability, and in particular wrong to use concepts like negligence or strict liability. The criminal law should always, the argument goes, use a higher and more subjective standard.

Not so. If strict liability is never to be used in the criminal law, the contract killer must be heard if the claim is that "I didn't know there was anything wrong with contract killing." Similarly, the rapist must be heard if the claim is that "I didn't know there was anything wrong with obtaining sex by force." If a defense of this sort could be advanced in a context where it was believable, it could not be rejected if strict liability is always inappropriate. Similarly, Holmes's construction worker and Hart's switchman cannot be convicted of a crime at any level if negligence is always an inappropriate basis for criminal liability. Never say never.

d. **Proportionality Is the Fighting Issue**
Everyone accepts the idea that the level of punishment for crime, that is the grade of the offense and the potential sentence following conviction, ought to be proportional to the conduct and culpability contained in the definition of the offense. No one would defend, at least after they cooled down, capital punishment for double parking.

The issues raised above need to be thought about in this context. The definition of each crime involves getting the right mix of conduct and culpability, of actus reus and mens rea, of behavior accompanied by subjective mental states judged by objective criteria, of conduct that confirms the resolution to violate societal norms and corroborates inferences of culpability. The definitions of the resulting crimes need to be placed in a complex set of consistent and proportional relationships so that murder is treated more seriously than theft, rape more seriously than fraud, robbery more seriously than embezzlement, and so on.

> ***Example:*** A famous example taught in many criminal law courses where the court got it wrong is Director of Public Prosecutions v. Smith, [1960] 3 All. E.R. 161, [1961] A.C. 290. The defendant killed a policeman by accelerating his car after the policeman ordered him

to stop, jumped on the car when the defendant pulled away, and was thrown off as the defendant picked up speed. Smith was convicted of murder on a jury instruction that used ordinary negligence as the standard of culpability. And then he was sentenced to death. Right result?

No way. The English House of Lords affirmed the conviction and sentence. But the case was later overruled by statute. Independently, the defendant's sentence was commuted to life imprisonment, which fixed the problem somewhat but hardly cured it. Whatever one thinks of capital punishment and/or life in prison as sanctions for crime, it is hard to think of them as appropriately proportional to a conviction based on ordinary negligence. And while it may be that Smith could have been convicted under a higher standard of culpability, or even that we could imagine a scenario under which the original or the substitute sentence was justified, the fact remains that both sentences were seriously disproportionate to Smith's conduct and culpability under the theory of the case submitted to the jury.

E.   CAUSATION

Causation is part of the actus reus of a crime whenever the definition of the offense requires that a result occur. Note that most crimes do *not* require the occurrence of a result. The various forms of criminal homicide are the principal examples of crimes where the defendant must cause a result, namely the death of the victim.

Determination of whether an act has "caused" a particular result requires an analysis in two steps. First, the defendant's conduct must be the "cause in fact" of the result. If it was, then the defendant's conduct must be the "proximate cause" of the result. Only if *both* conditions are satisfied can the defendant be said to have "caused" the result.

1.   CAUSE IN FACT
Whether the defendant's conduct is the "cause in fact" of the result is determined by asking whether the result would have occurred "but for" the defendant's conduct. The inquiry on this branch of the analysis is purely factual, namely whether the result would have happened if the defendant had not acted.

Example: The defendant shoots and wounds a victim with intent to kill. The victim is hospitalized, and after two weeks in the hospital undergoes an operation to repair the effects of the wound. The victim dies because the doctor is negligent in performing the operation. In this case the cause in fact standard is satisfied, since the operation would not have occurred if the defendant had not shot the victim.

a.   Exception: Concurrent Causes
There is one rare case where the "cause in fact" inquiry need not be satisfied. This is where two independent causes operate simultaneously, either of which would have caused the result.

Example: The defendant shoots a victim with intent to kill. The shot hits the victim in the heart. At exactly the same time, another bullet fired by a person not acting in concert with the defendant also hits the victim in the heart. The victim dies. It is clear that either bullet would have killed the victim. In this case, the defendant's shot was not the cause in fact of the victim's death, since the death would have occurred anyway. The defendant's shot is nonetheless treated as a "cause in fact" of the victim's death. And the shot of the other person would also be treated as a cause in fact of the victim's death.

2. PROXIMATE CAUSE

If the defendant's conduct is the cause in fact of the prohibited result, the next question is whether it is the "proximate" or "legal" cause of the result.

a. Dependent and Independent Intervening Causes

"Proximate cause" questions are usually analyzed by asking whether any "intervening" cause should be characterized as "dependent" or "independent."

1) Intervening Cause

"Intervening" cause means a contributing cause other than the defendant's conduct.

Example: The defendant shoots a victim with intent to kill. A bystander comes to the aid of the victim, but moves the victim in a manner that complicates the injury and hastens the victim's death. The bystander's conduct is an "intervening" cause.

2) Dependent Intervening Cause

A "dependent" intervening cause is an intervening cause that is sufficiently foreseeable or sufficiently related to the defendant's conduct so as to make it fair to hold the defendant responsible for the result. When the chain of causation between the defendant's conduct and the result includes a "dependent" intervening cause, the defendant's conduct is the "proximate cause" of the result.

Example: In the above example, the bystander's conduct would be a "dependent" intervening cause. The defendant's conduct would therefore be the proximate cause of the death.

3) Independent Intervening Cause

An "independent" intervening cause is an intervening cause that is sufficiently independent of the defendant's conduct so as to make it unfair to hold the defendant responsible for the result. When the chain of causation between the defendant's conduct and the result includes an "independent" intervening cause, the defendant's conduct is *not* the proximate cause of the result.

> *Example:* The defendant shoots a victim with intent to kill. The victim is hospitalized, but the wound is minor and plainly not life-threatening. While the defendant is in the hospital, another person puts poison in the victim's lunch and the victim dies from the poison. The conduct of the other person would be an "independent" intervening cause, and the defendant's conduct would therefore *not* be the proximate cause of death. A conviction of the defendant for murder thus could not be obtained, although the defendant could be convicted of attempted murder. [The person who poisoned the victim's lunch, assuming that it was an intentional act, could of course be convicted of murder.]

b. The Determinative Inquiry

The test for determining whether an intervening cause is dependent or independent requires that two questions be asked: (1) "What is the difference between what actually happened and what the defendant intended or foresaw?"; (2) "Does this difference make it unfair or unjust to hold the defendant responsible for the result?" If the answer to the second question is "no," then the intervening cause is dependent and the defendant's conduct a proximate cause of the result. If the answer to the second question is "yes," then the intervening cause is independent and the defendant's conduct is not a proximate cause of the result.

> *Example:* The defendant shoots a victim with intent to kill. The injury itself is minor, but because of a pre-existing medical condition unknown to the defendant, the injury is far more complicated and later causes the victim's death. The law will treat a preexisting medical condition as a dependent intervening cause, and thus convict the defendant of murder. The judgment is that the difference between what the defendant intended or foresaw and what actually happened ought to be regarded as immaterial to the gravity of the defendant's offense.

The most difficult cases are those where the independent conduct of another person intervenes after the defendant's conduct and where that person is also at fault in contributing to the victim's death. Such cases will turn either on the foreseeability from the defendant's point of view of the conduct by the other person or on the likelihood that the victim would have died anyway.

> *Examples:* The defendant shoots a victim with intent to kill. Even though the injury is not mortal, the victim cannot stand the pain and commits suicide. Here it is likely that the intervening cause will be "dependent."

The defendant shoots a victim with intent to kill. The injury is mortal, though the victim does not die immediately. While the victim lies dying, another person comes along and kills the victim instantaneously. Here too it is likely that the intervening cause will be "dependent."

The defendant shoots a victim with intent to kill. The injury is serious but not mortal. The victim dies on the operating table, however, because of the negligence of the physician. Again, it is likely that the intervening cause will be held "dependent." If the physician hated and therefore purposely killed the victim, however, it is likely that the intervening cause will be "independent."

F. PROOF OF THE ELEMENTS OF CRIME

Study of how the various elements discussed above are proved in a criminal trial will help you understand what it is that must be proved. The basic order of trial is that the prosecutor must first establish a "prima facie case" of guilt. Once that is done, the case will go to the jury unless the defendant seeks to rebut elements of that case or to raise an independent defense.

1. BURDEN OF PROOF
The term "burden of proof" refers to two quite different ideas. You should always indicate which you mean.

a. Burden of Production
The "burden of production" is placed upon the party who has the obligation first to introduce evidence on a given issue. A party who has not satisfied the burden of production will lose on that issue. The burden of production can be satisfied by introducing "some evidence" on the issue.

b. Burden of Persuasion
Once the burden of production is carried, the party on whom the "burden of persuasion" is cast must then undertake the obligation to persuade the jury on the issue. The "burden of persuasion" may or may not be placed on the same party who has the burden of production. A party who fails to carry the burden of persuasion will lose on that issue. The burden of persuasion can be satisfied by producing enough evidence so that, first, the trial judge is satisfied that a reasonable juror could find that the required "standard of proof" has been met and, second, the jury is satisfied that the required "standard of proof" has indeed been met.

1) Proof Beyond a Reasonable Doubt
There are two "standards of proof" used in most criminal cases. The first is "proof beyond a reasonable doubt." This means that the party who must

satisfy this standard on a given issue will lose on that issue if the jury has a "reasonable doubt" that a required fact has been proved.

It is often said that the prosecutor must bear the burden of persuasion in a criminal case "beyond a reasonable doubt." This statement is correct, but it is an overstatement because the prosecutor may not bear the burden of persuasion on every issue, and may be permitted on some issues to bear it by a preponderance of the evidence. It is critical that you ask on whom the burden of production and the burden of persuasion is placed *with respect to each separate issue* in a criminal case, as well as by what standard the burden of persuasion must be borne.

[Note that the Supreme Court has held that the prosecutor must bear the burden of persuasion beyond a reasonable doubt in some instances. The relevant cases are discussed beginning at page 414. It is best to postpone constitutional discussion for now, until you are familiar with prevailing practice. For this reason, constitutional limits are not considered at this point.]

2)   Proof By a Preponderance of the Evidence

The second standard of proof used in criminal cases is proof "by a preponderance of the evidence." This means that the party who must satisfy this standard on a given issue will lose on that issue if the jury believes it "more likely than not" that a required fact has not been proved.

Normally, when the burden of persuasion is placed on the prosecutor on a given issue, the required standard is beyond a reasonable doubt. And normally when the burden is placed on the defendant, the standard is by a preponderance of the evidence. There are rare exceptions, however. A given jurisdiction could require the prosecutor to prove facts relevant to proper venue, for example, by a preponderance of the evidence. And the same jurisdiction could put the burden of persuasion on the insanity defense on the defendant beyond a reasonable doubt. Finally, it is also possible that the "standard of proof" on a given issue could be by "clear and convincing evidence." This requires a level of proof intermediate between the other two standards, and is mostly used in civil cases. An example of its use in criminal cases is the federal insanity defense. The defendant in a federal court must bear the burden of persuasion on the insanity defense by "clear and convincing evidence." See page 237.

2.   THE ORDER OF TRIAL

The first evidentiary step is for the prosecutor to establish a "prima facie case." This means that the prosecutor must offer enough evidence of the actus reus, the mens rea, and any required causation elements to satisfy the "beyond a reasonable doubt" standard of proof. If the prosecutor does not do so, the case will be dismissed and the defendant acquitted.

Once the prosecutor has met this requirement, the case will either be submitted to the jury or the defendant will offer rebuttal evidence. This evidence can be an attempt to show that some element of the prosecutor's prima facie case does not exist. In this outline, this is called raising a "derivative defense." See page 143. Or the defendant may offer evidence of a defense like insanity or self-defense. These defenses are here called "collateral defenses." See pages 187, 221. The defendant will have the *burden of production* on all defenses. The *burden of persuasion* will be placed on the prosecutor to rebut some defenses and on the defendant to establish others. This varies from jurisdiction to jurisdiction, and from defense to defense.

3.   PROOF OF THE ACTUS REUS

The prosecutor must establish *each* separate actus reus element of the offense beyond a reasonable doubt. This requires independent proof of all conduct, circumstances, and results included in the definition of the offense.

Example: If the offense charged is common law burglary, the prosecutor must separately prove each numbered actus reus element: "(1) breaking (2) and entering (3) the dwelling house (4) of another (5) in the nighttime."

4.   PROOF OF THE MENS REA

The prosecutor must establish *each* mens rea element of the offense beyond a reasonable doubt. Satisfaction of this requirement is complicated by the fact that it will be rare that the prosecutor will have independent evidence of mens rea. Since only the defendant knows for sure what mental state accompanied the commission of the acts and since the prosecutor normally cannot use the defendant as a source of evidence, the prosecutor will usually be required to prove mens rea by circumstantial evidence and by asking the jury to infer mens rea from what the defendant did.

a.   Specific Intent

When the prosecutor must prove a specific intent and *what* the prosecutor must prove is established by the definition of the offense. *How* specific intent can be proved will be determined by the facts and circumstances of each case and the available sources of evidence. Normally, the jury will be asked to infer specific intent based on the circumstances under which the defendant's conduct was performed.

You should always distinguish *what* the prosecutor must prove from *how* the prosecutor may try to prove it. In the context of specific intent, there are two reasons why *what* the prosecutor must prove is important: (1) the finding the jury will be required to make is that the defendant actually entertained the required specific intent—without such a finding there can be no conviction; (2) since the prosecutor must show the defendant's actual intent, the defendant may deny the intent and the jury will be required to acquit if it believes the defendant's testimony. *How* the prosecutor will establish that the required intent exists, as stated above, usually depends on the circumstantial evidence and other sources of proof that are available.

b. General Intent

It is difficult to generalize about how the prosecutor must prove general intent because the courts are in such disarray about the meaning of the term. "General intent" sometimes means "recklessness" or "negligence," however, and it is instructive to focus on them.

1) Recklessness

Recall the definition of "recklessness" set forth on page 78. When applicable to a given element of an offense, it requires that the prosecutor prove three things, the second of which is that the defendant was *actually aware* of the risk that the element would exist or occur and the third of which involves understanding the facts and circumstances as they were known to the defendant at the time. Again, this is *what* must be proved; *how* it will be proved is normally by asking the jury to make inferences about what the defendant is likely to have realized given the nature and circumstances of the conduct. But (1) the jury will be required to acquit unless it can make an explicit finding that the defendant was actually aware of the relevant risk; and (2) if the defendant denies being aware of the risk, the jury will be required to acquit if the testimony is believed.

> ***Example:*** Common law arson might be defined as "the malicious burning of the dwelling of another." It is well settled that the word "malicious" cannot be read according to its dictionary definition to mean "ill will" or "intending harm." Instead, "malicious" is sometimes read to require that the offense be committed with "general intent." If this in turn is translated by a particular court into a concept of recklessness as defined above, the prosecutor would be required to prove that the defendant was actually aware of a risk that the burning was of the dwelling of another.
>
> This is *what* the prosecutor must prove. *How* the prosecutor will try to prove it most likely will be by asking the jury to infer awareness of the risk, given what the defendant did and the circumstances under which the conduct occurred. Again, the jury will explicitly be asked to find actual awareness and the defendant's testimony will be critical, if believed, to the recklessness finding.

2) Negligence

Recall the definition of "negligence" set forth on page 79. When applicable to a given element of an offense, it requires that the prosecutor prove three things, the second of which is that the defendant *should have been aware* of the risk that the element exists or would occur. The prosecutor must show, in effect, that a reasonable person in the defendant's situation—that is, a reasonable person who knew what the defendant knew about the context at the time—would have realized the relevant risk and, having done so, would presumably have refrained from the offending conduct.

Here, it will be noticed, *what* the prosecutor must prove comes very close to *how* it will be proved. The finding the jury will be asked to make is that a reasonable person in the defendant's situation would have appreciated the relevant risk. *How* this will be proved, most likely, is by re-creating what happened, and asking the jury what risks most people in that situation are likely to have realized.

Notice that this is probably exactly how the prosecutor would try to prove recklessness. The critical difference, however, is twofold: (1) In the case of negligence the jury is asked to make a finding only as to the risks of which a reasonable person in the defendant's situation would have been aware; (2) The relevance of the defendant's testimony is entirely changed: in the case of negligence, the defendant's testimony about actual awareness of the risk would be admissible, if at all, only to show that at least one person did not appreciate the risk. Whether the jury believed the defendant would not be critical, since the ultimate finding the jury will be asked to make is whether a *reasonable person* in the defendant's situation would have understood the risk. Thus, the jury would be entitled to convict *even if* it believed that the defendant was not actually aware of the risk.

On the other hand, the defendant's testimony as to what was believed about the context would be more directly relevant to the jury's task. It is their job to make findings about what the defendant knew at the time, and to work from that base in determining what else a reasonable person would have known about the facts and the risks. Thus if the defendant claims not to have known a critical fact, and the jury believes the claim to be true, the nature of the "reasonable person" inquiry will be critically changed. It will then be whether a reasonable person *who did not know the critical fact* would have understood the risks, *should have known* the critical fact, and would have refrained from acting.

> ***Example:*** Again consider the common law definition of arson as "the malicious burning of the dwelling of another." If this were interpreted as a general intent offense, and "general intent" were interpreted to mean "negligence" as defined above, the jury would be asked to find that a reasonable person who did what the defendant did and who knew what the defendant knew would have understood the risk that the dwelling of another would be burned. The defendant's denial of awareness of the risk, if admitted at all, would not exonerate even if believed.

c. The Presumption of Natural and Probable Consequences

A further complication is introduced by the so-called "presumption of natural and probable consequences." The prosecutor is frequently permitted to rely on this presumption to prove general intent, and sometimes specific intent. As developed in the discussion of the *Sandstrom* case (see page 416), it is unconstitutional to use the unadorned presumption in some contexts, perhaps for all specific intent crimes and maybe for general intent crimes too. But setting aside constitutional problems for the moment, what does the presumption mean and how can it be used? The answer is complex, but essentially it can be used in four ways:

1) Satisfying the Burden of Persuasion

The presumption could mean that the defendant is presumed *as a matter of law* to have intended the natural and probable consequences of conduct. This is often called a "conclusive" presumption. It is a legal fiction that is tantamount to a redefinition of the offense to say that the jury need only examine the defendant's conduct and ask whether normally one who engaged in such behavior would have intended what was done. In effect, this establishes a standard of negligence.

> ***Example:*** If arson is defined as "the malicious burning of the dwelling of another," the presumption if used in this manner to implement the meaning of "malicious" would mean that the jury would be asked, first, what the defendant did and, second, whether the burning of the dwelling of another is the normal consequence of such action. In effect, this is to ask whether the defendant was negligent, since a reasonable person would always know whether the burning of the dwelling of another would normally follow from particular behavior. For an example of a case that in effect follows this approach, see Director of Public Prosecutions v. Smith, [1960] 3 All.E.R. 161, [1961] A.C. 290.

2) Shifting the Burden of Persuasion

The presumption could also mean (1) that the prosecutor could establish a prima facie case by showing that the defendant engaged in the conduct defined by the offense and (2) that the jury would not be asked to make any mens rea inquiry unless the defendant undertook to prove that there was no "general intent." "General intent" could then be defined in terms of "recklessness" or "negligence" as the jurisdiction chose. The effect would be that the prosecutor established a prima facie case by proving the actus reus and causation, and the defendant could defend by proving a lack of mens rea.

> ***Example:*** If arson is defined as "the malicious burning of the dwelling of another" and this is taken to state a general intent offense, use of the presumption in this manner would mean that the prosecutor would prove a prima facie case simply by showing that the defendant burned the dwelling of another. The

defendant would then bear the burden of production *and* the burden of persuasion if lack of general intent is to be the defense.

3) Shifting the Burden of Production

The presumption could also mean (1) that the prosecutor could establish a prima facie case by showing that the defendant engaged in the conduct defined by the offense and (2) that the jury would not be asked to make any mens rea inquiry unless and until the defendant offered evidence that "general intent" was lacking. "General intent" could then be defined as "recklessness" or "negligence" depending upon the policy of the particular jurisdiction. In effect, this use of the presumption would remove the obligation of the prosecutor to prove mens rea as part of the prima facie case for general intent offenses, and would shift to the defendant the obligation first to introduce evidence on the point. Once the defendant did so, the burden of persuasion on general intent would be borne by the prosecutor in the normal manner.

Example: If arson is defined as "the malicious burning of the dwelling of another" and this is taken to state a general intent offense, use of the presumption in this manner would mean that the prosecutor would prove a prima facie case simply by showing that the defendant committed the actus reus of the offense. The defendant would be required to bear the burden of production if lack of general intent is to be the defense. This could be done by offering some evidence that the defendant was not reckless or negligent as to the element in question, depending on how "general intent" is defined in the particular jurisdiction. Once that was done, the prosecutor would be required to prove beyond a reasonable doubt that the defendant was reckless or negligent, as the case may be. For an example of a case that in effect follows this approach, see State v. Walker, 35 N.C.App. 182, 241 S.E.2d 89 (1978).

4) Permissive Inference

The fourth thing the presumption could mean is that the jury is entitled to infer that the defendant intended the natural and probable consequences of the proved conduct, but that it need not do so. In effect, the jury is told that people normally, but not always, intend the consequences that flow from their conduct. The jury is then admonished to make an explicit finding that the defendant was actually reckless or negligent as to the element in question, depending on the meaning of "general intent" in the jurisdiction, but that if it helps they may consider that most people understand and intend the normal consequences of behavior.

Example: If arson is again defined as "the malicious burning of the dwelling of another" and if this offense is again interpreted to require "general intent," use of the presumption as a permissible inference merely aids the prosecutor in bearing the burden of persuasion on the mens rea issue. The prosecutor will still have to prove as part of the prima facie case that the defendant acted with general intent, defined as recklessness or negligence depending on the law of the particular jurisdiction. The jury will be expected to make the required finding of general intent, but may do so with the aid of the inference that normally people understand and intend the natural consequences of behavior.

5.   PROOF OF CAUSATION

For any offense that contains a result element in the actus reus, the prosecutor must prove beyond a reasonable doubt that the defendant's conduct caused the result. There are no special problems in making this proof, beyond identification of the legal definition of causation in the jurisdiction and the practical evidentiary difficulties attendant to the proof of any issue in court.

G.   REVIEW QUESTIONS

[Answers Provided in Appendix A, page 419]

1.   T or F   The actus reus of all crimes includes conduct, circumstance, and result elements.

2.   T or F   Omissions may qualify as criminal acts in cases where a reasonable person in the defendant's situation should have acted.

3.   T or F   Specific intent always refers to a subjective state of mind actually reflected in the defendant's thoughts at the time of the offense, and identified with particularity in the definition of the offense.

4.   T or F   General intent refers to situations where the defendant did not act as a reasonable person would have acted in the defendant's situation.

5.   T or F   The presumption of natural and probable consequences means that the prosecutor need only establish that the defendant was negligent in committing any crime to which the presumption is applicable.

6.   T or F   A dependent intervening cause is a cause of the result that will not exonerate the defendant from liability.

7.   T or F   Strict liability is the only occasion in the criminal law where the defendant's liability is measured by a completely objective standard.

8.   Where should one begin the analysis of *every* criminal case?

9.   Identify the actus reus of the following offenses:

    a.   A person is guilty of theft for receiving property knowing it to have been stolen.

    b.   A person is guilty of theft for receiving property believing it to have been stolen.

    c.   A public official is guilty of extortion for corruptly receiving an unauthorized fee under color of office.

10. What are the elements of the prosecutor's prima facie case?

11. Why is it important to require conduct as a part of every crime?

12. *D* was prosecuted for violating a statute that punished one who "with intent to defraud an insurer, burns any building which is at the time insured against loss or damage by fire." *D* built a fire in the fireplace, but left the screen open. A spark jumped out of the fireplace, and ignited some papers nearby. *D* saw this happen, but decided to let the fire burn in order to collect the insurance and build a new house. If you were *D*'s lawyer, what would be your line of defense? If you were the prosecutor, what response would you make in order to gain a conviction?

III

THE MODEL PENAL CODE

Analysis

A. STARTING THE ANALYSIS

The Model Penal Code is much more analytically precise than the common law. The starting point is nonetheless the same: you need first to ascertain the definition of the offense, and then determine whether the actus reus, the mens rea, and any causation requirements have been satisfied.

Section 1.05(1) provides that no conduct can be a crime unless it is so designated by "this Code or another statute of this State." This means that there can be no separate, common law crimes under the Model Penal Code. Only those offenses specifically defined by statute can be punished. This does not mean, however, that the common law tradition is irrelevant. The Model Penal Code is a sophisticated amalgam of the common law tradition and modern insight into the proper purposes of the criminal law. As noted in the Introduction of this book, the Model Code is treated separately here in order to facilitate study of its highly integrated structure as an independent whole. It is assumed that you have access to the text of the Model Code, and indispensable that you read the cited sections as they are discussed.

B. THE ACTUS REUS

A person is not guilty of a crime under the Model Penal Code unless the charge "is based on conduct." § 2.01(1). Note also that the relevant provisions of § 1.02(1) are phrased in terms of "conduct" engaged in by an accused. Section 1.05(1) is also worded in terms of "conduct" that can constitute an offense. As at the common law, a crime cannot be predicated only on status, propensity, or desire.

1. ELEMENTS OF THE ACTUS REUS
Because of the portions of § 1.13(9) marked "(i)," "(ii)," and "(iii)," the actus reus of an offense under the Model Code is divided into "conduct," "results," and "circumstances." For reasons that will be elaborated later, it is important to be able to distinguish between these three kinds of elements, and you should get into the habit of doing so with each crime encountered.

a. Conduct
The conduct component of an offense is the physical activity in which the defendant must engage.

> ***Example:***   The conduct component of the offense of burglary defined in § 221.1(1) is "enters." All of the rest of that Subsection consists of circumstance or mens rea elements. Additional conduct elements are added for grading purposes by § 221.1(2), specifically "inflicts or attempts to inflict" in Subsection (a) and "is armed" in Subsection (b).

Note that some offenses do not describe with any specificity the nature of the conduct that must occur. It is nonetheless mandatory in such offenses that the defendant must engage in *some* conduct. This definitional tactic is employed only where a result must be caused, though it is not always employed in such a case.

Examples: The definition of criminal homicide in § 210.1(1) does not describe any specific conduct by the defendant that "causes the death" of another human being. Thus any conduct that causes a death will do.

The definition of causing a catastrophe in § 220.2(1), by contrast, provides that the result must be caused in one of a specified number of ways, e.g., by explosion or fire. Thus the defendant's conduct must cause a catastrophe, and must be such as to fit the additional legal labels "by explosion," "by fire," etc.

As in the common law, the conduct that will suffice under the Model Penal Code can be an act, an omission, or possession. See § 2.01.

1) Act

An act is any affirmative conduct sufficient to satisfy the definition of the offense.

Example: In the illustrations given above, the act required for burglary is "enters," for the grading of burglary is "inflicts or attempts to inflict" or "is armed," for murder is any act that causes the result, and for causing a catastrophe is any act that causes a catastrophe and that can be described as "by explosion," "by fire," etc.

2) Omission

Criminal liability can be based on an omission if the defendant is physically capable of performing the act (§ 2.01(1)), and if one of two conditions is met: (1) the omission is expressly made sufficient by the law defining the offense; or (2) a duty to perform the act is "imposed by law." See § 2.01(3). Any legal source of a duty to act will suffice for the second condition. A moral duty, which is not expressed in some provision of civil or criminal law, will not suffice.

Example: An example of the first condition, where an omission is expressly made sufficient by the law defining the offense, is contained in § 220.1(3)(b). An example of the second condition, where a duty to perform the act is "imposed by law," would be a charge of murder against parents who intentionally allowed one of their children to die of starvation. Both would have a duty of care arising from the family law to engage in positive action to prevent the death to the extent that they were physically capable.

3) Possession

Possession is a sufficient act for criminal liability if the definition of the offense so provides and if the item possessed was "knowingly procured or received" *or* if the defendant knew of the possession "for a sufficient period to have been able to terminate" it. See § 2.01(4).

> **Example:** Section 242.7(1) punishes an inmate who possesses an implement of escape, defined as a "weapon, tool or other thing which may be useful for escape." Note that the element "has in his possession" would require that the inmate "knowingly procured or received" the implement or knew of the possession for a sufficient period to have terminated it. § 2.01(4). Thus a mens rea of knowledge would be required, even though analysis of § 242.7(1) under the principles established by § 2.02 suggests that the mens rea would be recklessness. The principles established by § 2.02 are discussed in detail below.

b. Result

A result component of an offense is any consequence that must be caused by the defendant's conduct. Most crimes do not include a result element in the required actus reus.

> **Example:** "Bodily injury" is a result element in the assault offense defined in § 211.1(1)(b). There is no result element in the offense of theft defined in § 223.2(1), nor in most offenses in the Model Code.

c. Circumstances

The circumstance components of an offence are the external conditions that must exist when the defendant engages in the required conduct.

> **Example:** The circumstance elements in the offense of theft defined in § 223.2(1) are "unlawfully" (accompanying the conduct "takes"), "unlawful" (accompanying the conduct "exercises control over"), "movable property," and "of another." The circumstance elements in the offense of rape as defined in § 213.1(1)(d) are that the defendant is a male, that the victim is a female, that the victim is not the defendant's wife, and that the victim is less than 10 years old.

2. PROBLEMS OF INTERPRETATION

As with the common law, difficult problems of interpretation can arise in determining whether the defendant has committed the actus reus of a Model Penal Code offense.

Note, however, that many actus reus terms in the Model Code are defined. You should always look first for a definition before attempting any interpretation.

Definitions are contained in two places you might not think to look: in § 1.13 and in a section followed by the number "0" included in many Articles in Part II of the Code. See §§ 210.0, 211.0, 212.0, 213.0, and so on. In addition, definitions are sometimes contained in the section defining the offense itself (e.g., § 220.1(4)) or at the end of the Article in which the offense is defined (e.g., § 213.6(2)). Note also that § 213.6 contains other provisions stating how various elements of the offenses defined in Article 213 should be interpreted. Obviously, you need to look for special provisions of this sort too before you try to interpret a provision of the Model Penal Code on your own.

If a definition is not provided in a particular case, the general principles stated in § 1.02 are intended as an aid to construction. Note particularly the language of § 1.02(3).

Examples: Criminal homicide as defined in § 210.1(1) requires that the defendant cause the death of another "human being." Is it murder under the Model Penal Code to kick a pregnant woman in the stomach and cause the "death" of a viable fetus? The answer is "no," because "human being" is defined in § 210.0(1) as a "person who is born and is alive."

Is it burglary under § 221.1(1) for the defendant to reach through an open window for the purpose of stealing items within reach? Or must the defendant physically enter the premises in order to be a burglar? The term "enters" is not defined anywhere in the Model Code, and the case would thus turn on how it should be interpreted in light of the general principles stated in § 1.02. You ought to be able to argue this one either way.

Note that in a jurisdiction that has adopted a statutory structure based on the Model Penal Code and that uses an undefined word such as "enter" in a burglary statute, it is possible, perhaps even likely, that the courts will take the prior common law interpretations of such words into account in resolving the meaning of the term. One needs to be careful here, however, because it may be that the new statute was designed specifically to change prior common law interpretations. Lots of room for inventive argumentation here.

3. PROBLEMS OF CATEGORIZATION

It may look like the Model Penal Code places a premium on being able to tell the difference between actus reus elements that are properly described as "conduct," "result," and "circumstance" elements. Is it so clear which are which? Is it always easy to tell? Does it matter if you place an element in the wrong category?

The answer to all three questions is "no," at least most of the time. Though the category into which an element belongs is often intuitive, sometimes it is not easy to tell which is which. But usually it doesn't matter into which category an element is placed. The important thing is to isolate each element and treat it separately. It normally doesn't matter what you call it. But it matters a lot—it is the difference between guilt and innocence—whether each element occurred or was present.

When does it matter what an element is called? Under the Model Penal Code, only in one instance. As developed further on page 332, it matters in the crime of attempt whether an element is classified as embracing "conduct" or a "result" on the one hand or a "circumstance" on the other. Basically, therefore, so long as you focus on each element and put into the category that seems to you to fit, you are going to be ok. Where you need to watch out and be especially careful is in the crime of attempt.

C. THE MENS REA

The Model Penal Code contains a very precise and technical mens rea structure in § 2.02. You will need to study § 2.02 and its application to specific offenses with great care. If you can apply § 2.02 well and understand all of its implications, you can do any technical legal task in any subject. Indeed, one of the reasons to study the Model Penal Code is to learn how to read tightly integrated statutes. Mastering § 2.02 is good training in general, quite apart from what you will learn about the criminal law.

1. ELEMENTS OF THE MENS REA

The Model Penal Code does not use the terms "specific intent" and "general intent." Nor does it use the rest of the common law mens rea vocabulary. Words like "corruptly," "malice," "scienter," and the like will not be found in the Model Code.

Rather, the Model Penal Code establishes four levels of mens rea—purpose, knowledge, recklessness, and negligence—and defines each of them carefully. It then provides rules of construction to determine which of these mens rea terms applies to *each* actus reus element of an offense. *Note that, as will be illustrated, some offenses require extra mens rea elements that must also be satisfied.*

The judgment underlying the Model Penal Code culpability provisions is that the four concepts of purpose, knowledge, recklessness, and negligence—supplemented by strict liability in rare cases—are both necessary and sufficient for the job of defining the mens rea for crimes. If one were to take all of the definitions of all of the myriad common law mens rea terms, in other words, the argument of the Model Penal Code is that you could translate each one of them into one or another version of these five ideas. This is an important insight and, if adopted over time by osmosis in common law jurisdictions, will significantly enhance communication in the criminal law, particularly to juries. At the very least, it enhances one's ability to understand and communicate about the Model Penal Code because, unlike the words used by the common law to describe mens rea, mens rea words are used by the Model Penal Code with their ordinary language meanings and the meanings are consistent from offense to offense. No chameleons here.

a. Purpose

"Purposely" is defined in § 2.02(2)(a). Sections 1.13(11) and 1.13(12) state that words such as "with purpose," "designed," "with design," "intentionally," and "with intent" are equivalent to "purposely."

1) **Conduct**

A "purpose" to engage in particular conduct means that the defendant has a conscious objective or desire to engage in the conduct. The word is given its ordinary dictionary meaning.

2) **Result**

A "purpose" to cause a particular result means that the defendant has a conscious objective or desire to cause the result. Again, the word is given its ordinary dictionary meaning.

3) **Circumstances**

If "purpose" is the mens rea required for a circumstance element of a crime, the requirement is that the defendant be aware of the circumstance, or believe or hope it exists. This does not sound like an ordinary dictionary meaning of the word "purpose." But it does reflect the common sense of the matter. If one said that a person had a "purpose to keep the property of another," one would mean that the person had a purpose to keep property which was known to belong to another, or which was believed or hoped to belong to another. The Model Code definition thus accords with the ordinary meaning of the word "purpose" in this context.

A requirement that the defendant act "purposely" in the definition of an offense does not, unless the definition of the offense expressly so provides, mean that the defendant must "purposely" violate the criminal law. It means only that the actus reus components of the offense must be "purposely" committed, or that the defendant must have some other special purpose required by the definition of the offense (e.g., a "purpose to commit a crime therein" in burglary (§ 221.1(1))).

b. **Knowledge**

"Knowingly" is defined in § 2.02(2)(b). Section 1.13(13) provides that words such as "knowing" or "with knowledge" are equivalent to "knowingly."

1) **Conduct**

If "know" is the mens rea required for a conduct element of a crime, the defendant must be aware of the nature of the conduct. This accords with ordinary usage of the word "know." It does not mean that the defendant needs to know that the law applies the label used in the definition of the offense to the behavior, nor even that it matters what his belief on that subject might be. What it does require is that the defendant be aware of what is happening, aware of what is being done.

Example: Assume a defendant who reached through an open window in order to steal jewels that were sitting on a night stand in a house. If "enter" in the crime of burglary in § 221.1(1) means "break the plane" of the building or occupied structure (I haven't a clue if that is what a court would hold that "enter" actually means in this context—I merely want to make that assumption for purposes of the present illustration), then what the defendant must know is that the conduct engaged in on the occasion of the offense involved reaching through an open window. The defendant does not need to know that the criminal law calls such conduct "enters." The defendant needs to know the nature of the behavior, not the legal label applied by the criminal law to that behavior. Nor does the defendant need to know that such behavior would qualify as burglary. The defendant's beliefs about whether the legal label applies or whether the behavior counts as burglary would be irrelevant to guilt—the defendant is held to strict liability on these questions.

2) Result

If "knowledge" is the mens rea required for a result element of a crime, the requirement is that the defendant be aware that it is practically certain that the conduct will cause the result. The reason for this definition is that results are always a matter of probability. One can never "know" that a cause will produce a given effect—there can only be various degrees of likelihood. If knowledge is the mens rea for a result element, the degree of likelihood that the result will occur must be very high.

3) Circumstances

If "know" is the mens rea required for a circumstances element of a crime, the defendant must be aware that the circumstance exists. This again is ordinary usage. But there is a wrinkle.

Section 2.02(7) provides that knowledge of an existing fact (which means knowledge of a circumstance element of a crime) is established "if a person is aware of a high probability of its existence, unless he actually believes that it does not exist." This language is designed to deal with cases that have variously been referred to in the cases and the literature as "wilful blindness," "connivance," or "refusal to know." The paradigm case is where the defendant believes a fact is probably true, but doesn't want to know for sure and takes positive steps to avoid knowing.

Example: Assume a defendant who is hired for $1000 to drive a car across the Mexican border into Texas, and that the total length of the trip is two miles. No statements are made about why the payment is so high. The defendant asks no questions and says: "Yes, I will do it, so long as you don't tell me what is inside the car." Should the defendant be guilty of the offense of "knowing possession of narcotics" when stopped on the U.S. side by customs agents who find narcotics in the car? The answer given by § 2.02(7) is "yes," unless the jury believes that the defendant actually (and honestly) believed that there were no narcotics in the car. Under these circumstances, that seems unlikely.

c. Recklessness

"Recklessly" is defined in § 2.02(2)(c). Section 1.13(14) provides that words such as "recklessness" or "with recklessness" are equivalent to "recklessly." The distinctive characteristic of recklessness under the Model Code is that the actor must actually be aware of a risk that the element exists. The same analysis is applied to conduct, result, and circumstance elements. It requires three steps:

1) The Nature of the Risk

There must be a substantial and unjustifiable risk that the element exists or (in the case of result elements) will result from the defendant's conduct. The term "substantial" refers to the degree of likelihood that the element exists or will result. The term "unjustifiable" refers to the reasons one might have for taking the risk, and requires that these reasons not be good ones. How "substantial" and how "unjustifiable" must the risks be? That question cannot be answered in the abstract, but requires a judgment that is to be made by the jury in applying the criterion outlined in the third step of the analysis.

2) Awareness of the Risk

The defendant must be aware of the risk and of the facts that make it substantial and unjustifiable. The defendant need not, of course, conclude that the risk is substantial or unjustifiable; whether that legal label is placed on the risk is something for the jury to do. To repeat, all that the defendant need be aware of is the risk itself and the facts that make the risk substantial and unjustifiable.

3) The Ultimate Judgment

Once the jury has ascertained the nature of the risk created and that the defendant was actually aware of the risk and the facts relevant to how substantial and unjustifiable it was, the jury must make a judgment in the following terms: it must decide that in engaging in the conduct and disregarding the risk, the defendant made a "gross deviation from the standard of conduct that a law-abiding person would observe in the actor's situation." Two points should be noted about this judgment:

a) Defendant's point of view

The jury must make this ultimate judgment in light of "the nature and purpose of the actor's conduct and the circumstances known to him." That is, the jury must consider whether, given the facts and circumstances known to the defendant, the behavior was a "gross deviation" from what a law-abiding person would have done.

b) Defendant's situation

The words "in the actor's situation" in the last line of the definition of recklessness are meant to permit some personalization of the standard if there are characteristics of the defendant that ought to be taken into account. It may not be appropriate, for example, to measure a person with certain physical characteristics (blind, deaf, one arm or leg) against the standard of a person who does not share these physical characteristics. It is up to the judge, and ultimately the appellate courts, to decide what personal characteristics of the defendant should be taken into account. Unusual sensitivity, for example, most likely will not be considered, but physical characteristics of the sort mentioned above probably would be. The drafters of the Model Code deliberately said nothing about what the word "situation" meant, and intentionally left the matter to the courts to develop in the case law. They punted.

Notice the two places where subjective factors are considered in the application of this definition: the defendant must actually be aware of the risk; and the ultimate judgment that the defendant has deviated from appropriate standards of conduct must be considered in light of the purposes of the defendant's conduct and the circumstances that were known to the defendant. But the ultimate standard against which the defendant is measured by the jury is objective. And, so long as the defendant understands the characteristics of the risk, it does not matter whether the defendant believes it to be substantial or thinks that taking the risk is justified—these are judgments for the jury to make. Thus recklessness under the Model Penal Code is, like all standards of culpability used by the criminal law, a mixture of subjective and objective factors.

Example: Assume a doctor contemplating an operation on a comatose patient. The odds are 95% that the patient will die within the year if the operation is not performed. The odds are 60% that the patient will die from the operation. But the odds are 50% that the patient will live a normal life if the operation is successful. The operation is performed with the family's consent, but the patient dies. How would one determine whether the doctor and the consenting family members are guilty of manslaughter under § 210.3(1)(a) of the Model Code?

There is no doubt that the doctor's conduct created a "substantial" risk of death, and that the doctor and the family members were aware of the facts making the risk substantial. On the other hand, the justifications for undertaking the operation seem strong. Are they strong enough to justify taking the risk that the patient will die? That question would turn on whether a law-abiding person, knowing what the doctor and the family members knew, would have gone ahead with the operation, and whether it was a "gross deviation" from what a law-abiding person would have done for the operation to have been performed. The issue is of course for the jury, but here it seems clear that performing the operation was not a gross deviation from law-abiding behavior, and that the parties were not reckless and therefore not guilty of manslaughter. In fact, it is unlikely that such a case would be prosecuted.

d. Negligence

"Negligently" is defined in § 2.02(2)(d). Section 1.13(15) provides that words such as "negligence" or "with negligence" are equivalent to "negligently."

In addition, § 1.13(16) provides that "reasonably believes" or "reasonable belief" means a belief which the actor is "not reckless or negligent in holding." This would mean the same thing if it read "not negligent in holding" since, if negligence is an appropriate mens rea for an offense, a reckless defendant will always be regarded as satisfying the standard. See § 2.02(5). Thus a reasonable belief is the reciprocal of negligence: A person who reasonably believes is not negligent, and a person who is negligent does not have a reasonable belief.

> ***Example:*** Section 230.1(1)(d) provides that it is a defense to bigamy if the defendant "reasonably believes that he is legally eligible to remarry." Two things must thus be established in order to assert the defense successfully: (1) that the defendant actually believed "that he [was] legally eligible to remarry"; and (2) that the defendant was not negligent in so believing.

The distinctive characteristic of negligence under the Model Code is that the defendant *should be* aware of the risk that the element exists. The same analysis is applied to conduct, result, and circumstance elements. Like recklessness, it requires three steps:

1) The Nature of the Risk

The first step is identical to the first step in the analysis of recklessness. There must be a substantial and unjustifiable risk that the element exists or (in the case of result elements) will result from the defendant's conduct. How substantial and unjustifiable it must be is determined by the jury when it applies the criterion outlined in the third step of the analysis.

2) Should be Aware of the Risk
The second step is different from recklessness. In the case of negligence, the defendant *should have been* aware of the risk and *should have been* aware of the facts that make it substantial and unjustifiable. The jury determines whether the risk is one of which the defendant should have been aware when it applies the criterion outlined in the third step of the analysis.

3) The Ultimate Judgment
Once the jury has ascertained the nature of the risk created, it must make a judgment in the following terms: it must decide whether the failure of the defendant to perceive the risk involved a gross deviation from the standard of care that a reasonable person would have observed in the actor's situation. If so, then the defendant *should have* been aware of the risk, and presumably would have then known enough not to have taken it. Two points should be noted about this judgment:

a) Defendant's point of view
The jury must make this ultimate judgment in light of "the nature and purpose of his conduct and the circumstances known to him." That is, the jury must consider whether, given the facts and circumstances known to the defendant, it was a "gross deviation" from what a reasonable person would have done for the defendant to have been unaware of the risk and to have engaged in the conduct.

b) Defendant's situation
The words "in the actor's situation" in the last line of the definition of negligence have the same function as the identical words in the definition of recklessness.

Note again the combination of subjective and objective factors in this definition. The ultimate judgment that the defendant has deviated from appropriate standards of conduct must be considered in light of the purposes of the defendant's conduct and the circumstances that were known. Otherwise the standard is objective: the jury must decide that the defendant *should have been* aware of the risk, and that it was a gross deviation from appropriate behavior to have taken the risk and engaged in the conduct or caused the result (or in the case of circumstance elements should have been aware of the risk that the circumstance existed when the behavior occurred). As in the case of recklessness, and indeed all other measures of culpability used by the criminal law, negligence under the Model Penal Code thus involves a mixture of subjective and objective characteristics.

Example: Assume the defendant has the job of signaling oncoming cars that a bridge ahead has fallen down, leaving a 100—foot drop to craggy rocks below. Assume that lunchtime arrives, and that the defendant, knowing fully the condition of the bridge and what lies below, leaves the roadside without thinking about the consequences and without taking any precautions to assure that motorists who come along will be warned of the peril that lies ahead. If the occupants of a car are killed because they attempt to cross the bridge unaware of the impending danger, how would one determine whether the defendant is guilty of negligent homicide under § 210.4(1) of the Model Penal Code?

The first question is whether leaving the roadside for lunch created a substantial and unjustifiable risk of death. This would be up to the jury, but surely the risk of death from a 100-foot fall in a moving car to craggy rocks below is "substantial" and leaving for lunch is not a very good justification for creating such a risk. The next question is whether the defendant should have been aware of the risk. Given what the defendant knew about the conditions lying ahead, is the defendant's failure to be aware of the risk a gross deviation from the standard of care that a reasonable person would have exercised in the defendant's situation? This is the ultimate question for the jury, which surely on these facts would conclude that the defendant should have known the risks and should not have left for lunch without taking adequate precautions.

Note that the jury also would be likely on these facts to find that the defendant was reckless, that is, the jury very likely could be persuaded that the defendant was aware of the risk that someone would be killed. This observation merely makes the point that *how* the mens rea for an offense may be proved should be sharply distinguished from *what* must be proved. The difference between recklessness and negligence lies in the different findings that the jury must make. The *evidence* available to the prosecutor to establish recklessness or negligence may be substantially the same in a given case, and whether one or the other is found is a matter for the jury in evaluating the strength of the evidence. And note that the evidence available to the *defendant* may be substantially different depending on whether recklessness or negligence is the standard. In particular, the defendant's testimony about awareness of the risk assumes much greater significance if recklessness is the finding the jury must make.

2.   THE ANALYTICAL STRUCTURE

Section 2.02(1) is worth careful attention. It is where an analysis of mens rea under the Model Penal Code must start.

a. **Element of the Offense**

The term "element of an offense" is defined in § 1.13(9) to include all conduct, result, and circumstance components that are contained in the definition of the offense *and* in any defense. While the language of § 1.13(9) is capable of a contrary interpretation, it is the intention of the drafters that components of an offense that are included only for grading purposes also constitute an "element" of an offense.

> *Example:*   In the offense of burglary defined in § 221.1, all of the conduct and circumstance components of the offense set forth in the first sentence of Subsection (1) are "elements" of the offense. In addition, the circumstance components (that the building or structure was abandoned) of the affirmative defense set forth in the second sentence of Subsection (1) are also "elements." Still in addition, the conduct, circumstance, and result elements set forth under the heading "grading" in Subsection (2) are also "elements" of the offense.

b. **Material Element of the Offense**

An element of an offense is "material" when it is relevant to the harm or evil sought to be prevented by the law defining the offense. See § 1.13(10). This definition includes as a material element any conduct, result, or circumstance element used in defining the offense, in establishing its grade or severity, and in providing a defense.

c. **When Culpability Required**

The culpability structure of § 2.02 applies to all "material elements" of a crime. It does not apply, however, to violations.

1) **Culpability Not Required for Violations**

The opening phrase in § 2.02(1) excepts the offenses described in § 2.05 from the provisions of § 2.02. This means that the class of offenses described in § 2.05 does not require mens rea. The offenses dealt with in § 2.05 are classified as "violations" under the Model Code. Note that imprisonment cannot be imposed for a "violation" under the provisions of § 1.04(5), and that, also under § 1.04(5), a "violation" is not a crime for purposes of civil disabilities and the other consequences that follow conviction of a crime.

2) **Culpability Required for All Crimes**

By contrast, § 2.02(1) means that the culpability structure *does* apply to all crimes. As implemented by § 2.02(3), this has the effect of virtually eliminating strict liability from the Model Code. As will be illustrated (see page 125, in order for strict liability to be imposed, the definition of the offense must specifically do so.

d. Separate Consideration of Each Element

The final step in the application of § 2.02(1)—and a step of crucial importance to understanding the Model Code culpability structure—is that some level of culpability is required (absent express provision to the contrary in the definition of an offense) for *each* material element of *every* crime—that is, *each* conduct, *each* result, and *each* circumstance element contained in the definition of *every* offense, in its grading, and in any defense. The particular level of culpability required for a given element is determined by the definition of the offense and the principles of construction developed and illustrated below.

e. "As the Law May Require"

The phrase "as the law may require" in § 2.01(1) refers to (a) the law as stated in the definition of particular offenses; and (b) the principles of construction provided in the remainder of § 2.02. The Model Penal Code culpability structure is very tight and technical. Although no written statute is ever free from all ambiguity, the objective is to provide a structure under which the mens rea for any element of any crime can be derived from applying the logic of the specific provisions of the Code. By and large, it is successful in achieving this objective.

3. PRINCIPLES OF CONSTRUCTION

The place to start in applying the Model Code culpability structure is with the definition of the offense.

a. No Culpability Provided

The easy case is where the definition of the offense contains no culpability words. In this instance, § 2.02(3) provides that "recklessness" is the minimum culpability that will be required for each material element of the offense.

> *Example:* Examine the offense of escape defined in § 242.6(1) of the Model Code. What is the mens rea required for the element "official detention?" The answer is "recklessness," derived from the silence of the offense as to mens rea and the provision in § 2.02(3) that recklessness is the mens rea for each element when the offense is silent.

Note that one always describes the culpability for a given element in terms of the *minimum* that the prosecutor need establish. The prosecutor can always obtain a conviction by proving *more* culpability than is minimally necessary. See § 2.02(5). But what the prosecutor and defense attorney will focus on is the *minimum* culpability, since that sets the outer limits of guilt or innocence. Thus, while § 2.02(3) says that the mens rea required when the offense is silent is "purposely, knowingly, or recklessly," one would describe this as establishing a mens rea of recklessness.

b. Culpability Provided

If the definition of the offense contains culpability language, the case will be one of two types. In order to determine which type, you should ask why the culpability language was included in the definition.

1) Culpability Designated for One Actus Reus Element

If the culpability language was included in the definition of the offense in order to establish the mens rea for one of the actus reus elements of the offense, then the definition should be construed according to the principle stated in § 2.02(4). This principle is: the same mens rea should be applied to all other actus reus elements, *unless* it is clear from the grammatical structure of the definition that the mens rea term was meant to be applied only to a limited number of elements.

If the mens rea term was meant to apply to a limited number of actus reus elements, then it should be applied only to those elements. The mens rea for the remaining elements is determined by applying the normal rules of construction and will be recklessness if the terms of § 2.02(3) are satisfied.

Examples: Consider first the crime of incest defined in § 230.2. The word "knowingly" appears in the definition, and thus the offense contains culpability language. Why is this word included in the definition? Plainly it is included *at least* to describe the mens rea for the conduct element "marries." It thus is included in the offense in order to establish the mens rea for one of the actus reus elements of the offense. Given this, the question to which § 2.02(4) is designed to speak is *how many* of the other actus reus elements of the offense are meant to require the same mens rea? The answer in this case is "all of them." The grammatical structure of the offense does not plainly indicate that "knowingly" is meant to apply only to "marries" or only to "marries or cohabits or has sexual intercourse." "Knowingly" may or may not be meant to apply to "brother or sister." Since this is so, the word knowingly, in the language of § 2.02(4), "shall apply to all the material elements" of the offense. Thus, a male who has sexual intercourse with his sister is guilty of incest only if he knows that he is having sexual intercourse and knows that it is with his sister. Section 2.02(4) was designed precisely to provide a way of dealing with grammatical ambiguities of this sort *and only to perform this function.*

The false alarm offense defined in § 241.4 would be analyzed the same way. "Knowingly" applies to all of the actus reus elements of the offense. Similarly, "purposely" would apply to all the actus reus elements of the offenses defined in §§ 242.1 and 242.4.

Contrast, however, the offense of sexual assault contained in § 213.4(8). What is the mens rea for the element "in custody of law?" The section contains culpability words in several Subsections ("knows"). It is clear from the grammatical structure of the offense, however, that the word "knows" in Subsection (1) is meant to apply only to the elements in Subsection (1) (otherwise, why repeat it in Subsection (2) and why omit it in Subsection (4)?). Hence, the mens rea for the elements in Subsection (8) is not governed by the culpability stated in the other Subsections. One must therefore apply the normal rules of construction independently to these elements. Since no culpability words are included in Subsection (8), § 2.02(3) controls. The mens rea for "in custody of law" is therefore recklessness.

The mens rea for "incapable of appraising the nature of his or her conduct" in § 213.4(2), however, is "knows" because § 2.02(4) would apply to all of the actus reus components of Subsection (2) under the reasoning applied in the incest example above.

2) Culpability Required in Addition to Actus Reus Elements

One will get a different answer to the question "why is the culpability language included in the definition of the offense?" in a different class of offenses. These are offenses where the culpability language states a purpose or a belief that is *not* designed to specify the mens rea for a particular actus reus element, but that *is* designed to describe some mens rea the defendant must have *in addition to* whatever mens rea is required for the actus reus of the offense. One might describe this additional mens rea (in most cases) as a goal, purpose, or motive for committing the offense. The common law would call it a specific intent of one of the first two types described on pages 76–77.

Another way of saying the same thing is this: if the offense provides that one must "knowingly break and enter a dwelling," the purpose of the word "knowingly" is to state at least the mens rea with which the actus reus element "break" must be committed. What this means is that the defendant must commit the actus reus, i.e., must engage in conduct that the law describes as "breaking" *and* that the defendant must know that the conduct is of that nature (although as was said above and is repeated at page 176, the defendant need not know that the law attaches the label "breaking" to it). If the Model Penal Code culpability structure were applied to this definition, the word "knowingly" would apply to all of the actus reus elements of the offense under the principle of § 2.02(4) discussed above, that is, the defendant would have to "knowingly break" and "knowingly enter" and would have to know that the structure entered was a "dwelling."

On the other hand, if the offense says that one must "break and enter a dwelling with the intent to commit a crime therein," the purpose of the word "intent" is to describe a goal, purpose, or motive with which the defendant must commit the offense, i.e., in addition to whatever mens rea the law requires for "break and enter a dwelling," the defendant must *also* have the additional purpose to commit a crime inside the dwelling once entry has been achieved.

Note that it does not matter whether the defendant actually does commit a crime inside the dwelling once entry has been accomplished. The phrase "with intent to commit a crime therein" does not create an additional actus reus element of the offense. All it does is create an additional mens rea.

An additional mens rea of this type does *not* trigger the provisions of § 2.02(4). The mens rea for the actus reus elements is determined by temporarily ignoring this special mens rea and by applying the provisions of § 2.02(3) and § 2.02(4) to the remaining elements of the offense.

Thus, if the offense says that one must "break and enter a dwelling with the intent to commit a crime therein," the mens rea for the elements "break and enter a dwelling" would be recklessness under the Model Code structure. The phrase "with intent to commit a crime therein" must be temporarily ignored and the principles of § 2.02(3) and § 2.02(4) applied independently to the remaining elements. Since the remaining elements contain no culpability language, § 2.02(3) applies and recklessness is the mens rea for these elements. The complete mens rea for the offense, therefore, is recklessness as to all the actus reus elements *plus* "with intent to commit a crime therein." The complete actus reus is "break and enter a dwelling." These are the elements the prosecutor would have to prove to gain a conviction.

But if the offense says that one must "knowingly break and enter a dwelling with the intent to commit a crime therein," "knowledge" would be the mens rea for "break," "enter," and "dwelling." The language "with intent to commit a crime therein" would be temporarily laid to one side. Since "knowingly" clearly is designed to prescribe the mens rea for the element "break," § 2.02(4) would apply it to the remaining actus reus elements. The complete mens rea for the offense would now be knowledge as to all the actus reus elements *plus* "with intent to commit a crime therein." The actus reus, of course, would be the same as before.

Examples: Examine the definition of theft in § 223.2(2). What is the mens rea for the elements "unlawfully transfers movable property of another or any interest therein?" The answer is recklessness for each of these elements, under the provisions of § 2.02(3). The reasoning is as follows. The mens rea element "with purpose to benefit himself or another not entitled thereto" is included in the offense in order to state a goal or motive of the defendant's behavior. It is not designed to describe the mens rea for a particular actus reus element. Therefore, the provisions of § 2.02(4) are not triggered by the word "purpose" in the definition. Since this is so, the phrase "with purpose to benefit himself or another not entitled thereto" is temporarily ignored, and since no other culpability language is included in the remaining elements of the offense the provisions of § 2.02(3) are applicable. Recklessness is therefore the mens rea for all of the actus reus elements of the offense. The defendant must engage in all of the actus reus elements of the offense at least recklessly, and in addition must have the required purpose to benefit himself or another.

Note that it would not matter if the location of the "with purpose" language was moved in the definition of the offense. Suppose the definition read as follows: "A person is guilty of theft if, with purpose to benefit himself or another not entitled thereto, he unlawfully transfers immovable property of another or any interest therein." Would this change anything? No. The mens rea would still be the same based on the same analysis recited above. It is not the location of the "with purpose" phrase that matters in this instance, it is its function.

By similar reasoning, the mens rea for "false" in § 242.3(5) is recklessness. The "purpose" language in the offense is designed to state an impact which the defendant hopes the offense will have, and does not itself describe the mens rea with which a given actus reus element must be committed. The "purpose" language must be temporarily ignored, and since the definition of the offense contains no other culpability language, recklessness is the mens rea for "false" under § 2.02(3).

Contrast, however, § 241.5(1). What mens rea is required for "false?" The answer is "knowledge," derived in the following manner. The language "with purpose to implicate another" states a mens rea the defendant must have in addition to whatever mens rea is required for the actus reus elements of the offense. It does not therefore establish the mens rea for the remaining elements under § 2.02(4). One must look to the rest of the offense in order to determine the mens rea for these remaining elements. The word "knowingly" plainly modifies "gives" and is designed to establish the mens rea for that actus reus element of the offense. Does the word "knowingly" apply also to "false information to a law enforcement officer?" Purely as a grammatical matter, one could argue that the sentence is ambiguous: "knowingly" might modify only "gives" or it might modify the entire sentence. Section 2.02(4) is designed to resolve just such an ambiguity (and *only* for that purpose), and does so by providing that "knowingly" is applied to all of the remaining elements, unless a contrary purpose plainly appears from the grammatical structure of the offense. No such purpose here appears, and hence the element "false" requires a mens rea of "knowledge."

4. ADDITIONAL MENS REA PROVISIONS

Subsections (1), (2), (3), (4), and (7) of § 2.02 are discussed above. Subsection (9) is discussed at page 176. Subsection (10) has the same effect as § 3.09(2), which is considered at page 208. The remaining provisions of § 2.02 will now be considered.

a. Substitutes for Culpability Terms

Section 2.02(5) states the common sense proposition that if an offense establishes a given level of culpability, the prosecutor can obtain a conviction if it is shown that the defendant actually was *more* culpable than the level given. A person who acts with purpose is more culpable than a person who acts with knowledge. A person who acts with knowledge is more culpable than a person who acts recklessly. And a person who acts recklessly is more culpable than a person who acts negligently. Thus if negligence is the required culpability for a given element, the prosecutor is entitled to a conviction if purpose, knowledge, recklessness, *or* negligence is established. Similarly, if recklessness is the minimum culpability for a given element, a showing of purpose or knowledge will also suffice. And if knowledge is the minimum culpability, proof of purpose will do.

b. Conditional Purpose

Section 2.02(6) also states a common sense proposition. Assume a defendant charged with burglary under § 221.1(1) who defends on the ground that the required "purpose to commit a crime therein" was missing because the purpose was to steal a particular piece of jewelry only if it was there, the jewelry was not there, and the defendant therefore left without committing any crime. The defendant's purpose in this case was "conditional," i.e., conditioned on the jewelry being there. Section 2.02(6) denies a defense in such a case, "unless the condition negatives the harm or evil sought to be prevented by the law defining the offense." The "unless" clause is plainly inapplicable to these facts. The clause would be applicable only to a case where the condition changed the nature of the purpose so drastically that it no longer constituted the kind of purpose sought to be punished by the offense.

Note in this example that the offense occurs at the point of entry, and so the facts that the jewelry was not there and that the defendant left without committing any crime are irrelevant. The "conditional" purpose held at the time of entry is sufficient to warrant conviction for the offense.

c. **Wilfulness**

The term "wilfully" is equated with "knowledge" in § 2.02(8), unless a purpose to impose further requirements appears in the definition of the offense. The Model Code does not use the term "wilfully" in the definition of any of its crimes, so this provision is not important when dealing only with the Model Code. It was included, however, because the word is so common, and so commonly misunderstood, that it was thought desirable to take account of it in case a legislature using the Code as a model insisted on its retention as a mens rea term.

Note that the fact that the Model Penal Code defines "wilfully" as "knowledge" is entirely unrelated to the way a common law court might define of the term. Don't make the mistake of assuming that since the Model Penal Code treats "wilfulness" as "knowledge," it would probably have the same meaning at common law. No such luck.

5. **STRICT LIABILITY**

Understanding how the Model Penal Code treats strict liability requires first that one understand its use of the term "crime." The Model Code imposes strict liability for very few crimes. But it does create a class of offenses for which strict liability is the norm. They are called "violations." In some jurisdictions, they might be called "infractions," "regulatory crimes," or "public welfare offenses."

a. **Crimes vs. Violations**

Section 1.04 places the offenses defined by the Model Penal Code into two categories.

The first, called "crimes," consists of felonies, misdemeanors, and petty misdemeanors. Imprisonment is authorized for these offenses. Felonies are further broken down into three degrees. See § 6.01.

The second is called "violations." Sentences for violations can only consist of a fine, forfeiture, or other civil penalty. Section 1.04(5) specifically provides that a "violation *does not constitute a crime* and conviction of a violation shall not give rise to any disability or legal disadvantage based on conviction of a criminal offense." [Emphasis added.]

1) **Aside**

Section 1.04 is more important than it may seem. Section 1.04(7) provides that any offenses defined outside the penal code "shall be classified as provided in this Section and the sentence that may be imposed upon conviction thereof shall hereafter be governed by this Code."

One of the major purposes of the Model Penal Code was to invite American legislatures to re-examine their criminal codes, to rationalize inconsistent grading of criminal offenses, and to substitute a simple, consistent grading structure into which offenses could be placed. The hope, as new offenses were fitted into the structure, was that the structure could remain consistent over time.

Obviously, such consistency cannot be achieved if crimes can be scattered throughout other titles of the code and given grades and sentences that are not subject to the same discipline. Section 1.04(7) therefore invites a legislature to enter into a compact with itself—to agree over to time to stick to a consistent and rational structure for criminal offenses by imposing the regime of the penal code on any criminal offense no matter where it is placed in the many volumes of legislation in which laws are codified. See also the discussion of strict liability for violations, page 127.

b. Crimes

Section 1.05(1) reads as follows: "No conduct constitutes an *offense* unless it is a *crime or violation* under this Code or another statute of this State." [Emphasis added.] Section 2.05(1) says, with certain exceptions not relevant here, that the culpability requirements of § 2.02 do not apply to *violations*. And § 2.02(1) applies the culpability structure of § 2.02 to all offenses defined in the Model Penal Code except those covered by § 2.05.

The result when these three provisions are read together is clear: Offenses are either crimes or violations. The culpability structure of the Model Penal Code applies to crimes. It does not apply to violations.

Section 2.02(3) therefore means that recklessness is the default culpability level for all elements of all *crimes* defined in the Model Penal Code where the definition of the offense is silent as to mens rea. Thus, strict liability is never implied for a crime in the Model Penal Code, whatever the morality of the situation on the facts as the defendant believes them to be. Compare page 82. Moreover, since the culpability structure applies to all "elements" and since "element" includes grading components (see page 117), there will be no strict liability implied for grading components of a crime. Compare page 81. The only way strict liability can be imposed for a crime defined in the Model Penal Code is by explicit provision in the definition of the offense.

The Model Code rarely imposes strict liability in the definition of an offense. But it does so occasionally.

Examples: Section 213.6(1) is an example of the explicit imposition of strict liability by the Model Penal Code. Section 213.6(1) states that it is no defense if the defendant did not know the child's age or "reasonably believed" that the victim in certain sex offenses was over the age of 10.

                     The reasoning is fairly convoluted, but this translates into strict liability whenever "less than 10 years old" is an element of an offense. A defendant who is unaware of the child's age is explicitly denied a defense by the wording of § 213.6(1). A defendant who thinks the child is older than 10 is denied a defense even if the belief is "reasonable." "Reasonably believed" is defined in § 1.13(16) to mean a belief which the defendant is neither reckless nor negligent in holding. Since a "reasonable belief" is *not* a defense, the effect of § 213.6(1) is to deny a defense in cases where the defendant carefully and without fault formed a belief that the victim was older than 10. Since a non-culpable belief that the victim was older than 10 is not a defense, § 213.6(1) imposes strict liability for "less than 10 years old" in an offense where this is an element. For examples, see §§ 213.1(1)(d), 213.2(1)(d), and 213.4(4).

As one of my students pointed out, the same effect could have been accomplished if § 213.6(1) were more simply drafted, if it said that "it is no defense that the actor did not know the child's age or believed the child to be older than 10." The first part of this provision as redrafted is necessary to deal with the defendant who is agnostic as to age. If the victim is less than 10, the defendant is guilty even if the defendant had no idea how old the child was and whether the defendant cared about the age of the victim or not. The second part of the provision handles the case where the defendant thinks the child is older than 10. If it is no defense to believe the child older than 10, it doesn't matter whether the belief is carefully formed, or whether it was arrived at in a manner that the law would describe as recklessly or negligently. Belief that the child is older than 10 is not a defense no matter how that belief was formed. It doesn't matter, in other words, what the defendant thinks on this subject.

Compare the offense of perjury as defined in § 241.1(1). One might argue by applying § 2.02(3) that the mens rea for the element "material" was recklessness, and that it would therefore be a defense if the defendant thought the lie immaterial and was not reckless in so thinking. This defense is explicitly taken away, however, in § 241.1(2) by a provision similar to the language proposed for § 213.6(1) in the paragraph preceding this one. Section 241.1(2) says that it is not a defense if the defendant "mistakenly believed the falsification to be immaterial." The effect of § 241.1(2) is to impose strict liability on materiality—if the lie is material, the defendant is guilty. As § 241.1(2) goes on to say, materiality is a question of law for the court. What the defendant thinks doesn't matter.

c. **Violations**

In effect, strict liability cannot be imposed for *crimes* under the Model Penal Code unless the definition of the offense explicitly says that strict liability is to be used. The situation for *violations* is virtually the reverse. For them, strict liability is the norm.

1) **Decriminalization of Public Welfare Offenses**

Section 2.02(1) excepts § 2.05 from the culpability structure of the Model Penal Code. Section 2.05 is designed to decriminalize the class of offenses known as "public welfare" or "regulatory" crimes under the common law. See page 81. The Model Code thus retains the feature of strict liability that was their dominant characteristic, but reclassifies the offenses as "violations" and not "crimes." This is accomplished by the provisions in § 1.04(5). This treatment of "public welfare" offenses has been widely suggested in the literature.

2) **Strict Liability for Violations**

Section 2.05(1) provides, in effect, that no mens rea is required for violations, unless the definition of the offense explicitly says so or unless the court determines that enforcement will not be undermined by requiring culpability.

Section 2.05(2) has two effects:

a) **Reclassification of Offenses Defined Outside the Criminal Code**

Section 2.05(2)(a) reclassifies offenses that impose strict liability and that are defined outside the criminal code, for example, in a title of the State statutes regulating alcohol or traffic safety. All such offenses are punished as violations no matter what these statutes provided before the criminal code was enacted. Sections 1.04(7) and 1.05(2) are designed, moreover, to subject all offenses defined after the criminal code is adopted to the provisions of the criminal code. The purpose of these provisions is to prevent the imposition of strict liability for previously and subsequently defined public welfare offenses for which "criminal" punishment is imposed.

b) **Negligent Commission of Violations**

Section 2.05(2)(b) permits the imposition of misdemeanor sanctions for the commission of a violation *if* negligence as to all elements of the offense is established. This is accomplished by the interaction of § 2.05(2) with § 1.04(6). This too is a compromise that is widely suggested in the literature.

6. **CONCURRENCE OF ACTUS REUS AND MENS REA**

The Model Penal Code requires that the defendant's conduct be concurrent in time with the existence of any circumstance elements *and* with the formation of any required mens rea. Results required by the definition of an offense may occur later. The Model Penal Code and the common law are in full agreement on this point, and the discussion and illustrations of this principle on page 82 are equally applicable to the Model Penal Code.

7. TRANSFERRED INTENT
The Model Penal Code does not use the concept of transferred intent. The cases that the common law handled by this concept are treated by the Model Code as presenting issues of causation. See page 129.

8. THE RELATION OF MOTIVE TO MENS REA
The discussion of this topic beginning on page 83 is fully applicable to the Model Penal Code.

D. ACTUS REUS, MENS REA, AND PROPORTIONALITY

The principles and illustrations discussed on this topic beginning on page 85 are fully applicable to the Model Penal Code.

E. CAUSATION

Causation is governed by the provisions of § 2.03. As at common law, one determines whether conduct has "caused" a result by asking two questions.

1. CAUSE IN FACT
The first question is whether the defendant's conduct was "an antecedent but for which the result in question would not have occurred." § 2.03(1)(a). As with the "cause in fact" inquiry at common law, the question here is simply whether the result would have happened if the defendant had not acted.

a. Exception: Concurrent Causes
The problem of concurrent causes, which can be treated as an exception to the "cause in fact" requirement at common law, is not explicitly treated by the Model Code. It is made clear in the legislative history of the Model Code, however, that the drafters intend § 2.03 to be subject to an interpretation that will allow a concurrent cause to suffice as the basis for conviction. This result can be reached through a somewhat strained interpretation of the word "antecedent" in § 2.03(1)(a) to encompass multiple causes leading to a single result.

2. PROXIMATE CAUSE
If the defendant's behavior was the cause in fact of the result, then the second question must be asked. The Model Penal Code replaces the "proximate cause" inquiry of the common law with a different and more complicated series of inquiries. It also discards the terminology of the common law in favor of an explicit

focus on whether the defendant can properly be regarded as criminally responsible for the result. Section 2.03 requires the following analysis.

a. **Comparison of Actual Result With Designed, Contemplated, or Risked Result**
The first step in the analysis is to describe the details of the result as it actually occurred. The second step is to describe the details of the defendant's mental attitude towards the result. The third step is to compare the two in light of the culpability required for the result element in the offense with which the defendant is charged. There are four possibilities:

(1) if the offense requires purpose, then the details of the actual result should be compared to the details of the result the defendant intended to occur;

(2) if the offense requires knowledge, then the details of the actual result should be compared to the details of the result as the defendant thought it would occur;

(3) if the offense requires recklessness, then the details of the actual result should be compared to the details of the result that the defendant thought were risked by the behavior; or

(4) if the offense requires negligence, then the details of the actual result should be compared to the details of the result which the defendant should have known were risked by the behavior.

The purpose of making this comparison is to apply the provisions of Subsections (2)(a) and (2)(b) in the case of purpose and knowledge or the analogous provisions in Subsections (3)(a) and (3)(b) in the case of recklessness and negligence. Those provisions are applied as follows:

1) **Different Person, Different Property, or Lesser Harm**
If the comparison reveals one of three differences, then the defendant's conduct is regarded as the cause of the result. These differences are:

a) **Different Person**
The actual result involved harm to a different person than was intended (in the case of offenses that require purpose), contemplated (in the case of offenses that require knowledge), or risked (in the case of recklessness or negligence). This is the case which the common law treated under the doctrine of "transferred intent."

Example: The defendant shoots at A with intent to kill. The bullet misses A and kills B. The defendant would be guilty of murder under § 210.2(1)(a), since the mens rea of purpose is established by the intent to kill and the actus reus of causing the death of another is satisfied by the provisions of § 2.03(2)(a) in that the actual result (the death of *B*) differed from the designed result (the death of *A*) only in the respect that a different person was harmed.

b) Different Property
The actual result involved harm to different property than was intended, contemplated, or risked.

> *Example:* The defendant causes an explosion under circumstances that a reasonable person would have known to risk damage to *A*'s house. In fact, *A*'s house is not damaged, but *B*'s house next door is damaged. The defendant would be liable for negligent damage to *B*'s house by explosion under the provisions of § 220.3(1)(a), since the actus reus of the offense is satisfied (*conduct*: the employment of explosives; *result*: damage; *circumstances*: tangible property of another), the mens rea of negligence is satisfied, and the defendant's conduct was the cause of the result under § 2.03(3)(a). The actual result (damage to *B*'s house) differed from the result the risk of which the defendant should have been aware (damage to *A*'s house) only in the respect that different property was harmed.

c) Lesser Harm
The actual result involved less harm than the result intended, contemplated, or risked.

> *Example:* Defendant shoots at *A* with intent to kill. The shot results in a serious wound, but does not kill *A*. The defendant would be guilty of aggravated assault under § 211.1(2)(a).

Each of these three situations involves a discrepancy between the defendant's culpability and the event as it actually occurred that plainly should have no bearing on the defendant's criminal responsibility for what happened. The insight that underlies the Model Code causation provisions is that this is the critical question that ought to underlie the causation inquiry. Causation is a question of how the defendant's culpability matches up with what happened—whether in light of the defendant's culpability it is fair to hold the defendant responsible for what happened. In the three cases discussed above, this criterion is plainly satisfied. In the cases to be discussed below, it requires case-by-case judgment to determine whether the criterion is satisfied.

2) Similar Injury or Harm
The most numerous class of causation problems stems from the intervention of unexpected factors that lead to the same kind of result that

the defendant intended, contemplated, or risked. The Model Code resolution of these cases is to ask in §§ 2.03(2)(b) and (3)(b) whether the actual result is "too remote or accidental in its occurrence to have a [just] bearing on the actor's liability or on the gravity of his offense." This calls on the jury to make a judgment, which again involves a comparison between the details of the actual result and the details of the result the defendant intended, contemplated, or risked.

Examples: Consider three cases. In the first, the defendant shoots at *A* with intent to kill. In the second, the defendant shoots at *B* with intent to kill. In the third, the defendant shoots at *C* with intent to kill. In all three cases the victim is seriously wounded. In the first, doctors examine the victim and decide that a risky operation is necessary to save *A*'s life. They operate, and because of complications resulting from the surgery, *A* dies. In the second, doctors make the same decision, and *B* dies because the doctors were negligent in performing the operation; had they not been negligent, it is likely that *B* would have survived. In the third, the same decision is made, and a nurse who has always hated *C* puts poison in the anaesthetic. *C* dies from the gunshot wound complicated by the poisoning, though it is likely that *C* would have lived had the poison not been administered.

It is clear in the first case that the defendant should be guilty of murder under § 210.2(1)(a). The actual cause of death was complications from the operation, but a comparison of this actual result to the result intended by the defendant surely supports the judgment (which would be up to the jury, but it is likely that most juries would have no difficulty in coming to) that the actual result was "not too remote or accidental in its occurrence to have a [just] bearing on the actor's liability or on the gravity of his offense."

In the third case, on the other hand, it seems clear that the defendant should be guilty of attempted murder under §§ 5.01 and 210.2(1)(a). Attempted murder is graded as a second degree felony (see §§ 5.05(1), 210.2(2)), whereas murder itself is a first degree felony (§ 210.2(2)). This difference reflects the judgment of the those who drafted the Model Penal Code that the grade of the offense should turn on whether the result of death is caused by the defendant, a judgment that is consistent with current American law in most if not all jurisdictions. In the third case, the prospect that a nurse would intentionally poison *C* is not an event for which the defendant should properly be held responsible (so the argument would go), and is "too remote" from what the defendant intended so as justly to ascribe the result to the defendant's conduct. Though the question is one for the jury, it seems likely that the defendant would be acquitted of murder in this case.

The second case falls somewhere in between the first two, and seems arguable either way. Whether negligent human intervention should serve as a sufficient difference between what happened and what the defendant intended so as to preclude conviction of the more serious offense is not an easy question. The Model Code would answer it by leaving it to the jury under the criterion stated in § 2.03(2)(b).

Note that it would be possible to argue in all three cases that the defendant should be convicted of murder since the result was intended and the defendant is just as dangerous and just as culpable whether or not some intervening cause actually contributed to the death. This is a persuasive argument. Perhaps a legislature should accept it in the grading of attempt. But the difficulty with the argument is that it has been explicitly rejected by the drafters of the Model Code (and by most if not all criminal codes in America) when they established murder as a more serious crime than attempted murder. Surely one who believes that attempted murder is less serious than murder would not take the position that a defendant who shoots with intent to kill should be held liable for murder if the victim dies of natural causes entirely unrelated to the shooting. If this is so, some line needs to be drawn between deaths which properly can be regarded as "caused" by the defendant's behavior and deaths which are not so regarded. The Model Code draws this line in the terms reflected in §§ 2.03(2)(b) and (3)(b).

b. Strict Liability Offenses

Although the Model Code contains no strict liability offenses containing result elements, it does provide in § 2.03(4) how such an offense would work. Causation would be determined by asking whether the actual result was a probable consequence of the actor's conduct.

F. PROOF OF THE ELEMENTS OF CRIME

The structure of a common law trial described at page 94 is generally applicable to trials conducted in a Model Penal Code jurisdiction. The big difference is the *content* of what must be proved, since the Model Code does not use the concepts of "specific intent" or "general intent," nor does it use the presumption of natural and probable consequences. Several provisions of the Model Code related to proof of the elements of crime should be especially noted.

1. PROOF BEYOND A REASONABLE DOUBT

Section 1.12(1) requires that the prosecutor prove "each element" of an offense beyond a reasonable doubt. The term "element of an offense" is comprehensively defined in § 1.13(9) to encompass all actus reus elements, all mens rea elements, any causation element, any grading elements, *and* the absence of any defense. Thus, unless specific provision is made to the contrary, the Model Penal Code imposes on the prosecutor the burden of persuasion on *all* issues related to the "harm or evil . . . sought to be prevented by the law defining the offense" or the existence of any "justification or excuse" (§ 1.13(19)), and must prove them beyond a reasonable doubt. For an example of a specific provision to the contrary, see § 213.6(1) as it would apply to charges under §§ 213.3(1)(a), (1)(b) and 213.4(6), (7). See also § 2.04(4).

2. THE PROSECUTOR'S PRIMA FACIE CASE

The prosecutor's prima facie case under the Model Penal Code would be the same as at common law: all elements of the actus reus and mens rea, including any causation component. Elements related only to the grade of the offense would also be included in this requirement.

With respect to the mens rea, moreover, it is as important under the Model Code as it is under the common law to distinguish *what* must be proved from *how* it may be proved. *What* must be proved under the Model Code mens rea structure is derived from the definitions contained in § 2.02, and the jury will be instructed that it must make the findings required by those definitions. *How* mens rea will be proved normally will consist of the prosecutor asking the jury to make inferences about whether the defendant is likely to have met the required standard given the nature and circumstances of the conduct.

3. DEFENSES AND AFFIRMATIVE DEFENSES

As a formal matter, defenses under the Model Code are divided into "affirmative defenses" and "defenses." There is, however, no practical difference between them.

a. Affirmative Defenses

The Model Code uses the concept "affirmative defense" in a very unusual way. Normally, criminal codes designate a defense as "affirmative" when they wish to shift the burden of persuasion to the defendant to establish the defense by a preponderance of the evidence. Defenses called merely a "defense" normally require the defendant to bear the initial burden of production but leave the burden of persuasion on the prosecutor beyond a reasonable doubt. The Model Code structure, however, is quite different.

1) Definition

Section 1.12(3) defines "affirmative defense." An affirmative defense is any defense explicitly so designated. See, e.g., §§ 2.09(1), 3.01(1), 4.03(1), 221.1(1). And any defense of justification or excuse based on information "peculiarly within the knowledge of the defendant" is "affirmative" if it is fair to shift the burden of producing supporting evidence to the defendant. Virtually all defenses would seem to satisfy this criterion.

2) Consequence

The consequence of calling a defense "affirmative" is provided in § 1.12(2)(a). The result is that an "affirmative defense" *only* shifts the burden of production to the defendant. Once "there is evidence supporting such defense," § 1.12(1) requires that the prosecutor rebut the defense by proof beyond a reasonable doubt.

Effectively, therefore, this means that there is no practical difference between a "defense" and an "affirmative defense" under the Model Penal Code. The prosecutor must establish a prima facie case consisting of the actus reus, mens rea, and any causation elements of the crime charged. The burden of production on any relevant defensive evidence beyond these elements is on the defendant whether it is offered to establish an "affirmative defense," a "defense," or merely the rebuttal of some element of the prosecutor's prima facie case. The unique feature of the Model Penal Code, accomplished by the interaction of §§ 1.12(1) and (2)(a), is that the burden of persuasion remains on the prosecutor as to *all* of these matters, except those where a special provision shifts the burden of persuasion to the defendant. And such special provisions are rare.

4. PRESUMPTIONS

The Model Code also contains special provisions relating to the effect of a "presumption." For an example of a presumption under the Model Code, see § 210.2(1)(b): the required degree of recklessness is "presumed" if the defendant is engaged in one of the listed felonies. Presumptions work under the Model Code in the following manner.

a. The "Presumed Fact"

A "presumed fact" is an element of an offense the proof of which is aided by a presumption.

Example: In § 210.2(1)(b), the fact which must be proved is that the defendant committed the homicide "recklessly under circumstances manifesting extreme indifference to the value of human life." This fact is "presumed" if the defendant is proved to have been engaged in one of the listed felonies.

b. The Effect of a Presumption

The effect of a presumption is as follows:

1) Sufficient Evidence to Get to the Jury

The prosecutor must first offer enough proof of the facts which give rise to the presumption to satisfy the beyond a reasonable doubt standard. See § 1.12(5)(b).

Example: In a charge under § 210.2(1)(b), the prosecutor would offer enough evidence to persuade the jury beyond a reasonable doubt that the defendant was engaged in one of the listed felonies.

Once enough evidence of the facts which give rise to the presumption has been offered, § 1.12(5)(a) provides that the judge must take the position that enough evidence of the presumed fact has been shown to submit the case to the jury, unless satisfied that the evidence as a whole clearly negates the existence of the presumed fact.

Example: Assume in a charge under § 210.2(1)(b) that the prosecutor has offered enough evidence to justify a jury finding beyond a reasonable doubt that the defendant engaged in one of the listed felonies. At this point, the judge must submit to the jury the question whether the defendant acted "recklessly under circumstances manifesting extreme indifference to the value of human life." The judge need not do so, however, if the evidence as a whole clearly shows that the required level of indifference did not exist.

Thus, for example, if the evidence showed that the defendant shot the victim while engaged in an armed bank robbery, proof of these facts would justify submission of the case to the jury on whether the required level of indifference was established.

On the other hand, if the evidence showed that the defendant was the driver of the getaway car and believed that the actual robbers were not armed, the judge might conclude that the evidence as a whole "clearly negatives" a finding that the required level of indifference existed and might therefore refuse to submit the issue to the jury based only on proof of the defendant's involvement in the felony.

2) Instructions to the Jury

When the existence of the presumed fact is submitted to the jury, the judge is required to give two instructions: (1) that the presumed fact must be proved beyond a reasonable doubt on all the evidence; and (2) that the law permits the jury to regard proof of the facts from which the presumption arises as sufficient evidence of the existence of the presumed fact. See § 1.12(5)(b).

Example: Assume a charge under § 210.2(1)(b) where the prosecutor introduces evidence to show that the defendant was engaged in one of the listed felonies and where the judge has decided to permit the case to go to the jury based on this proof. In that event, the judge would instruct the jury (1) that the jury must find beyond a reasonable doubt on all the evidence that the defendant acted "recklessly under circumstances manifesting extreme indifference to the value of human life"; and (2) that the law allows the jury to regard proof of the defendant's involvement in the listed felony as sufficient evidence that the defendant acted with the required level of indifference.

G. REVIEW QUESTIONS

[Answers Provided in Appendix A, page 420]

1. T or F   The definition of "purpose" under the Model Penal Code requires a conscious desire that results and circumstances occur, and knowledge that the required conduct has occurred.

2. T or F   The term "situation" in the definitions of recklessness and negligence in the Model Penal Code is designed to permit the courts to personalize the objective standard against which the defendant is to be measured, but it is likely that the courts will be reluctant to carry this personalization very far.

3. T or F   The crimes for which the Model Penal Code permits strict liability are quite restricted. They include a narrow range of sex offenses and public welfare offenses.

4. T or F   An affirmative defense under the Model Penal Code shifts the burden of production to the defendant.

5. T or F   An affirmative defense under the Model Penal Code shifts the burden of persuasion to the defendant.

6. T or F   A presumption under the Model Penal Code shifts the burden of production to the defendant.

7. T or F   A presumption under the Model Penal Code shifts the burden of persuasion to the defendant.

8. T or F   The Model Penal Code is consistent with the common law in not requiring mens rea for grading elements.

9. T or F   If the word "purpose" appears in the definition of a Model Penal Code offense, the effect of § 2.02(4) is that "purpose" becomes the mens rea for all elements that follow that word. It does not apply "purpose" to elements that precede its use because the definition is not then ambiguous. Ordinary grammar rules do not apply modifiers to words that precede them.

10. T or F   The Model Penal Code provisions on causation handle the cases that the common law deals with through the doctrine of "transferred intent."

11. Answer Question 12, page 102. Change the offense to a charge under § 220.1(1)(b) of the Model Penal Code.

12. Describe all of the actus reus and mens rea elements of the offense defined in § 221.2(1) of the Model Penal Code.

13. What is the mens rea under the Model Penal Code for the elements "possesses" and "offensive weapon" in § 5.07?

14. You should practice application of the culpability structure on as many of the substantive offenses in Part II of the Model Penal Code as you have the patience to attack. In each case you should isolate carefully all of the actus reus elements, the mens rea required for each, and any additional mens rea requirements. Don't forget to include grading factors and any defenses. The only way to understand the Model Code culpability structure is to practice it repeatedly. You can check your answers with fellow students—this would be a good project for a study group if you are in one. If you can't figure out some of the offenses, perhaps you can get help from your Professor.

*

PART THREE

DERIVATIVE DEFENSES

Analysis

*

THE COMMON LAW

141

A. INTRODUCTION

The term "derivative defenses" is used here—perhaps invented here is the better way to put it since the phrase is unknown to the common law—to refer to defenses that are the obverse of the elements the prosecutor must show in order to secure a conviction. In effect they are an effort to rebut the prosecutor's prima facie case—to show that some necessary ingredient of the actus reus, the mens rea, or causation is missing. The prosecutor must prove beyond a reasonable doubt *all* of the actus reus, mens rea, and causation elements contained in the definition of the offense. The defendant may defend by seeking to rebut any one of them. The words "derivative defense" in these pages refer to the defendant's effort to undertake that rebuttal.

There is a substantial body of common law doctrine concerning some of the efforts by the defendant to rebut the prosecutor's case. This doctrine is developed below.

Start, however, with a simple case. If the prosecutor fails to prove that *each* of the actus reus elements of the offense occurred, there must be an acquittal. The first proposition, therefore, is that the prosecution must establish that each conduct element was committed by the defendant, that any required results were caused by that conduct, and that any required circumstances were present. One classic "derivative defense" is to show that one or more of the actus reus elements of the offense is missing, as by attempting to prove by establishing an alibi that the defendant was somewhere else at the time of the offense or attempting to prove in the crime of larceny that the property taken actually belonged to the defendant. An important thing to do in analyzing any crime, if not the first thing, is to isolate the actus reus elements contained in the definition of the offense and make sure they all occurred.

B. INVOLUNTARY ACTS

It is stated on pages 74–75 that crime requires conduct, and that the "conduct" requirement can be satisfied by an act, an omission where there is a legal duty to act, or possession. The actus reus elements of an offense must consist of at least some conduct in this sense. It needs to be added to that requirement that the conduct must include a "voluntary act."

This requirement is covered here rather than in Part Two because the prosecutor need not show as part of the prima facie case that the defendant's conduct included a voluntary act, even though a voluntary act is as much a part of every criminal offense as any other component of the actus reus. For practical reasons—why litigate the issue in every case when it will rarely be an issue?—the "voluntary act" aspect of the defendant's conduct will be assumed if the matter does not come up at trial, and there will be no instruction to the jury on the issue. However, it is a defense if the defendant claims that the conduct was "involuntary" (that is, that the conduct did not include a voluntary act) and produces some evidence to support that assertion. Once there is evidence on the point, the prosecution must prove beyond a reasonable doubt that the defendant's conduct included a voluntary act.

There is a clear moral basis for exonerating persons whose conduct is "involuntary," for not imposing criminal punishment on persons who are unable to control their behavior. Such persons are not blameworthy, and it is unfair to hold them responsible for criminal behavior. But how far should a defense based on this notion extend? Should it extend to a person of limited intelligence who doesn't really understand the consequences of choice? Should it extend to a person from a background in which socialization to the moral values of society were not properly inculcated? Do any of us ever *really* exercise conscious choice, or are all of our actions products of our environment, our background and upbringing, and our unconscious psyche in spite of the ways in which we might rationalize our behavior in the ways we think about it?

The meaning of "voluntary" as used by the criminal law in this context is quite narrow. It is limited to situations where the defendant engaged in *no act of will*, where literally and for a physically identifiable reason no choice or capacity for choice existed. Thus, cases of reflex actions or sleep-walking, bodily motions during epileptic seizures or complete blackouts, and the like, are paradigm examples of "involuntary" acts. Generally speaking, an act is "involuntary" if it is the product of a *physical* rather than a *mental* impairment. There is controversy over whether acts committed under hypnotic suggestion are voluntary or involuntary.

Why is the concept of involuntariness so narrow? One reason is based on the social control objectives of the criminal law. Persons acquitted by reason of an involuntary act generally are not subject to civil commitment or other confinement. If they are dangerous in spite of the involuntary character of their behavior, they will remain free to cause harm to other victims. The social control objectives of the criminal law would be undermined by the recognition of involuntariness based on limited intelligence or improper or defective socialization. They would be impossible to achieve if one or another notion of psychological determinism could provide the basis for an involuntary act defense.

Think also for a moment about the civil liberties consequences of a different regime for protecting society from criminal behavior. Would civil commitment of dangerous persons who were acquitted by reason of limited intelligence, unfortunate background, or psychological determinism be better or worse than the system we now have? For how long would the commitment last? Who would make the operative decisions?

Recognition of a theory of psychological determinism, or recognition of defenses based on limited intelligence or the constraints of background on socialization, would undermine the operating premises of the criminal law in another sense. There could be no responsibility, no blame, and no punishment in such a world. The criminal law is based on the capacity of the individual to make free choices and the assumption that virtually all of our behavior virtually all of the time is a result of free choice. This may or may not be a description of reality. But the criminal law as we know it cannot function without the hallmarks of responsibility, blame, and punishment as the working premises for most behavior. This is why the law assumes a voluntary act in the absence of evidence to the contrary. And this is why, when such evidence is forthcoming, the law will recognize a defense based on the lack of a "voluntary" act only in extreme cases of demonstrable lack of capacity to exercise free will based on identifiable physical characteristics that clearly differentiate the defendant's behavior from ordinary conduct.

1. INVOLUNTARY ACT IN VOLUNTARY COURSE OF CONDUCT

One situation that must be analyzed carefully occurs when the defendant's overall course of conduct includes both voluntary and involuntary behavior. The law may attach criminal consequences to the *voluntary* components of such behavior. Whether it does so is determined by closely examining the statute on which the prosecution is based to see whether the necessary actus reus occurred.

Examples: Assume that the defendant goes to sleep in a crowded hotel lobby armed with a gun, and that the defendant knows of a tendency when suddenly awakened to react immediately with violence. If the defendant is awakened suddenly, and while still in a somnambulistic state kills a person in the lobby, should the involuntary act defense be available against a charge of negligent homicide? Probably not, since the defendant's entire course of conduct included voluntary acts (going to sleep armed with a gun with knowledge of violent tendencies) and those acts alone could be said to have negligently caused the death. Conviction could not be based on the acts that occurred while the defendant was still asleep, but the fact that these acts were involuntary is not a defense if sufficient voluntary behavior had previously occurred. See Fain v. Commonwealth, 78 Ky. 183 (1879).

Another well-known, though more controversial case involving the same principle is People v. Decina, 2 N.Y.2d 133, 157 N.Y.S.2d 558, 138 N.E.2d 799 (1956), where the defendant, knowing he was subject to epileptic seizures, drove a car, suffered a seizure, and was held properly charged with negligent homicide by a motor vehicle.

2. RELATION TO OTHER DEFENSES

The voluntary act doctrine is not the only defense available to one whose conduct was in some sense involuntary. It is important to be able to distinguish when the voluntary act defense is appropriate and when these other defenses must be relied upon.

a. Insanity

The insanity defense *must* be used whenever the defendant proposes to assert a "mental disease or defect" as the basis for a lack of control over choice. The term "mental disease or defect" is an ill-defined word of art, which is further discussed in the section on the insanity defense. See page 226. For now it is sufficient to know that an involuntary act defense may not be predicated on the kind of "mental disease or defect" that serves as the basis for the insanity defense.

1) Physical Disease Leading to Recurrent Violence

Note that the consequence of an involuntary act acquittal is that the defendant goes free. There is therefore the possibility of continuing danger to the public if the defendant is suffering from a recurring condition and it is likely or possible that the defendant may, for example, kill again.

This has led one English court, in the case of Bratty v. Attorney General of Northern Ireland, [1961] 3 All. E.R. 523, to hold in a homicide case where psychomotor epilepsy was raised as a defense that "any mental disorder which has manifested itself in violence and is prone to recur" is to be treated as invoking the insanity defense and not the voluntary act defense. The consequence of invoking the insanity defense in most places is some form of automatic commitment, which thus reduces future danger to the public. The decision in *Bratty* was a practical one, born of the desire to limit the scope of the voluntary act defense in order better to protect the public from dangerous conduct, or in other words to promote the objective of social control. In effect it asserts that the way to tell the difference between a condition that gives rise to the insanity defense and a condition that gives rise to the involuntary act defense is to ask whether violent conduct is likely to recur. If it is, then the insanity defense must be used; if not, then the involuntary act defense.

There are few American decisions that have addressed this issue, although one that did held that psychomotor epilepsy, even though it may lead to future violence, could be asserted to support an involuntary act defense. See People v. Grant, 46 Ill.App.3d 125, 4 Ill.Dec. 696, 360 N.E.2d 809 (1977). It is clear in any event that the law needs some test for distinguishing the kinds of conditions that are relegated to the insanity defense from those which may be used to support an involuntary act defense. None as yet is widely recognized.

b. Duress

The defense of duress is discussed at page 245. It is available in some instances where the defendant had a hard choice (e.g., steal or be killed), but nonetheless is able to exercise will to make a choice. By contrast, the voluntary act defense is available *only* where it could be said that the defendant's conscious will was not operating at all. The difference is between a hard choice and no choice, between a capable person who must choose between two evils and a person who has no capacity to choose.

> *Example:*   A defendant who steals to feed the family will be guilty of theft. The act is voluntary because the defendant had a choice, though a hard one. (As will be seen, moreover, the defense of duress is unavailable in this case as well, since it requires that the coercion come from another person rather than from external events.)

c. Self Defense

The defense of self defense can be distinguished from the voluntary act defense on the same basis. A defendant who kills in self defense has engaged in a "voluntary act" as the law defines that term because the decision to kill is a conscious exercise of will. That it is a hard choice, and one that in some cases society is prepared to condone, is the reason for the existence of the separate defense of self defense, which is dealt with at page 191.

C. MISTAKE OF FACT

Most mistake defenses involve an effort by the defendant to show that a required mens rea element of an offense is missing. The crucial question, therefore, is what mens rea elements are required. Once this has been determined, application of most mistake rules is simply a matter of logic and common sense.

The common law approach to mistakes of fact does not always seem to follow this logic. It requires first that the offense be classified as one of specific intent, general intent, or strict liability, and second that certain specified rules be applied. Usually, the rules can be translated into the logic described above: if the prosecutor must prove X as the mens rea for an offense, the defendant can get off if a mistake of fact establishes not-X.

1. SPECIFIC INTENT
An honest mistake of fact is a defense to a specific intent crime. This assumes, of course, that the mistake relates directly to a specific intent required for commission of the offense. The word "honest" simply means that the defendant must have actually believed the mistaken fact to be true.

Example: Assume the defendant is charged with common law larceny, defined as "taking and carrying away the personal property of another with intent to deprive the owner of the property permanently." Assume that the defendant committed the actus reus of the offense, that is, took and carried away personal property that in fact belonged to another. But assume also that because of a mistake in identification the defendant thought that the property belonged to the defendant. Is the defendant guilty of larceny? The answer is "no," and it can be explained in either of two ways:

> (1) that the defendant has made an honest mistake, which is a defense to a specific intent crime.

> (2) that the defendant did not have the specific intent "to deprive the owner" of the property.

The first explanation is a statement of the common law rule. The second is the common sense of the matter.

a. Aside: Why Rules and not Logic?
The explanation for why the common law reasoned in this manner is lost in history, but is probably the result of the fact that the early judges thought

about such matters in terms of defenses rather than elements of crime. In modern terms, this could have been because of the way the burden of production of evidence was allocated. Or, as is more likely, it could have been that what we think of today as mens rea elements of crimes first emerged as defenses—that is, the judges initially thought of crimes in terms only of punishable acts, and mens rea emerged over time as the judges considered defenses to the criminalization of those acts.

Whatever the explanation, the tradition of the common law is to think of mistake of fact as a defense and to have a rule about it, in this case, "an honest mistake of fact is a defense to a specific intent crime." Other rules for other situations are described below. The fact that today we might convert some or all of these rules into logical corollaries of elements of offenses is a modern development, attributable more than any other source to the Model Penal Code. Importantly, you need to know, many courts in jurisdictions that have not recently revised their criminal law in response to the Model Penal Code still think and talk in the mode of the original common law. This is why you need to be able to do so too.

2. GENERAL INTENT

An honest and reasonable mistake of fact is a defense to a general intent crime. This assumes, of course, that the mistake relates directly to a general intent required for commission of the offense. The word "honest" means that the defendant must actually have believed the mistaken fact to be true. The word "reasonable" means that a reasonable person in the defendant's situation is likely to have made the same mistake.

> *Example:* Assume that arson is defined as "the malicious burning of the dwelling of another" and that "malicious" is held to require "general intent." Assume further that the defendant intends to raze an old house believed to belong to the defendant by burning it to the ground. Assume also a mistaken identification of the house, and that the defendant actually razes a dwelling that belongs to another. Is the defendant's mistake a defense? A categorical answer cannot be given. The mistake is a defense if it was honestly and reasonably made. It is up to the jury to determine whether these elements are present. The first question is whether it believes the defendant actually made the mistake. If so, the mistake was honest. The second question is whether it believes the mistake was reasonable under the circumstances, which probably translates into whether it was a mistake that any one of us might have made.

This answer too can be explained in either of two ways. One is in terms of the rule stated above: an honest and reasonable mistake of fact is a defense to a general intent crime. The other is that "ordinary negligence" is what "general intent" means when mistake of fact is the defense, and a defendant who honestly and reasonably believes facts that are inconsistent with the actus reus of an offense is not negligent.

Be careful with the application of this rule. As developed under the heading "Strict Liability" below, whether a particular element of an offense requires general intent or imposes strict liability may depend on the *kind* of mistake of fact that is made. Before dealing with strict liability, however, one other situation must be mentioned.

a. Mistakes as to Actus Reus Elements of Specific Intent Crimes

Note that specific intent crimes normally consist of specified actus reus elements in addition to the specific intent. What rules apply to mistakes as to those actus reus elements? The answer requires an analysis in two steps:

(1) Does the mistake show that the specific intent was not in fact entertained by the defendant? If it does, then the normal specific intent rule applies, and an honest mistake is a defense.

(2) If the mistake does not show that the specific intent is lacking, then the normal *general intent* rule applies, and only an honest and reasonable mistake is a defense.

Note that you must also be careful about application of the normal "general intent" rule in this context. As mentioned above and to be explained under the heading "Strict Liability" below, whether a particular element requires general intent or imposes strict liability may depend on the *kind* of mistake of fact the defendant makes. For now, however, the two steps described above can be illustrated as follows:

Examples: Assume a crime defined as "receiving property known to have been stolen." If the property received was in fact stolen, but the defendant believed that it was not, is the defendant's honest belief a defense? The answer is "yes," because in this instance the belief relates directly to the specific intent required by the definition of the offense and shows that the defendant did not have the specific intent. An honest mistake is a defense to a specific intent crime when it negates the specific intent.

Now assume a crime defined as "receiving criminal law books known to have been stolen." Suppose the defendant knows that stolen books have been received, but believes that the books cover English literature. Is the defendant's mistake a defense?

The first question is whether the mistake negates the required specific intent. Does it? Perhaps, if "known to have been stolen" means that the defendant must know *both* that books were stolen *and* that they were criminal law books. If the specific intent covers *both* of these things, then the mistake is a defense under the normal approach to mistakes of fact for specific intent crimes.

But now assume that the specific intent is interpreted to mean only that the defendant must know that books were stolen, and that the offense does not require that the defendant know they were criminal law books. Is the mistake still a defense?

Now the normal rules for general intent offenses will apply to the mistake. And we would now know that the mistake can be a defense only if both honest and reasonable. Note, however, that this answer will be qualified in the strict liability discussion below, specifically at page 153. For now, though, the point is that the specific intent rule does not apply to *all* mistakes of fact that relate to a crime containing a specific intent. Whether it applies depends on the meaning of the words used to describe the specific intent and whether the defendant's mistaken belief shows that the specific intent, as defined by these words as they are interpreted, is missing.

3. STRICT LIABILITY

A mistake of fact is not a defense if it relates to an element for which strict liability is imposed.

Example: Assume an offense defined as "serving alcohol to a person less than 18 years old." Assume further that the offense is interpreted as carrying strict liability with respect to age, and that the person served was reasonably believed by the defendant to be 19 but was in fact 17. Is the mistake a defense?

No. The prosecutor would need only to prove that the defendant served alcohol to a person who was less than 18 in order to establish a prima facie case. No mens rea for the age element would need be established. And a defense of mistake of fact as to the age would be disallowed.

This result can also be explained in either of two ways. The rule is that a mistake of fact is not a defense if it relates to an element for which strict liability is imposed, and that rule applies here. Alternatively, the mistake is not a defense because it is irrelevant. It does not negate any required mens rea element of the offense.

a. Immoral Behavior

Recall the class of cases involving immoral behavior discussed at page 82. Crimes like statutory rape and adultery are sometimes held to be general intent crimes and sometimes held to be crimes of strict liability. Which they are in a specific case depends on *the kind of mistake* asserted by the defendant as a defense.

Specifically, whether the rule for general intent crimes or the rule for strict liability crimes will be applied to a mistake of fact involving such an offense depends on the following calculus:

(1) If the underlying behavior is *immoral* on the facts as the defendant believed them to be, then the rule governing strict liability crimes will be applied;

(2) If the underlying behavior is *not immoral* on the facts as the defendant believed them to be, then the rule governing general intent crimes will be applied.

Bear in mind that this analysis does not apply to all offenses. Nor does it apply in all common law jurisdictions. Generally speaking, where used at all it is limited to offenses involving sexual intercourse outside the sanction of marriage, though it may not be quite as limited as that in all jurisdictions. For those jurisdictions that take this approach, the assumption is that all sexual intercourse outside of marriage is "immoral," even though perhaps not illegal.

Most of the precedents establishing this point of view are quite old. Whether they will or should survive can be doubted.

Examples: Assume a definition of adultery as "sexual intercourse with a person who is married to another or by a married person with a person who is not the married person's spouse." Compare two cases:

(1) A male defendant mistakenly believes that he is no longer married because the ship on which his wife had gone sailing was lost in a storm and she was thought to have died. He then has sexual intercourse with a woman to whom he is not married. His wife then shows up very much alive.

(2) A female defendant marries a man who, unknown to her, is already married. She then has sexual intercourse with the man. The law in such a case is that her marriage is void, since the man's marriage was bigamous. The law also is that the man remains validly married to his first wife.

The male's mistake would not be a defense. Since the male knew he was engaging in sexual intercourse outside the sanction of marriage, his conduct was "immoral" even on his belief as to what the facts were. Since that is so, no mens rea is required as to the element "married person" and he is guilty of adultery. The common law rule designed for strict liability offenses applies.

The female's mistake, on the other hand, would be governed by the rules applicable to general intent offenses. She would thus have a defense if her mistake was both honest and reasonable. She thought that she was engaging in sexual intercourse with her husband, and on the facts as she thought them to be no immoral act was committed. Normal "general intent" rules would therefore be applied.

b. Elements Not Central to the Criminality of Behavior

Recall now the class of cases discussed under the heading "Elements Not Central to the Criminality of Behavior" at page 81. The common law rule for mistakes of fact in general intent crimes is often stated in the following manner: "Mistake of fact is a defense to a general intent crime if the defendant's mistake is honest and reasonable *and* if the conduct would not be criminal if the facts were as the defendant believed them to be."

What this means is that, for general intent crimes, mistakes as to elements that are important to whether the behavior is a crime or not are a defense if honestly and reasonably made. But mistakes as to elements that are important only to the grading (or severity) of the offense are not a defense. To say the same thing another way, if the mistake relates to an element that distinguishes criminal from non-criminal behavior, the element requires general intent and the normal general intent rule applies. But if the mistake relates only to an element that affects the seriousness of the crime, the element carries strict liability and the normal strict liability rule applies.

Examples: Assume that arson of a dwelling house belonging to another is a second degree crime carrying a maximum sentence of 10 years, and that arson of an outbuilding belonging to another and not used as a dwelling is a third degree crime carrying a maximum sentence of 5 years. Assume further that the defendant in fact burns a building used as a dwelling, but believed that it was an outbuilding. If both classes of arson are general intent crimes, does the defendant have a defense to the more serious offense?

The answer is "no." Since a crime would have been committed even had the facts been as the defendant believed them to be, the mistake is no defense and the defendant is guilty of second degree arson. In effect, strict liability is applied to the element "dwelling house" in the major felony, since that element is of grading significance only.

Now compare the arson example used under the heading "General Intent" on page 147. On the facts as recited there, no crime would have been committed had the facts been as the defendant believed them to be, and hence the normal "general intent" rule applied.

1) Application to Specific Intent Offenses

Now consider another case. Assume that grand larceny is the stealing of property worth more than $100 and petty larceny the stealing of property worth $100 or less. Assume further that the defendant steals a ring that contains a precious stone worth several thousand dollars, but that the defendant believes the stone to be glass and the ring to be worth $20 or $30. Is the defendant's mistake, if honest, a defense to grand larceny, since grand larceny is a specific intent crime?

Recall the two-step analysis suggested for mistakes as to actus reus elements of specific intent crimes. See page 149.

(1)   The first question is whether the mistake relates to the specific intent. If it does, then an honest mistake is a defense. Here, however, it does not. The specific intent for larceny is an intent to deprive another of property permanently, and the defendant plainly had this intent.

(2)   The analysis therefore moves to the second step, which is to apply the normal general intent rule. The normal general intent rule is that the defendant would have a defense if the mistake were both honest and reasonable. But that rule applies only to elements of an offense that are central to the criminality of the offense, that is, to elements that determine whether a crime was committed or no crime was committed. It does not apply to elements that are only of grading significance, to elements that determine only how serious was the crime that the defendant committed. Here, the defendant's mistake relates only to grading. Petty larceny would have been committed had the facts been as the defendant believed them to be. Hence, liability on this element is strict and the strict liability rule applies. The mistake is not a defense and the defendant is guilty of grand larceny. The defendant is graded on what was done, not what was thought to have been done.

It was noted in a prior illustration—the one involving the defendant who mistook a criminal law book for English literature on page 150—that the answer given there would have to be qualified. This is the qualification: If it were a lesser (or, as of course it should be, a greater) crime to receive an English literature book knowing it to have been stolen *and* if the specific intent did not extend to knowledge of the nature of the book, then strict liability would be applied to that element of the actus reus and the mistake would not be a defense even if reasonable. In that case, the general intent rules would apply to the actus reus element "criminal law book." Those rules apply strict liability if the actus reus element involved relates only to how serious the crime might be, not whether there was a crime at all.

Note, however, that the rule that mistakes don't count if they relate to grading elements applies *only* to general intent. It does *not* apply to a required specific intent. Hence, if the statute in the criminal-law-book case were interpreted to require knowledge that the book was a criminal law book, as it well might be from its language, then an honest mistake would be a defense to that crime even if some other crime would be committed on the facts as the defendant believed them to be. In that case, the specific intent itself would encompass knowledge of the kind of book that was being received. Even though if would have been a less (or more) serious offense to have done what the defendant thought was happening, the mistake is still a defense because it shows that the required specific intent was not present.

Complicated stuff, but you need to get it straight.

D. MISTAKE OF CRIMINAL LAW

The maxim "ignorance of the law is no excuse" expresses the judgment that ignorance or mistake of law should not be a defense to crime. As so put, the maxim is an overstatement, for there *are* occasions when ignorance or mistake of law can be a defense to crime. The maxim would be far more accurate if it were changed to read "ignorance of the *criminal* law is no excuse." But even put in this way, it is an overstatement. Nonetheless, this revised version does state a principle to which, as a general matter, the criminal law adheres.

Why? The answer sometimes given is that "everyone is presumed to know the criminal law," but plainly this is the purest fiction if it purports to be an accurate explanation of what people in fact know. Do *you* know all the criminal law in your jurisdiction? Any of it? If you don't know it all, how about the average high school graduate? The average person who didn't finish high school? This fiction is also completely question-begging. It would not offer a policy reason for why people should be held to knowledge of the law even if it were true that most people did know the law.

There are, basically, two reasons for the principle.

The first is that it promotes the goal of prevention. To have a contrary rule would invite, indeed reward, ignorance of the criminal law. It would insulate from criminal liability all who could get the "right" legal advice from cooperative, if shady, attorneys. It promotes the objective of social control to require people to know the criminal law at their peril. It maximizes deterrence if people know that mistakes about the coverage of the criminal law will not be an excuse.

The second reason, as put by Jerome Hall in his book General Principles of the Criminal Law, is that the rule is an "essential postulate of the legal order." The very idea of law suggests that it should come from an authoritative source. Courts need to be empowered to make final and authoritative pronouncements on what the criminal law is. If ignorance of the criminal law were a defense, the criminal law in a very meaningful sense would be whatever any individual thought it was.

At the end of the day, this second reason is an application of the first: It undermines prevention (social control) for the law to be whatever criminals think it is. It promotes deterrence if people know that courts get to decide the meaning of the criminal law and what they think about it doesn't matter.

The major argument against the principle is that its application can sometimes be unfair. It is not unfair to deny a defense to a murderer or rapist who claims ignorance that murder or rape is a crime. All of us are socialized to know such things. But it might be unfair rigorously to enforce the rule in all contexts, as is illustrated below.

The important point for now is that what makes the principle acceptable in fairness terms is the fact that the vast majority of us who are law abiding citizens are socialized to know as a matter of common sense enough about right and wrong to know that behavior that amounts to murder, rape, robbery, burglary, theft, etc., is not to be tolerated. You can understand this point by asking yourself the following question: "Even though I have not memorized all of the crimes in all of the American jurisdictions in which I find myself from time to time (not to speak of foreign countries), why am I not in jail? Why don't *I* commit crimes every day out of ignorance if not intentionally?" The answer is socialization. By growing up in civilized society, you are taught enough about good and evil to know the fundamental boundaries that differentiate crime from ordinarily acceptable behavior. You know enough at least to ask when you get near the borders of what might be a crime. You know enough to keep out of trouble. Where this is not true—where the average citizen is not socialized to know that certain behavior might constitute a crime—there is, as is illustrated below, reason for questioning whether the "ignorance of the law" principle can fairly be applied.

1. THE PARADIGM CASE

Ignorance or mistake as to whether given conduct is a crime is not a defense. It should be emphasized that this principle also encompasses cases where the defendant knows perfectly well what the law says, but makes a mistake about the meaning or application of one of its terms.

The rule can be conceptualized in the following formula, where X, Y, and Z are actus reus elements of a hypothetical crime and the superscripted characters represent the mens rea (K for knowledge, R for reckless, and S for strict liability). Assume that:

$$X^K + Y^R + Z^R \ [= \text{crime}]^S$$

The paradigm illustration of the principle that ignorance of the criminal law is no excuse is a defendant who does not know that X + Y + Z is a crime. Since such ignorance is not a defense, in effect the law imposes strict liability for the "= crime" component of the equation.

Suppose the defendant knows the definition of the offense, but makes a mistake about whether particular conduct falls within the legal definition of "X." Can such a mistake be urged as a defense? "No" is the answer, but one must be careful: the mistake will not be a defense if the legal definition of which the defendant is unaware is one that is supplied *by the criminal law itself*. As will be seen under the heading "Mistake of Non–Criminal Law" beginning at page 159, if the mistake is as to a matter of property law, family law, or some other *civil* provision, the mistake might qualify as a defense.

Examples: Consider the common law definition of burglary as "breaking and entering the dwelling house of another in the nighttime with the intent to commit a felony therein." Assume that the defendant knows this definition. Assume also that the defendant reaches inside an open window in order to steal a valuable ring that is within reach. Assume that the decisions interpreting the burglary statute construe "breaking" as breaking the plane of the household, and that the defendant's conduct therefore constitutes burglary. Assume finally, however, that the defendant was convinced that the law of burglary was to the contrary: the defendant thought that one had to open the window or engage in some physical act of breaking in order to commit the crime. Would the defendant be entitled to a mistake defense?

"No." Mistake or ignorance of the criminal law is no excuse. The "ignorance of the law" maxim encompasses not only ignorance of the existence of the crime, such as would occur if the defendant did not know that "breaking and entering the dwelling of another in the nighttime with the intent to commit a felony therein" was a crime. It also encompasses mistakes about the meaning assigned by the criminal law to the terms used in the legal definition of the crime, such as occurred on the hypothetical facts. Liability is strict both on whether $X + Y + Z$ is a crime, and on the meaning assigned by the criminal law to X and Y and Z.

a. The Meaning of Mens Rea

This is a useful point at which to reinforce the meaning of mens rea in the criminal law. If it were required that the defendant have a mens rea of "knowledge" with respect to the "breaking" element of burglary, what would be meant is only that the defendant must know what happened. The defendant must know only what was being done. The defendant need not know that the criminal law attaches the label "breaking" to that behavior.

Example: On the facts in the preceding example, if the mens rea for the element "breaking" were knowledge, all the defendant would have to know is that the defendant was reaching a hand through an open window. The defendant would *not* have to know that the criminal law calls this conduct "breaking."

2. EXCEPTION: INTERPRETATION OF MENS REA TERMS

There are some situations where loose common law mens rea language employed in the definition of a crime has been interpreted to require that the defendant be culpable as to the criminality of behavior in order for a conviction to be obtained.

Example: In United States v. Murdock, 290 U.S. 389, 54 S.Ct. 223 (1933), the defendant refused to divulge certain information to the Internal

Revenue Service on the ground that to do so would incriminate him under *State* criminal laws and that the Fifth Amendment to the *federal* Constitution gave him a privilege not to answer any question which would have that effect. The Fifth Amendment question was resolved against him after litigation. He then was prosecuted for his previous failure to answer under a federal tax statute that punished one who "willfully" failed to supply requested information. He was convicted, but the Supreme Court held that the term "willfully" in this particular tax statute should have been defined in a manner that would preclude conviction of one who had a good faith belief in the lawfulness of conduct at the time it was undertaken. In effect, therefore, the Court interpreted the mens rea term "willfully" in the particular statute to prevent conviction of a person who believed that conduct was not criminal at the time it was committed.

Note that this is an extremely rare situation, and that the term "willfully" is not always so interpreted, even in federal statutes. Indeed, there are explicit holdings to the contrary in directly analogous situations involving other federal statutes. See, e.g., Barsky v. United States, 167 F.2d 241 (D.C.Cir. 1948). But as an analytical matter, it should always be kept in mind that the meaning of common law mens rea words is often sufficiently fuzzy so that, particularly with crimes not endangering the safety of another person, they are subject to an interpretation that will allow good faith mistakes of the criminal law to be asserted as a defense. The point is not that courts have often come to this conclusion, for they have not. The point is that this is a situation where effective advocacy might lead a court to produce a "fair" result that would otherwise be precluded by a rigid application of the common law rule. Remember that common law mens rea words can be chameleons.

3. EXCEPTION: MISLED BY OFFICIAL AUTHORITY

One case where the equities would seem to favor recognition of an exception to the rigid common law rule is where the defendant is affirmatively misled by public officials charged with enforcing the law in question. On the one hand, it could be argued that a defendant who knows enough to ask about the legality of behavior knows enough not to act if there is any doubt. On the other hand, there is a kind of entrapment when an official source says "go ahead" and the defendant takes the advice. Most common law courts have refused to recognize a defense in this situation. There are, however, some cases to the contrary.

Examples: One involved a situation where the defendant engaged in behavior in violation of a State statute that had been held unconstitutional by the State Supreme Court, but which was later revived by an overruling decision that occurred *after* the defendant's conduct. There the Court held, in effect, that the defendant had been misled by the highest authority there is in interpreting the law, and that it would be unfair to expect the defendant to anticipate the overruling decision. See State v. O'Neil, 147 Iowa 513, 126 N.W. 454 (1910).

Another involved a defendant who registered to vote in violation of laws precluding convicted felons from voting. He had in his possession, and showed to the election officials who then permitted him to register, papers which appeared to, but as it turned out actually did not, give him a pardon. His conviction was reversed on the ground that it was unfair to convict in these circumstances. See State v. White, 237 Mo. 208, 140 S.W. 896 (1911).

The Supreme Court has also addressed this situation in constitutional terms in the context of a civil rights demonstration. The defendant was convicted for demonstrating "near" a courthouse. The highest police officials, the sheriff, and the mayor were present at the demonstration. The demonstrators knew about the statute, and asked the officials where they could lawfully demonstrate. They were told that a certain place was ok, that it was not too "near" the courthouse to violate the statute. They demonstrated there, and their leader was later convicted for demonstrating too "near" the courthouse. The Supreme Court held that the conviction violated due process. Cox v. Louisiana, 379 U.S. 559, 85 S.Ct. 476 (1965).

Note that in none of these cases is the defense derived from the prosecutor's failure to prove an element of the offense. In each case, the court ordered acquittal of the defendant on the ground that a conviction would have been unfair. In effect, for these crimes in the circumstances present, the defendants were given a defense based on their mistakes as to the application of the criminal law to their behavior.

4. EXCEPTION: STRICT LIABILITY UNFAIR

It was stated above (page 88) that "strict liability is imposed in situations where, given what the defendant knows about the rest of what is going on, it seems appropriate to hold the defendant to strict liability for one or more aspects of the behavior. Strict liability . . . is appropriate only for defendants who are sufficiently aware of the context so that it is fair to hold them accountable even though they didn't know about—and may even have tried to avoid—one particular aspect of their behavior." This principle ought to be respected in all uses of strict liability, including its use in implementing the principle that ignorance of the criminal law is no excuse.

Suppose a defendant knows perfectly well that conduct being engaged in constitutes X and Y and Z but has no idea that X + Y + Z equals a crime. Suppose further that *none of us would have known either.* Is it fair in that circumstance to hold the defendant to strict liability on the "= crime" component of the equation? Should there be an exception to the "ignorance of the criminal law is no defense" principle for cases where no reasonably socialized individual would have known that the behavior might be a crime?

The question has not been litigated very often, but my answer would be "yes." Strict liability should never be permitted—on any issue—in situations where the defendant has no fair opportunity to obey the law. Turning it around, strict liability is only acceptable in situations where the context provides warning signals to the reasonably socialized individual that gives the individual a fair opportunity not to become a criminal.

Example: Lambert v. California, 355 U.S. 225, 78 S.Ct. 240 (1957), is a case that lots of people read for lots of purposes. What happened is that Ms. Lambert failed to register as a convicted felon in Los Angeles. Her defense was that she didn't know she had to register. No one told her, and registration, whether for convicted felons or anyone else, is not part of the culture in the United States. The California courts rejected her defense, but the United States Supreme Court reversed. Justice Douglas wrote the opinion for the Court in a style I have often described as "deliberate obfuscation." That is, he set out to say: "This conviction is reversed. I'm now going to say lots of stuff, but I'm not going to tell you why." And he did a good job of it.

There is language in the opinion that would stand for the proposition recited above, that is, that strict liability is impermissible—whether for an element of the offense or for whether the behavior is criminal—whenever the context is so innocuous that the average citizen would have no clue that behavior might implicate the criminal law. The context must provide warning to the average, socialized individual. Failing that, strict liability is impermissible.

Whether this is what *Lambert* means or not, the principle is sound and ought to be embraced by the courts in situations where it is applicable. The facts of *Lambert* were most likely such an occasion.

5. EXCEPTION: DUE DILIGENCE EFFORT TO ASCERTAIN THE LAW

There is some support for the proposition that a defense should be recognized in cases where the defendant made a reasonable mistake after diligently pursuing "all means available to ascertain the meaning and application of the offense to his conduct and honestly and in good faith concludes that his conduct is not an offense in circumstances in which a law-abiding and prudent person would also so conclude." N.J. Stat. Ann. § 2C:2–4(c)(3). In New Jersey, the defendant is required to prove this defense by clear and convincing evidence.

This is a controversial defense that is not widely accepted.

E. MISTAKE OF NON–CRIMINAL LAW

There are many questions of *non-criminal* law that can become relevant to the enforcement of penal policy. Property relationships are created by a separate body of non-criminal law. These relationships are protected by a variety of civil remedies and sanctions, but they are also protected in some respects by the criminal law, for example by the law of theft. Private legal relations are also regulated by the family law, the law of corporations, the law of contracts, and so on, each of which has also developed its own set of civil remedies. It is also true in many cases that the criminal law protects relationships created by these legal sources.

> ***Example:*** A bigamist is a person who marries while still married to another. When a divorce becomes effective and thereby entitles a person to marry again without becoming a bigamist will be determined by the family law.

The question arises whether mistakes of law involving legal relationships created by sources other than the criminal law should have any defensive significance. Should the maxim "ignorance of the law is no excuse" govern and deny the defense? Or are there differences between these legal errors and mistakes concerning the meaning of the criminal law that justify treating these cases differently? The common law answer to these questions begins with a differentiation between specific and general intent crimes.

1. SPECIFIC INTENT

An honest mistake of non-criminal law that negates a specific intent is a defense. As in the case of mistakes of fact in specific intent crimes, the word "honest" here means that the defendant actually believed the mistaken legal situation to be correct. And of course, again as in the case of mistakes of fact, the mistake of non-criminal law must relate directly to the specific intent required by the definition of the offense.

> ***Example:*** Assume a charge of common law larceny, defined as "taking and carrying away the personal property of another with intent to deprive the owner of the property permanently." Assume a mistake of property law which leads the defendant to believe that certain property belongs to the defendant when actually it belongs to another person. Can the defendant be guilty of larceny for taking and carrying away the property with intent to keep it permanently? The answer is "no," because the defendant did not have the specific intent "to deprive the owner" of the property.

The common law treats mistakes of the non-criminal law that negate a required specific intent exactly the same way it treats mistakes of fact that have the same effect. Compare the above example with the larceny example under the heading "Specific Intent" on page 147. Accordingly, it makes no difference to a larceny charge whether the defendant's mistaken belief that the defendant owns the property derives from a mistaken identification (a mistake of fact) or a mistake as to the legal relation of ownership established by the laws of property (a mistake of the non-criminal law). An honest mistake is a defense in either case.

2. GENERAL INTENT

When presented with mistakes of the non-criminal law in general intent crimes, however, common law courts frequently apply the "ignorance of the law is no excuse" maxim and deny a defense for the mistake.

Example: In State v. Woods, 107 Vt. 354, 179 A. 1 (1935), the court held that even though an honest and reasonable mistake of fact would be a defense to adultery (where no crime or immorality would have been committed had the facts been as the defendant believed them to be), a mistake of non-criminal law—no matter how reasonable and even though no crime or immorality would have been involved on the facts as the defendant believed them to be—could not be a defense to the adultery-like offense involved there. In addition to reciting the ignorance of the law maxim and the presumption that everyone knows the law, the court gave as a reason that the "public policy" underlying the non-criminal law at stake there would be undermined if a contrary result were reached.

Can this rule be defended? More particularly, are there valid reasons for treating mistake of fact and mistake of non-criminal law alike in specific intent crimes but differently in general intent crimes? Most modern statutes, following the lead of the Model Penal Code, treat mistakes of fact and mistakes of non-criminal law alike. This approach is explained in the Model Penal Code discussion of this issue, beginning at page 180. Some modern cases in common law jurisdictions also follow the same approach. The rationale for this position is that a mistake should be a defense whenever it negates mens rea, and that a mistake of non-criminal law can negate mens rea just as effectively as can a mistake of fact.

Examples: In the larceny example given under the heading "Specific Intent" above, whether the mistake is a result of misidentification of the property or of an error as to the meaning of property law, the defendant does not have the specific intent required for the offense and, the argument would be, should not be convicted whatever the reason the specific intent is lacking. Put another way, the crime of larceny is designed to protect society against those who ignore the property rights of others. The defendant who honestly thinks the property taken belongs to the defendant does not present the threat to societal interests sought to be punished by the offense of larceny.

Similarly, if the law of adultery recognizes honest and reasonable mistakes of fact as a defense, it establishes the policy that a person who is not negligent as to the elements of the offense should not be convicted. Consider the female defendant in the examples given under the heading "Immoral Behavior" in the mistake of fact discussion, page 151. She made a mistake of fact, and was entitled to a defense if the mistake was reasonably made. Now compare another defendant charged with the same offense who went to Reno, watched the divorce proceedings of another person, and then married that person after the divorce was final. If there was some legal defect in the divorce proceedings unknown to the parties, is the defendant in a different position, considering the kind of person the adultery offense is designed to punish? The modern answer to that question is "no," the two defendants are in the same position. The fact that one made a mistake of fact and the other a mistake of the non-criminal law has no bearing on their underlying culpability. If both acted reasonably, they should both be treated the same way when charged with adultery.

Is the common law position, then, completely indefensible? One could argue that punishing those who do not know the law will encourage them to learn it and that there is every reason to encourage people to learn the law of divorce, just as there is to encourage them to learn the criminal law. But the difficulty with this argument is that deterrence is *always* an argument for strict liability—one could argue with equal force that mistakes of fact should have no defensive significance either, since it is in the social interest to encourage people correctly to learn the facts before they act.

It may seem a stronger argument that we cannot have people deciding on their own whether divorces are valid, any more than we can have them deciding what the criminal law is. To permit them to do so would undermine the public policy of the law of divorce. Yet reflection will show that there is a big difference between the two situations. If a person makes a mistake as to the meaning of the criminal law and that mistake is given defensive significance, then the person will go unpunished, and the law really has become what that person thought it was. But if a person makes a mistake as to the validity of a divorce that is given defensive significance by the criminal law, recognition of the mistake in the criminal law has no significance within the family law itself. If the divorce is ineffective as a matter of family law, it remains so for family law purposes no matter what the disposition of any criminal proceedings. The civil consequences of the law of divorce are not undermined by recognition of the criminal law defense. All that is lost is an additional opportunity to enforce the divorce law, and this must be compared with the perceived unfairness of convicting a non-negligent defendant of an offense for which negligence is the announced standard. Since the unfairness of this differential treatment is thought to outweigh the incremental effect on enforcement of the divorce law, most modern lawmakers have rejected the common law rule that mistakes of non-criminal law are not a defense in general intent crimes.

a. Distinguishing Between Mistakes of Fact and Non–Criminal Law

It should be noted that the rule that treats mistakes of fact and mistakes of non-criminal law differently puts a premium on being able to tell the difference between the two kinds of mistakes.

Example: Consider the two adultery examples discussed on page 161 above. Is it so clear that the person who thought the Reno divorce was valid did not make a mistake of fact?

The answer is that it is not clear, and that there is no magical formula by which this crucial distinction can be made. One should not be surprised to find courts manipulating these two categories—forcing the mistake at issue into one pigeon-hole or the other—in order to reach the result deemed desirable on the facts presented.

b. A Word of Caution

It should also be noted that even if the conclusion is that mistakes of the non-criminal law should be treated the same way as mistakes of fact—as some courts will do—this does not automatically mean that any reasonable and honest mistake of non-criminal law will be a defense to a general intent crime. Recall the discussion under the heading "Strict Liability" beginning at page 150. Of course, if the situation is one where a reasonable mistake of fact is not a defense, a reasonable mistake of non-criminal law will not be a defense either.

F.   INTOXICATION

Evidence of intoxication might be offered by the defendant to show that both the actus reus and the mens rea of a given crime are missing. These potential uses of intoxication evidence are explored here. It is also possible that intoxication can establish an excuse for crime that is completely collateral to these definitional components of an offense. Discussion of this latter possibility is postponed to the heading "Involuntary Intoxication" in the discussion of collateral defenses, beginning on page 244.

1.   TERMINOLOGY

There are three terms that first need to be understood.

a.   Definition of Intoxication

Intoxication from any substances introduced into the body is treated in the same way. The criminal law relating to intoxication therefore includes alcohol, drugs, medication, and any other artificial substance which, when introduced into the body, produces intoxicating effects.

b.   Definition of Voluntary Intoxication

"Voluntary" intoxication is the voluntary introduction of substances into the body which the defendant knows or should know are likely to have intoxicating effects.

c.   Involuntary Intoxication

If intoxication is not voluntary, or if it is the result of an unanticipated and unforeseeable reaction to drink or drugs, or if it is so prolonged as to result in a settled mental illness, a defense might exist. Because this defense is so closely related to the test for insanity, its consideration is postponed to the heading

"Involuntary Intoxication" beginning on page 244. Note, however, that in cases where voluntary intoxication is admissible for defensive purposes, it would follow a fortiori that evidence of involuntary intoxication would be admissible for the same purpose.

2. ADMISSIBILITY TO NEGATE ACTUS REUS

There are two potential uses of evidence of intoxication to show that the actus reus of an offense is missing:

a. No Act

The first is to show that the defendant could not possibly have physically performed the conduct required by the definition of the offense. This showing could be made only in the case of intoxication so extreme that the defendant was literally comatose, and thereby physically unable to perform the required conduct. In the rare case where this could be shown, it would not matter whether the intoxication was voluntary or involuntary.

b. No Voluntary Act

The second is to show that the defendant did not engage in a voluntary act. The common law does *not* permit intoxication to establish that an act was involuntary. The Supreme Court has considered this issue in a constitutional context in Powell v. Texas, 392 U.S. 514, 88 S.Ct. 2145 (1968), which is considered on page 408.

3. ADMISSIBILITY TO NEGATE SPECIFIC INTENT

Several arguments can be made that evidence of voluntary intoxication should not be admissible on specific intent issues. The strongest is utilitarian. Deterrence is undermined if potential offenders know that intoxication can be an excuse for crime. Those who believe in a retributive basis for the criminal law might also take the same position. The choice involved in becoming voluntarily intoxicated, with knowledge of the possible consequences, may be regarded as manifesting sufficient culpability to justify holding the defendant accountable for whatever results ensue. Moreover, one could argue that avoidance of litigation over the effects of alcohol or drug use is desirable, given the imponderables involved in determining after the fact precisely what was taken, in what quantity and quality, what the defendant's physical and psychological condition was at the time, etc. Exclusion of the issue from litigation seems fair too, given the fact that many intoxicants, though certainly not all, act more to reduce inhibitions than to destroy perceptions.

On the other hand, the function of a specific intent component of an offense is to identify a special characteristic of dangerousness posed by the offender's behavior. One can question whether it is fair or necessary to punish an offender who did not in fact manifest that special characteristic, whatever the reason.

American jurisdictions have resolved these issues by taking one of three positions:

a. Admissible When Relevant

Many States, approaching 40%, take the position that evidence of voluntary intoxication is admissible to negate specific intent whenever the evidence is relevant to the particular specific intent required by the definition of the offense. Under this approach, the prosecutor is required to establish the specific intent beyond a reasonable doubt, and the defendant is entitled to acquittal if evidence of intoxication establishes the necessary reasonable doubt. The defendant, of course, must bear the burden of producing the initial evidence on this issue.

b. Admissible to Show Incapacity

Many States, also approaching 40%, take the position that evidence of voluntary intoxication is admissible in a specific intent offense only if it is offered to show that the defendant *lacked the capacity* to form the specific intent required by the definition of the offense. Under this approach, the *defendant* is required to establish the incapacity by a preponderance of the evidence. The defendant thus has *both* the burden of production *and* the burden of persuasion on this issue.

c. Inadmissible

In some States, around 20%, evidence of voluntary intoxication is *not* admissible to show the lack of specific intent. In at least one State there is the single exception that such evidence may be offered for the purpose of negating the premeditation and deliberation necessary for a conviction of first degree murder. But the Supreme Court has held that exclusion of evidence of intoxication on the issues of purpose and knowledge in a murder prosecution is constitutional. Montana v. Egelhoff, 518 U.S. 37, 116 S.Ct. 2013 (1996).

4. ADMISSIBILITY TO NEGATE GENERAL INTENT

Every American jurisdiction agrees that evidence of voluntary intoxication is inadmissible to negate general intent. The reasons for this conclusion include the arguments made above for the inadmissibility of such evidence on specific intent. In addition, evidence of voluntary intoxication will normally be relevant only to establish a mistake of fact. In many jurisdictions "general intent" means "negligence" in this context, which involves measuring the defendant's conduct against the standard of a reasonable person. Evidence of intoxication is thus irrelevant, unless the standard of behavior is to become that of the "reasonable drunk."

G.   EVIDENCE OF MENTAL DISEASE

The principal use of evidence of mental disease in the criminal law is to establish the separate defense of insanity, the discussion of which begins at page 225. However, evidence of mental disease can also be offered for other purposes.

1. DIMINISHED RESPONSIBILITY DEFINED

The term "diminished responsibility," or its synonym "diminished capacity," refers to the admission of evidence of mental disease for purposes other than establishing the insanity defense. The term is used in three quite different contexts:

a. Admissibility to Negate Mens Rea

The first refers to the admission of evidence of mental disease to negate mens rea. This is the topic that will be discussed now.

b. Mitigate Grade of Offense

The second refers to a junior version of the insanity defense, which has the effect of reducing the severity of a crime in a case where the insanity defense itself is not successful. The concept has been used for this purpose *only* in the case of criminal homicides. For this reason, it is discussed in that context, at page 371.

c. Avoid Capital Sentence

The third refers to a similar inquiry into the effects of mental disease for the purpose of assessing the desirability of the imposition of capital punishment upon a person already convicted of murder. This issue is discussed at page 381.

2. ADMISSIBILITY TO NEGATE MENS REA

The original common law position was that evidence of mental disease was *not* admissible to negate any mens rea components of a crime. The courts took a categorical approach to the question of mental disease. All persons were presumed to have the capacity to form a criminal intent. The only way this presumption could be rebutted was by establishing the insanity defense, and the only use to which evidence of mental disease could be put was to help in establishing this defense. The common law thus established two categories of people: those who were sane and those who were insane. The only relevance of mental disease was to help prove the defense that would move the defendant from one category to the other. Mental disease was therefore by definition inadmissible to show that a "normal" person could not or did not form the mens rea required for a given offense.

The law has been slow to retreat from this position, and many jurisdictions still have not done so. This result can be defended in modern terms for a number of reasons, among them:

(1) There must be some limits on the willingness of the law to personalize the question of guilt. The law cannot take into account the frailties, background influences, and peculiarities of each individual defendant. All persons must be judged to some extent by an external standard. Otherwise, the social control function of the criminal law would be undermined. The requirement of mens rea is a concession to arguments in favor of requiring blame as the basis for criminal punishment. But the law must draw the line somewhere between individualization that incapacitates the criminal law and unfairly holding all offenders to an external standard for all conduct. Requiring mens rea but not permitting evidence of mental disease to rebut it is an appropriate place to draw the line.

(2) Principles of personal autonomy postulate that all persons are to have the same basic freedoms and liberties. As a corollary, it is appropriate for the law

to treat people the same in many situations where rational arguments could be made for differentiation. While it is appropriate to provide a defense of insanity for those who are demonstrably and emphatically aberrational, it is more consistent with individual liberty to treat the rest of the population as alike in terms of psychiatric characteristics. The categorical approach of the common law, the argument concludes, is therefore right in principle.

(3) Psychiatry is hardly an exact science, and is unable to pinpoint the capacities of individuals with sufficient precision to warrant reliance on evidence of mental disease on all mens rea issues.

(4) Those who may lack mens rea because of mental disease nonetheless will have demonstrated by their behavior that they present a public danger. Though the law could be changed on this point, the present result is that a mens rea acquittal results in releasing the defendant, who may pose a significant risk of future danger to the public. Insanity acquittals, on the other hand, normally result in some form of commitment. Those who have a mental disease thus should be relegated to use of the insanity defense.

Most modern lawmakers have rejected these arguments. They have taken the position that evidence of mental disease should be admissible whenever relevant to any mens rea issue. This would mean that evidence of mental disease would always be admissible on any question of specific intent. Whether it would be admissible to negate general intent depends on what general intent means for the specific crime involved. If it means recklessness in a given case, then the evidence should be admitted on the question whether the defendant actually understood the risks. If negligence is meant, the evidence will probably be inadmissible, unless it is to be taken into account in formulating the objective standard against which the defendant's conduct will be judged or in understanding the context as it was perceived by the defendant. In cases of strict liability evidence of mental disease will be irrelevant to mens rea, since there is no mens rea requirement in the first place. But it might be relevant to the defendant's ability to understand the context, and therefore to the fairness of applying strict liability. See pages 88–89.

This position can be defended for a number of reasons, among them:

(1) Elements of specific intent and recklessness require the prosecutor to establish that the defendant actually had subjective state of mind at the time of the offense. It is illogical and unfair for the law to establish a subjective mens rea component and then to prohibit the use of probative sources of proof that it is lacking in a particular case. Those who suffer from some mental disease, through no fault of their own, should not be singled out for special treatment. The same arguments would suggest that evidence of mental disease should be admissible when considering the subjective components of negligence and strict liability.

(2) The exclusion of evidence of mental disease on mens rea issues is particularly ironic when compared to the way the law treats voluntary intoxication. In

most States, voluntary intoxication is a defense if it negates a required specific intent. All would agree that there some element of fault in the defendant who voluntarily drinks and then commits all of the elements of a crime except the specific intent. Yet one who is plainly *less* culpable—one who lacks the same mental ingredient due to a mental disease—is *more* harshly treated by the law. This is an intolerable result.

Current law on this question spreads across virtually the entire spectrum of possibilities:

a. Issues on Which Evidence of Mental Disease Admissible
A small number of States still do not admit evidence of mental disease on any mens rea issue. Some States will admit the evidence to negate mens rea only in homicide cases. Others will admit it to negate a specific intent only.

b. Limitation to Evidence of Mental Disease
In addition, the law is complicated by a further factor. Some States will admit expert testimony on mens rea issues only in cases where it is based upon the diagnosis of a recognized mental disease. Thus, evidence that the defendant was suggestive, dependent, childlike, or naive would not be admitted unless it could be related to some recognized disease, even though it may be supported by expert testimony and may be directly relevant to whether the defendant actually believed something that would negate mens rea.

c. Limitation to Proof of Lack of Capacity
In addition, some States will restrict evidence of mental disease to cases where it tends to show that the defendant lacked the capacity to form a required mens rea. This is to be contrasted with those States which admit the evidence whenever it supports a factual inference that the defendant actually lacked mens rea.

H. REVIEW QUESTIONS

[Answers Provided in Appendix A, page 425]

1. T or F   A person who acts under duress is engaging in a voluntary act.

2. T or F   If a defendant's conduct includes an involuntary act then criminal punishment cannot be imposed.

3. T or F   A person who has no control over criminal behavior is not entitled to raise a voluntary act defense if the reason for the lack of control is a recognized mental disease or defect.

4. T or F   An honest mistake of fact can negate the mens rea required for the actus reus elements of a specific intent crime.

5. T or F   In spite of the maxim "ignorance of the law is no excuse," there are instances where a mistake as to whether conduct is a crime can be asserted to negate mens rea.

6. T or F   In spite of the maxim "ignorance of the law is no excuse," there are a few cases which recognize that a defendant lacks mens rea when misled into committing a crime by the actions of a court or a high public official.

7. T or F   Mistakes of the non-criminal law are generally treated like mistakes of fact.

8. T or F   Evidence of voluntary intoxication is admissible to show that the defendant's conduct was involuntary.

9. The rule "an honest and reasonable mistake of fact is a defense to a general intent crime" is one of those rare maxims of the law that is subject to no exceptions. This statement is false. Why?

10. The common law relating to mistakes of fact can be stated by reciting rules or by applying logic. This statement is true. Why?

11. The definition of burglary is "breaking and entering the dwelling house of another in the nighttime with the intent to commit a felony therein." If the defendant claims a mistake as to whether it was nighttime when the offense was committed, the admissibility of the mistake evidence will turn on whether the mistake can be classified as one of fact, one of the meaning of the criminal law, or one of the civil law concerning the legal definition of sunset. True or False? Explain your answer carefully.

12. *D* was convicted of a criminal offense in Kansas and served a period of probation. *D* later possesses a firearm in California, and is convicted of a crime defined as "possession of a firearm by a convicted felon." It was not clear to *D* whether the Kansas offense was a felony, nor was it clear to the California prosecutor. After much research and consultation with Kansas officials, the prosecutor was able to establish to the Court's satisfaction that the offense was a felony. The defense is that *D* was told at the time of the prior conviction that the offense was not a felony. Also, on several occasions *D* was required by California officials to disclose whether there had been a prior felony conviction (e.g., when *D* registered to vote), and *D* had disclosed the situation and been assured by the officials that the offense was not a felony. Assuming *D* is believed, should the defense be successful?

13. Should evidence of mental disease or voluntary intoxication be admissible to negate the specific intent component of a common law crime? For which kind of evidence is there a greater claim for admissibility?

14. Mistakes as to the meaning or application of the criminal law cannot be asserted as a defense. Is this a good rule, or simply an outmoded relic of the past? Explain your answer.

V

THE MODEL PENAL CODE

Analysis

A. INTRODUCTION

There are counterparts in the Model Penal Code for each of the derivative defenses discussed in the preceding section. It is indispensable to the analysis of these defenses that the Model Code culpability structure discussed in Part Two be understood. For the most part, the defenses discussed below are simply logical applications of that structure. As at common law, however, there are special doctrines that must be learned.

B. INVOLUNTARY ACTS

Section 2.01(1) provides that a person cannot be guilty of an offense unless liability is based on conduct "which includes a voluntary act or the omission to perform an act of which he is physically capable." This language incorporates essentially the common law "involuntary act" defense into the Model Penal Code. The entire discussion of that topic, beginning at page 143, is thus fully applicable to the Model Code concept of a "voluntary" act, *including* the point that the content of the defense is quite narrow. Note that the Model Code gives narrow illustrations in § 2.01(2) of acts which are not to be regarded as voluntary. The language of Subsection (2)(d) comes about as close as one can to a generic definition of an involuntary act: "A bodily movement that . . . is not a product of the effort or determination of the actor, either conscious or habitual."

1. INVOLUNTARY ACT IN VOLUNTARY COURSE OF CONDUCT
Note the word "includes" in § 2.01(1). This word is intended to permit criminal sanctions to be imposed on the voluntary components of behavior that includes both voluntary and involuntary aspects, assuming of course that the actus reus of the offense is satisfied by the voluntary part of the conduct.

2. RELATION TO OTHER DEFENSES
The comments under this heading on page 145 are in general applicable to the counterpart defenses contained in the Model Penal Code. The only hard question is the role of evidence of mental disease or defect in an involuntary act defense. The Model Code is silent on this point. It could be inferred from § 4.01 and § 4.02(1) that evidence of mental disease or defect is admissible only for the purposes there specified. Even if this is so, where this leaves "physical" disabilities that pose the danger of recurrent violence is completely open.

C. MISTAKE OF FACT

The Model Penal Code provisions on mistake of fact are contained in §§ 2.04(1) and 2.04(2). The critical analytical step in the application of these provisions is to ascertain the mens rea required for the element as to which a mistake has been made. This is done by applying the Model Code culpability structure, the description of which begins at page 109. Once the mens rea for an element has been determined, the remaining steps are logical and straightforward.

1. MISTAKES THAT NEGATE MENS REA

Section 2.04(1)(a) provides that a mistake of fact is a defense if it negates any required mens rea element of the offense. Hence, if the prosecutor is required to prove a mens rea of *X*, it is a defense if the defendant makes a mistake that creates a reasonable doubt that *X* exists.

Examples: Assume a charge of theft under § 223.2(2), where the defendant believes that the property transferred belongs not to "another" but to the defendant. The mens rea for the element "another" would be recklessness. [If you are not sure why this is so, re-examine the discussion under the heading "Culpability Provided" on page 118.] This means that the defendant would have to be aware of a risk that the property belonged to someone else, and yet choose to disregard the risk under circumstances involving a "gross deviation from the standard of conduct that a law-abiding person" would have observed in the defendant's situation. § 2.02(2)(c). If the defendant made a mistake of fact in believing that the property did not belong to another, the mistake would be relevant as a defense only to the extent that it disproved recklessness in this sense. § 2.04(1)(a).

Now consider a charge of theft under § 223.2(1). Assume the same kind of mistake: the defendant believes the property belongs not to another but to the defendant. What is the relevance of the mistake? The first step is to determine the mens rea for the element "of another." Application of the analysis applied to § 223.2(2) in the preceding example would suggest that the answer is "recklessness." But further analysis is required. The definition of the offense in § 223.2(1) requires that the defendant also act "with purpose to deprive him thereof." The term "deprive" means "to withhold property of another." § 223.0(1). Hence, in addition to the mens rea required for each actus reus element, the defendant must also have the purpose to withhold the property of another. Since the ownership of property is a circumstance, the definition of "purpose" in § 2.02(2)(a)(ii) requires that the defendant be aware of the existence of the circumstance or believe that it exists. That is, here the defendant must believe that the property belongs to another. Since the defendant believed precisely to the contrary, the mistake would be a complete defense under the provisions of § 2.04(1)(a).

Note, by contrast, that § 223.2(2) requires only that the defendant have a "purpose to benefit himself." The defendant can have this purpose perfectly consistently with a belief that the property does not belong to another. Hence the mens rea for the "of another" element in § 223.2(2), as stated above, is recklessness.

Now assume a defendant charged with violating § 213.1(1)(d). The victim was actually 9, but the defendant believed she was 11. Of what relevance is the mistake? The answer is none. Section 213.6(1) specifically denies the defense, and hence in effect imposes strict liability for this element. The mistake is irrelevant since there is no mens rea for it to negate.

2. MISTAKES THAT ESTABLISH A STATE OF MIND CONSTITUTING A DEFENSE

Section 2.04(1)(b) provides that a mistake of fact is a defense when it establishes a state of mind that constitutes a defense. This provision applies when the definition of the offense, or some other relevant provision of the penal law, states that a certain belief is a defense.

Examples: Assume a charge of bigamy under § 230.1(1), and a mistaken but honest belief by the defendant that the prior spouse was dead. A defense based on this belief is explicitly given by § 230.1(1)(a). Hence, under § 2.04(1)(b), a mistake leading the defendant to this belief will be a complete defense.

An example of a place other than the definition of the offense where such a defense is provided can be found in § 223.1(3)(b). Assume a charge of theft under § 223.2(1). The defendant takes money from the cash register at work. The defendant knows the money belongs to the employer, but mistakenly believes that wages are due and that it is appropriate to take them from the cash register. Here the mistake establishes the belief given defensive significance by § 223.1(3)(b), which is the situation contemplated by the provisions of § 2.04(1)(b).

3. GRADING ELEMENTS

The culpability structure of the Model Penal Code applies to "each material element" of an offense. § 2.02(1). The term "element" is defined in § 1.13(9) to apply to each conduct, result, or circumstance element "included in the description of the forbidden conduct in the definition of the offense." While this language in § 1.13(9) is not unambiguous, it is clear that the drafters intended that actus reus elements relevant only to the grading of an offense be included as "elements." Since they are "elements," and since they are plainly not excluded by the provisions of § 1.13(10), they are "material elements" of an offense. In fact, the language of § 1.13(10) seems explicitly to contemplate the inclusion of grading elements by stating that the only elements that are not material are ones that are "unconnected . . . with the harm or evil . . . sought to be prevented by the law defining the offense." Plainly, grading elements directly relate to the harm or evil that a criminal offense is designed to prevent.

The consequence of this reasoning is that factors relevant only to grading require mens rea under the same analysis as any other actus reus element of an offense. [Another consequence is that grading factors must be proved by the prosecutor beyond a reasonable doubt under § 1.12(1).] Thus, and contrary to the result under the common law (see page 81), a mistake of fact relevant only to grading can be a defense if, as stated by § 2.04(1)(a), it negates the mens rea required for that element.

There is, however, a twist. A mistake as to a grading element is going to mean that the defendant is in the following situation: on the facts as they actually were, the defendant would have committed one crime; on the facts as the defendant believed them to be, the defendant would have been guilty of another crime.

> **Example:**   Examine the provisions of § 223.1(2). Assume the defendant steals jewelry believed to be worth about $300 that is in fact worth $3000. On the facts as they actually were, the defendant would be guilty of a felony of the third degree. On the facts as the defendant believed them to be, the defendant would be guilty of a misdemeanor.

Plainly in this situation the defendant should be guilty of something. The question is what. The common law response was that liability should be strict for grading elements, and the defendant should be convicted on the basis of what actually happened. The Model Penal Code result, provided in § 2.04(2), is that the defendant should be convicted of the crime that would have occurred if the facts were as they were believed to be. Thus, while mens rea is required for grading elements, establishing a lack of mens rea as to a grading element because of a mistake of fact is not a complete defense under the Model Code. Instead, it will have the effect of reducing the grade to the crime that would have been committed had the facts been as the defendant believed them to be.

> **Examples:**   Assume on the facts of the theft example given above that the defendant was charged with the felony and defended on the ground of mistake of fact as to the value of the jewelry. The mens rea for the value of the property, since none is provided by the definition of the offense, is recklessness. See § 2.02(3). If the prosecutor could prove beyond a reasonable doubt that the defendant was reckless as to the value of the property, then the mistake would not be a defense. As a practical matter in this situation, the defendant will have a hard time getting a jury to believe that the subjective valuation of the property was not reckless. Most thieves try to get all they can, and do not limit their ambitions to property of limited value. In any event, if the prosecutor proves that the defendant was reckless as to the value of the property, a conviction for the higher grade—a felony of the third degree—would follow.
>
> But what happens if the prosecutor *can't* prove recklessness? What should the jury then be told to do? The answer, under § 2.04(2), is convict of the misdemeanor.

Note that § 2.04(2) reinforces the conclusion that grading elements require mens rea under the Model Penal Code. If grading elements carried strict liability, as they do at common law, would § 2.04(2) be necessary? The answer is "no," since the mistake would not "otherwise afford a defense." Thus § 2.04(2) makes sense only if grading elements require mens rea in the first place.

D. MISTAKE OF CRIMINAL LAW

The Model Penal Code carries forward the common law position that ignorance or mistake of the criminal law is not a defense. It does, however, moderate its rigor by adopting several exceptions.

1. THE PARADIGM CASE

The Model Code states the rule in a rather convoluted, but ultimately logical, manner. Under § 2.04(1), a mistake of fact "or law" is a defense only when it negatives a mens rea element of an offense. In order for ignorance or mistake as to the criminality of conduct to be a defense, therefore, it would have to negate a mens rea element defined to be a part of the offense. Section 2.02(9) states that no mens rea is required "as to whether conduct constitutes an offense" or as to "the existence, meaning or application of the law determining the elements of an offense." This means that no mens rea as to the criminality of behavior is required by the structure of § 2.02. It follows that, unless the definition of a particular offense provides to the contrary, there is no mens rea element in the definition of an offense for a mistake as to criminality to negate. The circle is complete. Section 2.04(1)(a) cannot apply. Ignorance or mistake as to whether given conduct is a crime is not a defense.

Note that § 2.02(9) says that no mens rea is required "as to the existence, meaning or application of the law determining the elements of an offense." Thus, as is explained in connection with the identical common law position on this point at page 155, a mistake about whether particular conduct comes within the definition given *by the criminal law* to an actus reus element of a crime would not have any defensive significance. Mens rea under the Model Code, as at the common law, requires only that the defendant have the prescribed culpability as to certain physical behavior, results, and circumstances. It does *not* require that the defendant accurately attach legal labels supplied by the criminal law to those events.

Example: The defendant is charged with burglary under § 221.1(1) for entering a tent in the woods with intent to rape a person known to be sleeping inside. The offense requires that the defendant enter "a building or occupied structure," and recklessness is the required mens rea for this element. The defense is that the defendant did not believe that entry was made into a "building or occupied structure," and was unaware of any risk that the conduct was of that nature. Is the defense valid?

No. The defense is irrelevant. The first step in the analysis is to determine whether the actus reus of the offense was committed. It was, given the definition of "occupied structure" in § 221.0(1). That definition includes any "place adapted for overnight accommodation of persons," which would include a tent fitted for occupancy. The next question is whether the mens rea was present. It was, since the defendant knew perfectly well that a tent was being entered. This is

all the defendant must know. That the criminal law attaches the legal
label "occupied structure" to the tent is irrelevant to mens rea, and
specifically excluded as an element of the offense by
§ 2.02(9). Therefore, both the actus reus and mens rea are present,
and the defense evidence is inadmissible because not offered to
disprove any element of the offense or to establish any independently
recognized defense.

2. EXCEPTION: WHERE THE DEFINITION OF THE OFFENSE SO PROVIDES

Section 2.02(9) ends with an exception: "unless the definition of the offense . . . so
provides." This means that it is possible in the definition of a particular offense to
require some mens rea level as to the criminality of behavior, or as to the existence,
meaning, or application of the law determining the elements of an offense. Of
course, if the definition of the offense requires culpability as to one or more of these
matters, then a mistake that negates the required culpability will be a defense
under § 2.04(1)(a).

There are no Model Penal Code offenses that include such an element in the
definition of the offense. This is because the offenses defined in Part II of the Model
Code for the most part are traditional crimes, as to which it is not perceived as
unfair to hold defendants to knowledge of prevailing criminal (and moral)
standards. The kind of offense where such an element might be included would be
one where it would be regarded as unfair to expect a reasonably socialized person
to know not to engage in the proscribed behavior.

3. EXCEPTION: WHERE THE CODE SO PROVIDES

Section 2.02(9) also contains another exception: "unless . . . the Code so provides."
The Model Code contains a series of exceptions in § 2.04(3). See also § 2.13(1)(a),
discussed at page 258. The rationale for each of them is that it would be unfair to
the defendant to punish a violation of the criminal law in that context. Section
2.04(3) thus provides "collateral" and not "derivative" defenses. [See the Glossary if
you can't remember what these terms mean.] Section 2.04(1)(b) again completes the
circle by confirming the availability of the defenses recognized in § 2.04(3).

a. Law Not Reasonably Made Available

Section 2.04(3)(a) permits a defense of ignorance of the criminal law when the
law defining the offense is unknown to the defendant and "has not been
published or otherwise reasonably made available prior to the conduct alleged."
This exception of course would not apply to any offense defined in the criminal
code itself. It is mainly designed for situations where no reasonable access to
local ordinances is provided. It could also be applicable to administrative
regulations that are enforceable through the criminal process, again if no
reasonable access is provided.

b. Reliance Upon Official Statement

Section 2.04(3)(b) contains a narrowly drawn series of exceptions, all of which
consist of situations where it is reasonable for the defendant to rely on official
statements of the law. Note two things:

(1) The defendant must actually believe the conduct to be lawful and that belief must have been formed "in reasonable reliance" on an official statement from one of the prescribed sources. The term "reasonable" in this context is not explicitly defined by the Model Code, but one might assume that it was meant (by analogy to the term "reasonably believes" defined in § 1.13(16)) to require that the defendant's belief be measured against the standard of negligence defined in § 2.02(2)(d).

One could argue, however, that a lesser standard was meant—more akin to the lack of ordinary care used in the law of torts—since § 2.04(3)(b) does not use the term "negligence" or any of the variants of that term recited in § 1.13(15) or § 1.13(16). Could this therefore be a rare occasion where the drafters of the Model Penal Code introduced a culpability level different from the mainstay terms ordinarily used to define offenses?

(2) The list of official sources on which one may rely is explicit and exclusive. Importantly, it does *not* include a private attorney, though it does include a prosecuting official.

Why is the exception in § 2.04(3)(b) limited to official statements? Is it not equally unfair to punish people who rely in good faith on the advice of an attorney, or who simply are ignorant of the possibility that the criminal law might apply to conduct in which they engage? The answer to these questions involves the proper integration of a number of conflicting considerations:

(1) The rationales for denying a defense of ignorance of the criminal law, elaborated on page 154, must be considered. The strongest of these are deterrence and the need for official statements of the law to have determinative effect. Deterrence can easily be undermined in this context if shady defendants are allowed to rely on the advice of cooperative attorneys. And it is intolerable to permit defendants or their attorneys to state for themselves the criminal norms that will govern their behavior. That's what courts are for.

(2) The law already contains a number of doctrines designed to make it operate fairly: the vagueness doctrine, the principle of strict construction, the requirement of fair warning, and the principle of legality are designed to prevent unfair retroactive construction of statutes.

(3) There nonetheless are situations where it might be regarded as unfair to punish a defendant who acts in ignorance or mistake as to the meaning of the criminal law. It may be in this context that "ignorance" should be of more concern than "mistake." A defendant who is aware of the potential relevance of a criminal law but acts based on a mistaken interpretation of its meaning does have the option of not acting, an option that may not be available to one who is ignorant of the potential application of a criminal statute to contemplated conduct. On the other hand, the person who is

ignorant could perhaps have been more diligent in learning about potentially relevant criminal laws. A defense of ignorance of law both encourages and rewards ignorance. The traditional answer has been that the criminal law should do neither.

(4)   One of the consequences of strict liability is an increased "chilling effect" on behavior that is, so to speak, in the same neighborhood. If actors know that "ignorance of the law is no excuse," they will—at least if they are risk averse—avoid even coming close to behavior that might be criminal. They will refrain from engaging in behavior that is not criminal in order to be sure they do not engage in behavior that is.

Whenever strict liability is imposed, therefore, one must assess the social cost of the overdeterrence (or "chilling effect") that will be achieved. In many contexts, overdeterrence will be good. To pick an example from another area of the law, if men are deterred from sexual intercourse with 11 and 12 year olds by the imposition of strict liability on the age 10 element in § 213(1)(d), any overdeterrence that is achieved is a social good. Whether the same can be said for the overdeterrence achieved by the failure to recognize more exceptions to the "ignorance of the criminal law" rule is another issue that must be resolved in the debate, the terms of which will change as the context changes. The answer may be different if the ambiguity concerns where a demonstration can occur or whether a religious ritual is prohibited or protected.

How these issues should be resolved or compromised is not an easy question. The judgment underlying § 2.04(3)(b) of the Model Code is that the "need for official statements to have determinative effect" argument is weakened when the defendant's mistake is made in reasonable reliance on an official statement of the law. Moreover, the deterrence argument is weaker where there are objective indicia supporting the defendant's claim, and it can be met in part by shifting the burden of persuasion to the defendant. Thus the case for providing an exception for reasonable reliance on official sources seemed strong to those who drafted the Model Code.

Note that § 2.04(4) explicitly shifts the burden of persuasion to the defendant on the defense authorized by § 2.04(3). The defendant would in any event have the burden of production, and thus must in addition establish the defense by a preponderance of the evidence. This is one of the few instances in the Model Code where the burden of persuasion is shifted to the defendant. The rationale for doing so is compromise, as is often the case with debatable defenses. Those who would disfavor such a defense would argue in principle that the defense should not be provided, and would also make the point that it will be difficult for the prosecutor to prove awareness of the criminal law in this or any other context. Those who would favor the defense because it would be unfair to defendants to withhold it in these contexts might nonetheless be prepared to compromise on the burden of persuasion in order to ease the difficulties the prosecutor might face and at the same time introduce a desirable amelioration of a harsh rule.

E. MISTAKE OF NON–CRIMINAL LAW

Section 2.04(1) provides that ignorance or mistake of a matter of fact "or law" is a defense if it negates any required mens rea element or if it establishes a belief that constitutes a defense. To what kind of "law" does this provision apply? It can't be the criminal law, because that would undermine the effect (and precise language) of § 2.02(9). It must therefore be to the rest of the "law" that these words apply, that is, to the non-criminal law.

Thus the conclusion is that the words "or law" have the effect of treating a mistake of the non-criminal law *exactly* the same way as a mistake of fact. The Model Penal Code has resolved the debate summarized on pages 161–62 by assimilating mistakes of non-criminal law to mistakes of fact.

Note how § 2.04(1) integrates with § 2.02(9). Section 2.02(9) leads to the conclusion that mistakes of the *criminal* law are *not* a defense because no mens rea as to the *criminal law* is required as an element of most offenses. Section 2.04(1) permits mistakes of the *non-criminal law* to be a defense, however, because they can disprove mens rea required by the rest of § 2.02 to the same extent as can a mistake of fact. To turn the point around, the legal characterizations of the world by the non-criminal law are part of the mens rea of an offense under the Model Penal Code. The legal characterizations by the criminal law are not.

Examples: Assume a charge of extortion under § 223.4(1). Assume that the defendant, because of a legal error of property law, believes the property obtained belongs to the defendant. Is the belief, though a mistake of "law," a defense? Yes, under § 2.04(1)(a). The mens rea for "of another" in the definition of extortion would be knowledge, applying §§ 2.02(4) and 2.02(2)(a)(ii). Since the defendant's belief negated the required knowledge, even though it involved an error about application of the non-criminal law, the mistake would be a defense.

Now re-examine the illustrations given under the heading "Mistakes that Negate Mens Rea" on page 173. It was assumed in those examples that a mistake of fact was made, for example a mistaken identification. If the mistake were instead one of property law, the cases would nonetheless be analyzed in exactly the same manner.

F. INTOXICATION

If no special rules were provided, evidence of intoxication would be admissible in a criminal case whenever relevant to prove or disprove the existence of an element of the offense. The question for the lawmaker, therefore, is whether any special rules should be provided for application to cases where the defendant is intoxicated because of drink or drugs. There are two possibilities: a special defense could be created to preclude liability for crime in some or all cases of intoxication; and/or special limitations could be adopted that restricted the admissibility of evidence of intoxication short of its logical relevance.

The Model Penal Code adopts both of these strategies in § 2.08. The case where a special defense is created is dealt with in § 2.08(4). This provision is best understood if postponed until after consideration of the insanity defense. See page 255. Section 2.08(3) also relates to the insanity defense and is discussed at page 235. The remainder of Section 2.08 will be dealt with here.

1. TERMINOLOGY

There are three terms that need to be understood:

a. Definition of Intoxication

The term "intoxication" is defined in § 2.08(5)(a). It means any disturbance of mental or physical capacities resulting from the introduction of any substances—including drugs, alcohol, or medication—into the body.

b. Definition of Self–Induced Intoxication

The Model Code uses the term "self-induced" instead of "voluntary" to describe introducing substances into the body where the defendant knows or ought to know that they have a tendency to cause intoxication. This definition is contained in § 2.08(5)(b). The phrase "ought to know" probably incorporates the standard of negligence defined in § 2.02(2)(d), but this is not entirely clear. See the discussion of an analogous issue on page 178.

There are two exceptions, that is, two cases where knowingly taking drugs is *not* regarded as "self-induced" intoxication:

(1) where the substances are taken pursuant to medical advice; or

(2) where the substances are taken "under such circumstances as would afford a defense to a charge of crime."

The quoted phrase in the second exception is mainly meant to encompass (but is not necessarily limited to) situations of duress, as defined in § 2.09. That is, intoxicants which the defendant knowingly takes under the kinds of duress defined in § 2.09 are not regarded as "self-induced."

c. Definition of Pathological Intoxication

The phrase "pathological intoxication" is defined in § 2.08(5)(c). It refers to cases where the defendant suffers a grossly excessive reaction to an intoxicant, considering the amount taken and assuming that the defendant does not know of a susceptibility to such a reaction.

2. ADMISSIBILITY

Analysis of the Model Code position on intoxication begins with § 2.08(1). That section starts by stating that intoxication is not in itself a defense to a crime. Given that starting point, it then goes on to say two things:

(1) Evidence of intoxication is admissible whenever it is offered to disprove the existence of an element of the offense; and

(2) Evidence of intoxication is admissible whenever it establishes the special defense provided in § 2.08(4).

Implementation of the principle that evidence of intoxication is admissible whenever offered to disprove the existence of an element of the offense requires that a *special rule as to recklessness* be taken into account. The special rule is stated in § 2.08(2). It works in conjunction with § 2.08(1) as follows:

(1) If the required mens rea is purpose or knowledge, then evidence of intoxication—whether or not self-induced, and whether or not pathological—is fully admissible whenever offered to disprove the required purpose or knowledge.

(2) If recklessness is the required mens rea and the intoxication is *not* self-induced or *is* pathological, then evidence of intoxication is fully admissible to show that the defendant was unaware of the risk required by the definition of recklessness in § 2.02(2)(c).

(3) But if recklessness is the required mens rea and the intoxication *is* self-induced and is *not* pathological, then the defendant may *not* offer evidence of intoxication to show unawareness of the risk if the risk is one the defendant would have been aware of if not intoxicated.

(4) If recklessness is the required mens rea, and if the defendant testifies as to unawareness of the risk but does not mention intoxication, presumably the *prosecutor* can prove self-induced, non-pathological intoxication as the reason. Such proof would make unawareness of the risk immaterial if the defendant would have been aware of the risk if sober. One effect of the Model Code's special rule for recklessness, therefore, is to change the meaning of recklessness for the intoxicated defendant, and also to deny the intoxicated defendant a defense that would be available if the normal rules of logical relevance were applied.

(5) If negligence is the required mens rea, then the defendant would be measured against the standard of care that a "reasonable [sober] person" would have observed. The word "situation" in the definition of negligence in § 2.02(2)(d) would not be interpreted to encompass the defendant's intoxicated state.

The rationale for these provisions can be extrapolated from the arguments mentioned in connection with the various common law positions summarized beginning at page 164. The Model Code position on purpose and knowledge should be compared to the common law positions on specific intent. The Model Penal Code position on recklessness and negligence should be compared to the common law position on general intent.

a. Aside

An interesting point in connection with the intent of § 2.08(2) is how evidence of intoxication should be treated when offered on the *subjective* components of the definitions of recklessness and negligence other than the awareness-of-risk issue with which § 2.08(2) specifically deals. As defined in § 2.02(2), both of those provisions contain wording to the effect that the jury must consider "the nature and purpose of the actor's conduct and the circumstances known to him." Suppose the defendant offers evidence of intoxication to support an argument premised on unawareness of an important circumstance. Should that evidence be admitted to show unawareness of the circumstance on a recklessness or negligence issue if it is likely that the defendant would have been aware of the circumstance if sober?

The Model Penal Code contains no explicit answer to this question, though the logical inference from § 2.08(2) is that the drafters would not have wanted to permit the evidence to be admissible for this purpose.

G. EVIDENCE OF MENTAL DISEASE

The separate defense of insanity is discussed below, beginning at page 234. The use of evidence of mental disease to disprove mens rea is discussed here.

The Model Penal Code takes the position in § 4.02(1) that evidence of mental disease or defect is admissible to the extent relevant to establish or to rebut a required mens rea element. The rationale for this position can be extrapolated from the arguments for the modern point of view stated on page 167.

One could argue that the negative implication of § 4.02(1) is that expert psychiatric or psychological evidence falling short of an effort to prove that the defendant suffered from a "mental disease or defect" (terms which are not defined by the Model Code) is not admissible to establish or disprove mens rea. Compare the discussion under the heading "Limitation to Evidence of Mental Disease" on page 168. Given the general orientation of the Model Code towards requiring culpability and permitting the introduction of evidence logically relevant to its existence or rebuttal, however, it is doubtful that this interpretation was intended. But there are persuasive arguments for the proposition that speculation by psychiatrists and psychologists about conditions the defendant may have experienced short of a diagnosable "mental disease" should not be admitted. In a jurisdiction with a long tradition of excluding such testimony, a restrictive interpretation of a provision based on § 4.02(1) would not be surprising.

H. REVIEW QUESTIONS

[Answers Provided in Appendix A, page 428]

1. T or F The Model Penal Code treats mistakes of fact and mistakes of the non-criminal law in the same manner. Mistakes of the criminal law, on the other hand, are treated quite differently.

2. **T or F**   The voluntary act requirement is only that the defendant's conduct *include* a voluntary act. It is not that *all* of the defendant's acts are voluntary.

3. **T or F**   Although there are minor differences, the Model Penal Code and the common law take basically the same approach towards mistakes that are relevant only to grading.

4. **T or F**   Even though the Model Code accepts the basic thrust of the "ignorance of the law is no excuse" maxim, it does provide for limited exceptions in the case of certain kinds of official statements on which one can rely. The reliance must be reasonable, however, and the burden of persuasion to establish the defense is on the defendant.

5. **T or F**   "Pathological" intoxication is defined by the Model Penal Code to mean a degree of intoxication greater than would be caused in a normal person, caused by the excessive prior use of alcohol or drugs.

6. **T or F**   Evidence of self-induced intoxication is not admissible under the Model Penal Code to negate a mens rea of knowledge.

7. **T or F**   If the defendant claims unawareness of a risk essential to a finding of recklessness, the prosecutor can obtain a conviction by proving that the defendant was intoxicated at the time and would have been aware of the risk if sober. The intoxication in this instance, however, must have been self-induced and not pathological.

8. **T or F**   Evidence of mental disease is admissible under the Model Penal Code whenever it is relevant to negate mens rea. An unanticipated reaction to medication is treated the same way.

9. Answer question 11, page 169. This time change the offense to burglary under § 221.1 of the Model Penal Code, and assume that all other provisions of the Model Penal Code are in effect.

10. Answer question 12, page 169. This time assume that the California offense is contained in the Model Penal Code as it is worded in the question, and that otherwise all provisions of the Model Code are in effect.

11. *D* has been charged with tampering with a public record under § 241.8(1)(a) of the Model Penal Code. The defense testimony is that *D* did not know that the altered document was required by law to be kept by others for information of the government. Should this defense be submitted to the jury, and if so under what instruction? Explain your answer.

12. *D* has been charged with burglary under § 221.1(1) of the Model Penal Code. The defense testimony is that *D* believed that the building was abandoned. The

prosecutor has offered evidence that the building in fact was not abandoned. How should the jury be instructed on the abandonment question? Explain your answer.

13. *D* has been charged with theft under § 223.2(1). The defense testimony is that *D* did not believe that the property belonged to "another" because the property was jointly owned by *D* and two partners with whom *D* was engaged in a business partnership. The applicable partnership law on which *D* relied stated that each partner owned an indivisible joint share in all partnership property. *D* therefore believed, so the testimony went, that *D* was free to treat the property as though it belonged to *D*. The prosecutor has admitted that the property was indeed partnership property, but disputes that *D* believed it did not belong to "another." Under what instruction should the defense be submitted to the jury? Explain your answer.

14. Suppose a defendant called a psychiatrist to testify in favor of the defense that a required mens rea of purpose or knowledge was lacking. Suppose further that the psychiatrist proposed to testify that the defendant did not suffer from a recognized mental disease or defect, but that the defendant had certain personality characteristics that made it unlikely that the required mens rea was actually entertained. Specifically, the defendant was naive, extremely suggestive, and not very smart—in effect capable of being hoodwinked by another person on the occasion involved, and in fact, the psychiatrist will speculate, that is likely to have happened. Should the testimony be admitted in a Model Penal Code jurisdiction? Explain your answer.

*

PART FOUR

COLLATERAL DEFENSES: JUSTIFICATIONS

Analysis

*

VI

THE COMMON LAW

Analysis

A. INTRODUCTION

The common law recognized a number of exculpatory doctrines under the general headings of "justifications" and "excuses." These defenses were defined independently of the actus reus and mens rea of any crimes. It was always up to the defendant to raise one of these defenses, that is, to bear the initial burden of production of evidence. In addition, in some cases the defendant also was required to bear the burden of persuasion. The labels "justification" and "excuse" no longer have any legal significance, but are convenient theoretical categories because they suggest the moral bases of the various defenses.

1. JUSTIFICATIONS

A "justification" defense is provided when the defendant has engaged in conduct that the criminal law does not seek to deter or prevent. The conduct might be affirmatively desirable, as when the police make a lawful arrest (conduct that without a "justification" defense might well be kidnapping). Or it might be regrettable but not regarded as properly within the social prohibition of a given offense, as when a person kills another in self defense (conduct that without a "justification" defense might well be murder). The question posed by a "justification" defense is what social norms the criminal law should seek to enforce—how the prohibitions of the criminal law ought to be defined.

2. EXCUSES

An "excuse," on the other hand, is a defense provided because the defendant is not blameworthy for having engaged in conduct that is socially undesirable. A defendant who kills a person while insane or who commits a theft under physical coercion has not engaged in conduct that society would affirmatively encourage or desire. But such a defendant is not punishable because not deemed morally responsible for the otherwise criminal behavior.

B. SELF DEFENSE

A defendant is privileged to use force against another person in self defense when reasonably believed to be necessary to defend against immediate unlawful force employed against the defendant by the other person.

1. ELEMENTS OF THE DEFENSE

An elaborate body of doctrine has been developed to implement the defense.

a. Unlawful Force by Aggressor

The first rule of self defense is that the force used or threatened against the defendant must be *unlawful*. "Unlawful" force is force that is criminal or tortious. The force must be physical and must threaten violence against the defendant's person. Words and minor touching will not suffice.

1) Defendant as Aggressor

It follows from this requirement that if the defendant is the first to use unlawful force, the defendant may not then rely on the defense of self defense. Thus, if *D* attacks *V* and *V* responds in legitimate self defense, *V*'s force is not "unlawful" and *D* is not privileged to use force against *V* in self defense. There are, however, two situations in which an initial aggressor may assert the defense of self defense:

a) Response to Excessive Force

The first is when excessive force is used against the aggressor. Thus, if *D* attacks *V* with non-deadly force, and *V* overreacts and responds with deadly force, *V*'s use of excessive force would be "unlawful" and *D* may respond in self defense.

b) Withdrawal

The second is when the initial aggressor communicates a withdrawal from the affair but the other person continues to use force. Thus, if *D* attacks *V* and *V* responds with appropriate force, *D* has no defense. But if *V* gets the upper hand and *D* by words and deeds indicates a desire to quit, *V* would not then be privileged to keep pounding on *D* in retaliation for the initial aggression. Once *D* has communicated an effective withdrawal, any further use of force by *V* will be "unlawful," and *D* may then respond in self defense.

2) Response to Unlawful Arrest

In most jurisdictions, a person may respond to an unlawful arrest with non-deadly, but not deadly, force (these terms are defined below). However, if the person making the arrest uses deadly force, the defendant may respond with deadly force.

The emerging position on this issue, on the other hand, is different. It is the law in some jurisdictions that the defendant may not resist an arrest made by a known police officer, whether lawful or unlawful. The rationale is that society is better served by remanding the defendant to the various forms of legal redress provided for an unlawful arrest, particularly since it is frequently difficult for the defendant to determine the lawfulness of an arrest at the time and place it is made. Moreover, street violence is best avoided when peaceful means are readily available to resolve the dispute.

Nevertheless, even in these jurisdictions, a defendant may resist excessive force used to make an arrest, whether the arrest is lawful or unlawful. A police officer is privileged to use an amount of force necessary to make the arrest. Any force in excess of this amount is "unlawful," triggering the defendant's right to resist in self defense.

b. Imminence of Force by Aggressor

Any threat of force to which the defendant responds must be *imminent* or *immediate*. The other person must be threatening the defendant with bodily harm *now*. Thus it is insufficient if A threatens to attack D at some point in the future. D would have avenues of self protection other than the use of force.

c. Amount of Responsive Force Permitted

The defendant may respond only with proportionate force, enough to repel the attack and no more. Use of excessive responsive force by the defendant will make the defendant's force "unlawful," and will both deprive the defendant of the defense and permit the initial aggressor to respond in self defense.

The law has divided the use of force into two categories:

1) Deadly Force Defined

"Deadly" force is force used with an intent to cause death or serious bodily injury, or force that creates a substantial risk of death or serious bodily injury.

2) Non–Deadly Force Defined

"Non-deadly" force is any use of physical force that is not "deadly."

3) Rules for Use of Deadly Force

There are two rules limiting the use of deadly force:

a) Response to Deadly Force

The defendant may not use deadly force except in response to deadly force. This rule follows logically from the requirement that the defendant's use of force must be proportional to the force defended against.

b) Retreat

Some jurisdictions, probably less than half, do not permit the defendant to use deadly force if an avenue of safe retreat is available as an alternative. Retreat is required in those jurisdictions only if the defendant knows that it can be done with complete safety. Retreat is not required from the defendant's home, and usually not from the defendant's place of business unless the attack is mounted by someone who also works there.

d. Reasonable Belief in Necessity

The defendant must actually believe that the use of force in self defense is necessary, and the belief must be reasonable under the circumstances.

2. EFFECT OF MISTAKE

What happens if the defendant is mistaken as to one or more elements of the defense?

a. Reasonable Mistakes of Fact or Judgment

If a mistake of fact is "reasonable," the defense is unaffected. This rule also applies to mistakes of judgment, such as a mistaken estimate of the necessity to use force or of the amount of responsive force needed to repel the attack. The test of "reasonableness" in this context is ordinary negligence, that is, whether a reasonable person in the defendant's situation would have made the same mistake or the same judgment.

b. Unreasonable Mistakes; Imperfect Self Defense

If the mistake is "unreasonable," the defendant is in trouble. Generally speaking, an unreasonable mistake negates the defense, and the defendant is guilty of whatever offense is made out by the remaining conduct. In the typical self-defense situation the defendant will have intentionally used force against another with a purpose to injure (or kill), albeit in the belief that it was in necessary self defense. Thus an unreasonable mistake will usually result in a conviction for assault (or murder).

There is one mitigating doctrine, however. In some jurisdictions, but by no means in all, a defendant who makes an honest but unreasonable mistake will be guilty of manslaughter, and not murder, if the victim is killed. This is called the doctrine of "imperfect self defense" or, generically, "imperfect justification." See page 370.

c. Mistakes of Law

The ordinary rules are applicable.

1) Mistakes of Criminal Law

A mistake of the criminal law is irrelevant. For example, if the defendant fails to retreat in a situation where the criminal law requires retreat, the defendant cannot defend on the ground that the requirement of retreat was not known.

2) Mistakes of Non-criminal Law

Mistakes of non-criminal law are more complicated. The courts should treat them like mistakes of fact, but they might not do so. See page 159.

3. BATTERED WOMEN

There can be little doubt that the law of self defense was generated at a time and in a manner that did not take into account the situation faced by women who are physically and mentally abused by their husbands. The law has been increasingly responsive to this situation, but there remain many points of tension between evidence offered in support of the so-called "battered woman," "battered wife," or "battered spouse" syndrome and the traditional law of self defense.

There are two primary places in the traditional definition that can cause problems when self defense is raised by a battered spouse.

One is whether the belief in the need to use force in self defense was "reasonable." In part this involves potential debate over such questions as whether leaving the home was a realistic alternative to remaining in an abusive situation and responding with force. Increasingly, expert testimony is becoming admissible in support of the conclusion that departure from the home is in many contexts not a viable option, and that it was therefore "reasonable" under the circumstances for the spouse to believe that defensive force was the only available recourse.

The other is whether the "immediacy" requirement is satisfied. This point would arise, for example, in the case of a woman who kills her sleeping husband. The prosecutor might argue that there was no threat of "immediate unlawful force" when the defensive force was used, but the response could well be that it was entirely unreasonable to require the woman to wait until she was facing the "uplifted knife" that was certain to come on the morrow because at that point it would be extremely unlikely that she could prevail in the encounter. Requiring the woman to wait until a time when she would surely lose, perhaps her life the argument would go, is to refuse to recognize the reality of the situation.

It is difficult to generalize about the law in this context. It is probably best, first, to understand the dimensions of the common law in its traditional form and, second, to understand also that for many years now courts in a number of jurisdictions, but by no means all, have taken substantial steps to come to grips with the difficulties presented by the traditions of the law of self defense as they apply to the context of abusive relationships. Battered children can present the same situation, the same difficulties, and the same need for courts to understand that the law of self defense ought to be more complicated and responsive to real life situations than is required for it to deal with two macho men of the Old West facing each other on the street with holstered six-shooters.

C. DEFENSE OF OTHERS

There is disagreement in American jurisdictions on the scope of the right of one person to use force in defense of another.

1. ELEMENTS OF THE DEFENSE

Most jurisdictions permit a defendant to use force in defense of another when reasonably believed to be necessary to protect the other from immediate unlawful force. In general, the rules of self defense apply to this defense. Thus, the defendant may use deadly force only when the other person is reasonably believed to be threatened with deadly force. In retreat jurisdictions, the defendant must retreat with the other person before using deadly force whenever retreat is required and it is known that retreat can be accomplished with complete safety. Any use of force must be proportional, and must be in response to "unlawful" force that is reasonably believed to be "imminent."

a. Limitation: Relationship to Defender
By statute, some jurisdictions still follow the old English rule that force can be used to defend another only where the other person bears some stated

relationship to the defendant. Thus, the defendant might be privileged to defend a husband, wife, child, parent, employer, employee, or more distant relative, but not privileged to defend a neighbor, boy friend or girl friend, good friend or casual friend, or, to be sure, a complete stranger. These statutes are outmoded, and most have been repealed.

2. EFFECT OF MISTAKE

In jurisdictions where the defense is stated in terms of a "reasonable belief" in the need to defend another, the rules governing mistakes are the same as for self defense.

a. Limitation: Alter Ego Rule

In some jurisdictions, however, liability is strict: the defendant is privileged to defend another only where the other person is in fact privileged to make a defense. Any mistake in assessing the situation or estimating the amount of force required to repel the attack is fatal to the defense. This is called the "alter ego" rule: the defendant stands in the shoes of the person being attacked, and is privileged to use force only if, and to the extent that, that person may do so.

Recall that justification defenses state the appropriate social norm for the context involved. The purpose of making liability strict in this situation is to deter efforts to rescue. The rule could be justified only if mistakes were so frequent as to warrant discouraging rescue in all cases. The argument against strict liability here is the same as elsewhere: it punishes without fault. Indeed strict liability may be regarded as particularly unfair in this case, since it punishes persons who have the entirely laudable motive of rescuing others from danger and who most likely will be acting in concert with, rather than opposed to, conventional morality. A reasonably socialized person, in other words, might think it is praiseworthy to attempt to rescue another. To punish such a person using a standard of strict liability could well, in many contexts, be unfair.

D. DEFENSE OF PROPERTY

A defendant is privileged to use force against another person when reasonably believed to be necessary to protect real or personal property in the possession of the defendant from imminent and unlawful damage, trespass, or dispossession. The force may be used to prevent this harm before it occurs, or to re-enter real property or, immediately or in hot pursuit, to recapture personal property.

1. ELEMENTS OF THE DEFENSE

The defense is limited in the following respects:

a. Necessity to Use Force

Force is *not* permitted in two situations:

1) **Time to Invoke Law Enforcement**
   Force is not permitted if there is time to resort to more ordinary processes of law (such as calling the police) before any harm to the property occurs.

2) **Request to Desist**
   A request to desist must be made before force is used, unless the circumstances are such that it is clear that the request would be useless or dangerous to the property or the defendant.

b. **Amount of Responsive Force Permitted**
When force is permitted, the defendant may use that amount of *non-deadly* force reasonably believed to be necessary to protect the property.

1) **Limits on Use of Deadly Force**
   Most jurisdictions place severe limits on the use of deadly force to protect property.

   a) **Personal Property**
      They are likely to preclude the use of deadly force altogether solely for the purpose of protecting personal property. Of course a defendant who uses proper non-deadly force to protect property and who is met with deadly force from the person endangering the property may then respond in self defense. The deadly force used against the defendant would be "unlawful" and would trigger the normal defense of self defense—of course with its usual limitations.

   b) **Real Property**
      An early English decision took the position that deadly force could be used to prevent forcible entry of a dwelling if the intruder had been warned to stop and not to enter. This view is probably no longer followed.

      The more modern view is that deadly force can be used to prevent forcible entry of a dwelling only if the defendant reasonably believes that the intruder intends to commit a felony inside.

      Some jurisdictions have adopted a slightly broader rule, permitting *in addition* the use of deadly force if the threat is to harm some person inside the dwelling, even if the threat of harm does not involve a felony or the threat of serious injury or death.

2) **Use of Mechanical Devices**
   Mechanical devices, such as warning systems and electrified fences, may be used to protect property if they are reasonable under the circumstances, if there are warnings of any danger to intruders, and if they do not employ deadly force.

Some jurisdictions will permit mechanical devices that employ deadly force, but liability is strict: the force is permitted only if used in a situation where the defendant would have been permitted to use deadly force if present at the time.

2. EFFECT OF MISTAKE
The use of force to protect property is subject to the requirement that the defendant reasonably believe that all of the required conditions exist. This means that a reasonable mistake of fact or judgment does not deprive the defendant of the defense. But an unreasonable belief results in denial of the defense as does a mistake as to the legal scope of the defense.

E. ARREST, ESCAPE, AND CRIME PREVENTION

Police officers are permitted to use force when reasonably believed to be necessary to make an arrest, to prevent an escape, or to prevent a crime from being committed. Private citizens may also use force for these purposes under limited circumstances.

1. USE OF FORCE TO MAKE ARREST
A police officer is permitted to use *non-deadly* force when reasonably believed to be necessary to make a lawful arrest. A private citizen can assert any defense available to a police officer when called to the aid of a police officer. But a private citizen who acts alone may be privileged to use *non-deadly* force to make an arrest only when reasonably believed to be necessary to make an arrest for a felony that was in fact committed. If a felony was not in fact committed, the citizen may be strictly liable.

a. Use of Deadly Force by Police Officer
The defense of self defense can be triggered by the resistance of the person being arrested. Thus, deadly force may be used in response to deadly force.

1) Fleeing Felon
Deadly force may also be used, under the prevailing view, if the officer reasonably believes it necessary to prevent a fleeing felon from escaping arrest.

2) Fleeing Misdemeanant
Deadly force may *not* be used to prevent a misdemeanant from escaping arrest.

3) Fleeing Dangerous Felon
Some jurisdictions, on the other hand, have adopted a more restrictive view on the use of deadly force. They of course permit the police officer to respond in kind to the use of deadly force by a person sought to be

arrested. But if the person flees, deadly force may be used to prevent escape only if reasonably believed to be necessary to arrest a person who is dangerous to life or limb. Thus, deadly force may be permitted if the fleeing felon is reasonably believed to be guilty of murder or armed robbery, but not if the felon is believed an embezzler or a serious threat to continue a life of forgery.

b. Use of Deadly Force by Private Person
A private citizen who is called to the aid of a police officer can assert any defense available to the officer.

But a private citizen who acts alone may only be privileged to use deadly force when reasonably believed to be necessary to arrest a person who in fact committed a felony, and perhaps only one dangerous to life or limb. Liability is strict as to whether the felony has been committed: if the person in fact has not committed the felony, no defense is available.

2. USE OF FORCE TO PREVENT ESCAPE
The use of force to prevent an escape from custody is permitted if such force could have been used to arrest that person. In addition, it may be permissible for prison guards and others charged with responsibility to prevent escape from a secured custodial facility to use deadly force to prevent any escape.

3. USE OF FORCE TO PREVENT CRIME
A person who reasonably believes a felony or a misdemeanor involving a breach of the peace is being committed or is imminent may use *non-deadly* force when reasonably believed to be necessary to stop or prevent the crime.

a. Use of Deadly Force
There are two views on when deadly force may be used to prevent crime:

1) Any Felony
The older and still prevailing view is that deadly force may be used to prevent the commission of any felony.

2) Dangerous Felony
The modern and gaining view is that deadly force may be used only to prevent the commission of a felony that is dangerous to life or limb.

F. PUBLIC AUTHORITY

A public officer may use *non-deadly* force when reasonably believed to be necessary to enforce a valid law, court order, or process. The courts are divided on whether a mistake of law as to the validity of the law, court order, or process deprives the officer of the defense. But the emerging view is that such a mistake does not cost the officer the defense if it is reasonable under the circumstances.

G. DOMESTIC AUTHORITY

Persons who have responsibility for the care, safety, or discipline of others may use *non-deadly* force when reasonably believed to be necessary to the discharge of their duties.

H. CONSENT OR CONDONATION

Consent is sometimes a defense to crime because inconsistent with an element of the offense or because it precludes infliction of the harm at which the offense is aimed. Sexual intercourse is perhaps the paradigm illustration of an act which is regarded as an egregious crime when forcibly inflicted without consent, but which is regarded in a wholly different light when engaged in by mutually consenting adults. Boxing or football similarly involve activities which would not be welcome in other contexts.

Otherwise, however, consent is not a defense. Nor is it a defense if the victim is also guilty of a crime or is contributorily negligent. It is also not a defense if the victim retroactively consents to, or condones, the offense. Once an offense has been committed, subsequent action by the victim cannot undo it. There are statutes in some jurisdictions, however, that permit a defense of condonation in specified circumstances. For example, some permit subsequent marriage to be a defense to seduction. Others more broadly permit private compromise by formal court proceedings in the case of misdemeanors.

I. NECESSITY; CHOICE OF EVILS

In many ways the most interesting of the justification defenses is the so-called defense of "necessity" or "choice of evils." This is because this defense seeks to generalize the fundamental social question underlying all justification defenses: Should the prohibitions of the law be removed when a person commits what would otherwise be a crime but commission of the crime is a lesser evil than would occur if the person did nothing? The answer seems easy if the crime is running a red light and the justification is to get an imminently expectant mother to the hospital. On the other hand, considerably harder questions are raised if the defendant kills one person to save two.

1. DESIRABILITY OF GENERAL NECESSITY DEFENSE
There is dispute in the law over whether a general necessity defense actually exists. Many courts have assumed its existence, only to find it inapplicable to the case at hand. The British have debated for years whether such a principle is reflected in the common law, and not long ago a study commission rejected its adoption by statute. It is probable, however, that such a principle would be recognized by an American court in a proper case.

a. The Case For the Defense
The case for the defense is simple: it is wrong to punish a person for engaging in a socially desirable act. Recognition of the defense is thus essential to the

ethical integrity of the criminal law. From the standpoint of deterrence and social control, moreover, it is good for the law to encourage behavior that produces a net social gain.

b. The Case Against the Defense

On the other hand, it can be argued that the infrequency of successful invocation of the defense suggests little need for it. Recognition of the defense, moreover, invites people to take the law into their own hands—encourages them to engage in conduct *they* believe to be socially desirable that in fact may be quite harmful. One might predict, in other words, that the number of "mistakes" made by those purporting to act on this basis would produce more net harm than the good produced by those who get it right. In addition, the defense is most often asserted in an effort to use the courts as a public forum for political debate. Thus, the defense has been raised to justify trespass on nuclear power sites, to justify civil disobedience against the Viet Nam War, to avoid restrictions on use of certain drugs for medical purposes, etc. One can question whether it is efficient or desirable to use the criminal courts to resolve great social conflicts of this sort.

2. ELEMENTS OF THE DEFENSE

Curiously, there is general agreement about the essential elements of the defense even though it may not exist. There are three ingredients:

a. Emergency

The situation presented to the defendant must be an emergency threatening the imminent occurrence of a harm. And there must be no reasonable opportunity to avoid the harm without committing a crime.

b. Defendant Without Fault

The defendant must not be at fault in bringing about the situation that gave rise to the need to act.

c. Avoid Greater Harm

The harm that can only be avoided by committing a crime must be more substantial or more serious than that caused by commission of the crime.

This question is for the court to resolve, and not for the defendant or the jury. And it must be clear that the legislature has not previously balanced the respective harms contrary to the manner asserted by the defendant. The court must first determine whether the legislature, either in the formulation of a justification defense, the definition of a crime, or in other legislation, has previously resolved the "choice of evils" differently than the defendant. For example, the codification of a retreat limitation on the use of deadly force in self defense would foreclose any argument by the defendant that heroically standing one's ground does more social good than running from a fight. Only if the legislature has not previously resolved the stakes involved is the court then free to strike the balance of net social good.

3. EFFECT OF MISTAKE

The first element of the defense presents a question for the jury to resolve, probably based on the defendant's reasonable belief under the circumstances. Thus a mistake as to the nature of the emergency is likely not to deprive the defendant of the defense, if the mistake was reasonable under the circumstances.

But a mistake as to the third element—balancing the harm avoided against the harm committed—will deprive the defendant of the defense, since that balance is to be struck as a matter of criminal law by the courts.

J.   REVIEW QUESTIONS

[Answers Provided in Appendix A, page 432]

1. T or F   Some jurisdictions discourage rescue by permitting a defendant to use force to defend another only if the defendant is correct, that is, only if the other person in fact has the right to act in self defense. Liability is strict.

2. T or F   In most jurisdictions, deadly force can never be used to protect personal property.

3. T or F   A police officer is permitted to use whatever force is reasonably believed to be necessary to make an arrest, even deadly force if the defendant fights back.

4. T or F   The prevailing law is that deadly force may be used by any person to prevent the commission of any felony—even embezzlement, forgery, or tax fraud.

5. T or F   Contributory negligence by the victim is a defense to a crime for which negligence is the required culpability.

6. T or F   The existence of the emergency giving rise to a choice of evils defense is for the court to determine, and any mistake by the defendant will result in loss of the defense.

7. A defendant who makes an unreasonable mistake in assessing the need to use deadly force in self defense is negligent. But if death results, the defendant is convicted in many jurisdictions of murder and not negligent homicide. What are the arguments for and against this result? Which should prevail? Give reasons for your answer.

8. *V* curses at *D* and gets *D* mad. *D* shoves *V*, slaps *V* in the face, and threatens to do so again. *V* gets mad, pulls a knife, and charges at *D*. *D* avoids *V*'s charge, and

pulls a gun. *D* says to *V*: "Drop the knife or I'll shoot." *V* responds unprintably, and comes back at *D* brandishing the knife. *D* then shoots and kills *V*. *D* has now been charged with murder and you are *D*'s lawyer. Prepare a preliminary analysis of the likelihood that a defense of self defense will be successful, including an indication of any additional factual investigation you would have Paul Drake undertake.

*

VII

THE MODEL PENAL CODE

Analysis

A. INTRODUCTION

The Model Penal Code justification defenses are contained in Article 3. They are for the most part a morass of detail, though in general content they draw heavily on the common law tradition. They are so detailed, indeed, that it would unduly prolong this outline if each section were fully recapitulated here. Instead, only the highlights will be noted.

There is, however, an important innovation in Article 3 that should be understood before one addresses the details of the defenses. This is its approach to the problem of mistake. The results it reaches are likely to be reflected in most new criminal codes.

B. STRUCTURE

The Model Code approach to mistake is developed in two steps.

1. DEFENDANT'S BELIEF

Note first that each provision of Article 3 is stated in terms of the defendant's *belief* that the justifying factors exist. Self defense, for example, is permitted by § 3.04(1) when the defendant "believes" that force is immediately necessary for the purpose of protection against the use of unlawful force by another on the present occasion. Each of the other justification defenses is similarly defined in terms of what the defendant "believes."

Standing alone, these provisions would give the defendant a defense based solely upon subjective belief, no matter what the actual facts were and no matter how reasonably, how carelessly, or how irrationally the defendant arrived at the belief. Yet it is clear that the law cannot permit justification defenses to rest on the defendant's belief alone. A completely irrational and indefensible belief that one must engage in self defense should not be allowed to exonerate from a charge of assault or murder.

In the end, the Model Penal Code does not provide that the defendant's belief, standing alone, will constitute the defense. Focusing on the defendant's belief is only the starting point. If the defendant believes in the existence of the justifying factors specified in the Code and if they actually exist, the defendant would be entitled to a defense. It is where the defendant makes a mistake as to the existence of the justifying factors that further analysis is needed.

2. EFFECT OF MISTAKE

The insight reflected in the Model Code is that mistakes as to the elements of a *defense* should be treated the same way as mistakes as to the elements of an *offense*. Most importantly, moreover, the grading of any offense of which the defendant is convicted should take account of the defendant's culpability for any mistake relating to a justification defense.

a. Mistake of Fact or Judgment

Section 3.09(2) provides that if the defendant is negligent in forming any belief that would establish a justification under the Code, the defendant may only be convicted of an offense for which negligence is the required culpability if the elements of the offense are otherwise satisfied.

> *Example:* A defendant who intentionally killed another, but in the negligently formed belief that it was necessary to do so in order to save the defendant's life, could be convicted of negligent homicide under § 210.4(1).

Similarly, § 3.09(2) provides that if the defendant is reckless in forming any belief that would establish a justification under the Code, the defendant may only be convicted of an offense for which recklessness is the required culpability if the elements of the offense are otherwise satisfied.

> *Example:* A defendant who intentionally killed another, but in the recklessly formed belief that it was necessary to do so in order to save the defendant's life, could be convicted of manslaughter under § 210.3(1)(a).
>
> Alternatively, such a person could be convicted of negligent homicide, since it is always permissible for the prosecutor to prove that the defendant was *more* culpable than a given statute requires. Proof of recklessness, in other words, will warrant a conviction for an offense that requires only negligence. Cf. § 2.02(5).

It would also follow from § 3.09(2) that an honest (meaning actual) belief in the existence of justifying factors specified in the Code would be a defense to any crime requiring a culpability of purpose or knowledge. Thus, an honest belief in the factors that would justify the defense of self defense under the Code would be a defense to murder under § 210.2(1)(a). By extrapolation, a prosecution under § 210.2(1)(b) would be permitted if the defendant honestly believed in the existence of the justifying factors specified by the Code, but was so reckless in forming the belief as to satisfy the standards of that provision.

The rationale for these results is that the degree of the defendant's crime is proportionally matched to the degree of the defendant's culpability. Under the traditional common law view, a defendant who intentionally killed another in the negligent belief that it was necessary to do so in self defense was convicted of murder. The Model Code drafters thought this disproportionate. They reasoned that liability for the most serious crime known to the law was being imposed on the basis of negligence. It is true that the defendant intentionally killed, but not true that the defendant did so with the base motives that normally characterize the murderer who deserves the most serious sanctions known to the criminal law. Viewed in terms of culpability, the defendant believed—honestly if not reasonably—in the necessity to kill in self defense. Morally, therefore, the defendant is less culpable than the contract killer or the person who kills out of hate, and more like the person who kills negligently. If the defendant had been more careful no crime would have been committed.

But a death caused by negligence has occurred, and it seems appropriate in that event to convict the defendant of negligent homicide. This result is accomplished by § 3.09(2), which also generalizes the principle for application in cases where the defendant is more culpable towards the existence of justifying factors.

b. Mistake of Law

Consider three kinds of cases:

(1) The defendant is unaware of the requirement of retreat stated in § 3.04(2)(b)(ii) and uses deadly force without retreating when it was known that complete safety could have been secured by retreating.

(2) The defendant believes that force being used by another is unlawful and resists in self defense. The defendant is wrong. The force used by the other person was lawful.

(3) A person takes personal property from the possession of the defendant. The defendant believes that the property belongs to the defendant and uses moderate force to retake it in hot pursuit. The defendant is wrong. The property actually belongs to the person who took it from the defendant.

These cases would be analyzed as follows:

1) Mistake of Criminal Law

The first defendant made a mistake as to the meaning of the criminal law. The defendant did not know about the requirements of § 3.04(2)(b)(ii). One would expect that this mistake would not be a defense, and indeed the Model Code provides that it is not.

Section 2.02(9) provides that culpability is not required as to the "existence, meaning or application of the law determining the elements of an offense." The term "element of an offense" is defined in § 1.13(9)(c) to include such conduct as "negatives an excuse or justification." Here, the defendant's failure to retreat "negatived" a justification defense and hence is an element of any offense with which the defendant is charged. Culpability is therefore not required as to the "application" of the law determining the obligation to retreat. The mistake is therefore not a defense.

2) Mistake as to Lawfulness of Force

In the second case, the defendant made a mistake that could be characterized in a number of ways, depending on the facts. It could be a mistake of criminal law, of tort law, or of fact. Which is it? You can't tell from the facts as given. You need to know more about what happened.

If the mistake is one of criminal law, one would think that it would not be a defense. And § 3.09(1) so provides. A defense is denied when the defendant's "belief in the unlawfulness of the force or conduct against which he employs protective force . . . is erroneous; and his error is due to ignorance or mistake as to the provisions of . . . the criminal law."

On the other hand, if the mistake is one of tort law or of fact, then the case becomes just like the third situation, analyzed below.

3) Mistake of Non-Criminal Law

In the third case, the defendant's mistake as to the ownership of the property could be the result of a mistake of fact or a mistake of non-criminal law.

Under § 2.04(1)(b), either type of mistake is a defense if "the law provides that the state of mind established by such ignorance or mistake constitutes a defense." Here, § 3.06(1)(b) provides that the defendant's belief is a defense and such a mistake will therefore exonerate.

But note that the defendant's subjective belief is only a defense to crimes that require a culpability level of purpose or knowledge. The defense provided by the defendant's belief that the use of force is justified is taken away by § 3.09(2) in cases where the defendant is reckless or negligent and is prosecuted for an offense for which recklessness or negligence, as the case may be, is sufficient.

c. Innocent Party Injured

The Model Code also deals explicitly with another kind of mistake, namely one of aim. Under § 3.09(3), the defendant is liable for injury or risk of injury to innocent persons by the use of force that is otherwise justified under §§ 3.03 to 3.08. But the liability is limited to situations where the prosecution is for an offense that requires a culpability of recklessness and the injury or risk of injury was recklessly caused by the defendant, or where the prosecution is for an offense that requires negligence and the defendant was reckless or negligent.

Example: The defendant can be convicted of manslaughter under § 210.3(1)(a) if an innocent person is killed by a defendant who is acting in legitimate self defense and if the defendant is reckless as to the death of the innocent person.

Of course if a justification defense is unavailable to the defendant for some reason, the defendant's liability for injury or risk of injury to an innocent person would be assessed under normal principles of culpability and causation.

C. SELF DEFENSE

The defense of self defense is available if the defendant believes that force is immediately necessary for self protection against unlawful force on the present occasion. See § 3.04(1).

1. LIMITATIONS ON THE USE OF FORCE

Subsection (2) contains a series of limitations, first on the use of force in general (Subsection (2)(a)) and second on the use of deadly force (Subsection (2)(b)).

a. General Limitations

There are two general limitations:

1) Unlawful Arrests

Section 3.04(2)(a)(i) provides that the use of force is never permissible to defend against an arrest known to be made by a peace officer, whether the arrest is lawful or unlawful.

Note, however, that this provision would not preclude the use of force to defend against excessive force used by a police officer. The remainder of § 3.04(1) applies to such a case.

2) Defense of Property

Section 3.04(2)(a)(ii) contains a complex limitation on when force may be used against one who uses force to defend property under a claim of right. Essentially, force is permitted in the three situations listed in Subsections (a)(ii)(1), (2), and (3) and is otherwise prohibited.

b. Deadly Force

The term "deadly force" is defined in § 3.11(2). Note that a threat to use deadly force if necessary is not itself the use of deadly force.

Deadly force is *permissible* under § 3.04(2)(b) only if believed to be necessary to protect the defendant against "death, serious bodily harm, kidnapping or sexual intercourse compelled by force or threat." In addition it is *prohibited* in two situations:

1) Defendant Initiates With Intent to Kill or Seriously Injure

Deadly force is prohibited under § 3.04(2)(b)(i) if the defendant, with a purpose to kill or cause serious bodily harm, initiated the encounter.

2) Retreat

Section 3.04(2)(b)(ii) contains a carefully limited retreat provision. Note that retreat is required only when the defendant *knows* that deadly force can be avoided *with complete safety* by retreating. Note also the exceptions to the retreat requirement in the case of dwellings, places of work, and law enforcement.

D. DEFENSE OF OTHERS

Section 3.05(1) deals with the use of force in defense of others. Basically, it provides that force can be used to protect any third person when the defendant believes that the other person would be entitled to use force in self defense. Section 3.05(2) then fits the retreat rules of § 3.04 to the situation where one person is defending another.

Note that the common law limitation that only certain relatives can be defended is rejected. And note that the "alter ego" rule is also rejected. Mistakes in the context of defense of others are treated according to the general pattern of Article 3.

E. DEFENSE OF PROPERTY

Section 3.06(1) deals with the use of force in the protection of real and personal property.

1. DEFENSE AGAINST INITIAL AGGRESSION

Section 3.06(1)(a) covers cases where an aggressor seeks to enter or trespass upon land, or seeks to trespass upon or take away personal property. It permits the use of force against the aggressor when the defendant believes it immediately necessary to prevent or terminate the aggression *if* the land or personal property is, or is believed to be, in the defendant's possession or the possession of another in whose interest the defendant is acting. The concept of "possession" is defined in § 3.06(2).

2. RE–ENTRY OR RECAPTURE

Section 3.06(1)(b) covers cases where the defendant seeks to re-enter land on which another is present or recapture personal property taken by another. It permits the use of force when the defendant believes it is immediately necessary to re-enter land or recapture personal property under two conditions: (a) that the defendant believes the dispossession was unlawful and that the defendant is entitled to possession; and (b) that the force is used immediately or in hot pursuit, or the force is used where the aggressor has no claim of right to continued possession and, if the property is land, resort to the courts is not feasible.

3. LIMITATIONS ON THE USE OF FORCE

The remainder of § 3.06 is a complicated set of limitations on the privileges established by § 3.06(1). Three of the provisions should be especially noted.

a. Request to Desist

The common law requirement that, where practicable, a request to desist be made before force is used is continued. See § 3.06(3)(a).

b. **Use of Deadly Force**

The use of deadly force is severely restricted by § 3.06(3)(d), essentially to situations where the defendant's dwelling is being defended or a life endangering crime is threatened by the aggressor.

c. **Use of Mechanical Devices**

The use of mechanical devices is limited by § 3.06(5), essentially to situations where they are reasonable under the circumstances and not life endangering. Any such device must be one that is customarily used in the setting, or the defendant must take reasonable care to make it known that a mechanical device is being used.

F. ARREST, ESCAPE, AND CRIME PREVENTION

Section 3.07 deals with the use of force to make an arrest, to prevent an escape, or to prevent a crime.

1. **USE OF FORCE TO MAKE ARREST**

Section 3.07(1) permits the use of force when believed to be necessary to effect a lawful arrest. Section 3.07(2) contains a series of limitations on this privilege.

a. **Limits on Non-deadly Force**

No force is justified unless, where practicable, the person being arrested is told why the arrest is being made and if, when a warrant is used, the warrant is valid or believed to be valid.

b. **Limits on Deadly Force**

Deadly force is justifiable under four conditions:

1) **Felony**

The arrest is for a felony; and

2) **Status of Defendant**

The defendant is a peace officer or is helping a person believed to be a peace officer; and

3) **Risk to Innocent Persons**

The defendant believes that no substantial risk of injury to innocent persons is created; and

4) **Dangerous Person**

The person to be arrested is dangerous, as manifested either by the use or threat to use deadly force in the crime for which the arrest is made or by a threat to cause death or serious bodily harm if the arrest is delayed.

c. **Mistakes as to Lawfulness of Arrest**

Section § 3.09(1) provides that a justification defense is unavailable if the defendant erroneously believes that an arrest sought to be effected by force is lawful, and if the error is due to ignorance or mistake as to provisions of the law governing the legality of an arrest or search.

d. **Assistance by Private Persons**

Section 3.07(4) contains two provisions governing private persons who assist in making an arrest:

1) **Summoned to Assist Peace Officer**

The first protects the private citizen who is summoned to assist a peace officer in making an arrest. The citizen is likely to have no basis for knowing that an arrest is unlawful. The same protections are therefore given as would exist were the arrest lawful, unless the arrest is actually believed to be unlawful.

2) **Other Cases**

In other cases, where the private person is assisting another private person or is helping a peace officer without being summoned, a stricter position is taken. The defendant must believe the arrest lawful and is not protected if the arrest would be unlawful were the facts as the defendant believes them to be.

2. USE OF FORCE TO PREVENT ESCAPE

Section 3.07(3) governs the use of force to prevent escape.

a. **General Principle**

In general, the use of force to prevent an escape is governed by the provisions that would be applicable to an arrest of the person involved.

b. **Deadly Force**

But deadly force is permitted in the case of escapes from a jail, prison, or other institution used for the detention of persons *charged with* or convicted of a crime. Such force is limited to cases where it is believed to be "immediately necessary to prevent the escape" and can be used only by "a guard or other person authorized to act as a peace officer."

3. USE OF FORCE TO PREVENT CRIME

Section 3.07(5) permits the use of force if the defendant believes it immediately necessary to prevent suicide, self-inflicted serious bodily harm, or the commission or consummation of a crime involving or threatening bodily harm, damage to or loss of property, or breach of the peace.

a. **Limitations on the Use of Force**

Two limitations are imposed by § 3.07(5)(a)(i) and (ii):

1) **Other Justification Defenses Applicable**
   The fact that conduct is a crime does not displace any limitations on the use of force established by other justification defenses defined in Article 3.

2) **Deadly Force**
   Deadly force is not permitted unless the person against whom it is to be used is dangerous, as manifested in either of two ways:

   a) **Risk of Death or Serious Bodily Harm**
      The defendant must believe that there is a substantial risk that death or serious injury will be caused by commission of the crime, *and* that the defendant's force will not create a substantial risk of injury to innocent persons.

   b) **Suppression of Riot or Mutiny**
      The defendant must believe that the use of deadly force is necessary to suppress a riot or a mutiny. The rioters or mutineers must be ordered to disperse and warned that deadly force will be used.

G. PUBLIC AUTHORITY

Section 3.03(1) provides that conduct is justifiable when "required or authorized" by specified legal sources, as well as by "any other provision of law imposing a public duty."

Note that the use of force for purposes covered by other provisions of Article 3 must comply with those provisions. § 3.03(2)(a). And note that deadly force is permitted only when authorized elsewhere in Article 3, except in war or when expressly authorized by some other provision of law.

Section 3.03(3) deals with specified mistakes. It protects those executing legal process from lack of jurisdiction of the court or defect in the legal process. And it protects those who believe they are required or authorized to assist a public officer in cases where the public officer lacks authority.

Note also that there is a separate provision on the execution of military orders. See § 2.10.

H. DOMESTIC AUTHORITY

The use of force by persons who have responsibility over others is governed by § 3.08. In general, the force must be designed to accomplish objectives legitimately within the scope of authority of the person who uses it. Deadly force is prohibited, as well as force that is degrading, causes extreme pain or emotional distress, or is disfiguring.

I. CONSENT OR CONDONATION

Like the common law, the Model Code provides no defense for condonation or contributory negligence. And it is no defense that the defendant's victim was also guilty of a crime. Consent is dealt with in § 2.11.

1. **GENERAL PROVISION ON CONSENT**
   In general, consent is a defense if it "negatives an element of the offense or precludes the infliction of the harm or evil sought to be prevented by the law defining the offense." § 2.11(1).

2. **CONSENT TO BODILY HARM**
   Section 2.11(2) covers consent to cause or threaten bodily harm. Consent is a defense in any one of three situations:

   a. **Minor Harm**
      The harm is not serious.

   b. **Athletic Contests**
      The defendant's conduct and the harm caused are "reasonably foreseeable hazards" of "joint participation" in competitive sports.

      The "joint participation" limitation would exclude combat between spectator and participant. The "reasonably foreseeable hazards" provision would exclude the intentional infliction of serious injury outside of the rules and customs of the sport.

   c. **Authorized by Article 3**
      The consent establishes a justification under the provisions of Article 3, principally § 3.08.

3. **WHEN CONSENT INEFFECTIVE**
   Section 2.11(3) provides that consent is ineffective in four situations:

   a. **Legal Incompetence**
      Where the person is legally incompetent to consent.

   b. **Incapacity**
      Where the person is incapable of giving consent by reason of youth, mental disease, mental defect, or intoxication. Consent is ineffective if the defendant knows the person is "unable to make a reasonable judgment" as to the nature or harmfulness of the offense, or if the person is "manifestly unable" to do so.

   c. **Offense Protects Against Improvident Consent**
      Where the consent is given by a person whose improvident consent is sought to be prevented by the law defining the offense, e.g., statutory rape. See § 213.1(1)(d).

   d. **Force, Duress, or Deception**
      Where the consent is induced by force, duress, or deception which the law defining the offense seeks to prevent.

J. NECESSITY; CHOICE OF EVILS

The Model Code also includes a general "necessity" or "choice of evils" defense.

1. ELEMENTS OF THE DEFENSE
The elements of the defense are specified in § 3.02(1).

a. Belief in Necessity
Note that § 3.02(1) requires that the defendant "believe" that action is "necessary" to avoid a harm or evil. It does not explicitly require that the harm or evil be "imminent" or an "emergency," or that there be no reasonable opportunity to avoid the evil without committing a crime. But it is likely that these requirements will be read into the word "necessary" by courts and juries as they apply the provision.

b. Avoid Greater Harm
Section 3.02(1)(a) provides that the harm or evil sought to be avoided must be greater than the harm or evil that would be caused by commission of the offense.

Note that this language is *not* modified by the word "believes." This judgment is plainly for the courts to make, and not a question on which the defendant's or the jury's judgment will be determinative. If the defendant believes the harm avoided is more serious than the harm caused, but the court believes otherwise, the defendant will have no defense. Liability on this point is strict.

c. No Explicit Exclusion
Section 3.02(1)(b) states a principle of interpretation for the courts to follow. It instructs the courts not to strike a balance of harms which has been struck differently in an explicit provision of the criminal law. For example, the use of deadly force in self defense is carefully worked out in § 3.04. The courts are not free to strike a different balance in this area in the implementation of the general necessity defense.

d. Contrary Legislative Purpose
Section 3.02(1)(c) likewise states a principle of interpretation to guide the courts. They are free to hold one harm greater than another, and therefore a justification for crime, only if the legislature has not previously expressed a contrary intent. As is the case with § 3.02(1)(b), the point is that the courts should not feel free to strike a different balance of harms than one previously reached by the legislature.

2. EFFECT OF FAULT IN BRINGING SITUATION ABOUT
Section 3.02(2) provides a limitation on assertion of the defense in cases where the defendant was at fault in causing a situation that required a choice of evils:

(1) if the defendant was reckless in causing the need for choice, the defendant may not rely on the defense if charged with a crime requiring a culpability of recklessness or negligence; or

(2) if the defendant was negligent in bringing about the necessity, the defendant may not rely on the defense if charged with a crime requiring a culpability of negligence.

What happens if the defendant intentionally brings about the need for choice? Although the situation is not covered explicitly, it seems clear that the courts should deny the defense. For example, if the defendant wants to kill *A* for independent reasons, and maneuvers *A* into a situation where *A* must be killed in order to save the lives of 10 other people, an acquittal of the defendant for murder would clearly not be justified on a "choice of evils" rationale.

3. EFFECT OF MISTAKE

Section 3.02(2) also deals with the effect of mistakes in appraising the necessity for action. It does so in exactly the same manner that such a mistake would be treated under § 3.09(2). A mistake that is recklessly or negligently made is not a defense to an offense requiring recklessness or negligence, as the case may be. [Note that § 3.09(2) by its terms is not applicable to § 3.02. Hence the need for the separate provision here.]

And note, as developed above, that a mistake as to whether one harm outweighs another is not covered by § 3.02(2). This determination is to be made as a matter of criminal law and a mistake by the defendant is fatal to successful assertion of the defense.

K. REVIEW QUESTIONS

[Answers Provided in Appendix A, page 434]

1. T or F   The use of force is not permissible solely for the purpose of defending against an unlawful arrest by a police officer, even though both the police officer and the arrestee know the arrest to be unlawful.

2. T or F   *A* attacks *D* on a public street with deadly force. *D* pulls a gun and tells *A*: "Stop or I'll shoot." *A* stops and the encounter is ended. *D* is now prosecuted for assault under § 211.1(1)(c) on the ground that *D* threatened the use of deadly force and did not properly retreat when obligated to do so. *D* admits that a completely safe retreat could have been accomplished without pulling the gun, and that *D* realized it at the time. But *D* was unaware of any legal obligation to retreat under these circumstances. As unjust as it sounds, *D* is guilty. Ignorance of the criminal law is no excuse.

3. T or F   The Model Penal Code permits one to use deadly force in defense of a complete stranger, so long as the defendant reasonably believes that the

stranger would be entitled to use deadly force in self defense.

4. T or F   Force may never be used to defend real property against trespass unless a request is first made to the trespasser to withdraw.

5. T or F   A police officer would be guilty of no crime for shooting a felon who was fleeing from an attempted arrest if the police officer reasonably believed the felon used a weapon to threaten the lives of innocent people in the commission of the felony for which the arrest is sought to be made.

6. T or F   A person who is reckless in bringing about a situation in which a choice of evils must be made will have no defense to any crime committed, even though the commission of the crime resulted in a lesser evil than would have occurred if the crime were not committed.

7.   *A,* a basketball player, intercepts a pass and, with a substantial head start on the players from the other team, streaks for a slam dunk at the other end of the court. As *A* reaches an elbow above the rim, *B,* a player from the other team, catches up to *A* and intentionally pushes *A* from behind to prevent the score. *A* loses control and *A*'s head strikes the backboard, causing a severe concussion from which *A* later dies. You are an assistant to the local prosecutor. Your boss asks you for a preliminary analysis of whether *B* should be prosecuted for any crime. The entire Model Penal Code is in effect in your jurisdiction. Prepare the analysis.

8.   Prepare an essay in which you compare the common law approach to mistakes in the context of justification defenses to the approach of the Model Penal Code. Which is better? Give reasons for your answer, but be sure to consider the reasons that could be given by those who disagree with your conclusion.

*

PART FIVE

COLLATERAL
DEFENSES: EXCUSES

*

VIII

THE COMMON LAW

Analysis

A. INTRODUCTION

Recall that "excuses" are defenses provided because the defendant is not blameworthy for having engaged in conduct that is socially undesirable. See page 191. The label "excuse" has no modern legal significance, but is helpful in establishing a theoretical basis for thinking through the rationales of the various excuses recognized by the criminal law. The law recognizes excuses in two different contexts:

> First, there are cases of incapacity, cases where the defendant is regarded as so different from ordinary people that it is appropriate to recognize a lack of responsibility for crime. The defenses of infancy and insanity fit this category. These are cases where the defendant's capacities for normal behavior are limited or impaired.

> Second, there are cases where the defendant's capacities for normal behavior are secure but where it is recognized that an ordinary person would have had no fair opportunity not to engage in criminal conduct. The defenses of duress and entrapment fit this category. These are often called cases of "situational excuse."

The one case deals with abnormal people, the other with abnormal situations. Involuntary intoxication straddles the two. This defense is provided because a temporary and involuntary reduction in the defendant's capacity deprived the defendant of a fair opportunity not to engage in criminal conduct.

B. INFANCY

It is plain that the imposition of criminal punishment on very young children is inappropriate. This is not because children are incapable of conduct that has harmful social consequences, for clearly they are. Rather, it is because they are incapable of making rational, intelligent choices—choices upon which it is appropriate to visit the stigma and blame that follows from the conviction of crime. There are two basic approaches to the responsibility of children for crimes. The first emerged from the common law, and determines at what age a child can be held accountable for criminal behavior. The second is a product of modern legislation, and essentially diverts certain children from the regular adult courts to a different criminal process.

1. AGE OF CAPACITY
As originally formulated, the common law established three arbitrary limits based upon the child's chronological (not mental) age at the time of the offense:

a. Under Seven
A child under the age of 7 had no capacity to commit a crime. Sometimes this was expressed in terms of a "conclusive presumption," which is another way of saying that no proof will be admitted that a particular child under 7 was capable of making sufficiently rational choices to justify criminal punishment.

b. Between Seven and Fourteen
A child between the ages of 7 and 14 was presumed to be incapable of committing a crime, but this presumption could be rebutted by proof of capacity. It is not completely settled what was required to prove capacity, though it is clear that the burden of production and persuasion was on the prosecutor. The prosecutor was probably required to prove beyond a reasonable doubt that the child fully appreciated the nature and consequences of any behavior and what it meant to say that it was wrong.

c. Over Fourteen
Children 14 and over were treated as fully capable of committing crimes.

d. Rape
There was also a special rule for rape. Boys under 14 could not be convicted of this offense. The rule was based on a presumed physical immaturity rather than an incapacity to make moral choices.

e. Statutory Revisions of Common Law Structure
Statutes in a number of States have modified the common law structure summarized above. Most have raised the minimum age of capacity from 7 to somewhere between 8 and 16. A few appear to permit proof of capacity for all children below a specified age, usually 14.

2. JUVENILE COURT LEGISLATION
Today, Juvenile Courts have jurisdiction over all crimes committed by children below a certain age, usually 18. There is a division of authority on whether age is determined at the time of the offense or the proceeding. If the child is between two determinative ages, typically 14 or 15 at one end of the scale and 18 at the other, the Juvenile Court is usually permitted—and for serious offenses sometimes required—to waive its jurisdiction and transfer the case to an adult court for trial. In some States, transfer is mandatory depending on the offense committed. In others, a transfer hearing is held by the Juvenile Court to determine the amenability of the youth to treatment by processes available only to the Juvenile Court.

C. INSANITY

The insanity defense operates in a constant tension. On the one hand there is the compelling moral argument that the insane are incapable of making the kinds of rational, intelligent choices upon which it is appropriate to visit the stigma and blame of a criminal conviction. In a word, the insane cannot be blamed for what they do. On the other hand, there is a wide range of practical difficulties in administering the defense, difficulties which have led some American jurisdictions to narrow its operation significantly and others to abolish the defense completely. Some of these difficulties are:

(1) People who are mentally disturbed can be dangerous and can pose a significant public safety risk.

(2) Psychiatrists and other mental health professionals work from a set of operating assumptions that are not subject to empirical verification. There is therefore enormous range for subjective interpretation of mental illness and its relation to behavior. This can lead to shopping for, or perhaps even the purchase of, favorable expert testimony. And there is the constant fear that the defense can be faked or gamed by strategic behavior.

(3) The primary function of the insanity defense is to separate the sick from the bad, to separate those who cannot morally be punished from those who deserve to be punished. Mental health professionals are not interested in this objective, and do not gear their learning to be able to perform it. Their job is diagnosis and cure.

(4) In the end, a criminal defendant is either guilty or not guilty. There is no in between. Yet mental disorders are widely spread along a continuum of degree. And it is difficult, if not impossible, to identify precisely where along the continuum responsibility ends and "insanity" begins.

(5) One can search for deep psychological and sociological explanations for all deviant behavior, and before one knows it can arrive at the view that no one is morally "responsible" in some fundamental sense for any crime. There are thus tough lines to be drawn, lest the defense undermine all criminal punishment.

It would be easy to imagine an insanity defense that would exonerate most, if not all, criminals. But this is not practical. Most people who commit crimes are blameworthy and deserve to be punished—or at least the criminal justice system must so assume in order to perform its function. Even though, in an important sense, "normal" people don't commit crimes, the insanity defense must identify persons who suffer from gross abnormalities that set them apart from the "normal" people who do commit crimes. The definition of the defense must walk a difficult line between the limits of moral responsibility and the demands of an orderly society, and must do so with tools that are both not designed for the job and inadequate to the purpose. It is no wonder that the insanity defense is difficult and controversial.

1. THE TRADITIONAL FORMULATIONS

There have been five major attempts to define an insanity defense. Each has two components: (1) that the defendant must have been suffering from a qualifying mental disease or defect; and (2) that the mental disease or defect must have had a prescribed relationship to the defendant's behavior.

a. Mental Disease or Defect

The meaning of the term "mental disease or defect" is clear at the extremes. On the one hand, it includes the range of psychotic disorders, namely those disorders which seriously affect the ability of a person to perceive reality. On the other hand, it does not include temporary emotional strain due to anger, panic, grief, or stress, nor does it include defects of character, background, or moral development. Most agree that a "psychopath" (also called a "sociopath," and now usually called a person suffering from an "anti-social personality disorder") does not have a qualifying "mental disease." A "psychopath" is one whose only abnormality is the repeated commission of crime or other anti-social acts.

But this is about all that is clear. There is not a body of well-developed law concerning what counts as a mental "disease or defect." Some have argued that only psychoses should be included, while others that any "abnormal condition" having a substantial effect on emotional processes should suffice. It is probable that only medically recognized diseases will qualify, though it is not sufficient standing alone that a group of symptoms has a medical name.

Whatever the scope of the concept, it is clear that the term "mental disease or defect" is not limited to observable or measurable physical deficiencies. This invariably introduces a range of subjectivity into a diagnosis, and is one of the major reasons why so much inconsistent testimony can be offered in the trial of an insanity defense.

One way to think about the mental disease or defect required for the insanity defense is to view it as a gateway—as a necessary door through which any defendant must walk in order to introduce evidence relevant to an insanity defense. That doorway can be narrow or wide, can be extremely restricted or virtually unconstrained, depending on the generosity of a particular jurisdiction towards the defense. The relation of the disease to the defendant's behavior— the next topic to be considered—can also be broadly or narrowly defined, but most trial lawyers will tell you that the critical step is to get through the door, to get the evidence of the impact of mental disorder before the jury. Once inside—once the defendant gets to put on the expert testimony—the result is more a matter of common sense and advocacy than of the application of formal rules. As a practical matter, therefore, the "mental disease or defect" requirement is the critical threshold over which the defendant must cross. Most defendants who can cross that threshold have at least a fighting chance of success in establishing the defense, no matter what the jury is told about the impact that the disease or defect must have had on the defendant's behavior.

b. Relation of Disease to Behavior

A "mental disease or defect" standing alone is not enough. The disease must somehow be related to the commission of the offense. What this relationship must be, or what effect the mental disease must have had on the defendant, forms the substance of the various approaches to the defense.

The insanity defense still used in many States, probably a substantial majority, was originally formulated by the House of Lords in England in an advisory opinion in Daniel M'Naghten's Case, 10 Cl. & F. 200, 8 Eng.Rep. 718 (H.L.1843). The result of the decision in that case was the so-called

"*M'Naghten* rules." These rules are supplemented in some States by the so-called "irresistible impulse" rule. As explained below, the *M'Naghten* rules also provide the basis for the approach now taken in the federal courts.

As an alternative to *M'Naghten* (with or without the irresistible impulse supplement), two jurisdictions—New Hampshire and the District of Columbia—have used a different inquiry, called the "product test." This test was later abandoned in the District of Columbia in favor of the formulation proposed in the Model Penal Code. The Model Penal Code insanity defense was used for a time in the District and in all other federal courts, and was also adopted in a number of States. At one time, it probably was the prevailing view around the country. But it was displaced in the federal courts by an Act of Congress adopted in 1984 and, following the federal lead, a number of States have abandoned it as well.

So in summary there have been five major formulae for the insanity defense in American jurisdictions: *M'Naghten*, "irresistible impulse," the product test, the Model Penal Code, and the 1984 federal statute. In order to preserve a sense of historical evolution, each of these approaches is described below, including (in a departure from the general format of this book) a discussion here of the Model Penal Code. This departure is justified because, in a very real sense, the Model Penal Code insanity defense became, at least for a time, part of the common law in many American jurisdictions.

c. **The *M'Naghten* Rules**

It is worth quoting the *M'Naghten* test as announced by the Court in 1843:

> "[E]very man is to be presumed to be sane. . . . [T]o establish a defence on the ground of insanity, it must be clearly proved that, at the time of the committing of the act, the party accused was labouring under such a defect of reason, from disease of the mind, as not to know the nature and quality of the act he was doing; or if he did know it, that he did not know he was doing what was wrong."

M'Naghten has two branches. Either is a complete defense. The questions are whether the defendant at the time of the offense as a result of mental disease or defect was unable to know:

(1) the nature and quality of the act committed; or

(2) whether the act was right or wrong.

Both branches state a "cognitive" inquiry, that is, an inquiry that focuses upon the ability of the defendant to "know" certain things. This is to be contrasted with the focus of the "irresistible impulse" formula on the defendant's "volitional" capacities, that is, on the ability of the defendant to exercise "control" over behavior.

1) **Rationale for First Branch**

The theoretical justification for the first or "nature and quality of the act" branch of the *M'Naghten* rules is related to why the law requires mens rea. Mens rea is a mental attitude—purpose, knowledge, recklessness, or negligence—towards the elements of behavior. One reason mens rea questions are asked is that they provide a basis for imposing blame. The assumption of the law is that a person who knows the nature of particular behavior, or knows or is indifferent to its risks, is in a position to make rational choices. Persons who make wrong choices are blameworthy and therefore punishable by the criminal law.

However, one who is *incapable* of knowing the nature of behavior is not in a position to make proper choices, and therefore cannot be "blamed" for having made a wrong choice. The first branch of *M'Naghten* builds on this idea. It exonerates the defendant who is incapable of having mens rea. This is why this particular characteristic of mental disease was selected in the *M'Naghten* formula.

Note that this branch of *M'Naghten* does not duplicate common law mens rea defenses that were otherwise available. It is true that one who is incapable of knowing the nature and quality of conduct by definition will lack any *subjective* mens rea required by the definition of a particular offense. But recall that evidence of mental disease or defect was not admissible at common law on the ordinary mens rea inquiry, and thus could not be introduced to establish a lack of subjective mens rea. See page 166. But even if such evidence *is* admissible on mens rea questions, as it is today in many jurisdictions, the first branch of *M'Naghten* is still not completely redundant under the common law system. Recall also that, for general intent offenses and for some elements of specific intent offenses, only a *reasonable* mistake of fact can be a defense and sometimes strict liability is imposed. See pages 148–54. And recall that only a *reasonable* belief can support a justification defense, like self defense. See page 194. Virtually by definition the bizarre perceptions of one who is incapable of knowing the nature and quality of conduct will not be "reasonable." Thus, there are cases at common law where the first branch of *M'Naghten* will provide a defense where the simple argument "the defendant lacked mens rea" is not available. Were the insanity defense not available, in other words, it is likely that most defendants who could claim it would otherwise have committed the actus reus and mens rea of one or more crimes. It is for this reason that the insanity defense is classified in this book as "collateral" to an effort simply to disprove the elements of an offense as set forth in its definition.

2) **Rationale for Second Branch**

The theoretical justification for the second or "right-wrong" branch of the *M'Naghten* rules is closely related to why the maxim "ignorance of the law is no excuse" is an acceptable moral premise of the criminal law. The assumption for a "normal" person is that once the person "knows" the nature and quality of an act then correct moral choices can be made. The process of socialization—the development of a normal social conscience— tells most of us that murder, rape, and theft are wrong. All we need to know in order to make the correct moral judgment is that proposed conduct would be of that nature.

This branch of the *M'Naghten* formula is aimed at excluding from criminal responsibility those whose moral signals do not work in the normal manner. A person who is incapable of understanding the idea that murder, rape, or theft is wrong is not a fit subject for criminal punishment. Such a person cannot be blameworthy in the sense that a "normal" person can.

The second branch of *M'Naghten,* then, exonerates one who is incapable of knowing the moral basis of the law and hence is unable to make correct moral choices.

Note that the second branch of *M'Naghten* makes the first unnecessary. The purpose of the first branch of the inquiry is to exclude from criminal liability persons who do not perceive the correct data on which to make moral judgments. Since these persons will necessarily be excluded by the second branch—they will not be able to tell right from wrong because of incorrect information—the first branch becomes superfluous. It is partly for this reason, as explained below, that the Model Penal Code did not continue the first branch of the *M'Naghten* inquiry.

3) **Meaning of "Unable to Know"**
The words "unable to know" in both branches of *M'Naghten* require complete incapacity. There is no in-between: the defendant is either capable of knowing the nature of the act or that it is wrong, or is incapable of doing so.

As one would expect, this aspect of *M'Naghten* has been severely criticized, since it ignores psychological reality. While there is a lot we do not know about psychiatric disorders, one thing we do know is that they are not matters of black and white but virtually indistinguishable shades of gray along a spectrum between the two extremes. Nonetheless, the *M'Naghten* inquiry asks whether the defendant was completely "incapable" of performing either of the two mental tasks on which the inquiry focuses.

4) **Meaning of "Know"**
There is a dispute as to what is meant by the word "know" in both branches of *M'Naghten*. At one extreme, "know" could refer to a purely intellectual or cognitive capacity, an ability to recognize sights and sounds and to identify things by their right names. A person who was incapable of "knowing" in this sense would not be able to pass a purely descriptive true-

false test. At the other extreme, "know" could refer to what has been called "affective" knowledge. This kind of "knowledge" is meant to encompass a full emotional appreciation of the significance of what one "knows." A person with "affective" knowledge is not only able to describe what is happening, but also able to recognize the full emotional impact of the description and to internalize and act upon information correctly perceived.

Consider a small child, say a four-year-old. Such a child might "know" that a pet has died in the sense of being able to identify the phenomenon, but it would be rare for a child that young to have a full emotional appreciation of what death means. Similarly, the child may "know" in an intellectual sense that it is wrong to do something, and yet completely lack an "affective" understanding of the moral and emotional consequences of doing it anyway.

Some have argued that only cognitive or intellectual knowledge ought to be required for the *M'Naghten* inquiries. Yet if the purpose is to identify a person who is blameless in the sense that incorrect data is being internalized on which moral choices can be made, surely more than the extreme cognitive or intellectual meaning should be required. But how much more, and whether full emotional appreciation is what should be encompassed, has not been clearly resolved.

5) Meaning of "Wrong"
The courts are divided on whether the reference to right and wrong in the second branch of *M'Naghten* is to an ability to know right from wrong in a moral sense or to know whether conduct is legally wrong in the sense that it violates the criminal law.

d. Irresistible Impulse
The "irresistible impulse" test focuses on a different relationship between mental illness and the defendant's behavior, namely whether the defendant was able to maintain self control. In jurisdictions that use this test, the jury is instructed on *both* "irresistible impulse" and *M'Naghten* and is thus given, in addition to the two branches of *M'Naghten*, a third basis for acquitting the defendant. Indeed, the "irresistible impulse" formulation is sometimes referred to as the "third branch" of *M'Naghten*. Keep in mind that in jurisdictions that use this approach, an acquittal is warranted if any one of the three branches is satisfied.

The name "irresistible impulse" is misleading, because the jury is normally not told that the defendant's conduct must have been the result of a sudden impulse that was irresistible. What the jury is usually told was put as follows in an early case, Parsons v. State, 81 Ala. 577, 2 So. 854 (1887):

"[Even if the defendant could tell the difference between right and wrong, the defendant should be acquitted] if, by reason of the duress of . . . mental disease, he had so far lost the *power to choose* between the right and the wrong, and to avoid doing the act in question, as that his free agency was at the time destroyed [and] the alleged crime was so connected with such mental disease, in the relation of cause and effect, as to have been the product of it *solely.*"

In contrast to the "cognitive" inquiry of *M'Naghten,* this formula focuses upon the "volitional" capacity of the defendant, namely the capacity to exercise will to make choices. It is often called a "control" or "volitional" test for this reason. Bear in mind that, like *M'Naghten,* acquittal is warranted only if the defendant totally lacks the relevant capacity, i.e., if the defendant has totally lost the "power to choose" so that "free agency was at the time [totally] destroyed."

1) Rationale for Control Inquiry

The theoretical justification for inquiring into the ability of the defendant to exercise the "power to choose" is closely related to why the law requires a "voluntary" act. It is also closely related to the theoretical justification for the two branches of *M'Naghten.* People are blamed for having made wrong choices, and the premise of blame is that they have the capacity to choose in the first place. This is why persons who do not engage in a voluntary act—those whose conduct is the result of convulsion or sleepwalking—are not blamed and punished. They plainly lacked the capacity to choose to do other than they did. Similarly, both branches of *M'Naghten* are based on characteristics that affect the capacity of the defendant to make proper moral choices. The defendant who cannot interpret reality or cannot make moral distinctions is not a fit subject for blame or punishment. If psychiatry has the capacity to identify a third class of the mentally ill—persons who know what they are doing and know that it is wrong, but who still do not have the capacity to choose not to do it—then, the argument goes, they should be exonerated on the same basis as those who fit into the first two classes. It should not matter *why* one lacks the power to make choices. The fact of a disability to make voluntary and free choices should be sufficient.

Although this argument indisputably states a correct moral proposition, the difficulty lies in its administration. The difficulty emerges at least at three levels.

(1) The first is whether such a class of people exists in the first place— whether indeed there are people who know full well what is going on and the right and wrong of it (in an affective sense?), but who nonetheless cannot refrain from the illegal act because they completely lack the power to choose not to do it. It is this latter question— whether they completely lack the power not to do it—on which disagreement will occur.

(2) Second, if such people do exist, do we have the ability to determine whether a particular defendant is one of those people? How do we tell

the difference between the person who *did not* choose and the person who *could not* choose to refrain from criminal behavior? How can we distinguish the impulse that is irresistible from the impulse that was not resisted? This is an imposing, if not impossible, task for the psychiatrist.

(3) Finally, there is the closely related question of how and whether we can differentiate on rational grounds people who fall within the excused class from many others—a drug addict who steals or kills to feed a habit, an economically deprived person whose environment did not socialize to typical middle-class values—who may be regarded as having a claim to exoneration but who are not, and never have been, immune from blame and punishment.

Indeed, one of the real challenges for the insanity defense, in whatever form, is how to keep the defense from overwhelming the criminal law. All criminals—not just some but all—will have some form of a diagnosable mental illness, particularly those who engage in the most serious and violent crimes. If we are not to excuse *all* on the ground of mental illness, we need a way of drawing lines between most criminals and the few for whom the insanity defense is warranted. This is a formidable task.

In any event, the "volitional" inquiry is designed to exclude from the criminal process those who lack control over their behavior due to mental illness. It goes considerably beyond the voluntary act defense, since that defense is limited to cases where the defendant suffers from observable physical (and not mental) disorder or was literally unconscious at the time of acting.

Note, finally, that it would be possible to collapse the separate "control" inquiry into the *M'Naghten* formula, and that this may be one reason why some States do not supplement *M'Naghten* with the "irresistible impulse" test. If "know" in the two branches of *M'Naghten* means full emotional understanding and appreciation of the nature of conduct and its moral implications, presumably that implies a capacity to act upon such knowledge. Conversely, the person who lacks the capacity to exercise free choice over behavior can perhaps be said to lack full emotional appreciation of the nature of conduct and its moral implications. Most courts do not, however, interpret *M'Naghten* so broadly, and hence either reject the "control" inquiry or adopt some version of a separate "irresistible impulse" test by that name or some other.

e. The "Product" Test

The "product" inquiry was adopted largely as a result of the criticisms of *M'Naghten* by Isaac Ray, a pioneer in the relation of psychiatry to criminal law who wrote in the mid-19th century. It rejects the focus of the insanity defense on the cognitive and volitional consequences of mental disease as too narrow and unrealistic. Instead, it asks simply whether the crime was a product of the mental disease, that is, whether it was caused by the mental disease.

The "product test" was first adopted in State v. Jones, 50 N.H. 369 (1871), as a substitute for *M'Naghten*. The *Jones* court formulated the inquiry as follows:

> "No man shall be held accountable, criminally, for an act which was the offspring and product of mental disease."

The product inquiry was adopted by the D.C. Circuit in Durham v. United States, 214 F.2d 862 (D.C.Cir.1954), and is often called the "Durham test" after that decision. The test was abandoned in the District of Columbia in favor of the Model Penal Code inquiry in United States v. Brawner, 471 F.2d 969 (D.C.Cir.1972). It has been used in no other American jurisdictions, and is of little practical importance today. It has been so widely rejected for at least two reasons:

(1) It is too broad. No expert can say that a person had a mental disease but that particular conduct was somehow not caused by or not a "product" of the disease. In effect, therefore, the "product" test collapses the entire inquiry into whether the defendant had a mental disease.

And the product inquiry is particularly unmanageable when combined with a broad test for what qualifies a "mental disease." In McDonald v. United States, 312 F.2d 847, 851 (D.C.Cir. 1962), the court supplemented *Durham* in the District of Columbia by defining "mental disease or defect" as "any abnormal condition of the mind which substantially affects mental or emotional processes and substantially impairs behavior controls." This broad definition led to what one critic called "unstructured clinical speculation" and probably was the major cause of the downfall of *Durham* and the adoption of the Model Penal Code insanity defense by the D.C. Circuit Court. The fear was of too many acquittals of persons who posed serious threats to the social order and who were "deserving" of criminal punishment.

(2) It ignores the traditional moral criteria upon which the criminal law is based, reflected in doctrines like mens rea and the requirement of a voluntary act. Blame and punishment are central to the criminal law, and centuries of effort have been devoted to the development of proper criteria for judgment. Most people believe that these criteria should be reflected in the test used for the insanity defense.

f.   Model Penal Code

The insanity defense is defined in § 4.01 of the Model Penal Code. For a time, § 4.01 was one of the most influential single provisions of the Model Code. Its approach had been adopted by decision in every federal Circuit and by statute or decision in a majority of the States. It came dramatically to public attention when used as the source of the insanity defense in the trial of John Hinckley for his attempt to assassinate President Reagan.

The controversy surrounding Hinckley's acquittal by reason of insanity led Congress in 1984 to replace the Model Penal Code formula in the federal courts. Since then, many States have followed suit. The influence of the Model Code on the insanity defense in the United States thus has substantially declined, though there still remain a number of jurisdictions in which its approach is followed.

1) Elements of the Defense

Section 4.01 is derived from the common law. In effect, it merges the *M'Naghten* and irresistible impulse rules and modernizes the language in which they are stated. Like the rules from which it is derived, the test has two parts: the defendant must have been suffering from a "mental disease or defect"; and there must have been a specified relationship between the disease and the defendant's behavior.

2) Mental Disease or Defect

The term "mental disease or defect" is not defined by the Model Penal Code. Section 4.01(2) does, however, exclude the psychopath (also called a "sociopath" or person with an "anti-social personality disorder"). An "abnormality manifested only by repeated criminal or otherwise anti-social conduct" hence is not a mental disease or defect. Section 2.08(3) also provides that intoxication in itself does not constitute a "mental disease or defect," although this does not exclude diseases which repeated intoxication may cause or to which it may contribute. Beyond this, however, we are not told what constitutes a mental disease or defect. The issue was deliberately left to judicial construction—and to modification from time to time as psychiatric expertise matures.

3) Relation of Disease to Behavior

The Model Penal Code formula has two branches. Either is a complete defense. The questions are whether the defendant at the time of the offense as a result of mental disease or defect lacked substantial capacity:

(1) "to appreciate the criminality [wrongfulness] of his conduct"; or

(2) "to conform his conduct to the requirements of law."

The first branch states a "cognitive" inquiry derived directly from the second or "right-wrong" branch of *M'Naghten*. The second branch states a "volitional" or "control" inquiry derived directly from the irresistible impulse formula.

a) Lacked Substantial Capacity

The words "lacks substantial capacity" in both branches of the Model Penal Code formulation are in direct contrast to the "total incapacity" required by *M'Naghten* and irresistible impulse. The Model Penal Code formula is designed to recognize that few who raise the defense will be totally sane or totally insane. Most people who suffer from mental illness fit on a spectrum of lesser or greater severity. A defense is provided by the Model Code when the defendant is "substantially" incapacitated from performing the mental and physical operations on which the inquiry focuses. The indeterminacy of the word "substantial" is said to be offset by the increased accuracy of the medical information it invites.

b) Rationale for Cognitive Branch

The rationale for this branch of the Model Penal Code formula is the same as for the analogous branch of *M'Naghten*: it exonerates the defendant who is "substantially" incapable of knowing the moral basis of the law and hence "substantially" unable to make correct moral choices. Note that the word "appreciate" is used rather than "know," suggesting that it is "affective" knowledge on which the inquiry should focus, that is, knowledge the emotional significance of which the defendant is able to assimilate and act upon. Indeed, "appreciate" when used in an insanity defense has become a code word signifying an "affective" approach to knowledge. Note also that placing the word "wrongfulness" in brackets is designed to leave resolution of the "legal or moral wrong" question to individual legislators and courts. See page 231.

c) Rationale for Omitting "Nature and Quality of Act" Branch

The Model Penal Code does not contain an analogous provision to the first or "nature and quality of act" branch of *M'Naghten*. Why? There are two reasons:

(1) This ground is covered by the portion of *M'Naghten* that is included. The purpose of the first branch of *M'Naghten* is to exclude from criminal liability persons who do not perceive reality accurately and hence do not have a sufficient factual basis for making correct legal or moral choices. One who "substantially lacks" this ability will also "substantially lack" the ability to appreciate the criminality [wrongfulness] of the acts committed. Hence the second branch of *M'Naghten* includes the first, and the first becomes unnecessary as a separate inquiry.

In other words, persons who can't perceive facts correctly won't be able to make correct legal or moral judgments. Their misperceptions of the facts will qualify them for the defense under the second branch of *M'Naghten*. They don't need the first branch.

(2) Defendants who lack the ability to know the nature and quality of conduct can raise a mistake defense under § 2.04(1)(a). Since evidence of mental disease or defect is admissible under § 4.02(1) whenever relevant to mens rea, it is unnecessary to provide a separate insanity defense focusing upon this deficiency.

In other words, defendants who claim that mental disease or defect robbed them of the ability to know the nature and quality of conduct can use that evidence to establish a mistake of fact. For the most part, and particularly given the subjective focus of culpability under the Model Penal Code, they don't need a separate insanity defense.

d) Rationale for Control Branch

The rationale for this portion of the Model Penal Code inquiry is the same as the rationale for the "irresistible impulse" rule. The premise for blame is the capacity to have chosen to do otherwise than one did, and one who substantially lacks the power of acting by voluntary and free choice—one who substantially lacks control over behavior—cannot be morally condemned and should not be regarded by the criminal law as a responsible person.

g. Federal Insanity Defense

In the 1970s and 1980s, an insanity defense to a criminal prosecution in a federal court came to be governed by the Model Penal Code formula. This result was achieved when each of the federal Circuit Courts, acting independently, settled on the Model Code as the best approach to the question.

Following John Hinckley's acquittal by reason of insanity for his attempt to assassinate President Reagan, Congress for the first time enacted an insanity defense. This statute, enacted in 1984 and codified at 18 U.S.C. § 17, reads as follows:

"§ 17. Insanity defense

"(a) Affirmative defense. It is an affirmative defense to a prosecution under any Federal statute that, at the time of the commission of the acts constituting the offense, the defendant, as a result of a severe mental disease or defect, was unable to appreciate the nature and quality or the wrongfulness of his acts. Mental disease or defect does not otherwise constitute a defense.

"(b) Burden of Proof. The defendant has the burden of proving the defense of insanity by clear and convincing evidence."

1) The Federal Standard

The federal insanity defense is important for a number of reasons. First, it supplied for the first time by legislation a federal statutory standard for prosecutions that take place in federal court. Second, and more importantly, it acted as a beacon for reform of the substantive content of the insanity defense. The reaction to John Hinckley's acquittal by reason of insanity led to a narrowing of the insanity defense in at least half of the States, most of them in one respect or another following the federal approach. The following features of the federal statute are worth separate comment:

a)   Elimination of the "Control" Inquiry

The most important change in the federal statute was the elimination of the "control" or "volitional" (the "irresistible impulse") inquiry. This followed the recommendation of the American Bar Association, the American Psychiatric Association, and the National Conference of Commissioners on Uniform State Laws, and has been copied in a number of States.

The major reason for the elimination of this branch of the insanity defense was its administrability, that is, doubts that psychiatry has the forensic ability to distinguish between persons who *did not* and persons who *could not* control their behavior.

b)   Return to the *M'Naghten* Formula

Without the control inquiry, the federal standard essentially is a return to the old *M'Naghten* rules. Note the two questions asked under the statute: the focus is on the defendant's perception of "the nature and quality or the wrongfulness of his acts." This parallels the first and second branches of *M'Naghten*.

There are four points to be noted about the relation of the federal formula to the original *M'Naghten* rules:

(1)   "Severe" Mental Disease or Defect

The mental disease or defect must be "severe." This may be a signal to the courts to limit the qualifying mental disorder to psychoses, or it may mean less than that. But in any event "severe" is a qualifying term that was absent from the old *M'Naghten* formula, and that indicates a desire by Congress to place a restrictive emphasis on the "mental disease or defect" requirement. Having said this, it should be noted that many have thought that *M'Naghten* itself was meant to incorporate a similarly narrow notion of a qualifying mental disease or defect.

(2)   "Unable" to Perceive the Nature or Wrongfulness of Acts

The defendant must, under the federal formula, be "unable" to engage in the mental operations described in the statutory test. This follows the "complete incapacity" requirement of the original *M'Naghten* rules. It departs from, and rather clearly was meant to reject, the "substantial capacity" requirement introduced by the Model Penal Code.

(3) "Appreciate" the Nature or Wrongfulness of Acts

The word "appreciate" in the federal standard implies an "affective" meaning of the knowledge or understanding required by the test for insanity. This might be taken to mean that more than psychosis is included within the concept of a "severe" mental disease, since other mental illnesses can have severe effects on a defendant's "affective" understanding of the nature of conduct or its wrongfulness. It might also undermine to some extent the elimination of the "control" inquiry, since a person who lacks the capacity to exercise free choice over behavior may also be said to lack full emotional appreciation of the nature of conduct and its moral implications.

Inclusion of the word "appreciate" in the federal standard may seen anomalous, and is likely to lead to interpretational difficulties. In most respects, the federal standard is a tightening of the insanity defense—examples are the elimination of the "control" inquiry, the addition of the "severe" mental disease requirement, a return to the "complete incapacity" position of the original rules, and shifting the burden of persuasion to the defendant. Yet the word "appreciate" opens doors to arguments about the nature of the defendant's disabilities that are as generous to the defense as any previous formulation.

On the other hand, it could be argued that complete rejection of any affective content in the notion of "know" would so narrow the defense as to make it meaningless. At the end of the day, the combination of a narrow gateway (a "severe" mental disease) and a broad sense of what it is that the defendant must not be able to "know" may be the best narrowing compromise short of abandoning the defense altogether. That is, it could well be regarded that the best realistic choice if one is to retain the insanity defense is between the broad Model Penal Code inquiry and the narrower but far from meaningless federal test.

(4) Mental Disease or Defect Not Otherwise a Defense

The second sentence of § 17(a) provides that "[m]ental disease or defect does not otherwise constitute a defense." One could take this to embrace the original common law position that evidence of mental disease or defect is *only* admissible when offered to support an insanity defense and in particular is not admissible on mens rea issues. Most federal courts that have addressed this issue have not, however, so concluded. In general, psychiatric evidence is admitted in federal courts on mens rea questions.

2) Ultimate Issue Testimony

At the same time that it enacted its new formula for the insanity defense, Congress added Rule 704(b) to the Federal Rules of Evidence. Rule 704 provides:

> "Rule 704. Opinion on Ultimate Issue
>
> "(a) Except as provided in subdivision (b), testimony in the form of an opinion or inference otherwise admissible is not objectionable because it embraces an ultimate issue to be decided by the trier of fact.
>
> "(b) No expert witness testifying with respect to the mental state or condition of a defendant in a criminal case may state an opinion or inference as to whether the defendant did or did not have the mental state or condition constituting an element of the crime charged or of a defense thereto. Such ultimate issues are matters for the trier of fact alone."

Rule 704(b) forecloses expert opinion on the "ultimate" legal issues raised by an insanity defense, that is, the expert may not offer a conclusion as to whether the defendant's mental disease was in fact "severe" or whether the defendant was "unable" to "appreciate" the "nature and quality or the wrongfulness of his acts." The expert is thus limited in theory to diagnostic statements of a medical nature.

Enforcement of this limitation is difficult in practice, however, since defense attorneys try to get as close to the line as the trial judge will permit. As a practical matter, moreover, the defense strategy in insanity cases is to get as much evidence about the defendant's mental history before the jury as possible. The prosecutor is in a bit of a box too. The more prosecutors seek to exclude evidence on grounds of relevance to the narrow federal standard, the more the expert testimony is likely to sound like testimony on the "ultimate" legal issues.

Notice that the exclusion of Rule 704(b) also applies to whether the defendant has or does not have a mental state or condition "constituting an element of the crime charged. . . . " This language seems to imply that evidence of mental disease or defect *is* admissible (though testimony on the ultimate issue is not) on the mens rea components of a federal crime. This casts further doubt on the meaning of the second sentence of § 17(a).

2. TRIAL OF THE INSANITY DEFENSE

Normally both sides use expert witnesses in the trial of an insanity defense. Experts are not required, however, and it is permissible to rely partly or exclusively on lay witnesses who can testify about the defendant's conduct and demeanor. It is also typical for the defendant to take the stand.

a. Burden of Production

The burden of production on the insanity defense is on the defendant. In some jurisdictions, moreover, the defendant must give notice prior to trial of an intention to raise the insanity defense in order to give the prosecutor time to prepare.

b. Bifurcated Trial

In a few States, cases involving an insanity defense are required to be tried in two stages. In other States two trials are required if the defendant so requests, and in still others it is up to the trial judge whether to hold one trial or two.

The first trial, on "guilt or innocence," concerns whether the defendant committed all of the actus reus and mens rea elements of the offense, as well as whether any traditional defenses other than insanity (self defense, duress, entrapment) can be established. If the defendant is found "guilty" at this first trial, then a second "insanity" trial is held before the same jury at which evidence on the insanity defense is presented and the question of sanity is determined.

One difficult question that has arisen is whether evidence of mental disease can be offered on mens rea issues at the first trial. Plainly it can be relevant. It can also mean that the expert testimony becomes awkward, for the same diagnoses can lead to some characteristics that are relevant at the first trial and others that are relevant at the second. Some courts have resolved this question by admitting evidence of mental disease at both trials. Other courts have refused to allow any evidence of mental disease at the first trial.

c. Burden of Persuasion

Until recently, the States were about evenly divided on the allocation of the burden of persuasion on the insanity defense. In about half, the burden was on the prosecution to disprove the defense beyond a reasonable doubt. This rule was also followed in federal criminal prosecutions. In the remaining States, the defendant had the burden to establish the defense by a preponderance of the evidence.

Allocation of the burden of persuasion for the insanity defense is now tilted in favor of requiring the defendant to establish the defense. The change was begun in 1984 with the enactment of the current federal insanity defense. It is provided in 18 U.S.C. § 17(b) that the defendant must establish the defense by "clear and convincing evidence." Many States have followed the lead of the federal government in shifting the burden of persuasion to the defendant, but in most the "preponderance of the evidence" standard is used.

The Supreme Court has upheld the constitutionality of requiring the defendant to establish the defense rather than requiring the prosecutor to disprove it. Indeed, it has even upheld a requirement that the defendant bear the burden of proving the defense *beyond a reasonable doubt.* See Rivera v. Delaware, 429 U.S. 877, 97 S.Ct. 226 (1976); Leland v. Oregon, 343 U.S. 790, 72 S.Ct. 1002 (1952).

d. Verdict

At the close of the evidence, the jury is given the option of several verdicts depending upon its findings:

1) Traditional Verdict Options

Typically, the jury is given three verdict options in a criminal trial involving an insanity defense: Guilty, Not Guilty, or Not Guilty by Reason of Insanity. The jury is ordinarily told that it should not address the insanity defense until it is satisfied beyond a reasonable doubt that all other elements of the crime exist—that in effect the defendant would be guilty but for the insanity defense. The rationale for so informing the jury is that the normal effect of an insanity acquittal is commitment of the defendant, a commitment that could not be justified unless there was at least a finding that the defendant committed the criminal act. The prevailing view, on the other hand, is not to tell the jury that commitment will ordinarily follow an acquittal by reason of insanity.

2) Guilty But Mentally Ill

In recent years, a number of States have added a fourth verdict option: "Guilty But Mentally Ill." This verdict means that the jury has found the defendant guilty of the crime and has rejected the insanity defense, but that the jury nonetheless believes the defendant is mentally ill and should receive psychiatric treatment. Generally speaking, whether a defendant is "mentally ill" for purposes of this verdict is determined by a less stringent standard than the test in use in the particular jurisdiction for the insanity defense. And when the verdict is returned, it is usually discretionary with the trial judge, after psychiatric evaluation of the defendant and a hearing, what, if any, psychiatric treatment will be ordered. The defendant is in any event given a criminal sentence to be served either in prison if no treatment is ordered, or in an appropriate psychiatric facility if there is to be treatment.

Proponents of this verdict argue that it will facilitate treatment of disturbed criminals. Critics respond that treatment is still discretionary, that treatment can be obtained anyway at the initiative of either the judge or prison officials, and that the verdict is a transparent attempt to invite the jury to compromise the insanity defense—in effect an effort to invite a "guilty but mentally ill" verdict in cases where an insanity acquittal should be returned on the merits. The critics thus conclude that the verdict is a none-too-subtle effort by those who are opposed to the insanity defense to limit its operation.

3. EFFECT OF INSANITY ACQUITTAL

Traditionally, the effect of acquittal on grounds of insanity has been automatic commitment of the defendant in a psychiatric institution and release from that commitment only after it has been found that the defendant has been "cured." Some States still follow this procedure, although it has come under increasing constitutional attack on equal protection and due process grounds.

In most States today, some additional proceeding must be held before the defendant can be committed. Normally what happens is that the defendant is immediately committed for evaluation, often for up to 90 days. At the conclusion of the evaluation, a hearing is held at which the commitment decision is made, often under the same standards as would be applicable to a person sought to be civilly committed. If the defendant is then committed, the duration of the commitment is typically indefinite, even if the defendant had been originally charged with a crime that would permit only a short sentence. See Jones v. United States, 463 U.S. 354, 103 S.Ct. 3043 (1983) (offense charged carried one-year maximum; indefinite commitment upheld following insanity acquittal). Discharge of the defendant, moreover, is typically permitted only by judicial order following a hearing initiated by the custodial authorities or sought, at periodic intervals, by the defendant. A defendant who seeks discharge typically must bear the burden of showing— sometimes beyond a reasonable doubt—no need for further commitment under the prevailing civil commitment standards.

Provisions on the disposition of a person acquitted by reason of insanity and other related matters were added to the federal law in 18 U.S.C. §§ 4242–47 at the same time the insanity defense itself was modified in 1984. Three verdict options are provided: "guilty," "not guilty," and "not guilty by reason of insanity." 18 U.S.C. § 4242(b). Section 4243 adds that a person acquitted by reason of insanity will be committed for observation, and that a hearing will be held within 40 days. If the offense involved "bodily injury to, or serious damage to the property of, another person, or . . . a substantial risk of such injury or damage," then commitment will follow unless *the defendant* proves by clear and convincing evidence "that his release would not create a substantial risk of bodily injury to another person or serious damage to property of another due to a present mental disease or defect." For any other offense, the defendant must disprove the same standard by a preponderance of the evidence. If the defendant is committed, discharge is permitted only after a court hearing on motion of the director of the detention facility. The standard for release at such a hearing is the same as for the initial commitment.

4. EFFORTS TO RESTRICT OR ABOLISH INSANITY DEFENSE

The insanity defense has always been controversial, and from time to time efforts to restrict its operation, or even to abolish it, have been undertaken in various jurisdictions. Frequently these efforts have been in response to a visible and controversial insanity acquittal such as occurred at the trial of John Hinckley for attempting to assassinate President Reagan. There have been four major proposals:

a. Consider Only at Sentencing

Some have suggested that evidence of mental disease should not be admitted at the trial on guilt, but should be considered only at sentencing. This scheme was enacted in Washington in 1909, but held unconstitutional in 1910. State v. Strasburg, 60 Wash. 106, 110 P. 1020 (1910). It has not been adopted in any other State.

b. Consider Only on Mens Rea Issues

A small number of States have "abolished" the insanity defense, that is, they do not permit the defendant to raise a separate insanity defense. These States do, however, admit evidence of mental disease or defect to the extent that it is relevant to issues of mens rea.

c. Verdict of Guilty but Mentally Ill

Some States have introduced an additional verdict which critics believe is an effort to reduce the number of insanity acquittals. See page 242.

d. Eliminate Control Inquiry

A fourth proposal, which received a considerable boost by the Hinckley acquittal, is to abolish the "control test" in those jurisdictions in which it is in use. The basis for this view, essentially, is that psychiatry is unable to detect instances of volitional impairment that justify exoneration from crime—that psychiatry cannot distinguish those who cannot control themselves from those who will not do so.

Arguments for and against these propositions come down in the end to various considerations of ethics and social control. Those who like the insanity defense in one form or another argue that it is an essential ethical postulate of the criminal law. It is intolerable, they argue, to treat the sick as though they were bad. The ethical integrity of the criminal law demands an insanity defense that is focused upon appropriate criteria for making a moral assessment of fault, responsibility, and blame. Those who don't like the defense, or who argue for one restriction or another, usually start by emphasizing the danger posed by mentally disturbed people who engage in criminal behavior and the need to punish those who commit egregious social harms. They also point to the practical inability of psychiatry—indeed its disinterest, since the business of medicine is to cure not to judge—to identify those who should not be blamed.

5. NOTE ON DIMINISHED RESPONSIBILITY

The term "diminished responsibility," or its synonym "diminished capacity," refers to three quite different ideas. All, however, are concerned with the admissibility of evidence of mental disease on issues other than the insanity defense. These three ideas are identified and discussed under the heading "Diminished Responsibility Defined" at pages 165–66.

D. INVOLUNTARY INTOXICATION

Recall the prior treatment of the admissibility of evidence of intoxication to negate mens rea. See page 163. The term "involuntary" intoxication was there defined, and it was noted that under some circumstances involuntary intoxication could be a defense to a crime. But discussion of the content of that defense was postponed. The reason was that the content of the defense is closely tied to the insanity defense. In fact, the law is quite simple:

> Involuntary intoxication is a defense if it causes precisely the same conditions as are required by the insanity defense in the jurisdiction in question.

Thus, in a *M'Naghten* jurisdiction, involuntary intoxication is a defense if, as a result, the defendant was unable to know the nature and quality of the act committed or that it was wrong. The involuntary intoxication in effect substitutes for the "mental disease or defect" in the formulation of the insanity defense, and the rest of the insanity defense then governs.

E. DURESS

The law recognizes a separate defense of duress, although its rationale and hence its limits are a continuing source of debate. The defense is sometimes called "coercion" or "compulsion."

As discussed below, duress may or may not be closely related to the defense of necessity or choice of evils. However, it is definitely distinct from the involuntary act defense: The involuntary act defense is available when the defendant has made no choice—when the defendant is unconscious or unable to exercise physical control. The duress defense is available when the defendant is put to a hard choice—when the defendant must choose between committing an offense and an unpleasant consequence.

1. ELEMENTS OF THE DEFENSE
The elements of the traditional duress defense are:

a. Coercion by Another Person
Duress is a defense only if the defendant is coerced by another person. Coercion by circumstances or an event does not count.

b. Threat of Imminent Death or Serious Bodily Harm
The coercion must be a threat of imminent death or serious bodily injury to the defendant *or* to another.

c. Reasonable Person Would Have Been Coerced
The coercion must be such that a reasonable person in the defendant's situation would have been unable to resist committing the crime. It follows from this requirement that there must have been no readily available and reasonable alternative to committing the offense.

d. Defendant Not at Fault
The defendant must not have willingly participated in creating a situation where duress is likely. For example, a person who joins a conspiracy to buy

and sell illegal drugs will have no duress defense if later coerced by a co-conspirator to commit a crime that promotes the objectives of the conspiracy.

e. Intentional Killing

Duress is not a defense if the defendant intentionally kills another person. But it could be a defense to a murder charge framed on another theory, or to a lesser criminal homicide. For example, a defendant who has a valid duress defense to the underlying felony would not be convicted of felony murder. Nor would a defendant who was coerced into behaving recklessly be guilty of manslaughter so long as all of the elements of the duress defense are satisfied. Moreover, in a small number of States an intentional killing will be reduced from murder to manslaughter if duress can be proved.

f. Wife Presumed Coerced by Husband

Originally at common law, a wife was presumed to have been coerced if she committed a crime in the presence of her husband. This rule has long since been discarded by most States, but perhaps not yet by all.

g. Special Statutes

The definition of the defense of duress is different in some States by statute. For example, some States do not permit duress to be a defense to a specified list of serious crimes. Others require that the threat be to injure the defendant and no other person, while some specify that only threats to injure the defendant or a family member will be sufficient.

2. GUILT OF PERSON WHO COERCES

In situations where a successful duress defense can be asserted, it ought to be the case, and probably is in most jurisdictions, that the person who coerced the defendant is guilty of the crime as a principal in the first degree, as one who has caused an "innocent agent" to commit the offense. See pages 262–63.

3. RATIONALE OF DEFENSE

There is a dispute in the cases and the literature about the rationale for the defense.

a. Justification

Some argue that duress is a species of justification, a specific example of necessity or choice of evils. If this is so, the rationale for the defense is that it is better for the defendant to cause a lesser harm than a greater one—better, for example, to steal the money than let your child be killed. This rationale precludes assertion of the defense in cases where a greater harm will be caused by acting than will be caused if the threatened coercion is carried out. It also argues for broadening the defense to situations where less than deadly force is the instrument of coercion. So long as the defendant produces a net social good, why shouldn't any force suffice? Note, however, that the duress defense seems redundant if choice of evils is the underlying rationale. Why, then, is a separate defense required? Why can't the "necessity" defense do the job? The answer can only be that specific limitations are regarded as desirable where physical coercion is used, though it is difficult to see why physical coercion should be different from necessity arising from natural causes. Of course all this assumes that the jurisdiction in question recognizes a general necessity defense, something that is not always entirely clear.

b. Excuse

Others argue that the necessity defense can indeed take care of all choice of evils situations and that duress should be designed for something else, namely the case where a greater harm would be caused if the defendant acted but the defendant cannot fairly be blamed for succumbing to extreme coercive pressure. As it was put in an English study of the question, if the law punished in this situation "it would be making excessive demands on human nature and imposing penalties in circumstances where they are unjustified as retribution and irrelevant as a deterrent." Note that this rationale gives a distinctive purpose to the duress defense, and justifies the limitation to extreme coercive pressure. If the defense is to be available when giving in to the coercion will cause a greater harm than would be caused if the coercion is resisted, then it is in the interest of the law to encourage the defendant to resist. And one can expect most people to resist coercive pressure in the face of minor threats designed to coerce the defendant into doing serious harm.

Examples: Assume that *A* wants *B* to rob a bank, but *B* says "no." *A* then says to *B*, "Rob the bank or I'll (a) cry, (b) expose some secret about your private life, (c) break your arm, (d) shoot your child." In which cases should *A* be given a defense, and on what rationale should it be granted or denied?

Plainly *A* should have no defense in either situations (a) or (b), no matter the rationale for duress. *Justification*: Obviously a greater evil will be caused by acting than by suffering the consequences of the threat. *Excuse*: The law can expect deterrence to work in these situations, that is, it can expect (or demand) that reasonable people will resist the coercion and not commit the crime.

A defense should be provided in case (d), probably under either rationale. *Justification:* A greater evil is most likely avoided if *A* robs the bank, although more than one life may be endangered if *A* does so and perhaps the defense should be denied for this reason. *Excuse:* One would expect a reasonable person—you or me—to succumb to this kind of pressure. It would be unfair to punish *A* in this situation.

But what about case (c)? It is difficult under either rationale, but the rationale that is chosen helps in thinking through whether the defense should be provided.

c. **Ethical Gaps in the Law?**
Note that either rationale for the duress defense arguably leaves an ethical gap in the law.

1) **Justification**
If the justification rationale is chosen, then a defense is given if the harm avoided exceeded the harm caused and a defense is denied if the harm caused exceeded the harm avoided. This means that defendants can be criminally punished in situations where (a) a greater harm is caused but (b) any one of us, all presumably reasonable people, would have done the same thing. This result has been defended on two grounds:

(1) that virtually all cases where a defense should be given will involve situations where the evil avoided will be greater than the evil caused; and

(2) that persons who are put to hard choices should be encouraged to do the right thing—to cause the lesser harm.

2) **Excuse**
Even if the excuse rationale is chosen, defendants can still be criminally punished in some situations where any one of us, all presumably reasonable people, would have done the same thing. A necessity defense is given in any case where the harm avoided exceeded the harm caused. But a duress defense is given only where a *human agent* coerces another into causing more harm than would be avoided by not acting. No defense is provided where *natural forces* exercise a coercive pressure on an individual to cause more harm than would be avoided, even if the alternative is death and even if most of us would have avoided death by causing the greater harm. This result can be defended on the ground that it will rarely occur, but it is hard to see how to defend it in principle.

F. ENTRAPMENT

The defense of entrapment concerns situations where police unfairly invite or encourage the commission of crime. There is an unresolved disagreement as to its rationale and content.

1. COMPETING RATIONALES
The starting point is that there is nothing inherently wrong with police undercover work nor with police providing the opportunity for persons to commit crime who are ready and willing to do so. But plainly, on the other hand, it is not the function of the police to plan criminal offenses and then go out and find people to commit them. The purpose of the entrapment defense is to protect innocent people from being enticed by overreaching police behavior into the commission of crimes they would not otherwise commit. The question is how this purpose can best be implemented.

a. Subjective Inquiry

One view is that it is the defendant's character and predisposition that ought to be on trial. The theory is that the legislature did not mean to convict otherwise innocent persons who were enticed into the commission of crime by government agents and that this limitation, in effect, is an implied exception to the criminal statute sought to be enforced. On this view, the defense of entrapment requires, first, that the idea of committing the crime originate with the police and, second, that the defendant be an "innocent" person who would not have committed the crime anyway. Note that the first requirement cannot alone be sufficient, for it would outlaw "sting" operations, police purchases of narcotics, police delivery of a bribe, and other similar operations that in many contexts are regarded as proper police tactics—indeed necessary police tactics in the enforcement of crimes where there is no obvious victim or the victim is unlikely to complain. It is thus the combination of police instigation and defendant innocence that provides the rationale for the defense.

This is sometimes called the "subjective" view of entrapment. It is the view adopted by the United States Supreme Court for the federal courts. And it is the view currently in use by most States. Two important consequences flow from this view of the defense:

1) Defendant's Predisposition in Issue

Since the "subjective" approach focuses on whether the defendant is likely otherwise to have committed the offense, one of the principal issues it raises is the defendant's predisposition. The prosecutor is able to rebut an entrapment defense in jurisdictions that follow this view by offering evidence of the defendant's character, reputation, and prior criminal record, evidence that normally is inadmissible in a criminal case because it creates the risk that it will prejudice the jury.

2) Trial to Jury

It follows from this view of entrapment that the issues raised should be tried to the jury. The central question is the defendant's innocent disposition. This raises a question of fact about the particular defendant's guilt or innocence, not unlike others that are typically resolved by the jury.

b. Objective Inquiry

The competing view is that the police behavior should be on trial. The theory here is that it violates public policy to permit convictions based on outrageous police practices, and that the question should be whether the police have exceeded the bounds of proper investigative techniques. The defense of entrapment, on this view, again should require that the idea of committing the crime originate with the police, but this time should focus on whether the police behavior is likely to have enticed an innocent person to commit an offense.

This is sometimes called the "objective" view of entrapment. It asks not whether the particular defendant before the court is likely to have committed the offense anyway, but whether the average, innocent person would likely have been persuaded to commit the offense by the police tactics. This view of entrapment is followed by a substantial minority of the States.

1)   Defendant's Predisposition Inadmissible
By contrast to the "subjective" view, the defendant's character and predisposition are inadmissible under this approach.

2)   Trial to Court
And trial of entrapment is to the court, not the jury. The issue is usually raised by a motion to dismiss or some analogous pre-trial procedure.

2.   GENERAL LIMITATIONS

Whichever view of entrapment is followed, there are several points on which all jurisdictions seem to agree.

a.   Serious Crimes Excluded

The defense is normally raised in cases where there is no obvious victim or where the victim is unlikely to complain—offenses involving liquor, narcotics, prostitution, gambling, bribery, obscenity, and the like. It is probable that the defense would be rejected if raised to a crime of violence, although the issue has rarely been litigated.

b.   Burden of Proof

Normally, both the burden of production and the burden of persuasion are on the defendant. The burden of persuasion on factual issues is by a preponderance of the evidence.

c.   Limitation to Law Enforcement Agents

The defense applies only to entrapment perpetrated by a law enforcement officer or a person who at the time is working for law enforcement. Thus, the defense could be based upon the actions of a paid informant, but not upon the actions of a private citizen, no matter how outrageous the citizen's behavior.

One might question whether this limitation is consistent with either rationale for the defense. If its ultimate purpose is to protect against the conviction of "innocent" people—people who absent unusual pressures would not have committed the offense—then it arguably should not matter whether it was the police or someone else who applied the pressure.

3.   CONSTITUTIONAL STATUS

It is occasionally argued that entrapment should be recognized as a constitutional limitation on proper law enforcement. The Supreme Court has, however, consistently rejected this contention. See, e.g., Hampton v. United States, 425 U.S. 484, 96 S.Ct. 1646 (1976); United States v. Russell, 411 U.S. 423, 93 S.Ct. 1637

(1973). The Court has, on the other hand, recognized the possibility that police conduct could be so outrageous that a violation of due process would be found. But no such case has yet reached the Court.

G.   REVIEW QUESTIONS

[Answers Provided in Appendix A, page 436]

1. T or F   A child of eight was incapable of committing a crime under the common law rule.

2. T or F   The meaning of the term "mental disease or defect" as used in the insanity defense is not well defined. It is clear, however, that a psychopath has a qualifying disease.

3. T or F   The *M'Naghten* rules include a cognitive branch and a volitional branch.

4. T or F   Some States have rejected the *M'Naghten* rules in favor of the "irresistible impulse" formula.

5. T or F   The "product test" can be stated as follows: a person accused of crime is not guilty by reason of insanity if the power to choose between right and wrong has been destroyed by a mental disease or defect, and if the crime is the sole product of such a disease.

6. T or F   By constitutional compulsion, the burden of persuasion must be on the prosecution to disprove an insanity defense beyond a reasonable doubt.

7. T or F   The Model Penal Code insanity defense contains a cognitive branch and a volitional branch.

8. T or F   The term "mental disease or defect" is carefully defined in the Model Penal Code insanity defense to include psychoses and other medically recognized emotional disorders that affect reality perception and the capacity to exercise control.

9. T or F   The focus of the Model Penal Code insanity defense on persons who lack "substantial" capacity to meet the criteria of the defense is an improvement on the common law because it does a better job of recognizing medical reality.

10. T or F   The Model Penal Code insanity defense is a sophisticated and modernized restatement of the common law approach reflected in the *M'Naghten* and irresistible impulse rules.

11. T or F   The "nature and quality of act" branch of *M'Naghten* is restated in a more sophisticated and modernized manner in the Model Penal Code test for insanity.

12. T or F Involuntary intoxication is a defense if the defendant meets the same standards established by the insanity defense in the jurisdiction in question.

13. T or F The defense of duress protects against offenses committed as a result of coercive pressure exerted by people or by natural forces.

14. T or F The federal courts follow the "objective" view of entrapment, by which it is not the guilt or innocence of the particular defendant that is at issue but whether the police tactics were so overreaching as to have been likely to persuade an otherwise innocent citizen to commit the offense.

15. Why, over the years, have the *M'Naghten* and irresistible impulse formulas been more popular than the *Durham* or "product" test for the insanity defense? Explain your answer briefly.

16. At one point, the Model Penal Code formula for the insanity defense had been adopted in over half the States and in all federal courts. Many people must have thought that it was an improvement over the traditional approach to the insanity defense. Is it? Why was it later abandoned in the federal courts and many States? Explain your answer, with explicit attention to arguments likely to be raised by those who disagree with you.

IX

THE MODEL PENAL CODE

Analysis

A. INTRODUCTION

Each of the common law "excuses" is continued in the Model Penal Code. Infancy and insanity are defined in Article 4 under the heading "Responsibility." Involuntary intoxication, duress, and entrapment are defined in Article 2.

B. INFANCY

The defense of infancy, called "immaturity" in the Model Penal Code, is contained in § 4.10. Section 4.10(1) abandons the age-of-capacity structure of the common law and establishes 16 as the minimum age for the commission of a crime. No one who is less than 16 at the time of the act can be convicted of a crime. The Model Penal Code does not establish a Juvenile Court system, but it assumes that one exists or will be created. On that assumption, anyone less than 16 who engages in criminal behavior will be dealt with by the Juvenile Courts. And persons between 16 and 18 will be dealt with by the Juvenile Courts unless jurisdiction is waived to an adult court. Persons 18 and over will be tried as adults.

C. INSANITY

The Model Penal Code provision on insanity, contained in § 4.01, is discussed in connection with the common law insanity defenses on pages 234–37. Since it is so closely derived from the common law, and since the common law both embraced the Model Code insanity defense and, in substantial measure, has now backed away from it, study of its provisions is best undertaken in the context of study of the other common law insanity tests.

1. ELEMENTS OF THE DEFENSE
See pages 234–37.

2. TRIAL OF THE INSANITY DEFENSE
The Model Penal Code contains provisions on how the insanity defense shall be tried.

a. Burden of Production
Insanity is an affirmative defense under the Model Penal Code. This puts the burden of production on the defendant. See §§ 4.03(1) and 1.12(2)(a). Note, moreover, that under § 4.03(2) the defendant must give prior notice to the prosecutor before an insanity plea is entered. This is in order to give the prosecutor an opportunity to marshal a psychiatric case before trial. See §§ 4.05 and 4.07.

b. Burden of Persuasion
The burden of persuasion on the insanity defense under the Model Penal Code is on the prosecutor. The prosecutor must negate the defense beyond a reasonable doubt. See §§ 1.12(1) and 1.13(9)(c).

c. **Verdict**

Section 4.03(3) provides that the verdict and judgment shall so state when an acquittal is based on insanity. Under the Model Penal Code, therefore, the jury must be given three verdict options: guilty, not guilty, and not guilty by reason of insanity.

3. EFFECT OF INSANITY ACQUITTAL

The Model Penal Code requires mandatory commitment following acquittal on the basis of insanity. See § 4.08(1). Procedures for release from confinement are detailed by the remainder of § 4.08.

4. NOTE ON DIMINISHED RESPONSIBILITY

The terms "diminished responsibility" or "diminished capacity" are defined on pages 165–66. They are not used by the Model Penal Code, although the Model Code does address the three ideas they encompass:

(1) It permits evidence of mental disease or defect to be freely introduced on questions of mens rea. See § 4.02(1) and page 183.

(2) Such evidence may also be admissible to reduce a charge of murder to manslaughter. See § 210.3(1)(b) and the discussion of that section at page 379.

(3) And such evidence is admissible on the question of capital punishment. See §§ 4.02(2), 210.6(1)(e), 210.6(4)(b), and 210.6(4)(g). This question is discussed further at page 381.

D. INVOLUNTARY INTOXICATION

The Model Penal Code follows the common law approach to the defense of involuntary intoxication, though it does not use the term. The terms it uses are "self-induced" intoxication and "pathological" intoxication, which are defined in §§ 2.08(5)(b) and 2.08(5)(c). See the discussion at page 181. Section 2.08(4) provides that intoxication which is not self-induced or which is pathological is a defense if the standards of the insanity defense (§ 4.01(1)) are met.

E. DURESS

A defense of duress is provided by § 2.09.

1. RELATIONSHIP BETWEEN DURESS AND NECESSITY

Section 2.09(4) provides that § 2.09 does not by negative implication limit any defense that would be available under § 3.02. This means that the defendant may rely on the general choice of evils defense even though acting pursuant to the coercion of another person. Thus, if *A* tells *B* to "steal the money or I'll shoot your children," *B* could rely on a choice of evils defense under § 3.02 since stealing the money would be a lesser harm than the death of *B's* children.

Section 2.09, on the other hand, is based on an "excuse" rationale. See pages 246–48. It is premised on the view that extreme coercion may compel persons to do things that would not be justified by the choice of evils defense, but that may be excusable on the ground that a person of reasonable firmness would have succumbed to the pressure.

2. ELEMENTS OF THE DEFENSE

In order to facilitate comparison, the headings used to describe the common law defense will be repeated.

a. Coercion by Another Person

Section 2.09(1) does not explicitly say that the coercion must be applied by another person. But only people can use or threaten to use "unlawful" force. Coercion by another person is thus required by necessary implication.

b. Threat of Imminent Death or Serious Bodily Harm

Section 2.09(1) does not limit the required coercion to threats of death or serious bodily harm. Any "unlawful" use or threat of force will do, so long as it is directed to the person of the defendant *or another* and is force "which a person of reasonable firmness in [the defendant's] situation would have been unable to resist." Note that a threat to harm property will not suffice.

c. Reasonable Person Would Have Been Coerced

Like the common law, § 2.09(1) measures the defendant's capacity to resist the coercion against the standard of the reasonable person in the defendant's situation. The Model Code's wording in this respect is force "which a person of reasonable firmness in the defendant's situation would have been unable to resist."

d. Defendant Not at Fault

Section 2.09(2) denies the defense in situations where the defendant "recklessly placed himself in a situation in which it was probable that he would be subjected to duress." Note that the defense is denied even if the prosecution is for an offense that requires a culpability of purpose or knowledge. This provision thus departs from the general principle of the Model Code reflected in §§ 3.02(2) and 3.09(2). See pages 217–18 and 208. Note, however, that the general principle is adhered to in the case of negligence. Negligently placing oneself in a situation where duress might be imposed results in denial of the defense only where negligence is the culpability for the offense charged.

e. Intentional Killing

No offense is excluded from the coverage of § 2.09. Obviously, however, it would take a great deal more coercion to cause a "person of reasonable firmness" to kill than to commit some lesser offense.

f. Wife Presumed Coerced by Husband

Section 2.09(3) abolishes any special "husband-wife" rules in this context. Abolition of the common law presumption is in brackets because most States can be expected to have already abolished the presumption. Such a provision would be unnecessary in those States.

3. GUILT OF PERSON WHO COERCES

A person who causes another to commit an offense by duress would be guilty of committing that offense under § 2.06(2)(a).

4. RATIONALE OF DEFENSE

As noted above, § 2.09 is based on an "excuse" rationale rather than a "justification" rationale. These rationales are elaborated at pages 246–48. Note, moreover, that the "ethical gap" discussed in the context of excuses on page 248 exists under the Model Penal Code. Section 3.02 provides a defense in any choice of evils situation. And § 2.09 provides a defense in cases where a *human agent* causes a reasonable person to produce a greater harm than would occur if the threat were carried out. But there is no defense where *natural forces* cause a reasonable person to produce more harm than would occur if the forces were allowed to have their natural effect.

F. ENTRAPMENT

A defense of entrapment is provided by § 2.13.

1. RATIONALE

Section 2.13 follows the "objective" view described on pages 249–50. Note that § 2.13(2) specifically provides that the entrapment issue shall be tried to the court and not the jury. And implementation of the standard stated in § 2.13(1)(b) would make evidence of the defendant's predisposition to commit the offense inadmissible.

2. ELEMENTS OF THE DEFENSE

Section 2.13 contains the following elements:

a. Limitation to Law Enforcement Agents

The defense is limited to cases where the entrapment is perpetrated by a "public law enforcement official or a person acting in cooperation with such an official."

b. Serious Crimes Excluded

Section 2.13(3) makes the defense unavailable when causing or threatening bodily injury is an element of the offense if the victim of the offense charged is a person other than the person causing the entrapment.

c. Substantive Standards

Two kinds of behavior can constitute an entrapment:

1) Knowingly False Representations of Legality

The first is where police officials designedly misled the defendant as to the legality of the behavior now sought to be punished. § 2.13(1)(a). Note that this defense in effect becomes another exception to the principle that ignorance of the criminality of behavior is no excuse. Compare § 2.04(3) and page 177. Section 2.13(1)(a) implements the Supreme Court's decision in Cox v. Louisiana, 379 U.S. 559, 85 S.Ct. 476 (1965), discussed at page 158.

2) Substantial Risk That Innocent Persons Will Commit Offense

Section 2.13(1)(b) poses the typical "objective" inquiry adopted by those who follow this approach. The question is whether police tactics were employed which create a "substantial risk" that a criminal offense will be committed by persons "other than those who are ready to commit it." The question is not whether the particular defendant before the court was ready to commit the offense, but whether the tactics would place unwarranted pressure to commit the offense on the average citizen.

d. Burden of Proof

Section 2.13(2) explicitly places the burden of persuasion by a preponderance of the evidence on the defendant. The burden of production would also be on the defendant. See § 1.12.

G. REVIEW QUESTIONS

[Answers Provided in Appendix A, page 438]

1. T or F   A 15-year-old is incapable of committing a crime under the Model Penal Code.

2. T or F   The burden of persuasion under the Model Penal Code for entrapment is placed on the defendant by a preponderance of the evidence.

3. T or F   The Model Penal Code duress defense follows the "justification" rationale for that defense.

4. T or F   The Model Penal Code follows the "objective" theory of entrapment, focusing not on the defendant's prior disposition to commit the offense but on the likely effect of the police behavior on the average citizen.

5. T or F   The Model Penal Code entrapment defense contains an exception to the principle that ignorance of the criminal law is no excuse.

6. The Model Penal Code contains both a defense of necessity and a defense of duress. But arguably there is still an ethical gap, that is, an area where a defense might be warranted but is not. Explain why this is or is not the case.

PART SIX

PARTIES

*

X

THE COMMON LAW

Analysis

A. INTRODUCTION

When *P* commits all of the elements of a criminal offense, *P*, of course, is guilty of that crime and can be punished for it. The discussion to follow concerns the conditions under which others may be convicted of the same crime, not because they committed it but because *P* did. There are three situations that must be considered.

The most important is what one must do to become an "accessory" to *P*'s crime. The common law had a fancy vocabulary to describe various kinds of accessorial relationships, and specific consequences turned on the applicable term. Today, this terminology is less important, and what matters is the definition of the actus reus and the mens rea that will justify conviction of one as an accessory to the crime of another.

The other two situations arise less frequently. The first is called "vicarious" liability. It concerns the conviction of *B* for a crime committed by *A* based, not on any specific act committed by *B*, but entirely on a relationship between *A* and *B* that is itself noncriminal and usually socially desirable, as where *B* is *A*'s employer. The second is the imposition of criminal liability on a business entity—a corporation, a partnership, or an unincorporated association. Obviously in such cases the actual crime must be committed by a person purporting to act for the entity. The entity itself can only act through its employees. The question, therefore, is when employee conduct should justify the imposition of criminal sanctions on the entity itself.

B. LIABILITY AS AN ACCESSORY

The terms "liability as an accessory," "complicity," "accomplice liability," "aiding and abetting," and the like, are used today to refer generically to situations where one person helps another commit a crime. The common law, however, was much more structured.

1. THE TERMINOLOGY
There were four categories of parties to a felony at common law. Treason and misdemeanors were treated separately.

a. Principal in the First Degree
The principal in the first degree is the person who commits the crime—the person who personally engages in the actus reus with the required mens rea. But there are two situations where a person who did not actually commit the actus reus of an offense could nonetheless be guilty as a principal in the first degree. In both it is essential that the defendant had the mens rea required for the offense.

1) Innocent Agent Cases
The first is where an "innocent agent" is used. An "innocent agent" is a person (a) who engages in a criminal act, (b) who is coerced, is incapable of

committing a crime, or lacks mens rea for the crime, and (c) who is forced or duped by another person into committing the criminal act.

> ***Example:*** A says to B, "Please put some sugar in C's coffee. The sugar is right over there." B does so, and C dies because A wanted to kill C and, unknown to B, had put poison in the sugar. B is an "innocent agent" and A would be guilty of murder as a principal in the first degree.

2) Use of Animals or Inanimate Objects
The second is where an animal is trained to engage in the criminal act or an inanimate object is programmed to do so. In both cases, the trainer or programmer is guilty as a principal in the first degree.

b. Principal in the Second Degree
The principal in the second degree is a person who aids another to commit a crime, and is either physically present or "constructively" present at the time the offense is committed.

1) Constructive Presence
A person is "constructively present" when close enough to render assistance if needed, but far enough away so as not to be present at the immediate situs of the crime. For example, a lookout or a driver waiting in the getaway car might be "constructively" present and therefore a principal in the second degree.

c. Accessory Before the Fact
An accessory before the fact is a person who aids another to commit a crime, but is not present and not "constructively" present at the time of its commission. An example would be a person who helped plan the offense, but who stayed home while others went off to commit it.

d. Accessory After the Fact
An accessory after the fact is a person who aids a criminal *after* the crime is committed. The aid could come, for example, in the form of help to escape, to avoid detection, or to dispose of the fruits of the crime.

1) Persons Incapable of Being an Accessory After the Fact
At common law, a husband or wife could not be an accessory after the fact. They were expected to render aid, and excused for doing so. Under modern statutes, additional parties—usually other relatives—are also frequently made incapable of being an accessory after the fact.

e. Treason
Parties to treason were not classified, but were all treated as principals.

f.   Misdemeanors
No distinction among principals in the first degree, principals in the second degree, and accessories before the fact was made in the case of misdemeanors. All such parties were treated as principals. But it was not a crime to be an accessory after the fact to a misdemeanor.

2.   CONSEQUENCES OF CLASSIFICATION
Several important procedural consequences followed from the four felony classifications, among them:

a.   Place of Trial
An accessory before the fact could only be tried in a place where aid was given. This could well be a different location from the place where the crime was committed. A principal in the second degree, on the other hand, was tried in the place where the crime was committed, since that person was "present" there, either actually or constructively.

> ***Example:***   A purchases tools in County *X* for *B* and *C* to use to commit a burglary. *B* and *C* then drive to the victim's house. The plan is for *B* to stay in the car to serve as a lookout, and for *C* to commit the offense. As it happens, the County line is between the car and the house, and *B* remains in County *X* the entire time. *C* gets out of the car and commits the burglary, crossing into County *Y* to do so. Where can *A, B,* and *C* be prosecuted under the original common law rules?
>
> A is an accessory before the fact and can be prosecuted only where the aid was rendered, namely in County *X*. *C,* of course, will be prosecuted in County *Y*, since that is where the crime took place. And *B,* who is a principal in the second degree, will also be prosecuted in County *Y*, since *B* was "constructively" present in County *Y* at the time the aid was given.

Today, however, it would generally be permissible to prosecute an accessory of any kind either in the place where the aid was given or the place where the crime was committed. Thus, in the example given above, *A* and *B* could be prosecuted either in County *X* or County *Y*. If one leaves the possibility of a conspiracy charge out of the equation, *C* could be prosecuted only in County *Y*.

b.   Variance Between Allegations and Proof
Under the original common law structure, if it was alleged in the pleadings that the defendant was a principal in the second degree, a conviction was permissible if it was proved at the trial that the defendant was actually a principal in the first degree. Similarly, if it was alleged that the defendant was a principal in the first degree, a conviction as a principal in the second degree could be obtained.

The same was not true, however, if it was alleged that the defendant was an accessory before the fact and the proof was that the defendant was a principal in either the first or the second degree. Similarly, an allegation that the defendant was a principal in the first or the second degree would not support a conviction as an accessory before the fact. These variances between formal charge and proof were fatal to conviction.

These kinds of variances are generally not so critical today. Most though not all States have specifically changed this rule by statute, so that conviction can still be obtained even though a formal pleading error of this type is made.

c. **Prior Conviction of Principal in the First Degree**

It was an absolute prerequisite to conviction of a person as an accessory before the fact under the early common law rules that the principal in the first degree be tried and convicted first. They could be tried jointly, but in such a case a formal finding of guilt of the principal had to be made before the accessory's guilt could be considered.

The common law took this requirement to even further lengths. If the principal could not be prosecuted for some reason (for example, escape from detection or death), the accessory before the fact went free. If the principal was convicted and later pardoned, the accessory before the fact also went free. And if the principal was acquitted for any reason, or if a conviction was reversed on appeal, the accessory before the fact could not be punished.

These rules did not apply, however, to the relationship between a principal in the first degree and a principal in the second degree. They could be prosecuted in any order, and an acquittal of either did not affect the criminal liability of the other.

These rules have been abandoned in most jurisdictions today, though not in all. Note, however, that even where they have been abandoned it may still be necessary to allege and prove in the trial of a principal in the second degree or an accessory before the fact that a crime was actually committed by the principal in the first degree. More is said on this issue on pages 272–73.

3. **CURRENT LAW**

Current law distinguishes between the accessory after the fact and the other categories.

a. **Principal in the Second Degree and Accessory Before the Fact**

Most States have merged the categories of principal in the first degree, principal in the second degree, and accessory before the fact, calling them all "principals" in any crime committed. And, as noted above, many of the old procedural distinctions have been abolished. It is therefore possible to treat the elements of accessorial liability—the actus reus and mens rea of being an accessory—without reference to the presence of the defendant at the scene of the offense, as is done below under the heading "Elements of Liability as an Accessory." It is also common, as is done below, to speak of the "principal" as the person who committed the crime and the "accessory" as the helper, no matter which formal common law category (excluding the accessory after the fact) would be applicable to the accessory.

Note, however, that not all States have completely abandoned the old order. Some retain the common law terminology, but treat "principals" and "accessories" identically. And others retain various vestiges of the old procedural distinctions. It is therefore necessary in a particular State to examine carefully the approach that is followed on these issues. One cannot assume even from a statute that appears to abolish the old distinctions that they have all been discarded.

b. Accessory After the Fact

One point on which all States agree is that those who help the offender *after* the crime has been committed should be treated differently from those who help *before* or *during* its commission. For this reason, accessories after the fact are discussed separately below.

4. ELEMENTS OF LIABILITY AS AN ACCESSORY

There are three factors to focus upon in determining the liability of an accessory. The first two are the actus reus and the mens rea of the offense. The third is the approach taken by the particular jurisdiction on whether guilt of the principal must be shown. These three factors are discussed in order below. They are followed by treatment of the grading of accessorial liability and the effect of withdrawal after aid has been given.

a. The Actus Reus

A great many none-too-informative words have been used to describe the actus reus of accessorial liability: "aid," "abet," "incite," "encourage," "counsel," "command," "induce," "assist," and the like. The point, of course, is that the accessory must give some help or assistance to the efforts of another person to commit a crime. What these words obscure is the central issue: how much help is enough?

This question cannot be answered categorically. Nor has it attracted much attention in the cases or the literature. It has been answered case by case, with little attention devoted to the development of an analytical structure that focuses the question beyond simple recitation of the buzz-words used to describe the necessary actus reus. Aside from this problem, however, a number of special situations have arisen as the courts have spelled out the actus reus for accessorial liability, among them:

1) Affirmative Aid

It is clear that physical aid—supplying a weapon, driving the principal to the scene, standing lookout—can suffice for liability as an accessory. It is also clear that words of encouragement can be sufficient, such as "Why don't you beat up *A*. I'll come along and help if you need me." And merely standing by to help can be enough, so long as the principal knows the defendant is there for that purpose and is therefore encouraged or given moral reinforcement by the defendant's presence.

2) Omissions

The courts have held that an omission can suffice, but only if there is a legal duty to intervene to prevent the crime. Thus, one who stands by while a crime is committed is not guilty as an accessory, unless some provision of law imposes a specific duty to intervene. [Or unless, as noted above, the defendant is standing by in order to help if needed and the principal knows it. In this case, it is not the failure to intervene—the omission—that supplies the actus reus, but the positive acts of presence and encouraging the principal by expressing a willingness to help.]

3) Ineffective Aid; Principal Unaware of Aid

What happens if the defendant's aid actually does not assist the principal (e.g., a gun is supplied but not used)? Or suppose the principal does not know that help is being provided (e.g., the defendant makes sure the jewels are left where they can be found but the principal doesn't know that such help has been provided)? In general, these situations can be resolved by one of two rules of thumb:

a) Actual Help

It is sufficient if the defendant actually aids in the commission of the crime, even if the principal is unaware of the aid.

b) Communicated Encouragement

Alternatively, it is sufficient if the defendant communicates to the principal a willingness to help, and thereby encourages the commission of the crime, even if no actual help is given.

It is unlikely, though, that most courts would convict in a case both where the defendant provided no aid (though attempted to do so) and where the principal was unaware of the defendant's efforts. But there is no reason in principle why one should not be convicted of something in this situation, and some modern statutes (like the Model Penal Code) explicitly permit a conviction for "attempting" to aid in such a case.

4) Immunity From Conviction for Object Offense

Courts have sometimes inferred from a substantive offense that a "victim" cannot be convicted as an accessory to the commission of that offense.

Example: Statutory rape is traditionally defined as sexual intercourse with a person below a specified age, irrespective of consent. A "victim" who consents, even one who actively encourages the act, cannot be convicted as an accessory to the crime. Similarly, a person who agrees to pay ransom money to a kidnapper or extortion money to a racketeer is not an accessory.

5) Conduct Inevitably Incident to a Crime
Courts have also held that if the legislature imposed a punishment on only one party to a multiparty transaction, the other party cannot be convicted as an accessory.

> *Example:* Assume a crime of prostitution defined to punish the prostitute only, or a crime of selling alcohol to a minor that itself punishes only the seller. A court is likely to hold in such cases that only the prostitute and the seller were meant to be punished by the legislature, and that the person who uses the prostitute's services and the minor who purchases the alcohol cannot be convicted as accessories, no matter how actively they may have encouraged or contributed to the actual offense.

6) Incapacity to Commit Object Offense
Some offenses are defined so that they may be committed only by a person with certain defined characteristics. Rape traditionally was a crime that could not be committed by a female, nor by a male against his own spouse. An offense defined to punish a bankrupt for fraud on creditors could be committed only by a person who is bankrupt. Is it possible for one who does not have the defined characteristic to be an accessory to such offenses?

The answer is "yes." The principal, of course, must have the defined characteristic. But it is not essential for the accessory to have it. Thus, a woman may be an accessory to rape even in jurisdictions where only males can rape, as may a husband who assists another in the rape of his own wife even though it may not be possible, under the law of the relevant jurisdiction, for a man to rape his own wife. And a person who is not a bankrupt may be an accessory to a bankrupt who defrauds creditors.

b. The Mens Rea
The mens rea required for accomplice liability cannot be stated simply, and it varies widely. It is best to approach the issue in stages:

1) Mens Rea for Object Offense
It is reasonably clear that the defendant must have *at least* the mens rea required for the offense committed by the principal. Thus if the offense committed by the principal requires a specific intent, the accomplice must at least have that same specific intent.

2) **Purpose to Promote or Facilitate**

It is also clear that it is *sufficient* if the defendant has the intent to aid or encourage the commission of the offense, sometimes expressed as a purpose to promote or facilitate its commission.

> *Example:* Assume a principal who wants to commit a burglary, defined as "breaking and entering the dwelling of another at night with the intent to commit a felony therein." The accessory must have at least the mens rea required for commission of the burglary, that is, must intend that the principal commit a felony inside the house. It is clear that it is sufficient for conviction, moreover, if the accessory also has a purpose to promote or facilitate the burglary, that is, a purpose that the principal engage in each of the elements of the offense.

What is less clear is whether a purpose to aid or encourage the commission of the offense is a *necessary* predicate for liability as an accessory. Are there situations where some lesser mens rea will suffice? The answer is "yes, but not always."

3) **Knowledge That Crime Will be Promoted or Facilitated**

Perhaps the most debated question is whether knowledge that conduct will promote or facilitate an offense should suffice. Consider the following situations:

(1) *A* buys a gun and gives it to *P* because both *A* and *P* want *C* killed. *P* then kills *C*.

(2) *P* needs a gun to kill *C*. *A* sells a gun to *P*, knowing the reason why *P* wants it. *A* is indifferent, however, as to how the gun is used. *A* is interested only in the profit to be made from the sale.

(3) *P* needs huge quantities of sugar in order to make illegal whiskey. *A* supplies the sugar over the course of several years, charging extra because *A* knows of the illegal use. *A* doesn't care about the whiskey, but sure wants the profits from the sugar sales.

(4) *A* installs and repairs telephones in a day when that was done in the home by an employee of the telephone company. *A* is told by the phone company to install four phones in *P*'s house. It becomes obvious to *A* as the phones are installed all in one room that they are to be used in a bookmaking operation. *A* has no interest in the matter beyond doing a decent day's work and not rocking the boat.

In how many of these cases should *A* be guilty as an accessory?

The answer is that four distinct approaches to this question can be found in common law jurisdictions:

a) Require Purpose in All Cases

Some courts will never convict an accessory without a finding that the defendant had a purpose to promote or facilitate the offense committed by the principal. These courts would permit a jury to convict in the first case recited above. They also might let the second and third cases (but probably not the fourth) go to the jury and permit (but not require) the jury to draw the inference from what was proved that the necessary purpose existed.

b) Permit Conviction Based on Knowledge

Some courts would permit a jury to convict in all four cases. These courts would reason that in each case a crime has been committed with A's help, that deterrence of the offense will be promoted by discouraging those who would knowingly aid its commission, and that it satisfies at least minimum notions of fairness to hold A responsible for knowing assistance.

c) Intermediate Position

Other courts, however, would take a more discriminating approach. They would begin with a distinction between the first and fourth situations. They would agree that A should be convicted in the first case. There A has a "stake in the venture," a purpose to accomplish the goals of the criminal offense. In the fourth, however, A is merely an employee rendering an ordinary service and realizing no particular personal gain for doing so. While it would promote deterrence to convict A in that situation, it is, the argument would run, unfair to do so.

What of the second and third cases? A would probably be convicted in both instances. The reasoning in the second situation would be that the fact that aid is knowingly given to the commission of such a serious crime justifies maximizing the deterrence that the law can bring to bear on such behavior, and also makes it less unfair to base liability on mere knowledge. The law, in other words, wants to discourage murders as much as possible—even at some cost in individual fairness—and punishing those who knowingly aid a murder helps to do so.

In the third situation the deterrence argument is less strong because the crime is less serious, but there is still the fact that A is realizing a large profit from crime and is rendering a substantial amount of assistance to the illegal endeavor. Many courts would convict on this basis, reasoning either that knowingly rendering assistance to a crime in these circumstances is a sufficient mens rea or that purpose to promote or facilitate is required and the purpose can readily be inferred by the jury from A's large profits and the long-term nature of the relationship between A and P.

d) Facilitation Offense

Some legislatures have responded to the situation where aid is knowingly rendered by adopting a "criminal facilitation" statute. This statute usually punishes one who knowingly renders a substantial amount of aid to the commission of a serious offense. In these jurisdictions, the defendant can be convicted as an ordinary accessory only if a purpose to promote or facilitate the offense can be shown. The criminal facilitation offense, graded less severely, is reserved for cases where only knowing aid to a serious offense can be proved.

To summarize:

(1) All courts will convict in cases where a purpose to promote or facilitate the offense can be found, and many will be quite generous in letting cases get to the jury when the inference of purpose is sought to be drawn from knowing facilitation.

(2) Some courts, however, will convict in all cases where aid is knowingly rendered, and a fortiori in all cases where a purpose can be shown.

(3) Most courts, however, probably fall somewhere in the middle. They will convict in cases where purpose can be shown, as well as in cases where aid is knowingly rendered when (a) the crime is especially serious; or (b) the amount of aid given is significant and is important to the successful commission of the crime; or (c) the benefit derived by the accessory from the offense is especially significant.

(4) But some legislatures have adopted a "criminal facilitation" offense. In these States, conviction as an accessory is limited to purposeful aid. The separate facilitation offense permits a conviction for knowing aid, though it grades the offense less severely, usually requires a substantial amount of aid (more than would suffice for conviction as an accessory), and often is limited to aiding the more serious criminal offenses.

4) Recklessness or Negligence as to Results

Consider the following situation:

> A purposely renders aid to P in the performance of specific conduct. That conduct creates a risk of death, and in fact causes a death. P is convicted of manslaughter (based on a finding of recklessness in performing the conduct) or of negligent homicide (based on a finding of negligence). If A was equally reckless or negligent as to the possibility of death, can A be guilty as an accessory to P's offense?

It seems clear that A should be guilty, and most courts would so hold. Note, however, that A would not be guilty if the mens rea for accessorial liability is stated as a "purpose to promote or facilitate the crime" (or even if only knowledge is required). *A*'s purpose is not that *P* commit homicide. It is to aid the *conduct* in which *P* engages, not the *result* which that conduct causes. The question, therefore, is the mens rea that should be required of the accessory for result elements.

Although the cases are divided, the best answer is "the same as is required for a principal who commits that offense." Thus, if *A* has the necessary mens rea for aiding conduct, *A* should be liable as an accessory for any results caused by that conduct *if A* satisfies the mens rea for the result required for conviction of the principal.

5) Negligence: Unanticipated Offenses

Suppose *A* helps *P* commit a burglary by boosting *P* into the house. Their object is to steal jewelry. People are present in the bedroom, it turns out, and *P* commits an additional offense—a rape, a homicide, an assault, or a kidnapping—beyond what *A* and *P* initially contemplated. *A* is clearly liable as an accessory to the burglary. Is *A* liable as an accessory to the additional offense?

The traditional answer is "yes, if." The "if" is that the additional, unplanned offense must have been a "natural and probable consequence" of the offense the accomplice meant to aid or encourage. Essentially this states a negligence standard, and establishes the following rule: A person who satisfies all of the requirements for being an accomplice is an accomplice as to all offenses committed by the principal that were natural and probable consequences of the offense aided and that the accomplice should therefore have anticipated might occur.

Note that the accomplice is convicted on the basis of negligence, even though the principal may be held to a higher standard of culpability. Thus, in the burglary case above, *A* might well be held liable for a homicide, an assault, or a kidnapping as a "reasonably foreseeable" product of a burglary (and perhaps not a rape, though that would be a jury question). *P*, on the other hand, could not be convicted of any of these offenses on the basis of negligence. The "natural and probable consequences" rule has been justly criticized for this reason. Compare the treatment of this issue in the law of conspiracy, page 321 (the *Pinkerton* case).

c. The Principal's Behavior: Conduct or Guilt

What the principal did is also central to liability of the accessory in most jurisdictions.

1) Guilt of the Principal

The traditional common law theory was that the accessory's liability was derivative from the liability of the principal: if the principal was not guilty of the crime, then the accessory could not be guilty of aiding and abetting it. Thus it was an element of the accessory's liability that the principal actually be guilty of committing the aided crime. If the principal had a defense of mistake of fact, self-defense, or insanity, the accessory would not be liable even though the accessory rendered assistance to the act and fully meant for all elements of the crime to be committed.

Note that this requirement has survived in many jurisdictions long after the formal rule that the principal must first be prosecuted and convicted was discarded. In most jurisdictions today, it remains the law that the accessory's guilt is derivative from and requires proof of the guilt of the principal.

2) Aiding and Abetting an Attempt

It need not be, of course, that the principal is guilty of committing the completed offense. If the principal has gone only so far as to have committed an attempt, the accessory can be convicted of aiding and abetting the attempt. But if the principal has not committed the crime or attempted to commit it, or if the principal has a defense, then the accessory is not guilty under the traditional view.

3) Conduct by the Principal

However, some cases have taken the position that the principal need only engage in the actus reus of the offense in order for the accesssory to be guilty.

> ***Example:*** If A helped P kill V, A could be guilty of murder in such a jurisdiction based on A's intent to kill V, even though under the circumstances P had a defense of self-defense or insanity.

The rationale for this view seems obvious, and correct. Once A has engaged in the actus reus of accessorial liability (has rendered aid to another in the commission of certain behavior) and has done so with a sufficient mens rea (has done so with a purpose to promote or facilitate conduct that is a crime), A's fault and dangerousness have been established. Whether P, unknown to A, has a defense seems a fortuity that has little to do with whether A should be punished.

Note that, although a case could be made for convicting A of an attempt to aid and abet in this situation, the conviction in those jurisdictions that follow this rule is for the completed offense, probably on the ground that the harm has been accomplished by P's commission of the act.

4) Attempting to Aid and Abet; No Conduct by Principal

There seems to be no reason in principle why a conviction for attempting to aid and abet should not be permissible even in cases where the principal does nothing. Consider the following situation:

A agrees to help P commit a burglary, purchases the necessary equipment, goes to the scene, and waits for P. If the police arrive and arrest A at that point, having previously intercepted P before P has committed an attempt, should A be guilty of attempting to aid and abet a burglary?

Why not? As in the case where P engages in the conduct but unknown to A has a defense, A's blameworthiness and dangerousness have been sufficiently established to warrant a conviction. Yet there are few cases so holding. The reason is probably that A can be convicted of solicitation or conspiracy. There may, however, be a grading consequence. Attempt is often graded at a different level than solicitation or conspiracy.

d. Grading of Accessory's Crime
Of what level of offense can the accessory be convicted?

1) Traditional View
The traditional view is that the accessory is convicted of the same crime as the principal and is punishable to the same extent.

2) Exception for Homicide
The crimes of murder and manslaughter were regarded in the ancient common law as but different forms of a single generic offense, and for that reason it was possible for the accessory and the principal to be graded in a criminal homicide according to the culpability of each. Thus, if the accessory had the mens rea for murder and the principal the mens rea for manslaughter, they would be convicted of murder and manslaughter, respectively. Reversing the culpability would change the convictions accordingly.

3) Departures From the General Rule
Some modern cases and statutes have abandoned the traditional view in all cases, and regard it as appropriate to grade the principal and the accessory independently, each according to their own mens rea.

Example: Assume that arson in the first degree consists of burning with intent to destroy the dwelling house of another and that arson in the second degree consists of burning with intent to destroy any structure. A induces P to burn a particular building, which P believes to be an abandoned warehouse. A knows that it has been completely remodeled inside, and that V is using it as a dwelling house. Under the traditional view, P would be guilty only of second degree arson and therefore A's liability would be limited to that grade of arson as well. Under the more modern view, A could be convicted of first degree arson even though P was guilty only of the second degree offense. Both are graded according to their individual mens rea. And the same principle would hold if the mental states were reversed: if *A* had the mens rea for second degree and *P* the mens rea for first degree, they would be convicted of the second and first degree offenses, respectively.

e. Withdrawal of Aid
The common law recognizes a defense if the accessory, having given aid that would be sufficient for liability, withdraws that aid before the principal commits the offense. The requirements for an effective withdrawal are rigorous:

1) Communicate Repudiation
The accessory must inform the principal that the offense should no longer be committed.

2) Render Prior Aid Ineffective
The accessory must do all that is possible to render all prior aid ineffective. If the aid consisted of verbal encouragement, the accessory must attempt to persuade the principal not to commit the offense. If the aid consisted of physical assistance, the accessory must do what can be done to render that assistance ineffective.

3) Act in a Timely Manner
The accessory must accomplish the above requirements before it is too late to stop the chain of events leading to the commission of the offense. It is not necessary, however, that the offense actually not be committed— although, in effect, if the offense is committed it must be the result of the independent decision of the principal to go forward without the accessory's assistance or encouragement.

5. ACCESSORIES AFTER THE FACT
At common law, an accessory after the fact was also guilty of the offense committed by the principal. This position has been modified in virtually all jurisdictions today.

a. Elements of the Common Law Offense
The traditional actus reus and mens rea elements that associated one with a criminal offense as an accessory after the fact were:

1) The Actus Reus
The defendant must have given direct aid to a person who had in fact committed a felony. It was *not* enough if the person aided had been accused of a felony but was innocent, nor was it sufficient if the defendant mistakenly believed that the person had committed a felony. All elements of the felony must have been completed at the time the aid was given. Thus, aid given after the act but before the death did not make one

an accessory after the fact to murder. And the aid must have been given personally to the felon. It was not sufficient, for example, to give aid to another person who in turn aided the felon.

2) The Mens Rea

The defendant: (a) must have known that the person aided had committed specified acts—acts which the law designates a felony; and (b) must have rendered aid with the purpose of hindering the detection, apprehension, prosecution, conviction, or punishment of the person aided. The defendant need not, of course, come to the legal conclusion that a felony had been committed. Compare page 156 ("The Meaning of Mens Rea").

3) Persons Excluded From Conviction

A husband or a wife could not be convicted as an accessory after the fact. Most jurisdictions today have broadened the exclusion by adding other close relatives.

b. Modern Statutory Treatment

The modern statutes are of two types:

1) Accessory After the Fact

The first retains the common law terminology and the common law definition of the offense, but changes the punishment. The conviction is not for the offense of which the principal is guilty, but for a separate less serious felony or, in some cases, a misdemeanor.

2) Obstructing Justice

The second, and better, approach is to abandon the idea that the accessory is somehow a party to the principal's offense and substitute a different and more accurately descriptive crime. What the accessory is really doing is obstructing justice, interfering with or hindering the processes of law enforcement. The new offenses, often called "hindering prosecution," are addressed to this evil. They are usually graded as a lesser felony, and often defined to encompass a much broader range of conduct than would lead to conviction as an accessory after the fact. For example, they often apply to aiding misdemeanants as well as felons, and to aiding one who has been charged with an offense even though it turns out that the person aided is not guilty.

C. VICARIOUS LIABILITY

The term "vicarious liability" means the imposition of criminal liability on B for a crime committed by A based not upon conduct committed by B but upon B's relationship to A. Normally, vicarious liability is based on the relationship of employer to employee, although other relationships may suffice, for example, that between the owner and driver of a car or between parent and child. This is *not* to say that these relationships always lead to the imposition of vicarious liability, for they do not. It is to say, however, that when imposed vicarious liability is based on such a relationship.

1. WHEN IMPOSED

With minor exceptions that have been unimportant in this country, vicarious liability was unknown to the early common law. It emerged in response to the same factors that led to the development of public welfare offenses. See page 81. It is imposed only when a statute is construed specifically to impose it. Courts are reluctant to so construe a statute, but will do so when the penalty is mild, when the offense carries no significant moral overtones, and when it appears that the legislature intended such a construction. Most if not all of the characteristics of public welfare offenses will be shared by such statutes. See page 81.

2. WHY IMPOSED

In a word—deterrence. If employers are held accountable for acts of employees without direct participation by the employer in the offense, pressure will be placed on employers to engage in strict supervision and the incidence of the offense in theory will be reduced.

3. RELATION TO STRICT LIABILITY

Analytically there is a clear distinction between vicarious and strict liability. But vicarious and strict liability often are imposed together.

a. Nature of Vicarious Liability

Vicarious liability dispenses with the actus reus. It is imposed on a defendant who has engaged in no criminal act, based upon a crime committed by a person who stands in a specified relationship to the defendant. The relationships on which it is based are entirely legal, and usually socially desirable.

b. Nature of Strict Liability

Strict liability dispenses with the mens rea. It is normally imposed on one who has committed a criminal act, but who lacks culpability as to one or more components of the act. And it is normally imposed on a defendant who has engaged in socially undesirable conduct.

c. Imposition of Strict and Vicarious Liability

As a practical matter, however, strict liability normally accompanies vicarious liability—the employer is "without fault" both in the sense that no act was committed and no mens rea is required.

4. CRITICISMS OF ITS USE

Vicarious liability is commonly imposed in the law of torts, under the doctrine of respondeat superior. Indeed, as an historical matter, the criminal law probably borrowed vicarious liability from the law of torts. Widespread use of the doctrine can be justified in tort law on grounds that are unique to the law of torts and are not valid justifications for extending the principle to the criminal law. For example, the imposition of vicarious liability on a manufacturer can be justified on the ground that the manufacturer is in the best position to spread the cost of losses that are inevitably going to occur from injuries due to use of various products. This rationale is not, on the other hand, a suitable basis for the imposition of criminal sanctions. Thus vicarious liability must be justified—if at all—on grounds related to the purposes of criminal punishment. As noted above, deterrence is the principal ground usually asserted.

Vicarious liability has been criticized on the same grounds as strict liability. This criticism is based essentially on the idea that the imposition of criminal punishment can only be justified if the defendant is, to some degree at least, personally at fault. There is, to be sure, a sense in which one who has engaged in criminal conduct can be said to be at fault even though strict liability is imposed. See pages 88–89. The same could be said of certain forms of vicarious liability. While it is hard to say that one is at "fault" simply for being an employer in a legitimate business, a manufacturer that is in position to prevent widespread harm through extraordinary care could be regarded as at "fault" when injuries occur. And in any event making the manufacturer an insurer against injury, and imposing minor criminal sanctions when such injuries are widespread, could be regarded as a use of the principle of deterrence that is not unfair.

5. LIMITS ON ITS USE
The criticisms of vicarious liability have been recognized in various common law and constitutional doctrines.

a. Common Law Limits
In some contexts courts have permitted an employer to defend on the ground that all steps have been taken that could have been taken to prevent the occurrence of the offense. For example, the Supreme Court recognized such a defense in United States v. Park, 421 U.S. 658, 95 S.Ct. 1903 (1975), a case involving the imposition of strict and vicarious liability under the federal Food and Drug statutes. This same idea is reflected in a few decisions that permit an employer to defend on the ground that specific instructions had been issued to employees not to engage in the prohibited behavior.

In effect, these defenses are efforts to build an element of fault—close to employer negligence—into a scheme that otherwise would lack most indicia on which fault can properly be assessed.

b. Constitutional Limits
There is an emerging notion of proportionality in American constitutional law. This principle requires that punishment be proportioned to fault, and would forbid the imposition of serious criminal sanctions on the basis of vicarious liability. This idea is discussed at pages 410–14. For a well-known

example of its use in the context of vicarious liability, see Commonwealth v. Koczwara, 397 Pa. 575, 155 A.2d 825 (1959) (fine but not jail may be imposed on tavern owner for second offense of alcohol violations related to minors; decision based on State Constitution).

D. ENTERPRISE LIABILITY

Persons who commit crimes on behalf of or while working for a corporation or other business enterprise can be convicted on the same principles that apply to everyone else. And persons for whom they work can be liable as accessories under the same principles that apply to everyone else.

The same cannot, of course, be true for the enterprise itself. The enterprise, not being a natural person, cannot engage in an act except through its employees. Nor can it have a criminal intent except as those who work for it do. Thus, enterprise liability must by its nature be vicarious—both the act and mens rea of an employee must provide the basis for conviction. Liability, as in the case of other impositions of vicarious liability, is based on a relationship that is in other respects perfectly lawful and socially desirable, in this case between an enterprise and those who act in its name. And the above discussion of vicarious liability is thus fully applicable here.

1. LIABILITY OF CORPORATIONS AND OTHER ENTITIES

At common law, only natural persons could be convicted of a crime. This rule gradually changed, at about the same time that public welfare offenses first emerged and at first in order to impose strict and vicarious liability on business enterprises for public welfare offenses. The Supreme Court held in 1909 that it was constitutional to convict an enterprise of crime. New York Cent. & H.R.R. v. United States, 212 U.S. 481, 29 S.Ct. 304 (1909). And today it is well accepted that a corporation or other business enterprise can constitutionally be convicted of any criminal offense, even an offense like manslaughter.

This is not to say, however, that all criminal statutes apply to corporations. An act of construction is required in order to determine whether a particular legislative enactment was meant to encompass corporate liability. The fact that the word "person" is used will not be determinative, for "person" can be interpreted—and often is—to encompass artificial as well as natural persons. The construction will turn, on the other hand, on whether the legislature appears to have intended enterprise liability, an inquiry that will be guided by such factors as the authorized sanction (if only imprisonment is permitted, a corporation could hardly serve the sentence), whether the statute involved imposes a duty upon the corporation itself, whether additional deterrence is likely to be gained by the imposition of enterprise responsibility (for example, by publicity linking the corporate name to the conviction or from shareholder pressure that could be expected to be exerted on management), whether the offense is one that is likely to generate profits for the corporation, and the like.

An argument frequently made against construing a statute to impose enterprise liability is that the sanction falls on the wrong parties. For example, in the case of a corporation a fine is the most commonly imposed sanction, the cost of which is ultimately borne by consumers and shareholders—parties who themselves are likely to be innocent of the wrongdoing attributed to the enterprise. On the other hand, they may also be the parties who will benefit if the entity profits from the criminal conduct. And in a closely held enterprise the imposition of liability on the enterprise may serve as additional punishment for the wrongdoers.

It should be noted that enterprise liability has arisen most frequently in the case of corporations. Partnerships and other unincorporated associations are rarely held criminally liable, although there seems to be no reason why similar arguments and principles should not be applicable to all forms of association. The law is frequently stated, however, as follows: partnerships and other unincorporated associations are not criminally liable, unless a statute specifically imposes a duty on such an entity or unless it appears that the legislature intended such an entity to be liable.

Finally, there is the question of who within the organization may commit a crime for which the organization will be held responsible, and what that person must do. It is clear that the person who commits the crime must be an employee of the organization, that the offense must be committed in order to benefit the organization (rather than the employee personally), and that the offense must involve behavior that is within the scope of the actor's authority or responsibility. Some jurisdictions stop here, while others require in addition that the actor be a high-ranking official, one who is high enough in the organization so that it is fair to assume that the person is acting pursuant to official organizational policy.

2. RICO DISTINGUISHED

A comment about RICO should be added. The terms "enterprise liability" or "enterprise criminality" are sometimes used in connection with that offense. The discussion here concerns the conviction of corporations and other organizations of the array of traditional crimes for which individuals are ordinarily prosecuted, crimes like theft or manslaughter. RICO is a special criminal statute aimed at the predatory practices of "organized crime." It presents a series of distinct issues, different from those under discussion here, that are dealt with beginning at page 398.

E. REVIEW QUESTIONS

[Answers Provided in Appendix A, page 439]

1. T or F   It is appropriate for criminal liability to be imposed on a corporation when the legislature so intends, but we have not yet reached the point where we have held a partnership criminally liable.

2. T or F   Vicarious liability is most often imposed for public welfare offenses.

3. T or F   *P* engages in the actus reus of an offense, assisted by *A*. Unknown to *A*, *P* is insane, and is acquitted on that ground. *A* can nonetheless be

convicted of the offense as a principal in the first degree on the theory that *A* used an "innocent agent" to commit the crime.

4. **T or F**   Under the original common law rules, an indictment alleging that a person was guilty as a principal in the first degree would permit the conviction of one who aided and abetted the offense with a purpose to promote or facilitate its commission if it could be shown that the defendant was constructively present when the offense was committed.

5. **T or F**   *A* helped four people escape from prosecution in a jurisdiction that follows the original common law rules: one was guilty of a misdemeanor and *A* knew it, another was charged with a felony but was not in fact guilty, another was believed by *A* to be guilty of a felony but was in fact guilty of a misdemeanor, and another was believed by *A* to be guilty of a misdemeanor but was in fact guilty of a felony. *A* has done lots of bad things, but is not guilty as an accessory after the fact to any of these offenses.

6. **T or F**   A husband or wife could not be guilty as an accessory before the fact under the original common law rules.

7. **T or F**   The actus reus of accessorial liability requires that effective aid actually be given to the principal.

8. **T or F**   As odd as it sounds, it is possible in some jurisdictions for an accessory to be liable for aiding and abetting an offense that never occurred.

9. **T or F**   It is possible in some jurisdictions today for an accessory to be guilty of an offense that is more serious than the offense committed by the principal, as it was at common law.

10. **T or F**   At common law, it was not possible for a man to be convicted for the rape of his own wife.

11. What is the difference between strict and vicarious liability?

12. Once substantial aid has been rendered with the purpose to promote a criminal offense, is there anything a person can do to avoid being convicted as an accessory? If so, what? If not, why?

13. Name two different kinds of situations where a person who encourages the commission of an offense and actually helps another to commit it nonetheless cannot be convicted as an accessory. Can you state a rationale for each?

14. The cases are divided on whether knowledge that a crime will be promoted or facilitated is a sufficient mens rea for conviction as an accessory. What's the fuss all about, and what solutions have been developed? What's the best solution?

15. If the principal is not guilty of committing a crime because of mistake of fact, self-defense, or insanity, should one who assisted the principal in the commission of the act and who did so with at least the mens rea required by the object offense and with a purpose to promote the commission of that offense nonetheless be guilty as an accessory? Explain your answer.

XI

THE MODEL PENAL CODE

Analysis

A. INTRODUCTION

The Model Penal Code discards the traditional common law terms in which accessorial liability was described. It treats persons formerly called principals in the first degree, principals in the second degree, and accessories before the fact in § 2.06. Those who were called accessories after the fact are treated in the various offenses defined in Article 242. The Model Code does not deal explicitly with "vicarious" liability. But it does contemplate the possibility of its imposition. Enterprise liability is specifically covered by § 2.07.

B. LIABILITY AS AN ACCESSORY

Section 2.06 should be focused upon first.

1. THE TERMINOLOGY
The Model Penal Code unfolds the subject of complicity in stages:

a. Offense Committed by Conduct of Defendant
The easy case is where the offense "is committed by his own conduct." § 2.06(1). This includes the paradigm situation where the defendant engages in the complete actus reus and mens rea of an offense. It also includes cases where the defendant had the mens rea for an offense and trained an animal to engage in some or all of the acts, or programmed an inanimate object (like a robot or a computer) to do so.

b. Offense Committed by Conduct of Another for Which Defendant Is Legally Accountable
A person is also guilty of an offense if it is committed by the conduct of another for which the defendant is "legally accountable." § 2.06(1). There are three situations where one person is "legally accountable" for the conduct of another:

1) Innocent Agent
The first is where the defendant causes an "innocent agent" to engage in the actus reus of the offense. § 2.06(2)(a). The paradigm case that the drafters had in mind is where the defendant, acting with the mens rea required for a particular offense, coerces or dupes another person into committing the actus reus of an offense.

2) Made Accountable by Law
Section 2.06(2)(b) is a catchall provision allowing the legislature to broaden liability in specific instances beyond the terms of § 2.06(3). It would, for example, permit the imposition of vicarious liability based on the employer-employee relationship should specific legislation be adopted to that effect. Section 2.06(2)(b) is not important to an understanding of the Model Code approach to accomplice liability.

3) Accomplice of Another Person

Section 2.06(2)(c) makes one "legally accountable" for the conduct of another when one is an "accomplice" in the commission of the offense. The elements of liability as an "accomplice" are then spelled out in detail in § 2.06(3). They are addressed below.

2. CONSEQUENCES OF CLASSIFICATION

The Model Penal Code rejects the procedural complications that turned on the old common law classifications in this area. Specifically:

a. Place of Trial

Section 1.03 abolishes the old "place of trial" rules turning on the accessorial category into which the defendant fell. Under § 1.03(1)(a), an accessory can be prosecuted in the place where the principal committed the offense. Or under § 1.03(1)(d), an accessory can be prosecuted in a place where aid is given. The possibility of prosecution in *both* places is covered by § 1.10.

b. Variance Between Allegations and Proof

The problem of variance between charge and proof is not covered by the Model Code. It would therefore be dealt with under ordinary principles, and under no special rule turning on the appropriate accessorial category.

c. Prior Conviction of Principal

Section 2.06(7) specifically abolishes the old rule that prior conviction of the principal was necessary to conviction of the accessory before the fact. What happened in the prior trial of the principal is made irrelevant, so long as the proof in the trial of the accessory is adequate to establish liability.

3. ELEMENTS OF LIABILITY AS AN ACCESSORY

The elements of accomplice liability are set forth in § 2.06(3).

a. The Actus Reus

The words "solicits," "aids," "agrees to aid," and "attempts to aid" describe the actus reus of accomplice liability. None of them explicitly address the question of how much aid is enough. The following generalizations can, however, be made:

1) Affirmative Aid

Various forms of physical aid would be encompassed within the term "aids" in § 2.06(3)(a)(ii). Words of encouragement would satisfy the term "solicits," which probably is meant to encompass the behavior described in § 5.02(1) ("commands, encourages or requests"). Standing by to help, where the principal knows that is the purpose of the defendant's presence, also fits within the concept of positive encouragement. Note also that participation in a conspiracy is expressly made sufficient, by use of the words "agrees . . . to aid" in the planning or commission of the offense.

2) **Omissions**

An omission will suffice only if, "having a legal duty to prevent the commission of the offense," the defendant "fails to make a proper effort so to do." § 2.06(3)(a)(iii).

3) **Ineffective Aid; Principal Unaware of Aid**

The case where the aid is ineffective, or where the principal is unaware of it, is covered by the term "attempts to aid." The defendant is thus an accomplice where aid is ineffective for any reason, where the principal was in fact aided but didn't know it, or where the aid was both ineffective and unknown to the principal. Note that the word "attempts" is likely to invoke the definition of attempt in § 5.01, including the strong corroboration requirement. Thus in this one instance the question "how much aid is enough" may be answered by the attempt provisions, namely "enough aid to corroborate the required intent." See page 334.

4) **Immunity from Conviction for Object Offense**

Section 2.06(6)(a) provides that a person cannot be convicted as an accomplice if that person is a "victim" of the offense. Thus the examples given under this heading on pages 267–68 would come out the same way under the Model Penal Code, based on the offenses as there defined.

5) **Conduct Inevitably Incident to a Crime**

Section 2.06(6)(b) provides that a person cannot be convicted as an accomplice if "the offense is so defined that his conduct is inevitably incident to its commission." Thus the prostitution and selling-alcohol-to-a-minor examples given on page 268 would come out the same way under the Model Penal Code, based on the offenses as there defined.

6) **Incapacity to Commit Object Offense**

Section 2.06(5) provides that a defendant, who cannot commit a given offense because certain characteristics required for commission of the offense are lacking, may nevertheless be an accomplice in the commission of that offense, so long as the person who commits the offense has the necessary characteristics.

Examples: Rape under § 213.1(1) is committed when a male has sexual intercourse with a female not his wife. Nonetheless, a woman can be an accomplice to a rape committed by a male, and a husband can be an accessory to the rape of his own wife.

b. **The Mens Rea**

The mens rea for accomplice liability is a "purpose of promoting or facilitating the commission of the offense." § 2.06(3). As will be explained, and as modified by other provisions, this requires:

(1) a purpose that the principal will engage in the conduct elements of the object offense;

(2) knowledge or belief that the principal will do so in the presence of the circumstance elements of the object offense;

(3) in cases where the principal actually causes the result, the same mens rea as to result elements of the object offense as would be required if the accomplice were charged with committing that offense;

(4) in cases where the principal does not actually cause the result, a purpose that the principal cause any result elements required by the object offense; and

(5) a purpose that the principal act with any additional mens rea elements required by the object offense.

1) Mens Rea for Object Offense

The "purpose to promote or facilitate" required by the Model Code means that the defendant must have *at least* the mens rea required for the object offense. Most importantly, this means that the defendant must have a purpose that the principal will act with any separately stated mens rea requirements contained in the object offense.

2) Purpose to Promote or Facilitate

The defendant's purpose must extend to every conduct and circumstance element of the contemplated offense. Recall that defenses and applicable grading factors are "elements" of an offense for culpability purposes. See §§ 1.13(9), 1.13(10), 2.02(1), and pages 116–17. And recall that "purpose" applied to circumstance elements translates into knowledge or belief. See § 2.02(2)(a)(ii) and page 110.

> ***Example:*** Assume the defendant is charged with being an accomplice to second degree burglary as defined in § 221.1. The following mens rea would be minimally sufficient: (a) *Conduct elements of the object offense*: a purpose that the principal enter; (b) *Circumstance elements of the object offense, including defenses and grading factors*: knowledge that the entry is into a building or occupied structure (or separately secured or occupied portion thereof), knowledge that the premises are not open to the public, that the principal has no license or privilege to enter, that the premises are not abandoned, and that the offense was committed in the dwelling of another at night; and (c) *Additional mens rea required by object offense*: a purpose that the principal commit a felony inside the building. Of course alternative grading factors might be

asserted under § 221.1(2)(a) or (b), in which case the appropriate culpability could be substituted for knowledge that the offense was committed in the dwelling of another at night.

Note that these mens rea requirements are substantially higher than would suffice for the principal. And note that purpose or knowledge, as the case may be, would be required for the accessory even for a conduct or circumstance element that carried strict liability for the principal.

Why should the mens rea for the accessory be higher than for the principal? It is a sound general principle underlying the criminal law that the more the completed conduct and results, the less can be the culpability that can, as a minimum, fairly be required. Liability as an accessory is the obverse of this principle. Since less conduct is required of the accessory than for the principle, it is fair to require more culpability. These generalizations may not always fit the facts. Nor may they always be followed. But they do state general principles that can be found in the definitions of numerous crimes.

3) Knowledge That Crime Will be Promoted or Facilitated

An earlier draft of § 2.06 permitted conviction based on knowledge that aid was promoting or facilitating an offense. In the end, however, and after much debate, the American Law Institute decided to rest accomplice liability on a full-fledged purpose to promote or facilitate. Thus, mere knowledge will not suffice.

4) Recklessness or Negligence as to Results

Section 2.06(4) establishes the mens rea required for result elements of the object offense. It states that the accomplice must have the same mens rea for result elements as is required for the object offense.

But note that § 2.06(4) applies only to "an accomplice in the conduct causing such result." The effect of this language is to limit § 2.06(4) to cases where the principal actually causes the result. Otherwise—in cases where the result is not actually caused by the principal—the mens rea for result elements of the object offense is governed by the requirement that the accomplice have a "purpose to promote or facilitate" the offense. Thus, the effect of § 2.06(4) is that the mens rea for result elements differs depending on whether the principal actually causes the result. If the result is caused, the mens rea is the same as it is for the object offense. If the result is not caused, the mens rea is purpose.

The Model Penal Code takes this position in order to be consistent with its treatment of the principal. If the principal causes the result in an offense that requires recklessness, the mens rea of recklessness obtains. But if the principal does *not* cause the result, then prosecution of the principal for attempt under § 5.01 would require that the principal have a mens rea of purpose as to the result. See page 332. Thus, since the mens rea for the principal changes when the result is not caused, it makes sense for the mens rea for the accomplice to change too.

Examples: Assume that *A* helps *P* beat up *V* and that *V* dies. Assume that *P* is guilty of manslaughter under § 210.3(1)(a). *A* would also be guilty of manslaughter if *A* had a purpose to promote or facilitate *P*'s conduct and if *A* was also reckless as to the death. Or *A* could be convicted of negligent homicide if *A* was negligent as to *V*'s death, or murder if *A* intended *V*'s death. The degree of *A*'s liability is independent of the degree of *P*'s liability. Each is assessed based on their own culpability as to *V*'s death.

Now assume that *V* doesn't die. *P* can be convicted of attempted murder only if it is shown that *P* intended to kill *V*. *P* cannot be convicted of attempted manslaughter on a showing of recklessness as to death, nor of attempted negligent homicide on a showing of negligence. [For an explanation of this result in the context of the Model Code attempt provisions, see pages 333–34.] Similarly, *A* cannot be convicted as an accessory to an attempt unless it is shown that *A* intended to kill *V*—recklessness or negligence will not suffice since the result, *V*'s death, did not occur. [But, as developed below, if *A* did intend *V*'s death, *A* could be convicted of attempted murder even though *P* did not intend the death and was not guilty of an attempt.]

5) Negligence: Unanticipated Offenses
The Model Penal Code does not permit conviction merely because an offense was the "natural and probable consequence" of a crime which the defendant aided and abetted. The defendant can be liable as an accessory only if the mens rea as described above is satisfied.

c. The Principal's Behavior: Conduct or Guilt
What the principal did is not central to conviction of the accessory under the Model Penal Code. But it may affect grading. In each of the four situations discussed below, you should assume that the accomplice has committed the actus reus and mens rea sufficient for accomplice liability, as described above.

1) Guilt of the Principal
Plainly if the principal actually commits all elements of the object offense, the accessory would be guilty of the object offense under § 2.06.

2) Aiding and Abetting an Attempt

It is also clear from the language of § 2.06 that if the principal attempts to commit the object offense, the accessory is guilty of an attempt to commit the object offense.

3) Conduct by the Principal

Where the principal has engaged in conduct sufficient for the commission of the object offense, but is not guilty because the required mens rea is lacking or some other defense can be asserted, the accessory can still be convicted for the object offense. And where the principal has engaged in conduct sufficient for the commission of an attempt to commit the object offense, but is not guilty of an attempt because the required mens rea is lacking or some other defense can be asserted, the accessory can be convicted for an attempt to commit the object offense.

These results appear to follow from the use of the word "conduct" in § 2.06(1), although a contrary construction of the Model Code is possible. In effect, the accessory is liable for helping the principal engage in *conduct* sufficient for an offense or an attempt, no matter what mens rea the principal has towards that conduct and no matter whether the principal is guilty of committing or attempting the offense. This is a fair solution, moreover, since the accomplice is just as dangerous and culpable whether or not the principal is actually guilty. The accomplice has, recall, committed a sufficient actus reus and mens rea to be guilty as an accessory, and whether or not the principal is also guilty would seem an irrelevant fortuity.

4) Attempting to Aid and Abet; No Conduct by Principal

What of the situation where the defendant tries to aid and abet the commission of a crime by another, but the other person doesn't do anything? Or suppose the principal engages some conduct but not enough to constitute a "substantial step" for an attempt? These cases are treated by § 5.01(3) as attempts to commit the object offense.

Thus, when all is said and done, it doesn't matter to the *conviction* of the accessory what the principal does. But it may matter as to the *grading* of the accessory's offense. Attempts are graded the same as the object offense *unless* the object offense is a capital crime or a felony of the first degree. See § 5.05(1). Thus a grading consequence will turn on what the principal has done only when the object offense is an especially serious one. To summarize—and remember that in each instance the accessory has committed *both* the actus reus and the mens rea for accomplice liability:

(1) If the principal is guilty of the object offense or if the principal engaged in the conduct required by that offense, then the accessory can be convicted of the object offense under § 2.06.

(2) If the principal is guilty of an attempt to commit the object offense or has engaged in conduct sufficient for such an attempt, then the accessory is guilty of an attempt to commit the object offense under § 2.06.

(3) If the principal does nothing or engages in insufficient conduct for an attempt, then the accessory is guilty of an attempt to commit the object offense under § 5.01(3).

d. Grading of the Accessory's Crime

The grading of the accessory under the Model Penal Code is based on the conduct committed by the principal and the culpability manifested by the accessory. The principal's guilt is irrelevant and the principal can be convicted of a more serious or a less serious offense than the accomplice. Both, in effect, are graded on their own culpability.

Examples: These principles are illustrated in the summary of the relation between the accessory's liability and the principal's behavior which appears immediately above. They are also illustrated by the example given under the heading "Recklessness or Negligence as to Results," page 288, and by the example given under the heading "Departures from the General Rule," page 274 (applying § 2.06 to the definition of arson stated in the example).

e. Withdrawal of Aid

The Model Penal Code recognizes a defense if the accessory, having given aid that would be sufficient for liability, withdraws that aid before the principal commits the offense. The requirements for an effective withdrawal are stated in § 2.06(6)(c). They are that the actor "terminate" any complicity prior to the commission of the offense and in addition do one of three things:

(1) "wholly deprive" the aid of any effectiveness in the commission of the offense; or

(2) give timely warning to law enforcement authorities; or

(3) otherwise make proper effort to prevent the commission of the offense. [What constitutes an "otherwise proper effort" to prevent the offense is not elaborated upon.]

4. ACCESSORIES AFTER THE FACT

The Model Penal Code has abandoned the common law category of "accessory after the fact." It has substituted the offenses defined in Article 242, "Obstructing Governmental Operations."

a. Hindering Apprehension or Prosecution

Section 242.3 is the principal offense designed to punish those who were formerly accessories after the fact. Note, however, that the offense is much

broader than its common law counterpart. For example, it applies to aid given
to one who has committed any "crime" (recall that violations are not "crimes";
§ 1.04(5)), and it does not matter whether the person aided is in fact guilty so
long as the actor gives aid with purpose to hinder apprehension, prosecution,
conviction, or punishment of another for crime. Note also that the offense is
variably graded depending on the seriousness of the offense aided.

b. Supplementary Offenses

There are, moreover, a number of other offenses in Article 242 reaching conduct
that formerly could have justified punishment as an accessory after the fact,
including the following: §§ 242.1, 242.4, 242.5, 242.6(2), and 242.7.

C. VICARIOUS LIABILITY

The Model Penal Code does not deal explicitly with vicarious liability imposed on
natural persons. It does, however, seem to contemplate its imposition where the
legislature explicitly so intends. Section 2.05(1) states that the requirements of §§ 2.01
and 2.02 do not apply to violations. Section 2.01(1) is the provision of the Model Code
stating that "conduct" is the premise of criminal liability. Thus, the fact that the
provisions of § 2.01 do not apply to violations makes it possible for vicarious liability to
be imposed in such cases, since it is the lack of harmful conduct by the defendant that
distinguishes vicarious liability from more ordinary bases of criminal punishment. The
provisions of § 2.06(2)(b) make it possible for vicarious liability to be specifically
imposed for crimes as well.

D. ENTERPRISE LIABILITY

Section 2.07 covers enterprise liability.

1. LIABILITY OF A CORPORATION

Section 2.07(1) states four situations in which a corporation may be liable:

(1) the offense is a violation, and the criminal conduct is performed by an
employee acting for the corporation within the scope of office or employment; or

(2) the offense is defined outside the criminal code, there is a clear legislative
purpose to impose liability on a corporation, and the criminal conduct is
performed by an employee acting for the corporation within the scope of office
or employment [note that § 2.07(2) assumes such a legislative purpose, absent
contrary evidence, in all cases where "absolute" (read strict) liability is imposed
for the commission of an offense—in effect, this is designed to permit vicarious
corporate liability for public welfare offenses; and note that for both this
category of offense and the previous one an explicit statutory limit on the kind
of employee who can commit the offense must be respected]; or

(3) the offense consists of an omission to discharge a specific duty to engage in
affirmative conduct imposed on the corporation by law; or

(4) the offense was "authorized, requested, commanded, performed or recklessly tolerated" by the board of directors or by a high managerial agent acting for the corporation within the scope of office or employment. [Note that "high managerial agent" is defined in § 2.07(4)(c); and note that this provision applies to *any* offense in the criminal code.]

In summary, this provision applies to a narrow range of offenses—public welfare offenses, violations, situations where the legislature specifically intends liability, situations where affirmative duties are placed on the corporation and enforced by criminal punishment—except in instances where it can fairly be said that the offense is a product of official corporate policy (see the definition of "high managerial agent").

2. LIABILITY OF PARTNERSHIP OR UNINCORPORATED ASSOCIATION

Section 2.07(3) limits the liability of unincorporated associations to the second and third categories of offenses described above. Note that § 2.07(2) is limited to corporations, however. And note that for purposes of § 2.07(3) it appears that a partnership is an unincorporated association (otherwise, why include a partnership in the definition of "high managerial agent"?).

3. DUE DILIGENCE DEFENSE

Section 2.07(5) gives the corporation, partnership, or unincorporated association a defense that "the high managerial agent having supervisory responsibility over the subject matter of the offense employed due diligence to prevent its commission." But the defense is narrowly circumscribed:

(1) it does not apply in cases where strict liability is imposed; and

(2) it is limited to situations where the offense is committed by employees who are not themselves "high managerial agents"; and

(3) it does not apply to offenses involving an omission to perform a specifically imposed duty; and

(4) it does not apply if it is "plainly inconsistent" with the legislative purpose underlying the particular offense; and

(5) the defendant must prove the defense by a preponderance of the evidence.

4. LIABILITY OF EMPLOYEE

Section 2.07(6) deals with the liability of the employee. It provides in Subsection (a), as would be expected, that the employee is fully liable under ordinary principles for any crime committed, even though committed on behalf of or to benefit the enterprise. Subsection (a) also means that ordinary principles of accomplice liability could be applied to any supervisor of the employee.

Subsections (b) and (c) deal with the liability of the employee who has the primary responsibility of discharging a duty imposed on the enterprise. Under Subsection

(b) that employee is personally liable for a "reckless omission" to perform the duty. Under Subsection (c), the punishment may be any sentence authorized for imposition on a natural person for an offense of that grade and degree. [The reason for Subsection (c) is that the legislature is liable to have designed the penalties with only the corporation or other enterprise in mind, and thus may have authorized only a fine for commission of the offense. Under Subsection (c), one would look to Article 6 to determine the authorized penalty for an offense of that grade—which could include imprisonment.]

E. REVIEW QUESTIONS

[Answers Provided in Appendix A, page 442]

1. T or F   The employee of a partnership may be liable to imprisonment under the Model Penal Code for failure to discharge a duty imposed upon the partnership itself, if performance of the duty is the primary obligation of the employee and if the failure is at least reckless.

2. T or F   The "due diligence" defense may be asserted by an unincorporated association to a strict liability offense under the Model Penal Code, but the burden of persuasion is placed on the defendant by a preponderance of the evidence.

3. T or F   The liability of business enterprises—corporations, partnerships, and unincorporated associations—is the only place in the Model Penal Code where vicarious liability is specifically imposed.

4. T or F   Accessories after the fact are not punished as "accomplices" to any crime under the Model Penal Code. Rather, they are punished for a separate offense related to the obstruction of justice.

5. T or F   A member of a conspiracy who abandons the conspiracy and renounces any further association with its criminal objectives will no longer be liable for offenses thereafter committed pursuant to the conspiracy by other conspirators.

6. T or F   *P* marries *A* under circumstances that constitute bigamy in violation of § 230.1 of the Model Penal Code. *P* was already married to another. *A* cannot be convicted of bigamy, however, unless it can be shown that *A* had a purpose to promote or facilitate *P*'s bigamy. It is not enough to show that *A* merely knew of *P*'s prior marriage, and went ahead with the ceremony anyway.

7. T or F   *P*, a male, has sexual intercourse with a female less than 10 years old. *A*, a female, helps *P* commit the offense, with a purpose that the act be committed. *P* believes the victim to be 11 years old, and so does *A*. Oddly enough, under the Model Penal Code *P* can be convicted of violating § 213.1(1)(d) but *A* cannot.

8. T or F   On the facts of the previous question, curiously enough, *A can* be convicted if *P* is insane, because then *P* would be an "innocent or irresponsible person" under § 2.06(2)(a) and *A* would have acted with the culpability otherwise sufficient for commission of the offense.

[**Note**: the following two questions should be postponed until you have covered the materials on attempt in the next chapter, "Inchoate Crimes."]

9. *P* takes an umbrella believed to belong to *V*. Actually the umbrella belongs to *P. A* helped *P* take the umbrella with a purpose to promote its theft. Like *P, A* believed that the umbrella belonged to *V*. If the umbrella is worth $25, what is the maximum sentence, if any, that can be imposed on *P* and *A* under the Model Penal Code? [You will find the maximum sentences in Article 6 of the Model Code.]

10. Examine Question 13 in the Model Code materials on inchoate offenses, page 355. Assume in this instance that *D1* is charged as an accomplice to the commission of a violation of § 220.1. Assume further that *D1* purchased gasoline and gave it to *D2* so that *D2* could start the fire, but that *D2* arrested *D1* before engaging in sufficient conduct to constitute a "substantial step" towards setting the yacht on fire. Of what offense, if any, can *D1* be convicted? [Take your time on this one. It would be a 60 minute question on an examination.]

*

PART SEVEN

INCHOATE CRIMES

Analysis

*

XII

THE COMMON LAW

Analysis

A. INTRODUCTION

Attempt, conspiracy, and solicitation involve efforts to commit one or more of the array of offenses defined in the penal code. They are often called "inchoate" crimes because they do not require that the object offense be completed.

These offenses differ from most crimes in that they do not identify specific social harms they are designed to prevent. They are defined generically. Typically, they are defined to apply to all crimes that exist on the books. Thus there is a single definition of attempt that can be applied to an attempt to murder, or an attempt to rape, or an attempt to steal. The elements of a specific attempt charge will consist of the application of the generic definition of attempt to the definition of the offense that is its object. The same is true of conspiracy and solicitation. There is a law associated with all three that must be integrated with the law of the offense each is designed to commit before one can know what is required to obtain a conviction.

If you think about it for a minute, you will see why this must be so. Take attempted murder. How many ways are there to attempt to murder someone? How hard would it be to describe in advance the particulars of each and every different way that one could attempt to commit this crime? Now add attempted rape. And then attempted theft. And then an attempt to commit every other criminal offense on the books. How long and how complicated would the criminal code be if each of the particulars of each of the ways one could attempt to commit any offense were written down in advance? And how many gaps would exist in the law because the lawmaker didn't think of every possibility? Now do the same thing with conspiracy and solicitation. What kind of a mess would you have when you were finished?

You see the point. It makes much more sense to decide in the abstract what it takes to constitute an attempt, and then to apply that abstraction to the elements of any offense one might attempt to commit. That is a manageable task. And that is the approach the law takes to the crimes of attempt, conspiracy, and solicitation.

B. ATTEMPT

A separate crime of attempt was first formulated as a misdemeanor by common law judges in 1784. Today every American jurisdiction punishes the crime of attempt by statute. The definitions differ, but basically attempt consists of an act that falls short of completion of a specific criminal offense, committed with the intent to complete the offense. Though some courts get hung up on the point, it should not be a defense that the crime was actually completed. Rather, attempt should be regarded as a lesser included offense. A charge of the completed offense will permit a conviction of attempt, but the defendant cannot be convicted of both the completed offense and an attempt to commit it.

The first step in determining whether an attempt has occurred should be to ascertain whether the defendant had the required mens rea. The reason for asking the mens rea question first is that it will aid analysis of the so-called "impossibility" cases later to be considered. The second step is to ask whether the actus reus has occurred. The crime of attempt is complete once the mens rea and the actus reus have occurred.

1. THE MENS REA

Attempt is a specific intent offense.

a. The Specific Intent Requirement

The mens rea of attempt at common law is an intent to engage in all of the conduct, result, and circumstance elements that would constitute a completed criminal offense. Attempt is a "specific intent" offense, even though the crime attempted may only require "general intent." Moreover, if the offense attempted requires a specific intent, the defendant must *also* have the specific intent for that offense in order to be guilty of an attempt to commit it.

> *Examples:* Assume a general intent offense consisting of the elements "breaking and entering the dwelling of another." The mens rea for an attempt to commit that offense would be an intent to engage in conduct that the law would describe as "breaking and entering the dwelling of another." The specific intent required for the attempt would encompass all of the actus reus elements of the offense attempted.
>
> Now assume a specific intent offense defined as "breaking and entering the dwelling of another with intent to commit a felony therein." The mens rea for an attempt to commit that offense would be an intent to engage in conduct that the law would describe as "breaking and entering the dwelling of another" and *in addition* "an intent to commit a felony therein." The specific intent for the crime of attempt must encompass *both* the intent to commit all of the actus reus elements of the offense attempted *and* the specific intent (if any) required by the offense attempted.

b. The Meaning of Specific Intent

Remember as you consider these examples that the concept of "specific intent" ordinarily requires only that the defendant intend to engage in certain kinds of behavior under certain circumstances. The defendant need not know how the law characterizes that behavior, nor that the sum of the actus reus and mens rea amounts to a crime. The defendant is guilty so long as the intent encompasses the kinds of behavior that the law has resolved to punish.

> *Example:* Assume a crime defined as "breaking and entering the dwelling of another." The defendant tries to reach a hand through an open window to grab something inside the house, but is stopped before the act is completed. The defendant meant to do what was done, and meant to grab something inside. The defendant did not

believe, however, that reaching inside an open window constituted a "breaking" within the defined offense. If one assumes that the criminal law concludes that such conduct constitutes a "breaking," is the mens rea for an attempt satisfied?

The answer is "yes." Recall the normal response to mistakes of the criminal law (see page 156). The mens rea for an attempt to commit the defined crime consists of an intent to engage in conduct that the criminal law defines as breaking and entering the dwelling of another. What label the defendant places on the conduct is irrelevant.

c. Recklessness, Negligence, and Strict Liability

Designation of attempt as a specific intent crime means that one cannot commit an attempt recklessly or negligently. It also means that an attempt to commit a strict liability crime requires a specific intent to engage in all of the actus reus elements of the offense, including those which carry strict liability.

Examples: Assume a crime defined as "recklessly causing the death of another." Assume also that the defendant engages in conduct with sufficient recklessness to constitute this crime. Assume, however, that because of a medical miracle the victim does not die. Is the defendant guilty of an attempt to commit the defined offense?

The answer is "no." Attempt requires a specific intent, here an intent "to cause the death of another." The defendant did not have that intent, and is not guilty of an attempt no matter how close to killing the victim the reckless behavior came.

Assume a second offense defined as "sexual abuse of a person under the age of 10." Assume that strict liability applies to the element "under the age of 10." Assume further that the defendant tries to sexually abuse a person under the age of 10, but believes the victim to be 12 years old. Is the defendant guilty of an attempt to commit the defined offense?

The answer is "no." Attempt requires a specific intent, here an intent to "sexually abuse a person under the age of 10." The defendant intended to sexually abuse a person who was 12, and hence did not have the required specific intent.

d. Exceptions

The common law was as described above. There has, however, been some leakage in these requirements in American decisions.

1) Recklessness

A few courts have held that it is possible to have a "reckless" attempt. For example, in People v. Thomas, 729 P.2d 972 (Colo. 1986), the Court upheld a conviction of attempted reckless manslaughter. The defendant fired what he described as two warning shots and a third accidental shot at a person he thought was a fleeing rapist. Two shots hit the victim, but did not kill him. If the victim had died, the defendant's culpability was sufficient to warrant a conviction of reckless manslaughter. But since the victim did not die, was it permissible to convict him of attempted reckless manslaughter?

The Court held "yes." The argument in favor of this result is that the defendant intentionally engaged in conduct (firing the shots) that would have justified a conviction for the completed offense had the victim died. That the victim did not die was pure fortuity. The defendant was just as dangerous, and just as culpable, as one who recklessly killed. Both retributive and social control rationales warrant conviction.

The argument against this result is based on legislative intent. The legislature in Colorado (and in every other State) had defined an array of assault offenses that were graded based on various combinations of conduct, culpability, and results. The effect of the Colorado Supreme Court conviction was to permit the grading of Thomas's offense at a higher level than would have been warranted if he had been charged with the most serious of these assault offenses. So in effect what the Colorado Supreme Court did was undermine the carefully constructed grading structure established by the legislature.

For this and other reasons, most American courts that have confronted this issue have disagreed with the Colorado Supreme Court. They would follow the traditional common law rule, and convict of an attempt in the *Thomas* situation only if it could have been shown that he intended to kill.

2) Negligence

Courts have not extended the reasoning of the *Thomas* Court to negligence. Why not? It is not clear, but one reason might be that the offense of attempted negligent homicide would occur every time anyone (including the judges) was negligent in the operation of an automobile but was lucky that a fatal accident did not occur. Self-protection is a powerful incentive.

3) Strict Liability and Circumstance Elements

There are strong arguments that the mens rea for the circumstance elements of an attempt should be the same as they would be for the object offense being attempted. Assume that rape is defined to include sexual intercourse by a male with a girl who is less than 10 years old and that liability is strict as to the age of the victim. If the defendant completes his behavior, it will be no defense if he claims he thought the girl was 11 or 12. Should he have a defense if he is caught just prior to the act of penetration and makes the same claim to a charge of attempt?

The traditional common law response was "yes." The specific intent required for attempt meant that the defendant had to intend "the entire evil thing," which meant in turn that the defendant must know that all circumstance elements were present.

As described on page 332, the Model Penal Code would say "no." For circumstance elements, the Model Penal Code applies the same mens rea policy for the attempt as would be applied to the completed offense.

It seems clear that the Model Code has the better of it in terms of policy. Social control and retribution clearly point towards conviction. Can you think of any reasons why the traditional common law position should be followed on this point? It is hard, if not impossible, to do so. But the situation has not arisen very frequently, and decided cases that reject the traditional common law position on this issue are difficult to find.

2. THE ACTUS REUS

In the vocabulary of the common law, the task in determining whether the actus reus of attempt has occurred is to distinguish between acts which are mere preparation and those which constitute the beginning of an attempt. If one visualizes a time spectrum beginning with the defendant's first thought of committing an offense and ending with the completion of the crime, the question is when along the line between these two end points the defendant's conduct has come close enough to the commission of the offense to constitute an attempt. The actus reus of attempt is not set out in advance. What is required is a formula for determining how much conduct is enough.

a. The Common Law Tests

The common law has developed a number of tests for determining whether the actus reus of attempt has occurred, among them:

1) The Last Proximate Act

Early decisions asked whether the defendant had committed all of the intended conduct, whether the last act necessary to complete the offense had occurred. This inquiry is acceptable as a test of *inclusion,* but inadequate as a test of *exclusion.* That is, the last proximate act is clearly enough conduct, but courts today will convict of attempt when less conduct than that has occurred. The courts have accordingly discarded it as the test for the actus reus of attempt.

Examples: Assume a defendant who, with intent to kill, fires at a victim and misses. The "last proximate act" test is satisfied. The defendant did all that was intended, and completed sufficient behavior to constitute the crime of murder if the aim had been better. The defendant is guilty of attempted murder.

Now assume a defendant who, with intent to kill, aims the gun but is stopped by police before the trigger is pulled. Here the "last proximate act" test is not satisfied. The defendant has not committed the last act necessary to complete the offense. The defendant would be acquitted of attempt if that were the determinative inquiry. Yet plainly the defendant should be guilty of attempted murder, as all modern courts would hold.

2) The Physical Proximity Tests

A commonly used inquiry is to ask whether the defendant's act is sufficiently proximate to the completion of the crime to constitute an attempt. Put in this way the question is circular, for the very issue to be determined is whether the defendant has gone far enough to commit an attempt. Yet some courts have asked the unadorned "physical proximity" question, and focused on how much conduct remains to be done by the defendant (rather than how much conduct has already been completed). Presumably the rationale for this inquiry is that the more that remains to be done, the less likely it is that the defendant will complete the offense and the more likely it is that the harm sought to be prevented by the completed crime will not occur.

Some courts have also sought to sharpen the "proximity" inquiry by suggesting other criteria for determining whether what remains to be done should exonerate from liability for attempt.

a) The Indispensable Element Test

One technique is to ask whether the defendant has obtained control over all indispensable elements of the offense. Presumably, the defendant who does not yet have the capacity presently to commit all elements of the offense is "too far" from completion to be prosecuted for an attempt.

> ***Example:*** Assume a defendant charged with attempted assault with a deadly weapon. The indispensable element test would suggest that such a conviction could not occur until the defendant has obtained control over a deadly weapon, since that is an "indispensable element" of the completed offense.

b) The Dangerous Proximity Test

Another variation is to ask whether the defendant has come dangerously close to completion of the offense. This approach looks at four factors in addition to proximity to the ultimate goal: (1) the seriousness of the crime; (2) the uncertainty of its occurrence; (3) the apprehension caused to the victim; and (4) the amount of harm that would occur if the crime were completed. This test is generally associated with Oliver Wendell Holmes.

3) The Probable Desistance Tests

A contrasting approach is taken by those courts that focus upon the probability that the defendant will not commit the crime. Called the "probable desistance" test, this approach focuses more upon what the defendant has done (and the likelihood that the defendant will continue) than on what remains to be done. The question asked is whether the defendant has exhibited dangerousness of character (in the sense that the defendant is likely to commit the crime). The contrast with the proximity tests is a change in focus: from dangerous conduct to dangerous people, from whether what remains to be done shows that dangerous behavior has already occurred to whether what the defendant has done shows that the defendant is a dangerous person.

This inquiry has been criticized on the ground that it is too indeterminate, that there are no objective criteria by which one can measure the probability that a given defendant will desist from commission of the offense. In response to this criticism, at least one other approach has been developed:

a) The Res Ipsa Loquitur Test

Sometimes called the "equivocality" test, this inquiry asks whether the defendant's act speaks for itself, whether one who saw the defendant's behavior without knowing the defendant's intention would be able to guess what the defendant meant to do. The difficulty with this inquiry is that it may go too far: very few acts are completely unequivocal, and this test may exonerate too many defendants who ought to be convicted.

b. Conclusion

The fact is that the common law has yet to develop a satisfactory inquiry for determining when the actus reus of attempt has occurred. The issue is important, for all crime should require sufficiently unambiguous conduct so as to avoid unwarranted interference with innocent behavior. Yet the problem is intractable too, for the actus reus of attempt must necessarily remain indeterminate in order to encompass the vast range of inchoate behavior that may precede the commission of a crime. This is a good example of a hard problem with no easy answer.

3. IMPOSSIBILITY

The most frequently litigated and written about problem in the law of attempt concerns the so-called "impossibility" issue. This is an area of great confusion in the cases. Three different categories of situations can be identified, though it is "impossible," so to speak, to distinguish between the last two.

a. True Legal Impossibility

The easiest situation, and one where the cases are in unanimous agreement that a conviction for attempt is inappropriate, is called "true legal impossibility." This is where the defendant seeks to do something that is not a crime. "True legal impossibility" cases can easily be identified by asking whether the defendant had the mens rea required for an attempt to commit some criminal offense. When the answer is "no," then all "true legal impossibility" cases will be eliminated.

> *Example:* Assume a defendant who tries to smoke marijuana. The defendant believes this to be a criminal offense, but the legislature has repealed the law that formerly made it a crime. Is the defendant punishable for an attempt to smoke marijuana? No. The question to ask is whether the defendant had the mens rea for a crime. Here the defendant did not, since the intent was to smoke marijuana and that is not the mens rea for any crime. This is a "true legal impossibility" case because what the defendant tried to do is not a crime. The fact that the defendant *thought* it was a crime is irrelevant as an inculpating factor, just as a belief that conduct was *not* a crime will not exculpate.

b. Legal and Factual Impossibility

An attempt is said to present a case of "legal impossibility" if the act as completed would not constitute a crime. "Legal impossibility" is a defense to a charge of attempt. An attempt is said to present a case of "factual impossibility" if the crime cannot be completed because of some physical or factual condition unknown to the defendant. "Factual impossibility" is not a defense to a charge of attempt. The trouble is that any of the standard "impossibility" cases can be placed in either category.

> *Example:* Consider a case where a dummy is placed in a bed, and the defendant shoots the dummy thinking it the victim the defendant intends to kill. Is this a case of "legal" or "factual" impossibility? It could be either. The case presents a "legal" impossibility because the act of killing a dummy is not a crime. The act as completed would not constitute a crime. The case presents a "factual" impossibility because the defendant was prevented from completing the crime because of an unknown physical or factual condition. The victim wasn't there.

c. Primary and Secondary Intent

Some authors have sought to clarify this situation by distinguishing between the defendant's "primary" and "secondary" intent. The defendant's "primary" intent is to do what the defendant did, that is, in the example above, to kill a dummy. The defendant's "secondary" intent is to do what the defendant *thought* was being done, that is, in the example above, to kill a person. In this rather forced terminology, "secondary" intent is the defendant's actual intent. "Primary" intent is a purely fictional attribution of an intent to do what was actually done. "Primary" intent is then said to be the important "intent" for measuring liability for attempt.

This distinction is useless. And it is selectively employed by those who like it, since they do not want to measure the liability of *all* defendants charged with attempt by their "primary" intent.

Example: Assume a defendant who shoots at a victim with intent to kill, but who misses because of bad aim. Should the defendant be guilty of attempted murder? Of course. Would the defendant be liable if "primary" intent were the measuring rod? No, because the defendant's "primary" intent was to do what was done. Here what was done was to miss, and a defendant who has the intent to miss does not have the mens rea for attempted murder.

Advocates of the "primary"-"secondary" intent distinction would find some way to convict this defendant. They thus employ the distinction in a question-begging manner. Those defendants who ought to be convicted will be measured by their secondary intent. Those who ought to be acquitted will be measured by their primary intent. But there is nothing in the distinction that tells you which is which.

d. Proper Analysis of Legal and Factual Impossibility Cases

How, then, should impossibility cases be analyzed? The answer is quite simple. The cases do not present mens rea problems, but ought to be thought of as presenting an actus reus problem. The question is whether, under one's normal approach to ascertaining the actus reus of attempt, the actus reus is present. If so, the defendant should be convicted. If not, the defendant should not be convicted. One suspects that this is the issue that is submerged in the meaningless "legal-factual" and "primary-secondary" distinctions.

Consider how this approach would be applied to the example given above about the person who shot a dummy:

1) Mens Rea

The first question, as noted above, is whether the defendant has the mens rea for a criminal attempt. This question should be answered as it normally is, by asking what the defendant actually intended. In the example given above, the defendant intended to kill a person, and thus had the required mens rea.

2) Actus Reus

The second question is whether the actus reus is present. This depends on the approach one takes to that question.

a) The Physical Proximity Tests

If one normally uses one of the "proximity" inquiries, the issue is: "How close to killing a person did the defendant actually come?"

"Based on what remained to be done in order to effect a killing, was the defendant's conduct dangerous?" The answer to these questions is problematical. Since there was a dummy in the bed, the defendant really didn't come very close to a killing. On the other hand, if one takes the "dangerous proximity" approach and weighs all the factors involved in that inquiry, perhaps the defendant came close enough. The proximity inquiries ask, essentially, whether the defendant engaged in dangerous conduct. One can engage in a meaningful argument in these terms about this case, and decide—just the same way one normally does in the application of the proximity tests—whether defendants like this one ought to be convicted.

It is sometimes helpful in this respect to ask whether just prior to the last act that gave rise to the impossibility problem the defendant had already gone far enough to have committed an attempt. Thus, if the defendant had snuck into the victim's darkened bedroom and raised a pistol to fire into the victim's bed, one might, on the basis of what remained to be done in order to commit a murder, decide that an attempt had occurred at that point and regard the actual shooting of the dummy as irrelevant.

b) The Probable Desistance Tests

On the other hand, if one uses a version of the "probable desistance" inquiry, the defendant is almost certainly guilty. The question under this approach is whether the defendant has manifested a dangerousness of character, whether the conduct the defendant has already engaged in reveals that the defendant presents the danger at which the crime of murder is aimed. The answer in this case is surely "yes." People who are not dangerous simply do not fire guns into beds that appear to be occupied by a person.

Consider another example: the old saw about the absent-minded professor who, with intent to steal, takes from a stand an umbrella believed to belong to someone else when in fact it belongs to the professor. Here the defendant has the mens rea for attempted larceny. Is the actus reus present? Under the proximity approaches, probably not. The professor didn't come very close to committing theft, based on what remains to be done to accomplish that offense. The professor's conduct is not very dangerous. Nor is the actus reus present under the probable desistance approaches. What the professor did—take an umbrella from a stand—is ordinary, everyday behavior that does not manifest the kind of dangerousness of character that the law of theft is designed to prevent. Moreover, since the professor's conduct is objectively ambiguous, we cannot be certain that any inference of intent based on that conduct is accurate. We cannot be certain that the professor has the intent and the resolution of a thief. To punish the professor would effectively be to punish for thoughts alone, uncorroborated by actual behavior. It would run too great a risk of punishing innocent behavior.

4. ABANDONMENT

Once a criminal attempt has occurred, the common law does not recognize a defense based on a decision by the defendant to abandon the effort and not complete the offense. Plainly this is the right answer in cases where the defendant's decision is induced by a fear of getting caught or by the intervention of the police. Whether an abandonment defense ought to be recognized in the case of a truly voluntary change of heart presents a more difficult policy question.

5. GRADING

At common law, attempt was a misdemeanor. Modern statutes vary widely in their grading schemes. A few equate the grading of attempt with the offense attempted. Some statutes that place offenses in a small number of categories punish an attempt one category less severely than the offense attempted. Some statutes punish an attempt by a fixed proportion (e.g., one half) of the maximum for the offense attempted. And some statutes adopt a fixed penalty for attempts to commit either all or an identified class of offenses.

6. CUMULATIVE PUNISHMENT

A person cannot be convicted for both an attempt and actual commission of the offense attempted.

7. ASSAULT WITH INTENT

Many States punish numerous offenses of the "assault with intent" variety, for example, assault with intent to kill, assault with intent to rape, assault with intent to maim, etc. These offenses emerged at a time when attempt was punished as a misdemeanor. Misdemeanor penalties meant that there was a large gap between the punishment that could be imposed for an attempt and the punishment that could be imposed for some of the more serious completed offenses. Thus a person who murdered or raped could be executed or sentenced to life imprisonment. A person who attempted one of these offenses—and came very close to success—could only be convicted for a misdemeanor, the typical maximum for which was one year. The early statutory response was to create an attempt-like offense of intermediate gravity, such as assault with intent to kill. Basically, an assault with intent to kill is an attempt to kill that comes very close to completion. And typically, it will be punished by sanctions far more severe than an ordinary attempt.

Many modern statutes omit crimes of the "assault with intent" variety because they grade attempts more severely. If attempted murder can be punished under a flexible sentencing scheme by sanctions that approach those for murder, for example, then the crime of assault with intent to kill is not needed.

C. CONSPIRACY

A separate crime of conspiracy first emerged by statute at the turn of the 14th century. It became a common law misdemeanor by various stages during the 17th and

18th centuries, and is today punished by statute in every American jurisdiction. The common law definition of conspiracy is a combination between two or more persons for the purpose of accomplishing an unlawful act or a lawful act by unlawful means. Statutory definitions of the offense are generally of two types: those that punish an agreement to commit a crime; and those that, in addition to an agreement to commit a crime, punish agreements to accomplish other stated goals (such as "to commit any act injurious to the public health or public morals"). Many of these latter statutes would probably be held void for vagueness if actually used today to prosecute an agreement to accomplish a non-criminal objective expressed in such indeterminate terms. In any event, the important conspiracy cases today are those where the object of the conspiracy is to accomplish one or a series of crimes.

The offense of conspiracy has two primary functions. First, it is a means of imposing liability for the conduct of another. A person who participates in a conspiracy is liable for foreseeable substantive offenses committed in furtherance of the conspiracy. Second, it is an inchoate offense, one that—like attempt—allows the intervention of law enforcement in preliminary behavior that may lead to the commission of a crime. There is a big difference, however. An attempt is a lesser-included offense to the crime attempted, and one cannot be convicted both of an attempt and the offense attempted. But typically one *can* be convicted both of a conspiracy and the offense which is the object of the conspiracy.

The crime of conspiracy requires an actus reus and a mens rea like any other offense. The offense is complicated, however, by a wide range of special problems.

1. THE ACTUS REUS

The actus reus of conspiracy is an agreement between two or more persons to achieve an objective prohibited by the applicable law of conspiracy. The real difficulty with this requirement lies not in what must be proved, but in how it may be proved. Not many conspirators reduce their agreements to writing, nor make formal commitments that can be proved as a contract might be proved. Thus, proof of an agreement, as well as its terms, is normally left to inference from behavior, perhaps supplemented by the impressions of a party to the conspiracy who can be induced to testify. Moreover, it is often ambiguous just who agreed to what in multi-party conspiracies. As a practical matter, it is up to the prosecutor to formulate a theory of the case in which specific allegations are made as to the nature and scope of the charged conspiracy. Often the prosecutor will have numerous options depending upon the strength of the available evidence.

There are several special problems that have arisen concerning the actus reus of conspiracy:

a. Overt Act

The common law required only an agreement as the actus reus of conspiracy. Some statutes, however, require an overt act in addition to the agreement. See, e.g., 18 U.S.C. § 371. But the overt act requirement is not onerous. *Any* act committed in furtherance of the conspiracy by *any* member of it generally will suffice.

b. More Than One Agreement

The law is clear that a single agreement with multiple objectives constitutes a single conspiracy. But multiple agreements can constitute multiple conspiracies. The rub comes in the application of this simple principle to particular situations, and in who is regarded as a party to what agreements. Often the analogies of a "wheel with spokes" or a "chain" are invoked to describe the scope of multi-party agreements. These analogies are of minimal utility, but their paradigm operation is as follows:

1) The "Wheel With Spokes"

If one person or group of persons is at the center (the "hub" of a wheel), and a number of different and unrelated persons (or groups) have formed separate agreements with those at the "hub" (they become separate, unconnected "spokes"), then there is not one large conspiracy but a series of smaller ones. Those at the "hub" are involved in separate conspiracies with each group at the end of a "spoke." The reason this is not particularly helpful talk is that one must already decide that there is a series of independent conspiracies (which is the issue to be determined) before one can accurately draw this picture of the arrangement. Moreover, the wheel can have a "rim." That is, the spokes may be connected by an outer rim—an agreement by those who form the spokes that makes everyone a party to a single conspiratorial agreement.

2) The "Chain"

If one person or group of persons agrees with another person or group, which in turn agrees with yet another person or group (as in the arrangement that might exist between manufacturer, distributor, and retailer), then a "chain" agreement is said to be involved. Each person or separate group is said to be a "link" in the chain. What one knows when one knows this is unclear. For a "chain" arrangement can involve either a single conspiracy (as where three people get together, one to act as manufacturer, another as distributor, and another as retailer) or multiple conspiracies (as where one person sells to another, who unknown to the first sells to a third person for distribution).

The situation can get even more complicated when "wheels" and "chains" are mixed together, as where a manufacturer sells to an east coast and a west coast distributor, and each distributor then sells to five retailers. The manufacturer and each distributor are "hubs" in different wheels, and "links" in different chains.

What should be kept in mind amidst all this confusion is the issue sought to be resolved. The question is whether there is one agreement or several, and who is a party to each agreement if there are several. This is always a matter of evidence and proof, and often a function of the theory the prosecutor chooses to assert. The key is to identify a single crime—a single criminal act—to which all who are sought to be joined in one conspiracy have agreed. If the prosecutor can prove that a group is acting in concert towards a single prohibited objective, then one conspiracy can be found whether or not the arrangement can be described as a "wheel" or a "chain." If another group is somehow linked to the first, but does not share with it a particular criminal objective, then there will be more than one conspiracy.

c. Bilateral or Unilateral Agreement

The traditional crime of conspiracy required a bilateral agreement, that is, the actual agreement of two or more parties. Moreover, the common law also insisted that two parties actually be guilty of the offense. Under this view, if *A* feigned agreement with *B*, *B* could not be guilty of conspiracy even though *B* thought there was an agreement with *A*. Similarly, if *A* is not guilty of conspiracy because of some defense peculiar to *A* (for example, insanity, infancy, or duress), then *B* cannot be guilty either. The common law view was that it takes two to tango.

There is now, however, a division of authority on this point. Under some modern statutes and decisions, it is enough that there is a conspiracy from the point of view of one person. This "unilateral" view of the agreement requires only that *B* *think* there is an agreement with one or more additional parties. The fact that from the point of view of the additional parties there is no agreement does not matter to *B*'s liability.

d. Wharton's Rule: Object Crimes Requiring Concerted Action

The common law precluded a conviction of conspiracy where the object of the agreement was a crime that itself required concerted action. This is called "Wharton's Rule," after the author of the criminal law treatise that first articulated and explained the limitation. It would apply, for example, to offenses such as dueling, bigamy, incest, and adultery, where the action of two persons is necessary in order for the offense to occur. It is those two persons who cannot be convicted of conspiracy under Wharton's Rule.

1) Third–Party Exception

Some jurisdictions recognize an exception to Wharton's rule, called the "third-party exception," in cases where the conspiracy involves a greater number of people than is necessary for commission of the offense that is its object. Thus if four people agree that two of them will fight a duel, then all could be convicted of conspiracy to duel (assuming, of course, that dueling remains a criminal offense in the relevant jurisdiction).

2) Use of Wharton's Rule as Principle of Statutory Construction

In Iannelli v. United States, 420 U.S. 770, 95 S.Ct. 1284 (1975), the Supreme Court held that Wharton's Rule limited the federal conspiracy statute only as a presumptive matter. The relationship between that statute and any federal substantive crime requiring concerted action for its commission must be determined according to the Congressional intent when the substantive statute was adopted. Congress can be presumed to have intended Wharton's Rule to preclude an additional conspiracy conviction for those necessarily involved in the substantive offense, but this presumption should give way in the face of a contrary legislative intent.

e. Immunity From Conviction for Object Offense

Courts have sometimes inferred from a substantive offense that a "victim" cannot be convicted either as an accessory to, or as a conspirator with, the perpetrator of the offense.

> ***Example:***   A well-known illustration is Gebardi v. United States, 287 U.S. 112, 53 S.Ct. 35 (1932). The Mann Act punishes one who transports in interstate or foreign commerce "any woman for the purpose of prostitution . . . or for any other immoral purpose." The statute had been interpreted to punish only the transporter, and not the woman who was transported. In *Gebardi,* a man and a woman were charged with conspiring to transport the woman across a state line for the purpose of engaging in sexual intercourse with the man. The Court held that since the woman could not be convicted of a substantive violation of the Mann Act, the conspiracy statute should be interpreted to imply the same immunity from a conviction of her for conspiracy. The Court went on to hold that since it takes two to tango under federal law, the man could not be convicted of conspiracy either.

f. Incapacity to Commit Object Offense

To be distinguished from the preceding case is the situation where the substantive offense which is the object of the conspiracy can only be committed by a certain kind of person. In that case a person who would alone be incapable of committing the offense can be guilty of conspiracy to commit it.

> ***Example:***   Assume an offense punishing a bankrupt for certain kinds of fraud on creditors. Only a bankrupt can commit this offense. But *A,* who is not a bankrupt, can be convicted of a conspiracy to commit the offense if *A* agrees with a person who *is* a bankrupt that the bankrupt will commit the offense.

g. Agreement With Unknown Parties

There is no requirement in the offense of conspiracy that the co-conspirators actually know each other personally. It is sufficient if they know *of* each other, that is, it is sufficient if they know that another person has agreed to the same objectives even if they do not know who that other person is.

h. Husband and Wife

The common law precluded a conviction of conspiracy based on an agreement between husband and wife. Most jurisdictions no longer recognize this limitation.

2. THE MENS REA

Conspiracy at common law is a crime of specific intent. There are three dimensions of the intent requirement:

a. Intent to Agree

First, there must be an intent to agree.

b. Intent to Achieve Common Prohibited Objective

Second, there must be an intent to achieve a common objective or set of objectives that is within the prohibition of the crime of conspiracy as defined in the applicable jurisdiction. In most modern contexts the unlawful objectives that can be the object of a conspiracy are limited to crimes, but any crime will do. Thus, in such a jurisdiction, the parties must intend that they or one of them will commit, or otherwise bring about the commission of, *all* of the elements of any criminal offense. They need not, of course, know that the object of the agreement is a crime. Compare pages 302–03.

c. Proof of Intent

The most frequently litigated question concerning the intent required for conspiracy is how it can be proved. Actually, the issue is broader than this, for it involves the sufficiency of proof of three elements of conspiracy: the agreement, the intent to agree, and the intent to achieve a common prohibited objective. But the problem, upon reflection, is really no different from the problems of proof presented by any criminal case.

The question usually arises in the context of one who supplies goods and services to members of an on-going conspiracy, and concerns when that person can be regarded as a party to the conspiracy. The question is often put in terms of whether it is sufficient for the supplier to *know* that the goods and services are being put to an illegal use, or whether the supplier must in addition "have a stake in the venture," that is, actually have a conscious *purpose* that the unlawful objective be accomplished. Compare pages 269–70.

While varying positions can be found in the cases, the better view is that *purpose* is required, but that the required purpose can be inferred (as it can be in any case) from the facts and circumstances of the case. Thus, if the supplier has provided large quantities of goods and services over a long period of time, if there is no legitimate use for the particular goods or services supplied, and/or if a disproportionate part of the supplier's business consists of supplying goods or services for illegal use, it is usually appropriate to permit the jury to infer a purpose to promote the objectives of the conspiracy. Thus the issue properly is regarded not as one of *what* must be proved—it is generally clear that purpose to promote or accomplish the unlawful objectives is required—but *how* that purpose is to be proved. And to allow the jury to draw common sense inferences from the factual relationships of the parties is the normal manner in which purpose is proved in all cases where it is a required condition of liability.

d. Corrupt Motive

The third dimension of the intent requirement of conspiracy originated in the decision in People v. Powell, 63 N.Y. 88 (1875). The prosecution there was for a conspiracy by municipal officers not to advertise for bids before buying supplies. The defense was that the officers acted in good faith, and in ignorance of the statute that required advertising. This defense was accepted. The Court said that conspiracy did not only require an intent to agree and an intent to achieve a common prohibited objective—both of these elements were plainly satisfied. In addition, the Court held, a "corrupt motive" must be shown, in effect an intent to violate the law. The Court limited the requirement, however, to cases where the object of the conspiracy was not immoral and where its members were ignorant of the law they were violating.

The so-called *Powell* doctrine is not everywhere adhered to. Most modern commentators and courts believe it an inappropriate element of the crime of conspiracy.

3. IMPOSSIBILITY

Impossibility problems in the law of conspiracy are rare, but they can arise.

a. True Legal Impossibility

The "true legal impossibility" cases that sometimes arise in the law of attempt would be treated exactly the same in the law of conspiracy. If the unlawful objectives of a conspiracy are limited to crimes in a particular jurisdiction, plainly it will not be a punishable conspiracy for two persons to agree to do something which they *think* is a crime but which actually is not a crime.

b. Legal and Factual Impossibility

But what of the "legal" and "factual" impossibility cases that pose such a problem for attempts? These cases are not as difficult in the conspiracy context. This is because in the attempt cases the impossibility problem usually arises after the defendant has completed the planned behavior and for some reason beyond the defendant's control the crime has not resulted. The impossibility arises, in other words, in the implementation of the actor's proposed conduct. Since the crime of conspiracy focuses upon the *agreement* to engage in specified conduct, and not its implementation, the crime at that inchoate stage will in most cases be possible of commission.

Example: Recall the hypothetical considered in the context of attempt where the defendant shot a dummy believing it to be the victim (page 308). The defendant completed all planned behavior, but could not commit the crime because the victim was not present. If *A* and *B* conspire to kill someone, however, the crime of conspiracy is complete at the time of agreement (and, where applicable, once any overt act, such as obtaining the gun, is committed). The fact that they then may try to kill the victim by shooting into a bed in which a dummy has been placed does not change anything. The crime of conspiracy was completed when they agreed to try to kill the victim.

This is not to say that the impossibility problem cannot arise in the conspiracy context, but only that it is rare for it to do so. For it to arise, the parties would have to agree not only to commit a particular crime, but to commit it in a particular way. Such an agreement is unlikely, but it could occur.

Example: If *A* and *B* agree to steal *V*'s umbrella, the situation would be the same as in the dummy example above. The crime of conspiracy would be complete once the agreement is made (and any overt act, if necessary, has been committed). But suppose they not only agree to steal *V*'s umbrella, but also agree to take that particular umbrella over there in the umbrella stand (which they mistakenly believe to be *V*'s, but which actually belongs to *A*). In that case they have agreed to do something which, on the facts as they believe them to be, would be a crime, but which, on the facts as they actually are, would not be a crime. The "impossibility" situation is now presented. But given the convoluted nature of this hypothetical, you can see how rare it will be that it will actually arise.

How should the impossibility problem be analyzed when it does arise in the conspiracy context? The courts generally have not been as receptive to an impossibility defense to conspiracy as they have to attempt. Mostly this is for the reason that the danger of a conspiracy is thought to be the moral reinforcement that two persons will provide to each other. That danger still exists even though the particular object of the conspiracy may be impossible of achievement. This is but another way of saying that for purposes of a conspiracy prosecution, the defendants' liability should be measured by their perceptions of the facts. Conspiracy, like the probable desistance inquiries in the law of attempt, is designed to identify dangerous people, and the fact that for reasons unknown to the defendants the danger was not presented on a particular occasion does not mitigate the danger of future crime which they present. Thus, most courts will not recognize "legal" or "factual" impossibility as a defense to conspiracy.

4. ABANDONMENT AS A DEFENSE

Once a conspiracy has occurred, the common law does not recognize a defense based on a decision by the defendants (or one of them) to abandon the effort and not complete the object offense. As in the case of attempt, it does not matter whether the decision to abandon is voluntarily or involuntarily made.

5. DURATION: ACCOMPLISHMENT, ABANDONMENT, OR WITHDRAWAL

But there is an important issue that sometimes turns on abandonment or withdrawal from a conspiracy. This is the question of duration. A criminal conspiracy is a continuing offense, beginning with the point at which all of its elements concur and ending as described below.

a. Why Duration Matters
There are a number of reasons why the duration of a conspiracy matters, among them:

1) Statute of Limitations
The statute of limitations begins to run when the conspiracy is over. If it has ended at one time for one defendant and another time for another, the statute of limitations runs from the time the conspiracy ended as to each defendant.

2) Hearsay Exception
An exception to the hearsay rule provides that a statement against interest made by one conspirator is admissible against all conspirators. But the statement must have been made before the conspiracy was over.

> ***Example:*** Assume that A hears B say "C and I agreed that we would rob a bank, and last week we did it." Normally, A could repeat what was heard in court only as testimony against the person who made the statement, here B. But the "co-conspirator's exception" to the hearsay rule permits A's testimony to be offered against *both* B and C. The statement must have been made before the conspiracy was over, however, and here it would appear that the object of the conspiracy had been accomplished. If this is so, then the statement would have been made after the conspiracy ended, and A's testimony as to what B was heard to say would be inadmissible against C.

3) Venue
A conspiracy can be prosecuted in any place where an overt act has been committed in furtherance of the conspiracy. But the act must have been committed before the conspiracy was over.

4) Liability for Substantive Offenses
The rules for when a conspirator can be liable for substantive offenses committed by a co-conspirator are developed below. The offense must be committed prior to the end of the conspiracy, however, in order for such liability to attach.

b. How Duration Is Determined
There are two ways the conspiracy itself can be ended, as well as one way a single conspirator can terminate participation.

1) Accomplishment

A conspiracy is over when all of its objectives have been accomplished.

a) The Usual Case

Normally, this means when all of the planned crimes have been committed. It is not quite this simple, however, for it is clear that dividing the spoils or accomplishing a successful escape would still count as part of the conspiracy even though all of the object crimes may technically have been completed. The issue is when the objects of the conspiracy should be regarded as effectively accomplished.

b) An Agreement to Conceal

In addition, prosecutors have tried ingenious theories to extend the life of a conspiracy still further. The most common is an allegation that concealment of the completed crimes was an additional ingredient of the conspiracy, and that therefore the conspiracy should be regarded as over only after the statute of limitations on the completed offenses has run.

This theory can be successful if the prosecutor can offer one of two kinds of proof: either that an agreement to conceal was an express part of the original understanding of the parties to the conspiracy, or that the objective of the conspiracy was such that concealment was an integral part of its success.

Proof of an express agreement to conceal will be especially difficult. Proof of an overall objective to conceal, however, will not be difficult for some crimes. An example is Grunewald v. United States, 353 U.S. 391, 77 S.Ct. 963 (1957), where the Court accepted the government's theory (but remanded for a new trial because it had not been submitted to the jury) that the purpose of a conspiracy was to assure certain taxpayers that they would not be prosecuted for tax evasion, first by using improper influence to derail potential tax prosecutions and then to do whatever else was necessary to make sure that there was no prosecution until the statute of limitations had run on the underlying tax offenses.

2) Abandonment

A conspiracy is over when achievement of its objectives has been abandoned. The problem here is proof. Normally, an abandonment will be found if the prosecutor cannot prove any overt acts committed in furtherance of the conspiracy during period beginning with the last act that can be proved and ending with the expiration of the statute of limitations. But of course if the agreement was that the conspiracy should last longer, then a more explicit abandonment must be shown.

3) Withdrawal

Even though the conspiracy continues, it is possible for it to "end" as to any member if that person makes an effective withdrawal from the conspiracy. To be effective, a withdrawal must generally be communicated to *all* co-conspirators in time for them to abandon the conspiracy. The communication must be in a manner that would inform a reasonable person of the intent to withdraw. And one court has held that a defendant who seeks to withdraw must in addition successfully persuade the co-conspirators to abandon the conspiracy. See Eldredge v. United States, 62 F.2d 449 (10th Cir. 1932).

6. LIABILITY FOR SUBSTANTIVE OFFENSES

Those who commit the crime of conspiracy are punishable for that offense. In addition, they are punishable for the substantive crimes committed in furtherance of the conspiracy, under the following rules:

a. Offenses Agreed to

Under normal principles of accessorial liability, see page 269, any conspirator would be liable for the substantive offenses committed by a co-conspirator that were explicitly contemplated as part of the agreement. There is in any event a separate conspiracy rule that makes all parties to the conspiracy liable for these substantive offenses.

b. The *Pinkerton* Extension

The interesting question is whether a conspirator should be liable for additional offenses, offenses committed in furtherance of the conspiracy but not explicitly contemplated by the agreement. The traditional answer to this question is "yes," under a formulation articulated in Pinkerton v. United States, 328 U.S. 640, 66 S.Ct. 1180 (1946): a conspirator is liable for all offenses committed by other conspirators in furtherance of the conspiracy that were "reasonably foreseeable." The so-called *Pinkerton* rule can be justly criticized. It imposes liability for negligence where the mens rea for the person who commits the offense will often be higher. Compare page 272.

> ***Example:*** Assume that A and B agree to beat up C. They attack C, and A gets carried away, pulls a knife, and kills C. In order to convict A of murder, it will have to be shown that A had the mens rea for murder, which for present purposes should be assumed to be either an intent to kill or an extreme form of reckless indifference to the life of another. Must the same mens rea be shown to convict B of murder? Under the *Pinkerton* rule, the answer is "no." The issue in B's liability for murder will be whether it was "reasonably foreseeable" that A would pull a knife and kill C. Thus, B's liability will turn on a negligence inquiry, even though a higher culpability will have to be shown to convict the actual perpetrator of the offense.

The *Pinkerton* rule is not everywhere embraced, though it is often recited in the cases and has been adopted by statute in a few States.

7. GRADING

At common law, conspiracy was a misdemeanor. By statute today, it is punishable under a variety of schemes. In some States it remains a misdemeanor, but in others it is punished by a single authorized felony sentence. Still other States vary the maximum depending upon whether the object of the conspiracy is a felony or a misdemeanor, and an increasing number grade conspiracy at the same level as attempt.

8. CUMULATIVE PUNISHMENT

Originally at common law, a conspiracy merged into any felony that was committed in furtherance of it. Thus, conviction for both the conspiracy and the felony was not possible. The reason for this limitation was tied to outdated procedural differences between the trial of misdemeanors and felonies. The rule changed as the procedures changed, and the common law position came to permit conviction for *both* the conspiracy *and* any offenses committed pursuant to it. This rule is in effect today in many States.

A growing number of States disagree. They preclude cumulative punishment for a conspiracy and an offense that was its object. These States permit cumulative punishment, however, where the conspiracy contemplated a number of offenses, only some of which were committed. In this case, a defendant can receive separate convictions for each offense already committed, as well as for the conspiracy to commit those offenses still in contemplation.

Note also that in every State the number of convictions that will be permitted will turn on the number of separate conspiracies that can be proved. This issue is canvassed under the heading "More than One Agreement" at page 313.

D. SOLICITATION

The separate offense of solicitation emerged in its mature form at the turn of the 19th century. The definition of the offense is to encourage another person to commit a crime, with intent that it be committed by the other person. Solicitation is an inchoate offense. It is punishable whether or not the other person commits the offense or undertakes to commit it.

1. THE ACTUS REUS

The actus reus of solicitation consists of enticing, inciting, ordering, advising, counseling, inducing, or otherwise encouraging another to commit a crime. If the defendant tries to communicate the encouragement to the other person but for some reason fails, the defendant is still liable for solicitation or, in some jurisdictions, for an attempt to solicit.

a. Offenses It Is a Crime to Solicit

One must be careful in describing the actus reus of solicitation to identify the kinds of crimes in the relevant jurisdiction that can be the object of a criminal solicitation. A growing number of States, following the lead of the Model Penal Code, punish the solicitation of any offense. The statutes in other States vary. In some soliciting any felony is a crime, and in others there is a list of offenses it is a crime to solicit, either collected in a single provision or scattered in various sections throughout the penal code. At common law, it was a crime to solicit any felony, or any misdemeanor that constituted a breach of the peace, an obstruction of justice, or some other injury to the public welfare.

b. Immunity From Conviction for Object Offense

If a person is for some reason immune from conviction for a particular offense, it will not be a crime for that person to solicit the commission of the offense.

> *Example:* Reconsider the *Gebardi* case used to illustrate this point in the crime of conspiracy, page 315. If the woman in that case were charged with soliciting a violation of the Mann Act, the Court would hold, for the same reason that she was not guilty of conspiracy or as an accessory, that she could not be convicted of solicitation. Since she could not be convicted of a substantive violation of the Mann Act, it would undermine the policy that gives her immunity from that conviction if a conviction for solicitation were permitted.

2. THE MENS REA

Solicitation is a specific intent offense. The defendant must intend that the person solicited commit an offense that, in the relevant jurisdiction, can be the object of a criminal solicitation. Of course, the defendant need not know that the solicitation itself is a crime, nor that the offense solicited is one that can be the object of a criminal solicitation. It is enough that the defendant intend that the person solicited engage in specified behavior, behavior which the law describes as an object of a criminal solicitation. Compare pages 302–03.

3. IMPOSSIBILITY

The problem of impossibility is in general analyzed in the same manner as for conspiracy. Impossibility problems are rare, though they can arise.

a. True Legal Impossibility

As in both attempt and solicitation, "true legal impossibility" will be a defense to solicitation. Thus, if the defendant encourages behavior that is not a crime, a criminal solicitation will not have occurred, even though the defendant may believe that the behavior is criminal.

b. Legal and Factual Impossibility

The "legal" and "factual" impossibility problems that are so troublesome in the crime of attempt will rarely arise in the offense of solicitation. This is because the crime of solicitation is complete when the act and the intent concur. This normally will happen at such an inchoate stage that legal and factual impossibility, which generally are problems in situations where the defendant has completed all planned behavior but no crime has resulted, will not yet have arisen. Thus, solicitation is just like conspiracy in this respect. But, again as with the crime of conspiracy, there are rare situations where the problem can arise. If the defendant solicits a particular crime to be committed in a particular manner (as in, "why don't you steal that particular umbrella over there in that stand," when the umbrella in fact belongs to the defendant), the issue can arise. Again, as in the crime of conspiracy, it is likely that the defendant would be convicted in this situation. Compare the example given on this point in the conspiracy discussion, pages 317–18.

There is, however, a wrinkle. Suppose the defendant solicits another to commit a crime, where the other person is for some reason (unknown to the defendant) incapable of committing that crime. It could then be said that the object offense is "impossible" of commission. "Impossibility" in this sense is *not* a defense to solicitation.

> ***Example:*** It would not be a defense to an otherwise criminal solicitation that the person solicited was insane, or that the offense solicited could only be committed by a particular kind of person (a bankrupt, a trustee, a corporate officer) and the person solicited, unknown to the defendant, did not have that characteristic.

4. ABANDONMENT

It is not clear whether, once a criminal solicitation has occurred, abandonment or renunciation is a defense. It *is* clear that the defendant would at least have to communicate any recantation to the person solicited in time to avoid commission of the offense solicited. But it is likely, given that abandonment is not a defense to the other common law inchoate crimes of attempt and conspiracy, that it would not be a defense to solicitation either.

5. LIABILITY FOR SUBSTANTIVE OFFENSES

The defendant who solicits an offense will be liable, under normal principles of accessorial liability, for the commission of, or attempt to commit, any solicited offense. These principles are discussed beginning at page 262.

6. GRADING

Solicitation was a misdemeanor at common law. In most jurisdictions today, it is graded as a lesser offense than attempt or conspiracy.

7. CUMULATIVE PUNISHMENT

There are three situations that need to be considered:

a. Solicitation and the Object Offense

The defendant cannot be convicted of both solicitation and aiding and abetting either the solicited offense or an attempt by the person solicited to commit the solicited offense.

b. Solicitation and Attempt

There has been much debate whether mere solicitation constitutes an attempt. This issue can be of practical importance in a jurisdiction where solicitation is narrowly defined not to cover the solicitation of certain offenses or where there is a grading difference between solicitation and attempt. The question is whether the defendant's mere act of solicitation should be regarded as an attempt by the defendant to commit the offense. Most courts will answer "no." However this debate is resolved, it is clear that the defendant cannot be convicted for *both* solicitation and an attempt based on the same behavior.

c. Solicitation and Conspiracy

Solicitation can be regarded as an attempt to conspire, for if the person solicited agrees to commit the offense then a conspiracy has been formed. It is clear in that event that the defendant cannot be convicted of both solicitation and conspiracy.

E. OTHER INCHOATE OFFENSES

It is worth noticing that there are many other inchoate offenses beyond attempt, conspiracy, and solicitation. In fact, crimes are often defined in inchoate form. For example, both larceny and burglary are inchoate in the sense that they are committed before the ultimate harm sought to be prevented by the law has occurred. Larceny can be defined as "taking and carrying away the personal property of another with intent to deprive the owner of the property permanently." The offense is committed once the property is moved from its resting place with the requisite intent. The actual permanent deprivation need not occur, so the offense is inchoate in this sense. Similarly, burglary can be defined as "breaking and entering the dwelling house of another in the nighttime with the intent to commit a felony therein." The felony need not occur, and only the slightest entry need be made. Burglary can thus be viewed as a form of attempt to commit a felony inside a house, just as larceny can be seen as an attempt to deprive someone of property permanently.

It is clear, by the way, that a person can be convicted of an attempt, conspiracy, or solicitation to commit offenses, like larceny and burglary, that are themselves defined in inchoate terms. Sometimes courts get hung up on the question whether one can "attempt to attempt," but so long as actus reus and mens rea requirements are imposed that satisfy the minimum appropriate conditions of criminal liability, there should be no difficulty with such convictions.

There are a number of other offenses that have an inchoate character, many of which are designed to supplement the crime of attempt. Some, like the "assault with intent" offenses discussed at page 311, are designed to increase the penalty for an attempt that comes close to fruition. Others, like "possession of burglar tools" or "possession of narcotics paraphernalia," are designed to permit law enforcement intervention at a point in incipient criminality when an attempt to commit a crime has not yet occurred. Crimes of vagrancy have also traditionally served this purpose.

F. REVIEW QUESTIONS

[Answers Provided in Appendix A, page 446]

1. T or F   One who effectively withdraws from a conspiracy cannot then be convicted for the conspiracy.

2. T or F   One who solicits an offense can be convicted both for the solicitation and the offense solicited.

3. T or F   One who conspires to commit an offense can be convicted at common law both for conspiring to commit it and for an attempt to commit it subsequently committed by a co-conspirator.

4. T or F   One cannot be convicted of an attempted assault with intent to rape.

5. T or F   "Primary" intent, for purposes of analyzing impossibility cases in the law of attempt, is the defendant's actual intent.

6. T or F   Solicitation to commit any criminal offense is a crime in all American jurisdictions.

7. T or F   Some American jurisdictions permit a conviction for conspiracy where the object of the agreement is not a crime.

8. T or F   The "wheel with spokes" form of conspiracy necessarily involves a series of separate conspiracies between those at the "hub" and those at the end of each "spoke."

9. T or F   If one of the two parties to an agreement is insane, then neither party can be convicted of a conspiracy at common law.

10. T or F   Wharton's Rule states that one who cannot be convicted of a substantive offense also cannot be convicted of a conspiracy to commit that offense.

11. Explain the significance of abandonment in the common law offenses of attempt, conspiracy, and solicitation.

12. Assume that the relevant elements of perjury in a common law jurisdiction are: "a knowing, material falsehood in a trial or other official proceeding." *A* asks *B* to lie in *A*'s trial for statutory rape, which is defined as "sexual intercourse with a person under the age of 15." Strict liability applies to the element "under the age of 15." The lie that *A* wants *B* to tell is that they had discussed the age of the victim before *A* engaged in sexual intercourse, and had agreed that the victim appeared to be at least 17. *A* also wanted *B* to lie by saying that *B* heard the victim tell a schoolmate that "it sure was nice to be 17 on my last birthday." *B* agreed to tell these lies, and was prepared to do so on the stand at *A*'s trial. The trial judge excluded *B*'s testimony, however, on the ground that it was immaterial and irrelevant. *A* was convicted of statutory rape. Was the trial judge right to exclude *B*'s testimony? Of what inchoate offenses can *A* and *B* now be convicted?

13. Assume now that in *A*'s trial for statutory rape (see Question 12), *A* was able to show that the victim was in fact 17, and the prosecutor agreed that this was the victim's actual age. But the prosecutor offered evidence that *A* believed the victim to be 14. On what crime should the prosecutor now seek an instruction? If you were the lawmaker, would you write the law so as to convict *A* of anything if the prosecutor's evidence is believed? Why? [Assume in answering these questions that you have no quarrel with the law of statutory rape as represented in Question 12.]

14. Is the *Pinkerton* rule a sound extension of the liability of a conspirator? Explain your answer.

*

THE MODEL PENAL CODE

Analysis

A. INTRODUCTION

The Model Penal Code deals with attempt, conspiracy, and solicitation in Article 5. The function of these offenses is the same as at common law: to punish conduct that is preparatory to the commission of a crime but that nevertheless presents a sufficient threat to the social order to justify the intervention of the criminal law. The offenses are generically defined so as to reach efforts to commit any of the substantive offenses defined in the Model Code.

B. ATTEMPT

The definition of attempt in § 5.01(1) is impossibly drafted. There is no way you can derive its meaning by reading the language of the statute. Its meaning is clarified, however, in the commentary prepared to accompany its publication, and that meaning is reflected below.

The intended meaning can be forced into the words of § 5.01(1), but you can't do that until you already know what was desired to be accomplished. Basically, you just have to learn what the drafters had in mind and go from there.

It is helpful at the outset to notice that § 5.01(1) divides attempts into two categories:

(1) those where the defendant has completed all planned behavior, but nonetheless has failed to accomplish the object crime (dealt with in §§ 5.01(1)(a) and 5.01(1)(b)); and

(2) those where the defendant has not yet completed all planned behavior, and for that reason has failed to accomplish the object crime (dealt with in § 5.01(1)(c)).

The first category of cases will encompass most "impossibility" situations, that is, most situations where at common law a defense of "legal" impossibility might be applicable. The second category deals with the "preparation-attempt" problem, that is, at what point along the continuum between planning the crime and accomplishing its commission the law will say an attempt has occurred. Notice that an "or" separates the various subsections of § 5.01(1), meaning that the satisfaction of any one of them will constitute an attempt.

It is not a defense under the Model Penal Code that the crime was completed. As is elaborated under the heading "Cumulative Punishment" below, attempt is a lesser included offense to the completed offense. A charge of the completed offense will therefore permit a conviction of attempt, but the defendant cannot be convicted of both the offense and an attempt to commit it.

As with the common law, it will aid in recognition of "true legal impossibility" cases if mens rea questions are asked first.

1. THE MENS REA
The mens rea for attempt is a purpose to do what the defendant did, plus the required mens rea developed below.

a. Mens Rea Towards Elements of Object Offense

The first step is to divide the object offense into its conduct, result, and circumstance elements. This is a situation, moreover, where getting the elements into the right categories matters a lot. As revealed below, the mens rea for attempt is different depending on the kind of element involved. If you have trouble categorizing the elements—and inevitably you will since there is no magic formula for doing so—you should at least note the possibilities, point out what difference it will make to analysis of the case that concerns you, and think (on paper if it is an exam) about why one might want to choose one classification over another.

1) Conduct Elements of Object Offense

The defendant must have a purpose to engage in all conduct elements of the object offense.

2) Result Elements of Object Offense

In cases where the defendant has completed all planned behavior, the defendant must have a purpose to cause any result elements of the object offense *or* must believe that they will occur without any further conduct. See § 5.01(1)(b). In cases where the defendant has fallen short of completing all planned behavior, the defendant must have a purpose to cause any result elements of the object offense. See § 5.01(1)(c).

3) Circumstance Elements of Object Offense

The defendant must have the same mens rea for all circumstance elements as is required for those elements of the object offense. The language "acting with the kind of culpability otherwise required for commission of the crime" in the introductory clause of § 5.01(1) has this effect.

4) Additional Mens Rea Requirements of Object Offense

Another effect of the language "acting with the kind of culpability otherwise required for commission of the crime" is that the defendant must have *at least* the mens rea required by the object offense. Thus any additional mens rea requirements of the object offense must also be satisfied.

> ***Example:*** What are the mens rea requirements for a charge of an attempt to violate § 221.1(1)?
>
> The first step is to break down the actus reus of the object offense: *Conduct:* enters; *Results:* none; *Circumstances:* (a) building or occupied structure, or separately secured or occupied portion thereof; (b) premises not open to the public; (c) actor not licensed or privileged to enter; (d) building or structure not abandoned.
>
> From this information, one knows that the defendant must have a purpose to enter, since attempt requires that the

defendant have a purpose to engage in all conduct elements of the object offense. One also knows that no mens rea is required as to any results, since the offense contains no result elements.

The next step is to ascertain the mens rea required by § 221.1(1) for the circumstance elements of burglary itself. The answer is that recklessness is required for each of them, by application of § 2.02(3). [If you don't remember why, see the discussion under the heading "Culpability Required in Addition to Actus Reus Elements," page 120.] From this information, one now knows that the defendant must be reckless as to each circumstance element, since attempt requires that the defendant have the same mens rea for circumstance elements as is required for the object offense.

The final step is to ascertain whether there are any additional intent requirements for the object offense. The answer is that there is one: "with purpose to commit a crime therein."

One now has a complete picture of the mens rea required for an attempt to violate § 221.1(1): the defendant must have a purpose to enter, be reckless as to each of the circumstance elements, *and* have a purpose to commit a crime inside the building or structure. In addition, one must have a purpose to engage in all conduct actually undertaken, although this last element will rarely be in issue.

b. Recklessness, Negligence, and Strict Liability

In contrast to the common law, recklessness, negligence, or even strict liability might be a sufficient mens rea for attempt under the Model Penal Code—*but only for circumstance elements,* and then only when sufficient for a circumstance element of the object offense. Thus if strict liability is applied to a circumstance element of a crime—as it would be to the age element in § 213.1(1)(d) (see § 213.6(1))—then strict liability will also be applied to that element of an attempt to commit the crime.

Note, however, that recklessness or negligence *cannot* suffice for the result element of any offenses. Thus, conviction of an attempt to violate § 210.3(1)(a) cannot be based on proof that the defendant acted with sufficient recklessness towards the death of another so as to be guilty of manslaughter if the victim had died. A purpose to kill, or if the defendant had completed all intended behavior a belief that the victim would die, would be required—and that proof would justify a conviction for attempted murder. The same analysis would apply to a charge of attempted negligent homicide: such a charge would also require proof of a purpose to kill, or at the least a belief that the victim would die without further conduct by the defendant. Thus, there can be no crime of attempted manslaughter under § 210.3(1)(a) or attempted negligent homicide under § 210.4(1). [Note that perhaps there could be a conviction of attempted manslaughter under § 210.3(1)(b). If the defendant were charged with attempted murder, and defended on the ground that the purpose to kill was formed under the influence of an "extreme mental or emotional disturbance," then a conviction of attempted manslaughter might be warranted.]

2. THE ACTUS REUS

The Model Penal Code distinguishes between acts of preparation and acts that constitute the crime of attempt in § 5.01(1)(c), as elaborated in § 5.01(2). There are three aspects of the § 5.01(1)(c) standard that should be kept in mind:

a. Substantial Step

The defendant must take a "substantial step" toward the commission of the offense. This test resembles the "probable desistance" tests of the common law, in that it focuses upon what has been done (and the likelihood that the defendant will continue) rather than on what remains to be done. The focus is upon dangerous people, rather than on the dangerousness of the conduct itself.

b. Strongly Corroborative of Actor's Criminal Purpose

The defendant's conduct—the "substantial step" that has been taken—must be strongly corroborative of the defendant's purpose to engage in the object offense.

c. Illustrative Substantial Steps

Finally, § 5.01(2) contains examples of conduct that may be held to constitute a "substantial step." Most of the examples are taken from litigated cases which have given the courts difficulty under the common law approaches to the "preparation-attempt" inquiry. The phrase "without negativing the sufficiency of other conduct" means that the examples are not exclusive. Other conduct, not listed, can be sufficient. The phrase "shall not be held insufficient as a matter of law" is an admonition to the judge to let a case go to the jury if there is sufficient proof of one of the examples and if the conduct proved is "strongly corroborative of the actor's criminal purpose."

One interesting aspect of the Model Penal Code approach to the actus reus of attempt is its emphasis on social control. The reason for the list of situations in § 5.01(2) is strongly to suggest that they present facts that should at least get to the jury on whether an attempt has occurred. Many of them are based on situations where courts have applied a common law preparation/attempt test to preclude conviction.

Imagine a time line continuum where the left margin is the idea of committing a crime and the right margin is actual commission of the crime. Social control theory would suggest that one should find an attempt as far to the left along this line as is compatible with minimum fairness to potentially innocent defendants. Retribution theory, on the other hand, would suggest finding an attempt further to the right—only after a palpable harm or serious threat of harm has already occurred. This is the difference between focusing on a dangerous person and focusing on dangerous conduct.

The common law "proximity" tests tend to find the attempt further to the right along this line. The Model Penal Code is meant to suggest that the line should be drawn further to the left. This is backwards, one might conclude, from the normal impulses of the common law and the Model Code. In general, the Model Penal Code mens rea structure requires a higher mens rea for comparable offenses than does the common law. Mistakes of fact, for example, are normally measured at common law by a negligence or strict liability standard, whereas the default mens rea under the Model Code is recklessness. In the case of mistake of fact and most other issues turning on required levels of mens rea, it is the common law that is more motivated by social control than the Model Code. Interesting contrast.

3. IMPOSSIBILITY
The Model Penal Code does not use the "impossibility" vocabulary of the common law, nor is the word even mentioned in § 5.01.

a. True Legal Impossibility
It is not punishable under § 5.01 to attempt to do something that is not a crime, even if the defendant believes it is a crime.

b. Legal and Factual Impossibility
The Model Code answer to the "legal" and "factual" impossibility problems encountered by the common law is that the defendant is guilty of attempt if the offense would have occurred had the facts been as the defendant believed them to be.

Examples: The professor who, with intent to steal, takes an umbrella from a stand believing it to belong to someone else, when in fact it belongs to the professor, will be guilty of attempted theft under § 5.01(1)(a): the professor has "purposely engage[d] in conduct which would constitute the crime if the attendant circumstances were as he believes them to be."

The defendant who, with intent to kill, shoots at a dummy in a bed believing it to be the intended victim will be guilty of attempted murder under § 5.01(1)(b): the defendant has "when causing a particular result is an element of the crime, [done or omitted] to do anything with the purpose of causing or with the belief that it will cause such result without further conduct on his part."

If both defendants were stopped just before completing what they intended to do, they would be guilty of attempted theft and attempted murder, respectively, under § 5.01(1)(c): they would have "purposely [done or omitted] to do anything which, under the circumstances as [they believed] them to be, [was] an act . . . constituting a substantial step in a course of conduct planned to culminate in [their] commission of the crime." This assumes that in both cases their conduct was "strongly corroborative" of their intent.

c. Rationale for Model Code Solution

The rationale for the Model Penal Code resolution of these impossibility situations is that the defendant who believes the circumstances to be such that a crime will be committed presents the same social danger as would be presented if the belief were true. The fortuity that the belief was not true has nothing to do with the defendant's moral fault or dangerousness to society.

d. Innocuous Behavior

One difficulty with the Model Code approach to impossibility is that it literally permits conviction in what might be regarded as preposterous cases, for example, where the defendant "shoots to kill" with a water pistol or purports to kill another by sticking pins in a voodoo doll.

The Model Code response to this difficulty is found in §§ 5.05(2) and 2.12. Those provisions permit reduction of the grade of the offense, or in extreme cases outright dismissal of the charges, in cases where the defendant does not present the danger sought to be prevented by the object offense. It of course is not necessarily true that the water-pistol killer or the voodoo doctor is harmless. Either may resort to more effective means once they realize that their chosen tactics are not working. But the Model Code puts the inquiry directly whether a particular defendant presents a social danger, and permits mitigation or dismissal if the court concludes that there is no real threat to social interests.

e. Redefinition of Receiving Stolen Property

People v. Jaffe, 185 N.Y. 497, 78 N.E. 169 (1906), is a well-known "impossibility" case. In *Jaffe*, the New York Court of Appeals reversed a conviction for an attempt to receive stolen property where the property received had lost its character as "stolen" prior to the time the defendant received it. The Court held that the defendant's belief that the property was stolen was an inadequate predicate for conviction.

The Model Penal Code handles this case in its definition of the receiving offense. Section 223.6(1) provides that a person is guilty of theft if movable property of another is received knowing that it has been stolen or "believing that it has probably been stolen." Jaffe would thus be convicted, not of an attempt to receive stolen property but of the object offense itself.

f. Criticism of Model Code Approach

The Model Penal Code approach to impossibility has been criticized for failure, in the first two provisions of § 5.01(1), to take account of an essential limitation on its normal actus reus inquiry. Recall the discussion under the heading "Proper Analysis of Legal and Factual Impossibility Cases," page 309. There is in the typical legal or factual impossibility case no problem with the defendant's mens rea—what is intended would be a crime if the facts were as the defendant believed them to be. The problem is with the actus reus— because of some external event over which the defendant had no control, the defendant did not come very close to commission of the offense. The normal Model Code approach to the actus reus of attempt is to ask whether the defendant engaged in a substantial step toward the criminal objective, and did so in a manner that strongly corroborated the intent required for an attempt. The substantial step inquiry is designed to permit early intervention at a point when the defendant has manifested a clear social danger, and the "strong corroboration" requirement is designed to make sure that a sufficient actus reus has been shown to warrant criminal punishment.

The problem is that §§ 5.01(1)(a) and 5.01(1)(b) do not contain a corroboration requirement. They assume that a person who has completed all planned behavior will have engaged in conduct that "corroborates" intent. The question is whether a person who has engaged in the behavior described in these sections will necessarily have done so, that is, will necessarily have engaged in a sufficient actus reus to warrant criminal punishment.

The critics answer "no," offering the professor-umbrella situation as an example. There, objectively viewed, the professor's behavior is completely innocuous—the professor walks to an umbrella stand, and leaves with an umbrella that belongs to the professor. This behavior offers no corroboration of inferences of intent we may seek to draw, and thus presents a classic danger that the requirement of a minimum actus reus for crime is designed to guard against.

Compare the professor's case to the shooting of a dummy in the intended victim's bed. There the defendant's behavior is hardly innocuous—normal, non-dangerous people do not fire guns into other people's beds when it looks like a person is asleep in them. But normal, non-dangerous people *do* walk out of restaurants with their own umbrella. And therein lies the problem: conviction of the professor creates an unacceptable risk of convicting an innocent person because the underlying conduct is so innocuous.

The critics conclude that the addition of a "strong corroboration" requirement to §§ 5.01(1)(a) and 5.01(1)(b) would go a long way toward solving this problem. It would, for example, preclude conviction of the professor, while still permitting conviction of the person who "killed" a dummy in someone else's bed.

4. ABANDONMENT

Unlike the common law, the Model Penal Code provides that abandonment is a defense to attempt. Section 5.01(4) carefully circumscribes the abandonment defense. There are three important limitations:

a. Effective Abandonment

The defendant must abandon the effort or otherwise prevent commission of the offense. This explains the limitation of the defense to cases which would otherwise constitute an attempt under §§ 5.01(1)(b) and 5.01(1)(c).

The easy case is one covered by § 5.01(1)(c). If the defendant has engaged in a "substantial step" that "strongly corroborates" the criminal intent, an attempt has been committed. It is still possible, however, for the defendant to abandon the effort. Indeed, an abandonment at this point may be regarded as casting doubt on the firmness of the original intent to commit the crime, and is to be encouraged in any event because the defendant may be induced not to commit the crime.

It is also easy to see why cases under § 5.01(1)(a) are excluded. In these cases, the defendant has completed all planned behavior—there is nothing to "abandon." There is no change of heart, but a failure to commit the offense due to external fortuity.

The harder case, because it partakes of elements of both of the previous two, is presented by § 5.01(1)(b). In these cases the defendant has completed behavior designed to cause the result (or with the belief that the result will follow without additional behavior). Thus, one could argue, there is nothing to abandon, and the case is like those under § 5.01(1)(a). But the result has not yet occurred, and it may be possible for the defendant to do something to prevent its occurrence. Suppose, for example, the defendant has set a time bomb in a building with intent to kill the occupants. If the defendant has a change of heart and defuses the bomb before it goes off, the case is more like those covered by § 5.01(1)(c). The defense of abandonment is preserved in § 5.01(1)(b) in order to take account of situations like these.

b. Complete Renunciation

In order to be effective, the abandonment must involve a renunciation of the criminal purpose that is "complete." The meaning of the term "complete" is elaborated in the second paragraph of § 5.01(4). A renunciation is not complete if the motivation is to postpone the attempt until a more advantageous time (e.g., better to rob the bank when there are fewer cops around) or to transfer the attempt to a different but similar objective or victim (e.g., the bank up the street is likely to have more money).

c. Voluntary Renunciation

In order to be effective, the abandonment must involve a renunciation of the criminal purpose that is "voluntary." The meaning of the term "voluntary" is also elaborated in the second paragraph of § 5.01(4). A renunciation is not voluntary if the motivation is an increase in the probability of detection (e.g., let's quit—there are too many witnesses around) or of getting caught (e.g., let's quit—the cops just arrived), or if there is some change in circumstances that makes it more difficult to accomplish the criminal objective (e.g., let's quit—I didn't bring enough nitro to blow up the safe).

5. GRADING

Section 5.05(1) punishes attempts at the same grade and degree as the offense attempted. There is one exception: an attempt to commit a capital crime or a felony of the first degree is a felony of the second degree. Note that grading factors are "material elements" of an offense and are therefore covered by the culpability provisions of § 2.02. See pages 116–17. The consequence of this for attempts is that the mens rea required for an attempt must take into account grading factors as well as the basic elements of the offense.

Examples: Reconsider the burglary example given under the heading "Additional Mens Rea Requirements of Object Offense," pages 332–33. The mens rea described there would be adequate if the attempt were sought to be graded as felony of the third degree. See the last paragraph of § 221.1(2). But if the attempt were sought to be graded as a felony of the second degree, the mens rea for the attempt would have to include at least one of the alternative grading factors listed in the first paragraph of § 221.1(2): (a) the defendant would have to be reckless towards the circumstances "dwelling of another at night" (since recklessness is the mens rea for these circumstance elements in the object offense and the mens rea for the attempt is the same); *or* (b) the defendant would have to have a purpose to inflict bodily injury on another person, or in the case of completed behavior a belief that bodily injury would result without further conduct by the defendant (since this speaks to a result, and the mens rea for the attempt is therefore purpose or, in the case of completed behavior, a belief that the consequence will follow without further conduct by the defendant); *or* (c) the defendant would have to have a purpose to be armed with explosives or a deadly weapon when the offense is committed (since these seem to be conduct elements, and conduct elements of the object offense require a purpose for the attempt).

Note again that any ambiguity in the proper classification of these elements as conduct, results, or circumstances would have to be taken into account in a thorough analysis. For example, is "explosives" or "deadly weapon" a circumstance element, or is it part of the description of the conduct "armed with . . . "? "Who knows" is the answer, but it is clear that the mens rea for these elements would be different depending upon which classification is made. The saving grace here is that it probably won't matter whether recklessness or purpose is established as the mens rea. Most people will know perfectly well what it is that they are "armed" with, and will have intended to be "armed" in that manner.

6. CUMULATIVE PUNISHMENT

The Model Penal Code follows the common law in precluding conviction for both the attempt and the offense that was attempted. Section 1.07(4)(b) provides that attempt is a lesser included offense to the offense that is the object of the attempt. This means, for example, that a charge of burglary would permit a conviction of attempted burglary. And § 1.07(1)(a) provides that although one can be *prosecuted* for both an offense and a lesser included offense, a *conviction* for both is not permitted. Whether both charges will be submitted to the jury depends on the evidence. See § 1.07(5). Note also that § 5.05(3) prohibits conviction for more than one inchoate offense for conduct designed to culminate in the commission of the same crime. Thus, and contrary to the present result in many States, a conspiracy to rob a bank followed by an attempt to rob it can result in the conviction of either conspiracy or attempt, but not both.

7. ASSAULT WITH INTENT

The Model Penal Code does not include any "assault with intent" offenses. These offenses are made unnecessary by the equivalent grading of an attempt and its object offense. See pages 311, 339.

C. CONSPIRACY

Section 5.03 rejects the approach of older statutes that still punish combinations "to commit any act injurious to the public health or public morals," etc. It is limited to agreements to achieve objectives that are themselves criminal. The Model Code also departs from the traditional approach in precluding punishment both for conspiracy and for an offense that was its sole object. And conspiracy under the Model Code serves only the function of an inchoate offense. It is *not* an independent means of imposing liability for the conduct of another. Those who are parties to a conspiracy can be held liable for crimes committed in furtherance of the conspiracy only if the general standards for accomplice liability stated in § 2.06 are satisfied.

1. THE ACTUS REUS

The actus reus of conspiracy under the Model Penal Code consists of an agreement of one of two types: (1) that the defendant or another party to the conspiracy will commit, attempt to commit, or solicit a criminal offense; or (2) that the defendant will aid in the planning or commission of a crime, an attempt to commit it, or its solicitation. As at common law, the problem in the implementation of this definition is not so much *what* must be proved as *how* it can be proved. What must be proved is clear: persons are parties to the same conspiracy if the prosecutor can prove that there was a single criminal offense to which they agreed. As at common law, it is the prosecutor who shapes the charge, who designs the contour and scope of a prosecution for conspiracy to fit the available evidence.

a. Overt Act

If the charge is a conspiracy to commit a felony of the third degree or a misdemeanor, the Model Code requires proof of an overt act in furtherance of the conspiracy, committed either by the defendant or by any other party to the conspiracy. No overt act is required if the charge is a conspiracy to commit a felony of the first or second degree. See § 5.03(5). The Model Code does not elaborate on what will constitute an overt act. Presumably, however, use of the same term as has been traditional in this area will be construed to mean a continuation of the traditional content, the requirements of which do not impose a particularly onerous burden on the prosecution.

1) Sufficiency of Conduct

Any act should do to satisfy the overt act requirement, although in theory, by analogy to the Model Penal Code's treatment of the crime of attempt, it should in combination with the agreement be a "substantial step" strongly corroborative of the actor's criminal intent. The same case as for the crime of attempt can be made for the law of conspiracy to require corroborative behavior as a protection against unwarranted inferences of guilt in ambiguous situations. The act of "agreement" may well adequately perform this function on the facts, and may be helped in doing so when the law requires an overt act. The law of attempt puts the question explicitly to the jury, at common law by the various attempts to define the requisite conduct and in the Model Penal Code by the "substantial step" requirement. But nowhere in the law of conspiracy—either at common law or under the Model Penal Code—is the analogous question explicitly put to the jury.

The same can be said, by the way, for the law of solicitation, considered below. See page 351. The law of solicitation also does not explicitly contain a requirement that the jury focus on the issue of whether the defendant's behavior was sufficiently unambiguous so as to confirm the inference of "guilty intent."

Nor, it should be added, does the law of larceny or burglary or the other substantive offenses defined by the criminal law in inchoate terms. See page 325. To focus on larceny as an example, it may well be on the facts that "taking" the moveable property of another is confirmatory of an intent to achieve permanent deprivation, but there are many situations where the taking is entirely innocent and an inference of a purpose to steal would be wholly speculative if based on that conduct alone. Requiring that the jury make an explicit conclusion that the acts it finds to exist corroborate its guesses about the defendant's intent could add an important protection for the innocent.

> ***Example:***   One of your classmates picks up your Criminal Law book and leaves the classroom. Is the classmate guilty of theft?

Maybe yes, maybe no. The question would turn on the intent with which the book was taken. It could have been a simple case of mistaken identification ("I thought it was my book—they all look the same, after all") or it could be more nefarious ("I lost my book last week and I thought I could get away with taking another book that had no identifying marks in it"). The point is that the act of taking is ambiguous standing by itself. A strong case could be made that before convicting in such a case the jury should be required to find something in the defendant's behavior that corroborates its conclusion of guilt. See pages 85–86.

b.   More Than One Agreement

Section 5.03(3) provides that a single agreement with multiple criminal objectives constitutes a single conspiracy, not only if the crimes are the object of the same agreement but also if they are part of the same "continuous conspiratorial relationship." The quoted phrase means that multiple agreements over a long period of time between long-standing conspirators still should be regarded as consisting of but one conspiracy. On the other hand, § 5.03(3) leaves open the prosecution of multiple agreements as more than one conspiracy in other contexts (as between X and Y to commit an offense and between X and Z to commit the same kind of offense). The "wheel" and "chain" analogies are not expressly used by the Model Penal Code, and are no more helpful for analysis of its provisions than they are for the common law.

c.   Bilateral or Unilateral Agreement

The Model Code permits conviction on the basis of a "unilateral" agreement, that is, permits the conviction of a person who *thinks* an agreement was made with another, even though in fact it was not or even though for some reason the other party cannot be convicted for the conspiracy. This result is reached through the intersection of two provisions. First, the words "he agrees" in §§ 5.03(1)(a) and 5.03(1)(b) are meant to be interpreted in this manner. Second, § 5.04(1)(b) explicitly provides that the fact that one person is irresponsible or immune from prosecution is not a defense to anyone else, even though there remains only one to tango.

d.   Wharton's Rule: Object Crimes Requiring Concerted Action

The Model Penal Code contains no explicit reference to Wharton's Rule in its conspiracy provisions. One effect (and perhaps the overriding purpose) of Wharton's Rule is to prohibit multiple convictions for the same behavior. This result is reached by the Model Code. Section 1.07(1)(b) prohibits multiple convictions in cases of a conspiracy to commit a crime and the commission of that crime. Since there can only be one conviction, and since the conspiracy and any offense to which Wharton's Rule would apply will be graded at the same level, it does not matter for this purpose whether the conviction is for conspiracy or the object offense. Note, however, that the ability to charge a conspiracy may have a number of collateral effects, such as the admissibility of hearsay testimony, where the trial can be held, with whom the defendant may be tried, and when the statute of limitations begins to run. These advantages might be available under the Model Code in a context where a prosecution for conspiracy might not be possible in a traditional jurisdiction applying Wharton's Rule.

e. Immunity From Conviction for Object Offense

Section 5.04(2) provides that a person who cannot be guilty of an offense as a perpetrator or an accomplice cannot be guilty of a conspiracy to commit that offense.

Example: The result for the woman in the *Gebardi* case, page 315, would be carried forward under the Model Code. The man, however, could be convicted of conspiracy—since unilateral agreements count, and the case explicitly fits the language of § 5.04(1)(b). The man could not, on the other hand, be convicted of both the conspiracy and the substantive charges under the Mann Act. See § 1.07(1)(b).

f. Incapacity to Commit Object Offense

Section 5.04(1)(a) provides that a person can be guilty of conspiracy even though lacking a particular characteristic necessary for commission of the object offense, so long as the defendant believes that some conspirator has the characteristic.

Example: The bankruptcy example, page 315, comes out the same way under the Model Code. Note that the requirement is only that the defendant *believe* that some member of the conspiracy has the appropriate characteristic, not that the person actually has that characteristic.

g. Agreement With Unknown Parties

Section 5.03(2) continues the traditional position that the parties to a conspiracy need not know each other, so long as they know *of* each other. The paradigm situation is where *A* agrees with *B* that a crime will be committed, and *A* knows that another person has agreed with *B* that *the same crime* will be committed but does not know who that other person is. In that case, all three persons are parties to the same conspiracy.

Example: A distribution chain would provide an example. A manufacturer of an illegal substance who distributes to a wholesaler would be a party to a conspiracy with the wholesaler to commit the crimes involved in the sale to the wholesaler. The manufacturer would also be in a conspiracy with the retailer who actually sold the substance on the street after buying it from the wholesaler, even though the manufacturer was unaware of the identity of the retailer. It is enough that the manufacturer knows that the wholesaler will use a retailer to get the product on the street.

If multiple retailers are used, moreover, there could be one large conspiracy under the Model Penal Code involving all the parties. The entire organization (e.g., a manufacturer, a wholesaler, and 10 retailers) would be guilty of a single conspiracy to commit the crimes involved in making the product or transferring it to the wholesaler. In this case, all of the members of the organization would have agreed to commit the "same" crime or crimes, and they could be prosecuted as part of the same conspiracy even though they did not know everyone personally.

But could one retailer be charged with a conspiracy to commit the crimes involved in the street sales of another retailer? Or could the manufacturer be charged with one conspiracy to be involved in the sales of one retailer and another conspiracy to be involved in the sales of another retailer? Maybe yes, maybe no.

The answer depends on the available proof and the theory of the prosecution. What the prosecutor would be required to do is identify a specific crime to which all parties agreed. If, for example, the prosecutor could show that it was important to one retailer (R1) that another retailer (R2) sell the product on the street, it might be possible to construct a conspiracy in which R1 was guilty of conspiring with R2 to promote the crimes of R2. In this scenario, R1 could be said to have agreed with R2 that the "same" crime be committed, even if they did not know each other.

The factual variations that can be made on this simple distribution chain where crimes are committed by all parties at each step in the scheme illustrate a central point about the law of conspiracy. The shape and scope of a conspiracy does not exist in the abstract. A conspiracy can be established when the prosecutor can identify a specific crime or series of specific crimes that more than one person has agreed to commit. It is up to the prosecutor to select the theory of the prosecution. The prosecutor will choose the crimes on which the prosecution will focus, and will select the parties who will be proved to have agreed to commit those crimes. The canvas is empty until the prosecutor begins to paint. The conspiracy can have whatever shape and scope, and can involve whatever participants, that the prosecutor can prove to have been involved in an agreement to commit the *same* crime. There is enormous prosecutorial discretion and flexibility in choosing how to paint the picture.

h. **Husband and Wife**
There is no reason why husband and wife cannot be convicted of conspiracy under the Model Penal Code.

2. **THE MENS REA**
The only stated mens rea for conspiracy under § 5.03 is that the agreement must be formed "with the purpose of promoting or facilitating" the commission of a crime.

a. **Purpose to Promote or Facilitate Object Offense**
This means that each defendant must have a purpose to promote or facilitate each conduct and result element of the object offense, and must know (or believe or hope; see § 2.02(2)(a)(ii)) that all circumstance elements of the object offense will exist. Thus, and perhaps inconsistently with the Model Code treatment of this issue in the crime of attempt, a mens rea of knowledge or belief is required for circumstance elements of the object offense, even though for commission of the object offense itself recklessness, negligence, or strict liability will suffice. And note that, as in an attempt, the defendant must also satisfy any additional mens rea elements contained in the object offense.

Examples: Recall the burglary example discussed on pages 332–33. What is the mens rea for a conspiracy to violate § 221.1(1)? The answer is that the defendants must have a purpose to promote or facilitate an entry, must know, believe, or hope that each of the circumstance elements will exist when the entry is made, and must have a purpose that the perpetrator of the burglary will commit a crime inside the building or structure.

Now consider a charge of conspiracy to violate § 213.1(1)(d). The defendants agree that one of them will have sexual intercourse with an identified female who is in fact less than 10 years old but who is believed by the defendants to be 12. What mens rea would be required? Would the mistake be a defense? The required mens rea is that the defendants have a purpose to promote or facilitate sexual intercourse, and that they know, believe, or hope that the victim is a female who is less than 10 years old and is not the wife of a male perpetrator of the offense. Thus, even though strict liability is applied to the age element for purposes of the completed offense—see § 213.6(1)—knowledge or belief is required for the conspiracy. The mistake will therefore be a defense.

The result in this last example is perhaps inconsistent with the Model Code position for an attempt to commit the same offense. If the charge was attempt, the mens rea for the age element would be strict and the mistake would not be a defense. See pages 333–34.

This difference between the law of conspiracy and the law of attempt may be defensible on the ground that conspiracy is a crime more inchoate in nature than attempt—that is, it occurs at a point in time before a substantial step that strongly corroborates the defendants' intent has been committed. Higher culpability requirements may therefore be appropriate for conspiracy in order to avoid convicting the innocent. On the other hand, it is difficult to see exactly how the justness or fairness of a conviction is increased by accepting a defense of mistake in this context. And if conspiracy were to require a corroborative act by analogy to the law of attempt—as perhaps it should—this rationale for treating conspiracy differently from the law of attempt would disappear.

Note in any event that if an attempt is actually committed in furtherance of the conspiracy, the perpetrator will be guilty of the attempt in spite of the mistaken belief. See page 332. Ironically perhaps, the co-conspirators (is this inconsistent?) will *not* be guilty as accomplices under § 2.06. See pages 286–88.

b. Proof of Intent
Note again that all parties to a single conspiracy must have agreed to promote or facilitate the same criminal offense, and each must have had the required mens rea with respect to that same crime. This is *what* must be proved. *How* the required purpose to promote or facilitate can be proved depends on the ingenuity of the prosecutor and available sources of evidence.

c. Intent to Agree
It is not specifically required by the definition in § 5.03(1) that the defendant have a separate intent to agree. However, one could hardly have the required purpose to promote or facilitate a criminal offense and also make one of the agreements described in § 5.03(1) without intending to agree. An intent to agree therefore seems to be included in the offense by necessary implication.

d. Corrupt Motive
The Model Penal Code has discarded the *Powell* "corrupt motive" doctrine. See page 317. This means, as is generally the case in the criminal law, that it is irrelevant whether the defendants know that the object of their agreement is a crime. It is sufficient that they agree to engage in behavior which the law describes as criminal.

3. IMPOSSIBILITY
The Model Penal Code does not deal explicitly with impossibility in the context of conspiracy. Undoubtedly the reason is that the problem can be expected rarely to arise, as is explained on pages 317–18.

a. True Legal Impossibility
The defense of "true legal impossibility" would of course be recognized. Thus, an agreement to do something that was not a crime would not be a criminal conspiracy, even though one or more parties to the conspiracy believed it was a crime. This follows from the requirement in the definition of conspiracy that the object of the agreement be a "crime."

b. Legal and Factual Impossibility

It is also clear that the defense of "legal" impossibility would be rejected by the Model Code in a conspiracy case. Thus, the defendant will be guilty of conspiracy if the crime would occur on the facts as the defendant believed they will be.

This result is confirmed by the fact that a "unilateral" agreement is sufficient. The question is not whether two parties have actually agreed, but whether the defendant *thinks* there is an agreement with another. Thus, liability is measured on the facts as the defendant believes them to be, a posture that is consistent with rejection of the "legal" impossibility defense. The provisions of § 5.04(1) are also consistent with rejection of the defense, both specifically by focusing on the defendant's belief in § 5.04(1)(a) and generally by reinforcing the unilateral character of the agreement. Finally, note that the provisions of § 5.05(2)—provisions designed to allow mitigation in cases where the impossibility defense is rejected—are also applicable to conspiracy, thus implying that the defense should be rejected for conspiracy too.

4. ABANDONMENT AS A DEFENSE

Section 5.03(6) establishes an abandonment defense to conspiracy. Note the two requirements:

a. Thwart Success of Conspiracy

The defendant must have "thwarted the success of the conspiracy," that is, must have actively intervened to prevent the commission of the crime that was the object of the conspiracy. It is *not* enough that the defendant withdrew and permitted other conspirators to continue.

b. Complete and Voluntary Renunciation

The abandonment must constitute a "complete and voluntary renunciation" of the criminal purpose. Note that the terms "complete" and "voluntary" are elaborated upon in the second paragraph of § 5.01(4), and that this paragraph explicitly applies to all of Article 5. See pages 338–39 for illustrations of the meaning of § 5.01(4).

5. DURATION: ACCOMPLISHMENT, ABANDONMENT, OR WITHDRAWAL

Section 5.03(7)(a) provides that conspiracy is a continuing offense, beginning with the point at which all elements of the offense have concurred and ending when the criminal object is accomplished or abandoned. There is also provision for individual abandonment (withdrawal) in § 5.03(7)(c).

a. Why Duration Matters

The reasons why duration matters in a conspiracy charged under the Model Penal Code are essentially those canvassed in the discussion of the traditional conspiracy offense at pages 319–20. There are, however, differences of detail:

1) Statute of Limitations

The statute of limitations is dealt with in § 1.06 of the Model Code. Section 1.06(4), which is explicitly referred to in the introductory clause of § 5.03(7), starts the running of the statute for a conspiracy at the point at which its objects have been accomplished or the agreement has been abandoned by all conspirators. It is possible under § 5.03(7)(c) for an individual to terminate participation in a conspiracy—and for the statute of limitations to begin to run for that individual—even though others are going forward.

> *Example:*   Suppose, for example, an individual says to the other conspirators: "I'm out. My involvement in this agreement is ended." The statute of limitations will begin to run as to that individual from that point forward.

2) Hearsay Exception

The Model Code does not cover the admissibility of evidence, and hence does not address the hearsay exception one way or the other.

3) Joinder and Venue

There are explicit provisions for joinder and venue in § 5.03(4), some of which turn on when a conspiracy has been terminated.

4) Liability for Substantive Offenses

The liability of one conspirator for crimes committed by another is measured by § 2.06, not § 5.03. Note that there are independent requirements for renunciation in § 2.06(6)(c), and that they are more rigorous than the requirements for individual withdrawal from a conspiracy under § 5.03(7)(c). Thus, even though a conspirator has effectively withdrawn for purposes, say, of starting the statute of limitations, that withdrawal may *not* be effective for purposes of foreclosing liability for subsequently committed substantive offenses.

> *Example:*   Suppose an individual (C1) participated in a conspiracy to rob a bank by supplying the persons who were to commit the robbery with the floor plans of the bank and the combination of the lock on the vault. Then suppose C1 says to the others: "I'm out. My involvement in this agreement is ended. I don't even want any of the proceeds." The statute of limitations will begin to run as to C1 from that point forward. But is C1 guilty of the robbery thereafter committed by the other conspirators?
>
> The answer is "yes." Section 2.06(3) would govern C1's liability as an accomplice to offenses committed in furtherance of the original agreement. C1's attempt to

withdraw, while effective for purposes of starting the statute of limitations on the conspiracy, would not prevent conviction of C1 as an accomplice because § 2.06(6)(c) requires additional steps that C1 has not taken. On the facts as given, C1 has not wholly deprived the prior complicity of any effectiveness, has not given timely warning to law enforcement authorities, and has made no effort to prevent the commission of the offense.

b. How Duration Is Determined

The duration of a conspiracy is measured as follows:

1) Accomplishment

Section 5.03(7)(a) provides that a conspiracy is over "when the crime or crimes which are its object are committed." An agreement to conceal committed crimes thus could extend the life of the conspiracy only if in the course of concealing those crimes additional crimes are contemplated.

2) Abandonment

Section 5.03(7)(a) also provides that a conspiracy is over when the agreement that a crime or crimes be committed "is abandoned by the defendant and by those with whom he conspired." Thus if all parties to the agreement abandon the effort, but only if all parties do, the conspiracy is ended. Note that § 5.03(7)(b) explicitly continues the traditional rule that abandonment is presumed if no overt act in furtherance of the conspiracy is committed by any conspirator during the period of the applicable statute of limitations.

3) Withdrawal

Section 5.03(7)(c) deals with the conditions under which an individual may terminate participation in a conspiracy. Termination can occur in either of two ways: (1) when the individual "advises those with whom he conspired of his abandonment"; or (2) when the individual "informs the law enforcement authorities of the existence of the conspiracy and of his participation therein." But note, as illustrated above, that withdrawal by an individual from a conspiracy may not preclude conviction of that individual for crimes committed after the withdrawal by others who are still committed to the purposes of the original conspiracy.

6. LIABILITY FOR SUBSTANTIVE OFFENSES

The Model Penal Code has discarded the traditional conspiracy rules governing the liability of conspirators for substantive offenses committed in furtherance of the conspiracy. However, those who commit the offense of conspiracy will be liable for substantive crimes committed in furtherance of the conspiracy if the conditions of § 2.06, governing accomplice liability, are satisfied. The Model Code has thus integrated into a single provision those occasions when one person can be liable for the criminal conduct of another. Section 2.06 is discussed beginning at page 284.

7. GRADING

The grading of conspiracy is governed by § 5.05(1). A conspiracy is punished at the same grade and degree as the most serious offense that is its object, except that a conspiracy to commit a capital crime or a felony of the first degree is punished as a felony of the second degree. Note that grading factors are "material elements" of an offense, and are therefore covered by the culpability provisions of § 2.02. Thus the mens rea for conspiracy must also take account of grading factors as well as the basic elements of the offense. The content of this additional mens rea will be determined by dividing the grading factors into conduct, result, and circumstance elements, and applying the "purpose to promote or facilitate" requirement to each.

> ***Example:***   Recall the burglary example discussed in connection with the grading of attempts, pages 339–40. What would be the mens rea for a conspiracy to commit burglary, sought to be graded as a felony of the second degree?
>
> First, of course, the defendant would have to have the mens rea required for a conspiracy to commit the offense itself. See the example on page 345. In addition, the mens rea would have to encompass one of the three grading factors contained in § 221.1(2). Specifically, the defendant would have to know or believe that the offense would be committed in the dwelling of another at night; or the defendant would have to have a purpose that the perpetrator of the offense inflict or attempt to inflict bodily injury on another; or the defendant would have to have a purpose that the perpetrator be armed with explosives or a deadly weapon.

8. CUMULATIVE PUNISHMENT

The Model Penal Code does not permit conviction for both a conspiracy and an offense that is its object. This result is accomplished in § 1.07(1)(b). Note, however, that the defendant may be convicted for as many substantive offenses as are committed in furtherance of the conspiracy, either as a perpetrator or as an accomplice. And if the conspiracy contemplates the commission of additional offenses beyond those already committed or attempted, an additional conviction for conspiracy to commit those offenses can be obtained. Note also that § 5.05(3) precludes conviction both for conspiracy to commit a crime and an attempt to commit that same crime.

> ***Example:***   A and B conspire to commit crimes X, Y, and Z. B commits crime X. B attempts to commit crime Y. Assuming that A satisfies the requirements of § 2.06 and is an accomplice as to all crimes committed or attempted, of how many offenses may A and B be charged? Of how many may they be convicted?
>
> Note that § 1.07(1) is *not* a limitation on the number of offenses with which a person may be *charged*. In fact, it specifically permits

prosecution for as many offenses as have occurred. Thus, A may be *charged* with: (1) conspiracy to commit crime X; (2) conspiracy to commit crime Y; (3) conspiracy to commit crime Z; (4) conspiracy to commit crimes X and Y; (5) conspiracy to commit crimes X and Z; (6) conspiracy to commit crimes Y and Z; (7) conspiracy to commit crimes X, Y, and Z; (8) attempt to commit crime X (if the offense was committed, necessarily an attempt was committed along the way); (9) the commission of crime X; and (10) the attempt to commit crime Y. B can be charged with the same offenses.

But both A and B can only be *convicted* of a lesser number of offenses. They can both be convicted for the substantive offenses committed in furtherance of the conspiracy, namely the completion of crime X or an attempt or conspiracy to commit it (but not more than one of these offenses, because of §§ 1.07(1)(a) and 1.07(4)(b)) and the attempt or conspiracy to commit crime Y (but not both). Since a single agreement with multiple objectives was involved, there can be only one conspiracy conviction under § 5.03(3). And since the agreement contemplates the commission of a crime not yet attempted or committed (crime Z), a conviction of conspiracy remains permissible even though some of the objects of the conspiracy have been accomplished. (This conviction will be graded at the level that crime Z is graded, even if crimes X and Y are more serious). At the end of the day, both A and B can be convicted, in effect, for three offenses: committing crime X, attempting crime Y, and conspiring to commit crime Z.

D. SOLICITATION

Solicitation of any crime is punished by § 5.02.

1. THE ACTUS REUS

The actus reus under § 5.02(1) occurs if the defendant "commands, encourages or requests" another person to (a) commit a crime; (b) attempt to commit a crime; or (c) become an accomplice in the commission of or attempt to commit a crime. See page 341 ("Sufficiency of Conduct"). Under § 5.02(2), the defendant is still guilty of solicitation even if the encouragement is not actually communicated to the person solicited, so long as it was designed to be communicated.

a. Offenses It Is a Crime to Solicit
Section 5.02 makes it an offense to solicit any crime. Recall that violations are not crimes. See § 1.04(5).

b. Immunity From Conviction for Object Offense
Section 5.04(2) provides that a person who cannot be guilty of an offense as a perpetrator or an accomplice cannot be guilty of a solicitation to commit that

offense. Thus, the hypothetical variation of the *Gebardi* case discussed at page 323 would come out the same way under the Model Penal Code, based on the offense as there defined.

2. THE MENS REA

The mens rea for solicitation under § 5.02 is a "purpose to promote or facilitate" the commission of a crime. This means that the defendant must have a purpose to promote or facilitate the occurrence of the conduct and result elements of the object offense, and know, believe, or hope that all circumstance elements will be present when the offense is committed. See § 2.02(2)(a)(ii). And the defendant must also satisfy any additional mens rea requirements of the object offense. Compare the discussion of conspiracy at page 345. The defendant need not, of course, know that the solicited conduct is a criminal offense; it is enough to solicit behavior which the criminal law makes a crime.

3. IMPOSSIBILITY

Impossibility is not dealt with in the context of solicitation, undoubtedly for the reason explained in connection with the common law on pages 323–24.

a. True Legal Impossibility

"True legal impossibility" would be a defense. Thus, the solicitation of another to do something that was not a crime would not be criminal under § 5.02(1), even though the defendant believed that the act solicited was a crime. This follows from the definition of solicitation as commanding, encouraging, or requesting another to engage in specific conduct which would constitute a "crime."

b. Legal and Factual Impossibility

The defense of "legal" impossibility would be rejected by the Model Code in a solicitation case. The defendant would thus be guilty of solicitation if the crime would occur on the facts as the defendant believes they will be. This result is consistent with the approach taken by the Model Code to attempt and conspiracy. It also follows in this context from the fact that an uncommunicated solicitation is sufficient, that is, the defendant's liability is measured from the facts as the defendant believed them to be rather than as they might actually have been. As in the case of conspiracy, moreover, the provisions of §§ 5.04(1) and 5.05(2) suggest that impossibility is not a defense to a criminal solicitation. See the inferences drawn from these provisions with respect to conspiracy, page 347.

4. ABANDONMENT

Section 5.02(3) explicitly provides an abandonment defense to a charge of solicitation. Note the two requirements:

a. Prevent Commission of Crime

The defendant must have persuaded the person solicited not to commit the offense "or otherwise prevented the commission of the crime." A change of heart is thus not effective if the person solicited rejects a request to abandon and proceeds to commit the offense.

b. **Complete and Voluntary Renunciation**

The abandonment must constitute a "complete and voluntary renunciation" of the criminal purpose. Note that the second paragraph of § 5.01(4) applies to solicitation, and elaborates on the meaning of "complete" and "voluntary." See the illustrations of that provision on pages 338–39.

5. LIABILITY FOR SUBSTANTIVE OFFENSES

A person who solicits an offense will be liable under normal principles as an accomplice to the person who commits or attempts the offense. See the discussion of § 2.06 beginning at page 284.

6. GRADING

The grading of solicitation is governed by § 5.05(1). Solicitation is punished at the same grade and degree as the offense solicited, except that the solicitation of a capital offense or a felony of the first degree is punished as a felony of the second degree. Note that since grading factors are "material elements" of an offense, the defendant's mens rea as to these factors will be important. Compare the discussion of the grading of conspiracy, page 350. A solicitation of burglary would require the same mens rea for the elements of the object offense as would a conspiracy to commit burglary, and would be analyzed in the same manner.

7. CUMULATIVE PUNISHMENT

Normally, a person who solicits an offense will be liable as an accessory under § 2.06 for the commission or attempt to commit that offense. However, the Model Penal Code does not permit a conviction for both the solicitation of an offense and for (1) the commission of that offense by the person solicited; (2) an attempt by the person solicited to commit that offense; or (3) a conspiracy with the person solicited to commit that offense. These results are derived from §§ 1.07(1)(a), 1.07(4)(b), and 5.05(3), by precisely the same reasoning used in the context of attempt, page 340. Under § 1.07, solicitation is a lesser included offense to the object offense, and though both solicitation and the object offense may be charged, the defendant may be convicted of only one or the other. And under § 5.05(3), a person may be convicted of only one Article 5 offense—attempt, solicitation, or conspiracy—for conduct designed to culminate in the commission of the same offense.

E. OTHER INCHOATE OFFENSES

The Model Penal Code continues the tradition of defining many crimes in inchoate terms. Thus, the definitions of burglary in § 221.1 and the counterpart to larceny in § 223.2 are inchoate in the sense that they are committed before the ultimate harm sought to be prevented by the law has occurred. It is also clear, moreover, that one can be convicted under the Model Code for an attempt, solicitation, or conspiracy to commit burglary or theft.

Since attempt, solicitation, and conspiracy are graded so severely, it is not necessary for the Model Code to contain any offenses designed to increase the penalty for efforts to commit a crime that come close to fruition. Thus, there are no offenses of the "assault with intent" variety.

The Model Code contains a few inchoate offenses of a more generic nature than burglary or theft, designed to punish incipient criminality. Section 5.06 punishes possessing weapons and other instruments of crime and § 5.07 covers a variety of acts with a list of prohibited offensive weapons. And several of the offenses in Articles 250 and 251—most notably §§ 250.6 and 251.3—are also designed to deal with incipient crime.

F. REVIEW QUESTIONS

[Answers Provided in Appendix A, page 448]

1. T or F   Under the Model Penal Code, a solicitation or conspiracy to commit a violation would be graded as a violation.

2. T or F   One cannot be convicted of attempt under the Model Penal Code unless the conduct that is the basis of conviction strongly corroborates the intent required for conviction.

3. T or F   Unlike the common law, abandonment can constitute a complete defense to attempt, solicitation, and conspiracy under the Model Penal Code.

4. T or F   An attempt to commit a felony of the second degree is graded as a felony of the second degree under the Model Penal Code.

5. T or F   Unlike the common law, a defendant under the Model Penal Code cannot be prosecuted for both a conspiracy to commit an offense and commission of the same offense.

6. T or F   It is a defense to conspiracy under the Model Penal Code if the only person with whom the defendant is charged with conspiring is a juvenile incapable in law of being prosecuted for crime as an adult.

7. T or F   A and B agree to commit five bank robberies, which they successfully complete over a period of nine months. After the last one, they decide to commit one more. A and B can be convicted for two conspiracies under the Model Penal Code, one to commit the first five bank robberies and a second to commit the last additional one.

8. T or F   On the facts of the last question, A and B can be convicted for the five completed bank robberies and can also be convicted for conspiracy.

9. T or F   In order to justify a conviction for conspiracy to commit burglary under § 221.1 of the Model Penal Code and a grading of the offense as a felony of the second degree, it would be insufficient for the prosecutor to show that the defendants were indifferent as to whether the planned offense would take place at night.

10. T or F   A, B, and C agree to commit a bank robbery. Two days before the planned offense, A advises the others that they can go ahead and commit the

offense if they want to, but that *A* wants no part of it. *B* and *C* then commit the offense as planned. *A* can nonetheless be convicted of conspiracy to commit bank robbery.

11. **T or F**   On the facts of the previous question, the statute of limitations for prosecuting *A* for conspiracy to commit bank robbery begins to run on the day the object of the conspiracy is accomplished, namely the day the bank robberies are committed.

12. *D* has been charged under § 5.01 of the Model Penal Code with an attempt to violate § 220.1. *D* sought revenge against *A* for stealing *D*'s spouse, and decided to get back at *A* by destroying *A*'s 50–foot yacht. *D* approached the yacht at night, spread gasoline on the deck, and was about to light it when caught by the police. *D* was aware that *A* and *D*'s spouse might have been below deck at the time, and though *D* did not want to go so far as to wish them physical harm, *D* had decided to go ahead with the offense anyway. On what issues would *D*'s liability for the attempt turn, and, if *D* can be convicted, of what grade would the offense be?

13. *D1* has been charged with conspiracy under § 5.03 to violate § 220.1. The charge is that *D1* agreed with *D2* to burn *A*'s 50–foot yacht because *A* had stolen *D1*'s spouse. They agreed that they would use gasoline to make sure the fire would catch and the yacht would be destroyed. *D2* asked *D1* what they should do if *A* and *D1*'s spouse were aboard that night, and *D1* responded that, though there was no intent to do them harm, they would have to take that risk and go ahead anyway. As soon as the agreement was made, and before anything could be done to carry it out, *D2* arrested *D1*. *D2* was a cop who had merely feigned agreement.

Analyze this situation from two perspectives:

(a) On what issues would *D1*'s liability for conspiracy turn, and, if *D1* can be convicted, of what grade would the offense be?

(b) Does the Model Penal Code provide the right answer to a situation like this?

14. Describe and evaluate the Model Penal Code's approach to impossibility in the crime of attempt.

*

PART EIGHT

CRIMINAL HOMICIDE

Analysis

*

XIV

THE COMMON LAW

Analysis

359

A. INTRODUCTION

A criminal homicide occurs if the defendant causes the death of another person without justification or excuse. There were two grades of criminal homicide at common law: murder and manslaughter.

1. JUSTIFICATION AND EXCUSE

The terms "justification" and "excuse" have no legal significance today. They describe all defenses that would make a homicide non-criminal (self defense, a legal execution, etc.) and a killing that is without the minimum culpability for murder or manslaughter (a truly "accidental" killing).

2. PERSON

The term "person" has given some problems at both ends of the spectrum: at what point does a fetus become a "person" and hence a potential victim of a criminal homicide? And at what point does death occur so that a "person" is no longer a potential victim of a criminal homicide?

a. Birth

Traditionally, a baby must be born alive and be capable of life independently of its mother before it can be a victim of murder or manslaughter. There have been some departures from this rule. For example, a California court held in People v. Chavez, 77 Cal.App.2d 621, 176 P.2d 92 (1947), that a healthy baby in the process of being born was a "person" who could be a victim of criminal homicide. And when in Keeler v. Superior Court of Amador County, 2 Cal.3d 619, 87 Cal.Rptr. 481, 470 P.2d 617 (1970), the California Supreme Court refused to extend the *Chavez* principle to an unborn but viable fetus, the California legislature amended the law to provide that a killing of a fetus without the consent of the mother could be murder. See Cal. Penal Code § 187. New York has also modified the common law rule by statute to include "an unborn child with which a female has been pregnant for more than twenty-four weeks." See N.Y. Penal Code § 125.00. In most States, however, the common law "born alive" requirement still obtains.

Note, however, that there are other criminal offenses specifically directed to the termination of life before birth. The offenses are called "feticide," "infanticide," or "abortion." As a formal matter they are not classified as "criminal homicide" because they do not involve the death of a "person." In practical terms, however, they are distinguished from the traditional homicide offenses—murder and manslaughter—only by the fact that they are less severely punished. This area of the law is complicated, of course, by the Supreme Court's holding in Roe v. Wade, 410 U.S.113, 93 S.Ct. 705 (1973), that a woman's right to an abortion is constitutionally protected up to a certain point in the pregnancy. Basically, however, it is still permissible for the criminal law to punish the killing of a viable fetus. And most States do so, though killing a viable fetus is usually regarded as a lesser offense than the killing of a "person" who has been "born alive."

    b.   **Death**
    The killing of any person who is still alive can be a criminal homicide. Thus, pulling the plug on a life-sustaining respirator or premature removal of a vital organ for transplantation can be a criminal homicide, even though it is perfectly clear that the victim would soon die anyway. There is no generally accepted definition of when death occurs for this purpose. There are cases that talk about brain death or about the cessation of heartbeat and respiration, but there are problems with both tests. The area is difficult and unresolved, and subject to constant change in any event because of medical advances.

3.   CAUSATION
The definition of criminal homicide is drafted in terms of a specific result that must be "caused" by the defendant's behavior. Any behavior by the defendant will do, as indeed will an omission where there is a legal duty to act, so long as there is a proper causal relationship between the defendant's act (or failure to act) and the death of a person. The principles of causation discussed at pages 91–94 will govern this issue.

    a.   **Year and a Day Rule**
    At common law, a death that occurred more than a "year and a day" after the defendant's conduct was not regarded as "caused" by the defendant. A few States have extended this period by statute, but most no longer follow it at all.

    Retroactive abolition of the "year and a day" rule by the Tennessee Supreme Court was upheld by the United States Supreme Court in Rogers v. Tennessee, 532 U.S.451, 121 S.Ct. 1693 (2001). See page 410.

B.   MURDER

Murder is causing the death of another person "with malice aforethought."

1.   MEANING OF "MALICE AFORETHOUGHT"
The first thing to understand is that "malice aforethought" has nothing to do with "malice" or "aforethought." It has become over the years a completely arbitrary verbal formula encompassing four distinct kinds of behavior having nothing in common except that they have been regarded as morally equivalent for purposes of grading. As elaborated below, they were originally developed as a means of isolating those forms of murder that warranted capital punishment.

    a.   **Intent to Kill**
    The first category includes cases where the defendant intended to kill, or knew that death would almost certainly result.

        1)   **"Deadly Weapon" Presumption**
        "Intent to kill" has been presumed in cases where the defendant intentionally used a deadly weapon on another person. As usually

interpreted, this "presumption" is merely a permissive inference—the jury is entitled to draw the inference of an intent to kill from such behavior, but is not required to do so.

b. Intent to Inflict Serious Injury

The second category includes cases where the defendant intended to inflict grievous bodily harm, or knew that such harm would almost certainly result. This category could easily have been collapsed into the third, but the usual definition of "malice aforethought" did not do so.

c. Extreme Recklessness

The third category includes cases where the defendant was extremely reckless—where the defendant manifested an extreme indifference to the value of human life. These cases have been colorfully described over the years in many different ways, for example, as situations where the defendant had a "depraved mind," an "abandoned and malignant heart," or manifested a "wickedness of disposition, hardness of heart, and a mind regardless of social duty."

1) Actual Awareness of Risk

It is unclear whether the recklessness referred to in this category of murder requires an actual awareness by the defendant of the risk that death might result. Most cases and jury instructions do not speak to the point, but simply recite the various colorful formulas quoted above. Scholars who have addressed the question have disagreed. Actual awareness of the risk should be required, however, for a grading reason. It makes sense to treat the defendant who is aware that death is extremely likely, but doesn't care, as morally equivalent to the defendant who intends death. But it does not make sense to treat the person who is negligent— the person who ought to perceive the risk of death but does not—as morally equivalent to the defendant who intends death.

d. Felony Murder

The fourth category includes cases where the death occurred while the defendant was engaged in a felony. This is the so-called "felony-murder rule." It is elaborated below.

Bear in mind that satisfaction of any one of these categories constitutes "malice aforethought." There is also some authority that there was a fifth category consisting of cases where the defendant intended to resist a lawful arrest, but there have been few if any convictions on this basis and the other categories are adequate to deal with the situation. This "fifth" category is no longer of importance.

2. HISTORY

It is important to understand a bit of the history of murder. Originally (up until 1496, to be precise), murder was the only homicide offense. It included all criminal homicides, and the penalty was death. The history of criminal homicide since that time consists of: (a) the gradual peeling away of layers of criminal homicides that were thought not to deserve the death penalty; (b) the emergence of more detailed grading schemes placing various types of criminal homicide along the spectrum of available criminal punishments; and (c) the development of various justifications and excuses making certain homicides non-criminal. The third point is dealt with elsewhere. See pages 187, 221. The first two will be discussed here.

a. Manslaughter

The first development was the emergence of the offense of manslaughter. Over the years, murder—still punished by the mandatory death penalty—came to consist of all criminal homicides committed with "malice aforethought." Manslaughter became all criminal homicides that were not murder. It was not punished by death.

b. The Degree Structure

The next significant development was the emergence of "first degree" and "second degree" murder. This is an American invention, first used in Pennsylvania in 1794. The original Pennsylvania statute, still in force in many States today, provided that:

> "[A]ll murder, which shall be perpetrated by means of poison, or by lying in wait, or by any other kind of wilful, deliberate and premeditated killing, or which shall be committed in the perpetration or attempt to perpetrate any arson, rape, robbery, or burglary, shall be deemed murder in the first degree; and all other kinds of murder shall be deemed murder in the second degree."

The most important categories of "first degree murder" were (and still are where this structure is used) "wilful, deliberate and premeditated" killings and those felony murders placed in the first degree category. First degree murder was punished by the mandatory death penalty at first. Second degree murder was not punished by death.

1) "Wilful, Deliberate, and Premeditated"

The meaning of these words is unsettled. In some States, they encompass any intentional killing. See, e.g., Commonwealth v. Carroll, 412 Pa. 525, 194 A.2d 911 (1963). At the other extreme, they describe a particular method by which the defendant formed the intent to kill, described by the California Supreme Court as " 'a result of careful thought and weighing of considerations; as a *deliberate* judgment or plan; carried on cooly and steadily, [especially] according to a *preconceived design.*' " People v. Anderson, 70 Cal. 2d 15, 73 Cal.Rptr. 550, 447 P.2d 942 (1968). Many States fall somewhere between these two extremes. This is a typical point of confusion in those States that retain the Pennsylvania degree structure.

2) **Second Degree Murder**

Second degree murder includes "all other kinds of murder." This means that *any* killing with "malice aforethought" that is not on the first degree list will be punished as second degree murder.

c. **Discretionary Death Penalty**

Beginning with Tennessee in 1838, the death penalty gradually became discretionary for murder (or first degree murder as the case may have been) in all States.

d. **Note on Model Penal Code and the Death Penalty Decisions**

The other two major events of historical importance in the development of the law of murder are the drafting of the Model Penal Code and the death penalty decisions of the United States Supreme Court. The Model Penal Code homicide provisions are discussed at page 375 and the death penalty decisions at page 411.

3. FELONY MURDER

Literally stated, the felony murder rule permits a murder conviction if a death results during and as a result of any felony committed by the defendant. The rule also makes any accomplice in the commission of the felony guilty of murder.

a. **Rationale for the Rule and for Its Limitations**

The rule is never this broadly implemented, however. The reason is that the felony murder doctrine is not based on the defendant's culpability as to the death of another.

At its broadest, the rule means that a person who has the culpability for any felony will be convicted of murder if, during the course of the felony, another person is killed. Of course if the victim were intentionally killed or "malice aforethought" could otherwise be shown, no special doctrine would be required to obtain a conviction for murder. Thus, the felony murder doctrine is necessary only in those cases where the culpability for murder cannot independently be established. Its effect is to elevate to murder a homicide that would otherwise be manslaughter or that perhaps, because it was accidental, would not be criminal at all. And the basis for this elevation is the conduct and culpability required for commission of the underlying felony.

If there were a correspondence between the culpability manifested by the defendant in committing the felony and the culpability required for a conviction of murder, the felony murder rule would make sense. For this reason, the rule does make more sense in the context of armed robbery, for example, than tax fraud. Ironically though, the felony murder rule is also less needed in the case of armed robbery, because it is more likely that the minimum culpability for murder—extreme recklessness as to death—can independently be proved.

The felony murder rule can be defended only on grounds of deterrence—that it deters the commission of felonies and adds to the protection of life if a felon knows that any resulting death will lead to a conviction of murder. However, the less likely it is that the particular felony will result in violence, the more disparity there will be between the defendant's culpability and the culpability otherwise required for murder. There is great pressure, therefore, to limit the scope of the offense. The history of the doctrine is accordingly marked primarily by acceptance of the rule in order to achieve its deterrent effects, but at the same time an increasing reduction of its literal content in order to make its coverage ever more narrow. As a result, a large body of doctrine has emerged, consisting principally of limitations on the literal scope of the rule—limitations that will do a better job than the unadorned felony murder rule of matching the defendant's actual culpability to the culpability otherwise required for murder. In England and at least three States (Hawaii, Kentucky, and Michigan), moreover, the doctrine has been abolished completely.

b. "Inherently Dangerous Felony" Limitation

In States that have adopted a degree structure for murder, the first degree category will usually include a list of dangerous felonies that will support a first degree conviction on the felony murder theory. The original Pennsylvania statute quoted above, for example, included arson, rape, robbery, and burglary.

Note, however, that second degree murder consists of "all other kinds of murder." Thus, unless the felony murder doctrine is independently constrained, the concurrence of a death and any other felony will constitute second degree murder. And in a State that has not adopted a degree structure, an unconstrained felony murder doctrine will convert the concurrence of a death and any felony into a conviction for murder.

Because the list of modern felonies has grown so large, because so many felonies are not in the least bit life-endangering, and because application of the felony murder rule to felonies that are not life-endangering increases the disparity between actual culpability and the culpability otherwise required for murder, the rule has emerged that the felony murder doctrine can only be based upon a felony that is dangerous to life.

There is a division of authority on whether this rule means that the felony must have been committed in a manner that was in fact dangerous to life, or whether it means that the felony must be one that in the abstract is usually or "inherently" dangerous to life. Some jurisdictions approach the same objective by excluding offenses that were not felonies at common law, or that are "mala prohibita" rather than "mala in se." Virtually all jurisdictions, in any event, constrain their general category of felony murder by some such doctrine.

c. "Proximate Cause" Limitation

In addition, many courts require that the felony be a "proximate" cause of the death, that is, that the manner in which the death occurred be reasonably foreseeable from the manner in which the felony was committed. Thus a particularly convoluted chain of events that literally connected a death to a felony but that was so bizarre as to have been utterly unpredictable would not support a conviction for felony murder. But an accidental discharge of a gun by an armed robber would support a murder conviction if a victim or a bystander were killed.

d. **"Independent Felony" Limitation**

In addition, many courts require that the felony be "independent" of the homicide. This means that the felony must be independent of any acts which were necessarily a part of the homicide. Under this rule a lesser included offense to murder—manslaughter or an assault—cannot trigger the felony murder rule.

e. **When the Felony Begins and Ends**

Application of the felony murder rule requires a determination of when the underlying felony "begins" and when it "ends." For example, is a killing a felony murder if it occurs while the robbers are on the way to the bank or two hours after the offense while they are trying to hide the loot? Probably the most common statement of the rule is that the felony starts when an attempt has been committed and stops when the period of immediate flight from its commission is over. But some courts have drawn arbitrary lines at the beginning or the end of the felony in order to limit the operation of the doctrine. Thus a categorical answer cannot be given. It depends on how generously the court involved views the felony murder doctrine.

f. **"Killing Committed by Felon" Limitation**

A frequently litigated situation involves the following fact pattern:

> *A*, *B*, and *C* agree to commit an armed bank robbery. They do so, and during the robbery *V*, a victim, and *P*, a police officer, resist and engage *A*, *B*, and *C* in a gun battle. During the battle a bullet from *P*'s gun kills *V*, or a bullet from *P*'s gun kills *I*, an innocent bystander, or a bullet from *V*'s gun kills *B*. Are the surviving felons guilty of felony murder?

Two answers have been given:

1) **"Proximate Cause" Theory**

Under what has been called the "proximate cause" approach to this issue, it has been held that the surviving felons are guilty of felony murder. Their commission of a felony set in motion a chain of events which led to a death, and the manner in which the death occurred was reasonably foreseeable.

2) **"Agency" Theory**

Under what has been called the "agency" approach to the issue, it has been held that the surviving felons are *not* guilty of felony murder. In order for the felony murder doctrine to be applicable, these courts hold, the death must have been "directly caused" by the act of a felon, that is, the bullet that killed must in fact have been fired from a felon's gun.

3) Prevailing View

The prevailing view these days is the "agency" theory. It has been adopted in California and Pennsylvania, which are the jurisdictions in which the most famous cases have arisen.

4) Competing Rationales

If one likes the felony murder rule, the "proximate cause" theory makes sense. It *is* perfectly foreseeable that people will get killed in a gun battle, and also foreseeable that armed robbers will be killed by victims or cops, or that during an armed robbery a bullet from a victim's or a cop's gun will kill a cop, a victim, or an innocent bystander. Thus, the "proximate cause" theory might be regarded as a reasonable and minimally "fair" way of implementing the deterrence objectives that underlie the felony murder rule.

On the other hand, if one doesn't like the felony murder rule, then a sensible way to limit its operation is by the "agency theory." The reason the felony murder rule is criticized, as noted above, is the potential disparity between the defendant's actual culpability and the culpability otherwise required for murder. The additional deterrence cannot be "fair," the argument goes, if this disparity is too great. If it is required that the bullet that causes death actually come from a felon's gun, then it is more likely that the felon will actually be culpable as to the death, and more likely that the "culpability disparity" of the felony murder rule will be minimized. This will eliminate, for example, cases where the robbers are "armed" with a toy pistol in order to avoid killing someone, but a victim or a cop fires at them with real bullets. Under the "proximate cause" theory, the robbers in this case would still be guilty of felony murder.

5) Independent Liability for Murder

Courts that adopt the "agency theory" are quick to point out that a conviction of murder may well be possible in these situations without resort to the felony murder rule, that is, by proof of the extreme recklessness that will establish the culpability required for murder. Thus, the California Supreme Court noted in People v. Washington, 62 Cal.2d 777, 44 Cal.Rptr. 442, 402 P.2d 130 (1965), that "[d]efendants who initiate gun battles may . . . be found guilty of murder if their victims resist and kill." In effect, the court stated, police officers and victims should not be regarded as an "independent intervening cause" (see page 92) of the death in the situation posed, *if* the felon started the gunplay and otherwise manifested the culpability required for murder.

g. **"Culpability" Limitation**

At least one State (Delaware) has limited the felony murder rule by the statutory requirement that some culpability be shown towards the death. A first degree murder conviction can be obtained only if in addition to committing the felony the defendant is "reckless" towards the life of another in the Model Penal Code sense of that term. See Del.Code Ann. tit. 11, § 636(a)(2). It is second degree murder if the defendant is "negligent." See Del.Code Ann. tit. 11, § 635(2).

h. **"Liability of Accomplices" Limitation**

The traditional statement of the felony murder rule is that the felon "or any accomplice" is liable for a death resulting from the felony. As would be expected, limitations on the co-felon's liability have also been adopted.

1) **Judicial Limitations**

Courts sometimes require that the death be a "natural and probable result" of the felony (compare page 272) or that the killing be "in furtherance of the felony" (compare page 321).

2) **New York Limitation**

New York has limited the liability of an accomplice by statute. The limit is an "affirmative defense," a term which in New York means that the burden of persuasion is on the defendant by a preponderance of the evidence. It is an affirmative defense to a charge of felony murder if the defendant can prove four things:

(a) that the defendant did not commit the homicidal act or in any way encourage or aid in its commission; and

(b) that the defendant was not armed; and

(c) that the defendant had no reasonable ground to believe that anyone else was armed; and

(d) that the defendant had no reasonable ground to believe that any other participant in the felony intended to engage in life-endangering conduct.

N.Y. Penal Code § 125.25(3). This limitation has been copied in a number of other States.

C. MANSLAUGHTER

Manslaughter is any criminal homicide committed without malice aforethought. Modern statutes tend to divide manslaughter into two grading categories, voluntary and involuntary.

1. VOLUNTARY MANSLAUGHTER

Voluntary manslaughter consists of cases where "malice aforethought" would exist but for the presence of certain extenuating circumstances. It was often said that "malice aforethought" was disproved when these circumstances existed, but they are not logically inconsistent with any of the states of mind that constitute "malice aforethought."

a. Provocation

The defendant is entitled to have a killing reduced to voluntary manslaughter if it was committed in the "heat of passion" caused by "adequate provocation" and committed before a reasonable "cooling time" has expired.

1) "Heat of Passion"

There are three steps involved in determining whether "heat of passion" has been caused by "adequate provocation." Each must be satisfied.

A) Defendant Actually Provoked

The defendant must have lost control of normal restraints in response to some provoking event—must have acted in the "heat of passion."

B) Provocation Legally Adequate

The provocation must have been "legally adequate." There is a large body of doctrine as to what this means. Words alone are never sufficient in most jurisdictions, though they can be in some if they inform the defendant of the occurrence of some event that would itself be adequate. Perhaps the classic case of "adequate" provocation is the discovery of one's spouse in the act of adultery. Another common situation involves assaults (a threat to harm), batteries (an actual touching of another, minor or serious), and mutual fights. Essentially, all three of these occurrences can be "adequate" provocation in most jurisdictions, unless the event is trivial (e.g., a minor or accidental touching) or the defendant is at fault in initiating the encounter. In some instances, moreover, an injury to another person, particularly a family member, may constitute "adequate" provocation. In any event, the question whether the provocation is "legally adequate" will be resolved by the court in determining whether to allow the provocation issue to be submitted to the jury.

C) Defendant's Reaction must Have Been Reasonable

The provocation must have been such that it was reasonable or understandable that the defendant lost control and committed the act. This is an objective standard against which the defendant is measured. The mitigation does not exist to reduce the grading of homicides committed by hotheads who lose their cool at the slightest provocation. Rather, it exists to mitigate the penalty for persons who lost control more as a result of "the extraordinary character of the situation . . . than to any extraordinary deficiency [of their] character." Wechsler & Michael, A Rationale of the Law of Homicide II, 37 Colum.L.Rev. 1261, 1281 (1937). There is disagreement in the cases and the literature about how "objective" the standard should be— whether the defendant should be measured against the standard of a reasonable person or whether the standard should be a reasonable person with some or all of the defendant's emotional and physical characteristics.

2) Cooling Time

The issue of "cooling time" involves the same three kinds of questions. First, the defendant must not in fact have calmed down. Second, a period of time must not have passed that will lead the court to say as a matter of law that the defendant should have calmed down. And third, the jury will be asked to decide whether the defendant, as a reasonable person, should have calmed down and not committed the homicide.

3) The Effect of Mistake

There are surprisingly few decisions concerning the effect of mistake in the context of provocation. Three views can be found in the cases and the literature: (a) that an honest mistake in understanding the factual situation does not affect the availability of the mitigation; (b) that any mistake must be both honest and reasonable in order not to affect the availability of the mitigation; and (c) that any mistake is fatal to the availability of the mitigation (strict liability). It is probable that most courts would take the second position, although the case that is always cited for this proposition was decided in 1901. See State v. Yanz, 74 Conn. 177, 50 A. 37 (1901).

b. Imperfect Justification

Recall the "imperfect justification" situation. See, e.g., page 194. Where this doctrine is recognized, the conviction is for voluntary manslaughter.

c. Presumption of Malice

It is frequently stated that once the prosecutor has proved an intent to kill malice aforethought is "presumed." In most jurisdictions it is probable that this means only that a conviction of murder will be justified unless the defendant comes forth with evidence of a complete defense (such as self defense) or with evidence that will justify reducing the offense to voluntary manslaughter (such as adequate provocation or "imperfect" justification). If the defendant does so, normally the burden of persuasion will then be on the prosecutor to show that a conviction of murder should nonetheless be entered. As developed on page

414, however, one court got itself into trouble by placing the burden of persuasion on the defendant to show that the offense was voluntary manslaughter and not murder.

2. INVOLUNTARY MANSLAUGHTER

Involuntary manslaughter is a homicide that is neither murder nor voluntary manslaughter but is still criminally punished. There are two types of cases:

a. Recklessness or Negligence

There is a level of recklessness or negligence that will support a conviction for involuntary manslaughter, but the courts have never been very precise in defining its content. It is usually described with epithets: "gross" negligence, "willful and wanton" negligence, etc. Most courts would agree that more than the ordinary negligence that would suffice for a civil action is required, though some would permit a conviction on the basis of ordinary negligence if a deadly weapon is used. There is also a separate offense of vehicular homicide in some jurisdictions, usually based on some form of negligence.

b. Misdemeanor Manslaughter

There is a counterpart to the felony murder rule in the case of misdemeanors: any death that occurs during the commission of a misdemeanor will be involuntary manslaughter. Some courts have even stated the rule more broadly: any death that occurs during the commission of *any unlawful act* will be involuntary manslaughter. As would be expected, most jurisdictions have limited the scope of the misdemeanor-manslaughter rule for the same reasons that felony murder has been limited. And the limitations have followed the same lines, e.g., by limiting the doctrine to misdemeanors that are malum in se, that are inherently dangerous, that were committed in a manner that was dangerous to life, etc. The doctrine has been abolished, moreover, in about half of the States.

D. DIMINISHED RESPONSIBILITY

The concept of "diminished responsibility," sometimes called "diminished capacity," encompasses three quite separate ideas which are set forth on pages 165–66. One of them is relevant to the grading of criminal homicide. The idea is that persons who are not entitled to be acquitted by reason of insanity may nonetheless be entitled to a mitigation of their offense to a lesser crime based on the effects of a mental disease or defect. This use of the term thus describes a "junior version" of the insanity defense or an "intermediate degree" of insanity—not enough for complete acquittal but enough to reduce the grade of the offense. Like the insanity defense, it involves two steps: the defendant must be suffering from a "mental disease or defect"; and the mental disease or defect must have had a prescribed relationship to the defendant's behavior that is regarded as warranting a mitigation of the offense to a lesser grade.

This notion of diminished responsibility was adopted in England, by the Homicide Act of 1957, 5 & 6 Eliz. 2, c. 11, § 2. The statute provided that a homicide will be reduced from murder to manslaughter if the defendant was suffering from such an "abnormality of mind . . . as substantially impaired his mental responsibility." England uses the *M'Naghten* rules for the insanity defense, and among other things the quoted language has been interpreted to permit a "control" or "volitional" inquiry to reduce an offense to manslaughter.

Two California decisions illustrate how a similar idea has been developed in the United States:

1. MITIGATION OF FIRST DEGREE MURDER TO SECOND DEGREE

The first case is People v. Wolff, 61 Cal.2d 795, 40 Cal.Rptr. 271, 394 P.2d 959 (1964). This case defined the terms "wilful, deliberate and premeditated" to include an additional ingredient: that the defendant have the ability "maturely and meaningfully" to reflect upon the killing. This was designed to take account of the degree of "personal depravity" and the "quantum of personal turpitude" manifested by the defendant. The court then held that evidence of mental disease or defect could be considered on this issue and that, even though the defendant was legally sane under the *M'Naghten* rules, the defendant was entitled to have a conviction of first degree murder reduced to second degree based on the medical evidence. This case was overruled in California by statute. See Cal.Penal Code § 189.

2. MITIGATION OF MURDER TO VOLUNTARY MANSLAUGHTER

The second case is People v. Conley, 64 Cal.2d 310, 49 Cal.Rptr. 815, 411 P.2d 911 (1966). The defendant had been convicted of first degree murder based on a finding of an intent to kill that was formed wilfully and with deliberation and premeditation. The court nonetheless redefined the concept of "malice aforethought" to include an "awareness of the obligation to act within the general body of laws regulating society" and held that evidence of mental disease or defect, while not indicating insanity under the *M'Naghten* test, was sufficient to justify a manslaughter instruction under this standard. This case too was overruled in California by statute. See Cal.Penal Code § 188.

E. REVIEW QUESTIONS

[Answers Provided in Appendix A, page 452]

1. **T or F** At common law, the intentional killing of a healthy child in the process of being born was murder.

2. **T or F** The phrase "wilful, deliberate, and premeditated" in a first degree murder statute means that the defendant must carefully and thoughtfully have formed an intent to kill.

3. **T or F** The "inherently dangerous felony" limitation on the felony murder rule has no application in a jurisdiction where the first degree murder statute limits felony murder to crimes like robbery, burglary, rape, and arson.

4. **T or F** A defendant can establish a provocation sufficient to reduce what would otherwise be murder to voluntary manslaughter by showing that the

offense was committed in the heat of passion and that a reasonable person in the defendant's situation would have done the same thing.

5. **T or F** In most jurisdictions, involuntary manslaughter consists of a residual category of criminal homicide offenses based on recklessness, negligence, or the concurrence of a death with certain kinds of misdemeanors.

6. *A* and *B* are married. *A* is extremely jealous, and is always checking up on *B*. *A* hears that *B* is messing around with *C*, and follows *C* to a motel room. *A* listens at the door and when heavy breathing is heard, *A* barges in with gun drawn. In the dark, *A* sees *C* in a compromising position with a member of the opposite sex, and believing it to be *B* shoots and kills them both. It turns out that *C* was really with *D*, who looked a lot like *B*. In a typical common law jurisdiction, what legal issues would be presented if *A* were charged with murder? On what principles would a jury be charged before *A* could be convicted of murder? In your opinion, how should this situation be resolved?

7. Write a short essay in which you identify all legal errors made in the following statement and indicate what should have been said:

"Malice aforethought" is one of those wonderful phrases of the law the meaning of which has nothing to do with a literal rendition of the words. Actually, it means intent to kill, knowledge that death will almost certainly result, intent to inflict serious bodily injury, knowledge that serious bodily injury will almost certainly result, a category of extreme recklessness usually described with colorful but equally meaningless words, or, as implemented in most jurisdictions, the occurrence of a killing during the commission of certain kinds of felonies, felonies which are described in an elaborate body of doctrine designed to mitigate the disparity between the culpability in fact manifested by the defendant and the culpability that otherwise constitutes "malice aforethought." And in order for "malice aforethought" truly to exist, the defendant must not have acted in the heat of passion based on adequate provocation, unless an adequate cooling time had occurred, and must not have acted in an honest but unreasonable belief that some justification which the law recognizes as a defense existed.

8. *A* and *B* agree to commit an armed bank robbery. They do so, and *P*, a police officer, tries to stop the robbery while it is in progress. *A* and *B* engage the police officer in a gun battle, during which a bullet from the officer's gun kills *B*. Describe the pros and cons of convicting *A* of murder on a felony murder theory. Which side has the better of it? Explain your answer.

*

XV

THE MODEL PENAL CODE

Analysis

A.   INTRODUCTION

Section 210.1(1) of the Model Penal Code provides that a defendant is guilty of criminal homicide who "purposely, knowingly, recklessly or negligently causes the death of another human being." Section 210.1(2) provides that criminal homicide shall be punished as murder, manslaughter, or negligent homicide. Sections 210.2, 210.3, and 210.4 implement this grading structure.

1.   JUSTIFICATION AND EXCUSE

The definition of criminal homicide in § 210.1 does not explicitly refer to the absence of justification or excuse, but that is because under the structure of the Model Code it does not have to. Under Section 1.13(9)(c), facts which negate a justification or an excuse are an "element" of every crime. Thus, self defense, insanity, and all of the other justification and excuse defenses, if raised by the defendant, must be disproved by the prosecutor beyond a reasonable doubt before a "criminal homicide" can occur. See § 1.12(1).

2.   PERSON

The Model Penal Code defines "human being" as "a person who has been born and is alive." § 210.0(1). It thus follows the common law in this respect. The Model Code does not address the other end of the spectrum, that is, when a person is regarded as too "dead" to be a victim of a criminal homicide.

3.   CAUSATION

Questions of causation are dealt with in § 2.03 and discussed at page 128. The "year and a day rule" is abolished.

B.   MURDER

The term "malice aforethought," like most other common law culpability terms, has been abandoned by the Model Penal Code. But the Model Code does take account in § 210.2 of each category that was included in the term "malice aforethought."

1.   TREATMENT OF CASES INCLUDED IN "MALICE AFORETHOUGHT"

Recall that four types of cases were included in the concept "malice aforethought:"

a.   Intent to Kill

Cases where the defendant intended to kill or knew that death would almost certainly result are explicitly included in § 210.2(1)(a). See § 2.02(2).

b.   Intent to Inflict Serious Injury

Cases where the defendant intended to inflict serious injury or knew the practical certainty of that result are collapsed into the concept of extreme recklessness contained in § 210.2(1)(b).

c. Extreme Recklessness

Section 210.2(1)(b) covers cases where the death is caused "recklessly under circumstances manifesting extreme indifference to the value of human life." This is an ordinary English rendition that parallels the common law concept of an "abandoned and malignant heart," etc. It expresses agreement with the common law that there is a moral equivalence between those who intend to kill and those who act with an extreme form of reckless indifference. For example, a person who randomly discharges a machine gun on a crowded street, not intending to kill but not caring one way or the other, is regarded as at least as culpable as a person who intends to kill. Note that the word "recklessly" in § 210.2(1)(b) incorporates the concept of recklessness defined in § 2.02(2)(c), and thus involves an actual awareness of the risk of death. The intent is that the definition of "recklessness" in § 2.02(2)(c) will apply in this context, but that in addition the defendant's conduct must manifest the required "extreme indifference to the value of human life."

d. Felony Murder

The Model Penal Code abolishes the felony murder rule on the rationale that it can produce too large a disparity between the defendant's actual culpability and the culpability otherwise required for murder. See pages 364–65. The judgment of the drafters was that felons who cause death ought to be convicted of murder only in those cases where they intend to kill, knew that death would result, or manifested the level of indifference to human life identified in § 210.2(1)(b). Hence, one who would be accused of felony murder at common law will be tried under § 210.2(1), or if a lesser culpability is shown, under the standards of §§ 210.3(1)(a) or 210.4(1). Normal principles of causation under § 2.03 will be applied. The person who formerly would have been accused of felony murder will thus be tried under no special substantive doctrine under the Model Penal Code.

The Model Code does, however, make one concession to the momentum of the felony murder rule. It permits a "presumption" that the requisite degree of recklessness exists in cases where a death occurs during the course of several specified felonies. For the effect of a presumption under the Model Code, see § 1.12(5) and page 134.

It should be added that this provision of the Model Penal Code has had little impact on modern legislation. Most states with revised penal codes have retained the felony murder rule in some form.

2. RATIONALE FOR REJECTION OF DEGREE STRUCTURE

Note that the Model Code does not include the degree structure first adopted in Pennsylvania and later reflected in many codes in other States. This judgment was partly based on the difficulty, after nearly two centuries of effort, of giving distinctive content to the critical phrase "wilful, deliberate, and premeditated." More importantly, however, the reason was that the concept of "wilful, deliberate, and premeditated," if taken literally and seriously, was not regarded as stating a particularly useful criterion for distinguishing the relative moral culpability of various offenders. Consider, for example, the person who randomly discharges a machine gun on a crowded street, not intending to kill anyone but not caring either. On any scale of moral values that person is as dangerous and culpable as the contract killer who coldly dispatches the targeted victim, perhaps moreso. Yet the "premeditation-deliberation" standard sharply distinguishes between the two, and convicts only the latter of the highest form of murder. And that standard would also convict of first degree murder the mercy killer who after weeks of torment finally puts a loved one away, while remanding the machine gunner to a lesser offense.

C. MANSLAUGHTER

The Model Penal Code abandons the terms "voluntary" and "involuntary" manslaughter. It drops the "misdemeanor-manslaughter" rule completely. And it resolves the "imperfect justification" situation in terms of the defendant's culpability as to the mistake. See page 194. It also puts reckless and negligent homicide into different grading categories. See §§ 210.3 and 210.4.

1. PROVOCATION
The provisions of § 210.3(1)(b) are derived from the common law "provocation" mitigation. A defendant whose offense would otherwise be murder may nonetheless be convicted of manslaughter if the offense is committed "under the influence of extreme mental or emotional disturbance for which there is a reasonable explanation or excuse." And the reasonableness of the defendant's explanation or excuse "shall be determined from the viewpoint of a person in the actor's situation under the circumstances as he believes them to be." This provision has been widely copied in new penal code revisions. It departs in five major ways from the common law rule of "adequate provocation":

  a. **Source of Provocation**
      It does not focus upon a particular act of provocation by the victim, but upon the defendant's emotional condition at the time of the offense.

  b. **Eliminate "Adequacy" Limitation**
      There is no requirement that any provoking events be "adequate," and hence no occasion for the courts to build a body of doctrine that excludes some types of provocation from the defense. Thus the second step (see page 369) in the common law analysis has been eliminated.

  c. **Moderate Objectivity of Standard**
      The defendant is measured against an objective standard by the Model Penal Code. This is the function of the language "for which there is a reasonable explanation or excuse." But the standard is less rigorously objective than the

common law, in large part because of the word "situation" in the second sentence of § 210.3(1)(b). Courts and juries are admonished to consider a person in the actor's "situation," and this term was deliberately left undefined so that particular aspects of the defendant's physical or emotional makeup could be taken into account in judging the reasonableness of the defendant's "explanation or excuse." Blindness, shock, or extreme grief, for example, could easily be read into the word "situation." The extent to which the court as opposed to the jury will give decisive content to the term is also left open.

d. Eliminate Separate "Cooling Time" Inquiry

There is no separate "cooling time" inquiry. The thought was that, once the standard of § 210.3(1)(b) was met, nothing was added by asking the "cooling time" question. If the defendant had in fact calmed down and was no longer under the influence of extreme mental or emotional stress at the time of the offense, then the mitigation by its own terms would not apply. And whether the defendant should have calmed down by the time the offense was committed can be taken into account in determining whether there was a "reasonable explanation or excuse" for the defendant's behavior.

e. Effect of Mistake

The effect of mistake is governed by the language "under the circumstances as he believes them to be." This means that the defendant will be judged on the basis of the facts as perceived. Any mistake will not deprive the defendant of the benefit of the mitigation. The rationale for this position was put well by Professor Glanville Williams in Provocation and the Reasonable Man, [1954] Crim.L.Rev. 740, 753, when he said that the purpose of measuring the defendant against an objective standard was to exclude from the mitigation those who suffer from "unusual deficiency of self-control, not the making of an error of observation or inference in point of fact."

2. DIMINISHED RESPONSIBILITY

The Model Penal Code does not explicitly incorporate the English concept of diminished responsibility. See page 371. But the ambiguity of the word "situation" in § 210.3(1)(b) would permit a court interested in the concept to take mental disease or defect into account in considering the standard against which the defendant is to be measured. Thus, the reasonableness of the defendant's "explanation or excuse" might be considered by a court sympathetic to the idea of diminished responsibility from the viewpoint of a person with the particular mental characteristics of the defendant. It should be emphasized, however, that the Model Code does not require or even invite this result. It merely includes a deliberately ambiguous word that will allow courts to make their own policy through its interpretation.

D. CAPITAL PUNISHMENT

The American Law Institute decided to take no position on whether capital punishment should be authorized for murder. Accordingly § 210.6 and the other references to capital punishment in Article 210 were placed in brackets. But the Institute was realistic enough to understand that, whatever position it took, capital punishment was likely to be a feature of American criminal law for some time to come. It did therefore think it important to speak to how capital punishment should be imposed by those jurisdictions that elected to retain it, hence § 210.6. Section 210.6 has been widely influential, both before and after the death penalty decisions of the United States Supreme Court. Those decisions, and how the Model Penal Code fares under them, are dealt with at page 411. Here the Model Code structure will be briefly described.

1. THE NATURE OF THE PROCEEDING

There are two fundamental ideas on which the approach to capital punishment in § 210.6 is based:

a. Bifurcation

The first is that the capital punishment decision should be made in a separate proceeding, normally held before the same jury that determined the defendant's guilt, at which evidence is specifically directed by both parties to the capital punishment question. [Note that there are alternate versions of § 210.6(2), permitting each jurisdiction to decide whether it wants the trial judge or the jury to make the capital punishment decision. Virtually all States that follow this procedure let the jury do it and the Supreme Court has since held that Apprendi v. New Jersey, 530 U.S. 466, 120 S. Ct. 2348 (2000), means that a jury, not a judge, must find the aggravating circumstances that will justify a capital sentence. See page 412.] Thus, the prosecutor will have an opportunity to introduce the defendant's prior record, evidence that is usually not admissible on the question of guilt. And the defendant will have the opportunity to offer evidence in mitigation, and in particular will be able to take the stand without worrying about self-incrimination with respect to the offense in question since guilt will already have been decided.

b. Criteria for Decision

The second is that the capital punishment decision should be regulated by announced criteria. Note first that § 210.6(1) sets forth criteria for the judge to use in determining whether to permit the second stage of the proceeding to go forward. Thus, under § 210.6(1)(d), if the defendant was less than 18 at the time of the offense, the court is instructed not to impose a sentence of capital punishment. If the capital punishment hearing is held, § 210.6(2) and its alternate state an ultimate standard for imposition of the capital sentence: the court or jury is to take the aggravating and mitigating considerations into account, but is not to impose or recommend a sentence of death "unless it finds one of the aggravating circumstances enumerated in Subsection (3) and further finds that there are no mitigating circumstances sufficiently substantial to call for leniency." The aggravating circumstances, one of which thus must be found to exist before a capital sentence can be imposed, are listed in § 210.6(3). A list of potential mitigating factors is suggested by § 210.6(4), but this list is not exclusive and the defendant is free to offer anything thought relevant to mitigation.

1) **Diminished Responsibility**
   Note that there are three places under § 210.6 which specifically address the introduction of evidence of mental disease or defect short of insanity for the purpose of avoiding the death penalty:

   a) **Preclusion of Death Penalty by Court**
      The first is § 210.6(1)(e), under which the court can preclude the death penalty without going through the second hearing if "satisfied that . . . the defendant's . . . mental condition calls for leniency."

   b) **Extreme Mental or Emotional Disturbance**
      The second is § 210.6(4)(b), which is derived from the provocation standard as stated in § 210.3(1)(b). Note, however, that the standard here is completely subjective. The defendant must have been acting under the influence of extreme mental or emotional disturbance, but need not have had a "reasonable explanation or excuse."

   c) **Cognitive or Volitional Impairment**
      The third is § 210.6(4)(g), which is derived from the insanity defense as stated in § 4.01(1). Note, however, that mere impairment is sufficient for mitigation (the impairment need not be "substantial" as in the case of the insanity defense itself) and that intoxication (both voluntary and involuntary) that leads to cognitive or volitional impairment can also be considered.

E. REVIEW QUESTIONS

[Answers Provided in Appendix A, page 454]

1. **T or F** The Model Penal Code follows the common law in determining when a fetus becomes a "person" for purposes of the criminal homicide statutes.

2. **T or F** Although the Model Penal Code abolishes the concept of "malice aforethought," it does punish as murder all cases that were included in the common law rendition of that term.

3. **T or F** The Model Penal Code rejects the English concept of diminished responsibility, that is, the idea that evidence of mental disease or defect short of proving the insanity defense can mitigate an offense from murder to manslaughter.

4. **T or F** But the Model Penal Code does adopt the idea of diminished responsibility in another sense, that is, as evidence to be offered in mitigation of an offense for purposes of avoiding a capital sentence.

5. Re-examine Question 6 on page 373. How would the mistake issue in the case be resolved under the Model Penal Code?

6. The Model Penal Code "provocation" standard is quite different from the common law notion of "provocation." Write a short essay in which you explain the differences, the case that can be made for both the Model Code and the common law, and which you think is the better approach. Be sure to state your reasons.

PART NINE

OTHER CRIMES

*

383

XVI

OTHER CRIMES

Analysis

A. INTRODUCTION

This section departs from the format of the rest of the book by combining discussion of the common law and the Model Penal Code in the consideration of two additional substantive offenses—rape and theft—that are commonly included in criminal law courses. The Model Penal Code definitions of the offenses have been chosen as the organizing principle because most students will have access to its text.

The format is to contrast some of the more important features of the Model Penal Code to the common law counterparts of these two offenses. Not all aspects of these crimes can be covered without turning this portion of the book into a morass of detail. The purpose, instead, is to provide a general overview of important principles.

The section concludes with discussion of the cumbersomely named Racketeer Influenced and Corrupt Organizations Act, better known as RICO. RICO is a federal statute aimed at organized crime. It has served as the model for a number of State statutes with the same objectives. Because of the success of RICO, it has become popular to include coverage of its provisions in criminal law courses, usually in connection with—and in contrast to—materials on conspiracy. RICO has no common law or Model Penal Code counterpart.

B. RAPE

Section 213.1(1) contains the Model Penal Code counterpart to the traditional offense of rape. The heart of the definition is in § 213.1(1)(a): it applies to a male who has sexual intercourse with a female not his wife if he "compels her to submit by force." This definition and its companion provisions carry forward the common law in some respects and depart from the common law in others. Some of its provisions are also substantially out of date, incomplete, or just wrong when measured against recent legislation or judged by contemporary critics.

1. THE COMMON LAW
The traditional definition of rape at common law, from Blackstone, is "the carnal knowledge of a woman forcibly and against her will."

a. Theory of the Offense
There are two competing modern justifications for punishing rape.

1) Offense Against the Person
One is that rape is an offense against the person, a form of physical assault of a kind with other forms of aggression by one person against another. This conception leads to a focus on the amount of force used by the aggressor and to a grading structure based on the amount of physical harm caused or threatened.

2) Offense Against Sexual Autonomy

The other is that rape is an offense against sexual autonomy, a crime that occurs whenever the sexual act is completed without full and willing consent. This conception leads the focus away from the amount of force by an aggressor towards a focus on the element of consent. On this view, force sufficient to engage in the sexual act would be sufficient, whether or not it causes or threatens physical harm to the victim beyond the sexual act.

3) Rape as a Defense to Adultery or Fornication

In addition to these two justifications for punishing rape, it should also be noted that consideration of the relationship of rape to other early crimes has explanatory power in understanding the evolution of the law. Another theory that may explain some of the surviving doctrines of rape—explicated in Anne M. Coughlin, *Sex and Guilt*, 84 Va. L. Rev. 1 (1998)—is that, since sex out of wedlock was itself an offense of adultery or fornication, the woman who cried "rape" was essentially in the position of advancing an excuse for her own potential criminality. If her act was not the result of coercion by another, in other words, she was herself guilty of a crime. She could only escape her own conviction by shifting the blame to the other party to the sexual act.

b. Elements of the Offense

The offense at common law could only be committed by a man, and was not committed by a man who had "carnal knowledge" with his wife, no matter the circumstances. "Carnal knowledge" was limited to penile-vaginal intercourse where "some" penetration, however slight, was accomplished. It is difficult to quantify the amount of force that was required, but clear that it was more force than necessary to accomplish the act of penetration. Lack of consent was a separate element.

Various statements have been advanced to establish how far the woman must have gone in order to establish her lack of consent, even where the act was consummated by force. One State still adheres by statute to the early common law requirement of "utmost resistance." Variations such as "earnest resistance," "reasonable resistance," and the like, can also be found in common law decisions. More was certainly required than the modern variants of "no means no" or "the absence of yes means no" that are expressed in the literature—and very occasionally in the law—today.

Note that a requirement of "utmost" resistance might have made sense if, by analogy to the law of duress, its function was to establish an excuse for what otherwise would be criminal behavior by the woman. A law of rape informed by the two modern justifications of the offense recited above, by contrast, would substantially reduce, or eliminate, the common law resistance requirement.

c. Mistakes of Fact

There was disagreement at common law about the effect of mistake on the element of consent. Although rape was commonly called a "general intent" crime, in many courts this element was satisfied by the intentional act of carnal knowledge by force, and a mistake by the defendant about the woman's consent was irrelevant and no defense. Liability was strict on this element, in other words, a result that can perhaps be explained if the defendant was engaging in criminal or at least immoral behavior (adultery or fornication) whether or not the woman consented. The act was a crime or a breach of prevailing morals, in that perception, even on the facts as the defendant believed them to be. See pages 150–52.

But there were other jurisdictions where the ordinary mistake of fact rules applied, where an honest and reasonable mistake of fact as to the woman's consent was a defense. And in England, as the result of the interaction between a 1976 case and legislation later in the same year, the standard for mistake on the consent issue is "recklessness" in the Model Penal Code sense of that term. See page 112.

2. THE MODEL PENAL CODE

There are a number of different aspects of the relationship of the Model Penal Code to the common law that deserve separate comment.

a. Force and Consent

Notice that § 213.1(1)(a) does not contain a requirement that the act be "against her will" or without the woman's consent. It instead requires that the man "compel" the woman "by force."

The theory of the Model Penal Code is that the offense should focus on the physical aggression of the male rather than the state of mind of the victim. The question is whether the defendant engaged in behavior that "compelled" the victim to submit. Consent is of course relevant to this concept, but the idea is that remanding it to subsidiary status as part of an inquiry into whether the defendant was seeking to compel compliance will provide proper focus for the evidence and the jury's thinking. It also avoids focus on the resistance issue, as well as the varieties of formulae in which preceding versions of the law expressed this requirement.

1) Backwards?

Some modern critics respond that the Model Penal Code has it backwards. If rape is viewed primarily as a form of physical assault, perhaps the Model Code is right. But if it is viewed as a protection of sexual autonomy, as the critics argue it should be, then the focus should be on the woman's lack of consent, not the behavior of the actor. If the woman says "no," in other words, it should not matter how much "force" is manifested by the defendant's behavior or whether the woman resisted to the point that one can conclude that she was "compelled." "No" means "no," and that should be enough.

2) The Grading Response

Model Penal Code defenders, and other commentators on the law of rape, are likely to respond that the way to handle this point is by establishing different grades of sexual assault. Obtaining sex by violence should be punished as a more serious offense, this argument would go, than obtaining sex without the full consent of the other party.

Under the Model Penal Code, rape is a first degree felony if the actor "compels" the victim to submit "by force" and if either (a) he inflicts serious bodily injury on the victim or another or (b) if the victim was not a voluntary social companion of the actor and had not previously permitted him sexual liberties. It is a second degree felony if both of these factors are missing and if the sex is compelled by force. See § 213.1(1).

The offense is called "gross sexual imposition" and punished as a felony of the third degree if the actor "compels her to submit by any threat that would prevent resistance by a woman of ordinary resolution." § 213.1(2). And the offense is reduced to the misdemeanor of "sexual assault" if it involves "sexual contact" which the actor "knows . . . is offensive to the other person." § 213.4(1).

The interplay between the elements of force and consent is reflected in a variety of provisions enacted in recent years. Some have followed the Model Penal Code and emphasized the "force" side of the equation. Others have done the opposite, by focusing on lack of consent and de-emphasizing the requirement of force. Still others have required various mixtures of the two, often complicating the picture even further by various sorts of grading distinctions between different levels of the offense.

b. Alternatives to Force

Rape has always recognized situations where physical assault was unnecessary and "consent" by the victim was ineffectual. The Model Penal Code, and modern statutes, have extended this notion.

1) Threats

"Force" under the Model Penal Code can consist of physical compulsion, or it can consist of threats to kill, to cause serious bodily injury, to cause extreme pain, or to kidnap someone. The threat need not be to harm only the victim. It is sufficient if the threats are directed at "anyone." § 213.1(1)(a).

Lesser threats can result in conviction for a lesser offense. Gross sexual imposition is committed if the defendant "compels [the victim] to submit by any threat that would prevent resistance by a woman of ordinary resolution." § 213.1(2).

2) Impairment

Section 213.1(1)(b) deals with situations where the defendant has engaged in behavior designed to impair the ability of the victim to "appraise or control her conduct." The Model Penal Code language on this point is quite narrow. It applies to the situation where substantial impairment occurs through the use of drugs, intoxicants, or other means only if (a) they are administered by the defendant (b) "without her knowledge" and (c) "for the purpose of preventing resistance." Other modern statutes extend this notion by focusing on the victim's substantial impairment due to drugs or intoxicants but dropping one or more of the Model Penal Code's limiting conditions.

The Model Penal Code also punishes as rape in situations where the victim is "unconscious" (§ 213.1(1)(c)) and as gross sexual imposition in situations where the defendant knows the victim suffers from a mental disease or defect that renders her incapable of appraising the nature of her conduct (§ 213.1(2)(b)) or where he knows that the victim is unaware that a sexual act is being committed upon her or where she submits because she mistakenly supposes that the defendant is her husband (§ 213.1(2)(c)).

There are similar provisions for the misdemeanor of sexual assault. See § 213.4.

3) Age

The common law punished "carnal knowledge" as rape if it was committed by a man with a girl of less than 10. Liability on the age element was strict. The Model Penal Code continues this prohibition in its crime of rape, punishable as a second degree felony, in § 213.1(1)(d). It also continues the tradition of strict liability as to age. See § 213.6(1).

The Model Penal Code also punishes as a third degree felony called "corruption of minors and seduction" sexual intercourse by a male with a female not his wife if the victim is less than [16] years old and the actor is at least [four] years older than the victim. § 213.3(1)(a). Brackets are used in the definition in order to suggest that different legislatures may wish to use a different age for the victim and a different relationship between the victim's age and the actor's age.

Offenses of this type are often called "statutory rape." They are quite common in modern legislation, with considerable variation as to age of the victim and the relationship of the victim's age to the age of the defendant. Often liability is strict on the victim's age, no matter how high it is set. Notice that the Model Penal Code uses strict liability only where the age of the victim is set at 10. Where the victim's age is higher than 10, it is a defense if the defendant proves non-negligence by a preponderance of the evidence. See § 213.6(1).

c. Sexual Act

The common law offense of rape was limited to penile-vaginal penetration. The Model Penal Code, as do many modern statutes, extends the definition of sexual intercourse beyond this to include "intercourse per os or per anum, with some penetration however slight; emission is not required." § 213.0(1). The common law agreed that emission was not required.

d. Spousal Exclusion

The Model Penal Code retains the common law notion that a man cannot rape his wife. It expands on this idea in § 213.6(2) by providing that the exclusion extends to persons living together as man and wife, regardless of the legal status of their relationship. But persons still legally married who are living apart under a decree of judicial separation are not within the exclusion. A man who compels sexual intercourse by force after such a separation can, under the Model Penal Code, be guilty of rape.

Many modern statutes have eliminated this exclusion, and permit prosecutions for rape even though the parties are married.

e. Sex Neutrality

It is also common today for rape statutes to be drafted in sex neutral terms, that is, to apply to male-male and female-female encounters, as well as to situations where a female is the aggressor and a male the victim. Neither the common law nor the Model Penal Code crimes of rape were written in these terms. The Model Penal Code does, however, include as a felony of the second degree the crime of "deviate sexual intercourse by force or imposition." See § 213.2. This crime is drafted in sex neutral terms, and applies to the same kinds of overreaching covered as rape in § 213.1.

A number of recent statutes have changed the terminology as they have achieved this reform. Some have abandoned the word "rape" and substituted "criminal sexual assault," "criminal sexual abuse," "aggravated sexual abuse," "criminal sexual conduct," and the like. Most have adopted a degree structure of some sort.

f. Procedural Provisions

1) Prompt Complaint

Section 213.6(4) continues the "prompt complaint" requirement of the common law. A prosecution for rape cannot be filed if the woman does not file a complaint with the public authorities within a prescribed period of time. Three months is suggested by the Model Penal Code as a reasonable period.

This is a much-criticized feature of the law of rape. It has been abandoned in many jurisdictions.

2) Corroboration of Victim's Testimony

Section 213.6(5) also contains a controversial aspect of the law of rape. It provides that no felony conviction under Article 213 can be obtained based upon the uncorroborated testimony of the victim. It also provides that the jury "shall" be instructed to evaluate the testimony of a complaining witness "with special care in view of the emotional involvement of the witness and the difficulty of determining the truth with respect to alleged sexual activities carried out in private." This too is a much-criticized feature of the law that has been abandoned in a number of jurisdictions.

3) Rape Shield Laws

One aspect of the law of rape that has drawn constant criticism is the defense practice of attempting to shift the focus of the trial from the acts of the defendant to the sexual history and character of the victim. The result of such criticisms has been a succession of so-called "rape shield" laws which have placed severe limitations on the ability of the defense to engage in such tactics.

C. THEFT

Article 223 of the Model Penal Code consolidates an array of common law theft offenses into one overarching crime with many variations of detail. The distinctive feature of common law theft was a series of maddeningly arcane distinct offenses, with whisper thin distinctions between them, that had to be properly charged on pain of losing the case. It is a bit of a caricature, but not too much of one, to say that if the indictment charged embezzlement, it was reversible error if the appellate court thought the facts showed larceny. And then if subtle differences in the facts shown on retrial on a charge of larceny persuaded the appellate court that the offense really was embezzlement, the conviction was reversed and the defendant went free. In an influential recasting of a single law of theft, the Model Penal Code set out to fix this problem.

1. THE COMMON LAW

The law of theft began with the offense of larceny, which was created by early English common law decisions and embellished over the years to embrace different forms of acquisitive behavior. The courts backed off from further expansions and Parliament entered the scene with the first false pretenses statute in 1757 and the first embezzlement statute in 1799. Additional statutory enhancements followed shortly, both in England and America.

a. Larceny

In its simplest form, common law larceny involved the taking and carrying away of the personal property of another with intent to effect a permanent deprivation. The taking had to be a trespass against the rights of the person in possession of the property. The carrying away, often called "asportation," need only have involved slight movement once the defendant obtained control of the property by the taking. There is a lot of law on what counts as personal property—it had to be tangible (a deed or a bond didn't count) and it couldn't be fixed to real property (crops didn't count, unless they were harvested first). The specific intent to steal had to be to effect a permanent deprivation, or at least a deprivation for a long time or for an intended use (selling it to another, betting it at the track) that was likely to lead to permanent loss. Each of these elements resulted in hundreds of decisions over the years parsing the details of this and that situation in this way and that.

b. Common Law Ingenuity

The law of larceny grew over the years to encompass wider and wider varieties of acquisitive behavior.

1) "Breaking Bulk"

To describe the situation in modern terminology, a person who gave packages to others for transportation to distant places still, in the law's eye, had possession of the contents. All the transporters possessed was the outer wrapping. So when the transporters broke open the package to steal its contents, the view of the law was that the offense of larceny occurred because the taking was a trespass against the possession of the owner of the property. Pretty neat example of the early use of fictions to achieve a proper result in policy. The transporter who "broke bulk" to steal was indeed a thief.

2) "Constructive" Possession

The usual fiction employed by the early law to expand the law of larceny was the notion of "constructive possession," i.e., lets pretend a person possesses property who really doesn't. Then it will be larceny to steal the property because it will be a trespass against possession.

The notion of "breaking bulk" explained above is a form of constructive possession. Over the years, the courts found lots of other situations where it was appropriate to pretend that the owner of property still had possession so that it was ok to return a conviction of larceny.

Again to use modern terminology, suppose an employer gave property to an employee for delivery to another location. Or suppose a pen, a sweater, or a criminal law book with the owner's name in it is lost or misplaced. Or suppose someone handed a $10 bill to a bank teller for deposit or a cashier for a purchase and the $10, after possession is obtained, is pocketed. Or suppose one rents a car intending at the time of rental to keep it rather than bring it back at the end of the rental period.

In each of these situations, over a long and painfully slow series of decisions, the courts were able to find that the owner of the property really still had possession of it. The last case had a name: "larceny by trick." And fine distinctions emerged as testing cases at the margins were presented to the courts for decision.

Suppose, for example, the finder of the criminal law book picks it up intending to return it to its owner, and then later has a change of heart (because, for example, the written notes in the margin of the book are better than the finder's). Or suppose the car renter decides for the first time to keep the car after driving it for two days. Or suppose the $10 is taken after the person who handed it over has left the premises or after it has been placed in the cash drawer.

These situations strained the judicial notion of constructive possession too far. And they illustrate the fine distinctions—fodder for Charles Dickens, indeed—that the courts developed as the law evolved. Because larceny was the only theft offense during this period, no crime was committed in cases where the judicial imagination was unable to find a constructive possession. Where, for example, lawful custodians—a bank teller, the car renter—converted property in their custody, larceny was not permitted because there was no trespass against possession. In cases where someone duped another to part with title to property, there was also no offense of larceny. Where the finder of the criminal law book decided later to keep the book, there also was no crime because there was no offense against possession.

c. False Pretenses

The first major legislative expansion of the law of theft occurred in 1757 with the creation of the offense of obtaining property by false pretenses. Basically, it covered cases where the thief stole by obtaining title to property by deception. As with the crime of larceny, there were numerous technical limitations on the scope of the offense.

As this offense has come down to us in various forms, it can usually be committed, for example, only by a false representation of material fact—a statement of opinion or prediction will not do, nor will silence in the face of expected confirmation or denial. The defendant must know the statement to be false and must intend to defraud the victim. And typically the victim must rely on the false statement—a statement made but not heard or not believed will be insufficient.

d. Embezzlement

Parliament enacted the first crime of embezzlement in 1799, dealing with situations where employees in lawful custody of their employers' property converted it for fraudulent purposes. The crime was generalized into the form in which we know it today, applying to any people who are in lawful possession of another's property and then convert it with intent to defraud the owner (usually expressed as "fraudulently converts"). And—by now you are not surprised—there were technical issues here too as the law of embezzlement evolved. One who borrowed money and thereafter could not repay it, for example, was not an embezzler, although larceny by trick might have been committed if there was no intent to repay from the outset. And, as already observed, it made all the difference in the world that the prosecutor got it right when charging the defendant with one of the three types of theft offenses.

2. The Model Penal Code

As noted above, the Model Penal Code is premised on the view that there should be one crime of theft and that people can commit it in a variety of different ways. The Model Code does not eliminate issues of coverage that can arise at the margins—no offense could—nor does it eliminate serious questions of policy about what should count as criminally punishable theft and what should count as a civil wrong for which remedies such as breach of contract or restitution should be adequate. But the conclusion is that there should be one theft offense and that the edges of the common law distinctions should be smoothed so as to develop a unitary and coherent policy on when behavior can justly be characterized as theft.

a. Consolidation of Theft Offenses

The most important provision in Article 223 is § 223.1(1), which is worth quoting in full:

> "Conduct denominated theft in this Article constitutes a single offense. An accusation of theft may be supported by evidence that it was committed in any manner that would be theft under this Article, notwithstanding the specification of a different manner in the indictment or information, subject only to the power of the Court to ensure fair trial by granting a continuance or other appropriate relief where the conduct of the defense would be prejudiced by lack of fair notice or by surprise."

In effect, § 223.2(1) combines the common law offenses of larceny and embezzlement in a single definition and § 223.3 deals with obtaining property by false pretenses. The remainder of Article 223 covers related offenses that involve different methods of stealing the property of another: § 223.4 covers crimes sometimes called extortion and sometimes called blackmail, § 223.5 covers when finders of lost, mislaid, or misdelivered property can be convicted of theft, § 223.6 covers receiving stolen property (the fence), § 223.7 covers theft of services, and § 223.8 covers theft by failing properly to dispose of property received subject to a known legal obligation. There is a single grading provision applying to all of these various ways of committing theft, contained in § 223.1(2).

[Section 223.9 covers unauthorized use of vehicles (joyriding). But notice that § 223.9 does not call this behavior "theft." For that reason, it is not covered by § 223.1(1) and it is graded as a misdemeanor independently of § 223.1(2).]

The result of § 223.1(1) is that the indictment will charge "theft" and issues concerning the particulars by which one or the other forms of the offense occurred are left to the evolution of the trial, with proper protection against unfair surprise to the defense falling to the supervisory role of the judge.

b. Analytical Exercise

Just as little would have been accomplished by marching through all of the particulars of each of the twists and turns taken in the evolution of the common law of larceny, embezzlement, and obtaining property by false pretenses, little would be accomplished here by marching through the details of each of the forms of theft reached by Article 223. But a useful analytical exercise can be performed by examining the relationship between §§ 223.0(1), 223.1(3), and 223.2(1).

> ***Example:*** Assume that I hire you to sell a table and chairs for me and offer you a 15% commission on whatever you can get for them. You sell the items for $3,000, keep $450, and give me the rest of the money. The purchaser, as you knew would happen, is long gone and cannot be traced. My response when you hand me the money is: "Nice job, but I just learned that you sold the wrong table and chairs. I wanted you to sell the maple set, but you sold the cherry set. I want the full $3,000 and I'm going to have you prosecuted for theft." You apologize for the mistake, give me the rest of the money, and hire a lawyer. Do you have a defense to a charge of theft under the Model Penal Code?

Let's walk through it. Is the actus reus of § 223.2(1) present? If you forget the word "unlawfully" for a moment, the answer is "yes." You have taken my moveable property. Is the mens rea present? The answer again is "yes." The word "deprive" is defined in § 223.0(1) to include disposing of property so as to make it unlikely that the owner will recover it. That's what you did, albeit innocently in your own mind. So are you guilty of theft? No. Why not? Because of § 223.1(3)(b): You acted under an honest claim of right to dispose of the property in the manner in which you did.

Now return to the word "unlawfully." What does it mean? Well, one thing it means is that the actor does not have a claim of right as defined in § 223.1(3). Is that all it means? No. According to the Model Penal Code commentary, it means lack of consent or authority, and specifically the absence of a claim of right defense under § 223.1(3), or a defense under § 2.11 (consent) or Article 3 (justification).

What's the point of this exercise? My guess is that you thought all along that you shouldn't be guilty of theft—but in order to demonstrate the correctness of this intuition, you need carefully to parse the language of the Model Penal Code. And "reading the statute" involves more than reading the definition of the crime. It involves checking to see whether words used in that definition are themselves defined in other sections of the Code and involves also checking to see whether there are other general provisions that include or exclude liability for the case in front of you. In this exercise, your behavior is literally covered by the definition of the crime of theft. But a defense is provided—and appropriately so, I am sure you agree—by a provision of general applicability stated in a different section of the statute. "Read the statute" means "read the *whole* statute."

c. Robbery, Burglary, and Fraud

Note that the Model Penal Code also covers other acquisitive behavior that might, in common sense terms, seem a part of the law of theft. The common law tradition, of course, included comparable offenses.

1) Robbery

Essentially, robbery is theft from the person accompanied by violence or the threat of violence. It typically is graded more seriously than theft, for the obvious reason that it combines a form of assault—the threat or actuality of physical harm—with the act of theft. See § 222.1 of the Model Penal Code.

2) Burglary

Essentially, burglary is an attempt to commit a theft (or indeed, any other crime) combined with a trespass to property. It is especially serious, as you can readily imagine if you let your mind wander, if committed in a dwelling at night. Section 221.1 of the Model Penal Code covers this offense in more or less traditional terms.

3) Other Forms of Fraud

Article 224 of the Model Penal Code covers a number of other different ways in which one can steal the property of another. Forgery (which in the Model Penal Code offense includes counterfeiting) is covered in § 224.1. And there is a range of other offenses—bad checks (§ 224.5), credit card offenses (§ 224.6), rigging a basketball game or a horse race (§ 224.9), etc. The Model Penal Code is typical of modern statutes in its coverage of an array of different kinds of fraudulent behavior. It does not cover internet fraud explicitly, but there's a good reason. It was written when its drafters wrote with a typewriter or a pencil on a yellow pad, well before the days of word processing and the reality of the internet. All of which goes to say that the law of theft, like the law in other respects, needs to worry about the admonition of the Supreme Court of Pennsylvania in Commonwealth v. Taylor, 5 Binn. 277, 281 (Pa.1812):

> "It is impossible to find precedents for all offenses. The malicious ingenuity of mankind is constantly producing new inventions in the art of disturbing their neighbors. To this invention must be opposed general principles, calculated to meet and punish them."

The Pennsylvania Court made this observation in defense of the practice of judicial invention of new common law crimes to meet the "malicious ingenuity of mankind." Today we respond to such ingenuity by enacting new statutes, often choking on redundancy but often addressing new ways to violate old norms that otherwise might fall between the cracks. Such is the history of the law of theft, and such will be its future.

D. RICO

Congress passed the Racketeer Influenced and Corrupt Organizations Act (RICO) as part of the Organized Crime Control Act of 1970, but it was not until the decision in United States v. Turkette, 452 U.S. 576, 101 S.Ct. 2524 (1981), that it was armed with the primary weapon that has made it the most effective organized crime statute in history. The lore is that the awkward title of the statute was chosen to produce the acronym "RICO" based on the title character played by Edward G. Robinson in the first Hollywood movie about organized crime, *Little Caesar*.

RICO is codified at 18 U.S.C. §§ 1961–1968. Its highlights are summarized below.

1. STRUCTURE OF THE STATUTE

The heart of the statute is in three provisions of § 1962. The original objective was to punish the infiltration of legitimate businesses by organized crime.

a. Buy or Operate a Business with Dirty Money

Section 1962(a) is a long and complicated provision that in essence makes it a crime for a person who has received money from a "pattern of racketeering activity" to use or invest that money to acquire, establish, or operate any "enterprise" engaged in or affecting interstate commerce. The idea is to reach money laundering by purchasing and operating legitimate businesses. [Note that the buzz word "affecting" commerce is usually taken to mean "to the maximum reach of Congress's power under the interstate commerce clause."]

b. Acquire a Business by Extortion

Section 1962(b) makes it a crime to acquire or maintain an interest in or control of an "enterprise" through a "pattern of racketeering activity" if the enterprise is engaged in or affects interstate commerce. The idea was to reach racketeering acts that force owners of legitimate businesses to sell out to organized crime.

c. Operate a Business by Organized Crime Tactics

Section 1962(c) makes it a crime for any person employed by or associated with an "enterprise" engaged in or affecting interstate commerce to conduct or participate in the affairs of the enterprise "through a pattern of racketeering activity."

In effect, both subsections (a) and (b) were, in the original conception, efforts to punish acts preparatory to those punished in subsection (c). Subsection (a) punished buying one's way into a legitimate business by using the profits of organized crime. Subsection (b) punished forcing one's way into legitimate business by threats or violence. And subsection (c) punished what Congress expected organized criminals to do once they had infiltrated a legitimate business, namely to run it to the detriment of ordinary commerce by using threats, force, and other illegitimate competitive tactics.

A neat package, but it didn't work that way.

2. *UNITED STATES v. TURKETTE*

In United States v. Turkette, 452 U.S. 576, 101 S.Ct. 2524 (1981), the Supreme Court gave federal prosecutors a new and exceedingly effective weapon to use against organized crime. The key to its holding was its reading of the word "enterprise" to apply to *illegitimate* as well as *legitimate* businesses. So read, § 1962(c) applied to persons who were employed by or associated with *organized crime* who conducted or participated in the affairs of *organized crime* through a "pattern of racketeering activity."

In other words, it became a violation of RICO for organized crime to operate as organized crime. The overriding purpose of RICO—protection of legitimate businesses from being corrupted by the tentacles of organized crime—was served by going after organized crime itself. In effect, subsection (c) now punished acts preparatory to those covered by the original purpose of subsection (c)—it kept organized crime from distorting competition among legitimate businesses by punishing organized crime itself.

The effect of *Turkette* is that virtually all RICO prosecutions now proceed under § 1962(c). It is rare that subsections (a) or (b) are used as the basis of a criminal prosecution.

3. DEFINITIONS

The keys to the operation of § 1962(c) are the definitions of "enterprise," "racketeering activity," and "pattern" contained in § 1961.

a. "Enterprise"

"Enterprise" is defined as any individual, partnership, corporation, association or other legal entity and "any union or group of individuals associated in fact although not a legal entity." The material in quotes was the basis for the Supreme Court's conclusion in *Turkette* that organized crime itself can be an "enterprise" for RICO purposes. Of course this doesn't say too much, because it isn't easy to determine what counts as "organized" crime. How about two people who decide to rob a series of banks and spend a lot of time thinking about it? How about the owners of a mom and pop store who promote their business by engaging in illegal activities?

A group of people can be an "enterprise" if they share three characteristics. They must have a common or shared purpose. They must function as a continuing unit over time. And there must be an ascertainable structure different from the organization required simply to commit a series of crimes. Individuals can come and go, but there must be an "entity," some continuity of structure and people, that exists apart from an ordinary conspiracy to commit multiple criminal acts.

Even this description, you will observe, is none too helpful at the margins. But it's about as precise as one can get.

Notice that the statutory definition of "enterprise" also includes lawful entities. It is possible for a legitimate corporation to be a RICO enterprise, for a unit of government to qualify, for a partnership to count, and indeed for any group of individuals who are organized in a manner that meets the criteria stated above. Thus, if a local police department operates a protection business through a "pattern of racketeering activity" (e.g., bribes and extortion), participating police officers and officials can be prosecuted for RICO violations.

b. "Racketeering Activity"

The definition of "racketeering activity" is extremely broad. It includes a long list of federal crimes, including mail fraud, securities fraud, bribery, currency offenses, counterfeiting, and on and on. It also includes acts or threats involving a list of State offenses, including murder, kidnapping, gambling, arson, robbery, bribery, extortion, and dealing in obscenity or drugs.

c. "Pattern"

The statutory definition of "pattern" is also extremely broad. It says that a "pattern" of racketeering activity "requires at least two acts of racketeering activity" that occur within 10 years of each other (excluding any period of imprisonment). So, literally, a person who commits an offense, gets caught and goes to jail for 20 years, and who commits another offense after getting out of jail (or sometime within the 10 years) has engaged in a "pattern" of criminality if the two criminal acts are on the long list contained in the definition of "racketeering activity."

The Supreme Court narrowed the notion of "pattern," somewhat, in Sedima, S.P.R.L. v. Imrex Co., Inc., 473 U.S. 479, 105 S. Ct. 3275 (1985). In a famous footnote (number 14), the Court said that "while two acts are necessary, they may not be sufficient. Indeed, in common parlance, two of anything do not generally form a 'pattern.'" So what makes two or more acts a "pattern"? The Court's answer was *continuity plus relationship*." That is, there must be the fact of continuous criminal activity or the threat of it, and the various crimes must be related in the sense that there are common goals, similarity of method, temporal proximity, etc. Again, as with the concept of "enterprise" not a terribly precise definition at the margins.

So at the end of the day, one who conducts the business of an enterprise through a pattern of racketeering activity is guilty of a violation of RICO. The enterprise can be a group of people who work together in a structured organization over time for the purpose of committing crimes, or it can be a lawful enterprise the primary purpose of which is to sell products or perform government services. Almost any serious crime will count as "racketeering" activity. And there is a "pattern" if there is a relationship between the offenses or to some core purpose and if there is a reasonable measure of continuity over time.

4. RELATION TO CONSPIRACY

One of the overriding difficulties in the law of RICO is to tell the difference between an ordinary conspiracy (see pages 311 (common law), 340 (Model Penal Code)) and a violation of RICO. The simple, perhaps simplistic, way to put the difference is to say that RICO is a "conspiracy plus." Anyone who is guilty of a RICO violation is also likely to be part of at least one conspiracy, but the RICO violation requires additional elements that meet the criteria described above—continuity and relationship of the offenses, and a more structured organization than is required for the conspiracy standing alone. The challenge the courts have faced is to describe the nature of the "plus," a challenge that has been met with mixed success.

Notice that the law of conspiracy requires something that the law of RICO does not. To connect two people to the same conspiracy, the prosecutor must prove that they agreed to commit *the same criminal offense*. By contrast, the hit man who is the murder specialist can be prosecuted in a RICO case together with the bag man who collects the numbers proceeds. Both are engaging in a pattern of racketeering activity in the conduct of the same enterprise. Moreover, § 1962(d) permits a prosecution for a conspiracy to violate RICO, so the hit man and the bag man can be seen as co-conspirators in the RICO offense itself—the crime they both have agreed to commit is conducting an enterprise through a pattern of racketeering activity.

5. SANCTIONS

A violation of RICO is a serious offense. The maximum penalty is 20 years (or life if one of the racketeering offenses is punishable by life). In addition, there is a very broad forfeiture provision that authorizes the government to seize any property associated in any way with the illegal activity (e.g., the house or the boat or the airplane bought with money that cannot be shown to have come from legal activity). Fines can also be assessed for up to twice the profits that can be shown to have come from the illegal activity.

6. CIVIL REMEDIES

RICO has been a great success in the government's efforts to prosecute organized crime. It also contains civil provisions, however, that are more noted for their abuse than their successes.

RICO authorizes a civil suit by any "person who has been injured in his business or property by reason of a violation" of RICO. Successful plaintiffs can collect treble damages and attorneys fees, both of which are unusual in American tort recoveries.

The difficulties to which this provision has led are unrelated to organized crime. There are very few cases where a plaintiff has attempted to recover civil damages from a Mafia boss (would you try?). What has happened, instead, is that RICO counts have become common in ordinary commercial litigation—over contract issues, for example—where it can plausibly alleged that mail or securities frauds occurred. (Both the federal mail and security fraud statutes are so broadly drafted that such allegations are plausible in more cases than you might think.)

The result is that the treble damages and attorneys fee provisions of RICO are distorting ordinary civil litigation in ways that are not likely to have been intended by Congress. But neither Congress nor the Supreme Court has been persuaded to do anything about it. The Supreme Court has been afforded numerous opportunities to interpret the civil provisions in a way that would limit them to real organized crime situations, but it has repeatedly declined to do so. The result is that decided cases under civil and criminal RICO are interchangeable as precedents, a situation that has substantially distorted civil litigation when the plaintiff can plausibly attach a RICO claim to the complaint.

PART TEN

CONCLUSION

Analysis

XVII.   *Constitutional Limits on Punishment for Crime*

*

XVII

CONSTITUTIONAL LIMITS ON PUNISHMENT FOR CRIME

Analysis

A. INTRODUCTION

The United States Constitution contains numerous limitations on the capacities of State and Federal Government to punish people for crimes. One crime, treason against the United States, is defined in the Constitution itself (Article III, § 3). Specific guarantees contained in provisions such as the freedom of speech clause of the first amendment have frequently been interpreted to place a substantive limitation on the power of the Federal Government, and through the 14th amendment on State Government, to punish particular conduct as a crime. And rights which the Supreme Court has managed to discover in such vague clauses as "due process" and "equal protection" have precluded national and local government from passing criminal laws punishing conduct ranging from abortion to miscegenation.

These provisions of the Federal Constitution are typically studied in courses in Constitutional Law, and will not be considered here. There is also, of course, a range of procedural protections contained in the Bill of Rights, traditionally studied in separate courses in Criminal Procedure. They will not be pursued here either.

In recent years particularly, the United States Supreme Court has addressed itself in numerous contexts to general principles that limit the way crimes are defined and punished. Some of these principles are identified below.

B. THE DEFINITION OF CRIME

One question that might be asked is whether the Constitution sets forth minimum components that must be contained in the definition of any crime. The answer is that it does, but that the limits operate only at the fringes. They are not in play in the average criminal case.

1. VAGUENESS

The Supreme Court has held many times that criminal laws are unconstitutional if so vaguely drafted that their meaning cannot fairly be determined from the words used. The standard reasons given for this requirement are that persons are entitled to "fair notice" of the content of the penal law so that they can govern their conduct accordingly, and that persons are entitled to protection from the "arbitrary enforcement" that can occur if police, prosecutors, juries, and courts are permitted to give retrospective content to poorly defined criminal statutes after they see what a potential defendant has done.

Three practical points should be made about the vagueness doctrine:

(1) The first is that the Supreme Court has never used it to strike down conduct that is within the area of what might be called a "core crime." No murder, theft, or rape statute has ever been held unconstitutionally vague, even though there is plenty of uncertainty in the phrases of the common law and in modern

legislation as well that have been used to define these offenses. If the legislature is making a good faith attempt to attack a serious social problem, particularly where there is an identifiable victim who has suffered real harm, it is unlikely that the law will be held unconstitutionally vague.

(2) The second is that the Supreme Court has rarely if ever used the vagueness doctrine in a manner that would effectively prohibit the legislature from accomplishing a legitimate law enforcement objective. It is always relevant to a vagueness issue whether it is possible to draft a narrower statute that will still accomplish the legitimate legislative objectives. And law enforcement need is always a powerful argument against the vagueness of any statute.

(3) The third is that law students *always* overuse the vagueness doctrine. It is a doctrine of very limited scope, a doctrine that the Supreme Court is willing to apply only in very limited contexts. The classic situation is one where the crime defined by the legislature seems to be aimed at no particular evil, where the average citizen may well violate the law by engaging in perfectly innocuous conduct, where there is large opportunity for law enforcement officials to pick and choose the persons they would like to arrest, and where there is no serious law enforcement need for a statute drafted in the terms before the Court.

The point is that all laws (indeed all words) are vague, and inescapably so—there is ambiguity everywhere. If "vagueness" (in the sense of indeterminacy at the margins) were the test for holding a statute unconstitutional, all statutes would fail the test. The vagueness doctrine, instead, involves a balance of factors having to do with society's need for the statute on the one hand and the risks the statute poses to individual liberty on the other. Merely reading the statute and exploring the ambiguity that can be teased from its words is never enough.

Successful invocation of the vagueness doctrine is therefore a very rare occurrence.

Examples: Coates v. City of Cincinnati, 402 U.S. 611, 91 S.Ct. 1686 (1971), and Papachristou v. City of Jacksonville, 405 U.S. 156, 92 S.Ct. 839 (1972), are paradigm examples of the vagueness doctrine in operation. The statute in *Coates* made it a crime for "three or more persons to assemble . . . on any . . . sidewalks . . . and there conduct themselves in a manner annoying to persons passing by." The statute in *Papachristou* punished such dangerous characters as "lewd, wanton, and lascivious persons," "rogues and vagabonds," and "persons able to work but habitually living upon the earnings of their wives or minor children."

No serious law enforcement objective is impeded by striking such laws down, and they are capable of enforcement with great unfairness. Both of these concerns are central to most vagueness determinations.

2. AN ACT

The Court held in Robinson v. California, 370 U.S. 660, 82 S.Ct. 1417 (1962), that it cannot constitutionally be a crime for a person to "be addicted to the use of narcotics." The proposition for which this case stands is that all crime requires some "act" by the defendant. The criminal law cannot punish a mere status or condition. It must be based upon physical conduct.

Note that this requirement does *not* preclude basing criminal liability on omissions. A failure to act where there is a duty to act has traditionally been punished by the criminal law, before and after *Robinson*. *Robinson* is satisfied if the defendant has engaged in some physical behavior, *or* if the law is written so that some physical behavior can be performed that will remove the defendant from the coverage of the statute. "Being an addict" is not physical behavior, nor is there any physical behavior in which one can engage to stop the present status of "being an addict." The question of liability for omissions was not addressed, nor meant to be precluded, by the Court in *Robinson*.

Nor does this decision stand, at least alone, for the proposition that the act must be "voluntary" or somehow within the capacity of the defendant. That was the issue in *Powell,* considered immediately below.

Finally, note that *Robinson* will have no application to most criminal statutes. The criminal law traditionally has required an actus reus, consisting of some affirmative conduct by the defendant or an omission where there is a duty to act. Possession crimes, moreover, usually require that the defendant be aware of the possession for a sufficient period to have been able to terminate it, and hence can be analyzed as cases of a failure to act in the face of a duty. See Model Penal Code § 2.01(4). Only in the rare case where a legislature specifically departs from this well-entrenched common law tradition is *Robinson* likely to have any application.

3. A VOLUNTARY ACT

The question in Powell v. Texas, 392 U.S. 514, 88 S.Ct. 2145 (1968), was whether a chronic alcoholic could be prosecuted for being drunk in public. The *Powell* majority was divided. Four Justices held that *Robinson* stood only for the proposition that some "act" was required and that the defendant in *Powell* had in fact engaged in public behavior. One Justice (White) held that there was no evidence in the record before the Court that Powell had lacked control over the "public" aspect of his drunken behavior, and that even if *Robinson* stood for a broader proposition it would not be applicable on the facts as presented.

The broader proposition for which *Robinson* might have been construed to stand is that the Constitution requires not only that each criminal defendant engage in physical conduct but that the defendant must have had the power to choose to do otherwise.

Four Justices in dissent thought *Robinson* stood for some such proposition, and Justice White indicated that he was inclined to agree. Thus, on paper at least, five

Justices seemed at that time to support the proposition that perhaps the Constitution requires a "voluntary" act, or something approaching it, although for one the issue was not properly presented by the record.

Powell, though of great theoretical interest, has no pr actical importance today. Nothing has come of it, and the Court has not gone on to find a "voluntary act" principle in the Constitution. The reason is practical, and is elaborated in the plurality opinion by Justice Marshall and the concurrence by Justice Black. If the Court read the Constitution to require that the defendant have the capacity to control behavior before criminal liability could be imposed, either some arbitrary lines would have to be drawn or, for example, the Court would have constitutionalized the "volitional" or "control" aspect of the insanity defense, would have enmeshed the Constitution in the rules governing intoxication as a defense, and would soon be choosing as a matter of Constitutional law how far the defense of duress was required to extend. Thus in spite of the moral appeal of the idea that it is unfair to punish someone who lacks the capacity to choose not to commit a crime, its implementation is so fraught with difficulty that the Court has wisely refrained from enshrining it in the Constitution. The criminal law has struggled for centuries to integrate this idea into the fabric of a law that also has strong objectives of social order and control, and will likely do so for some considerable time yet to come. The Court is not ready to pronounce a solution for all time as a matter of federal Constitutional law.

4. MENS REA

The Supreme Court has never addressed in so many words the question whether the Constitution requires some minimum notion of mens rea before conduct can be punished as a serious crime. It has held many times that "public welfare" or regulatory offenses need not require mens rea. But it has never dealt with the question in the context of a serious crime that imposed strict liability. One reason, of course, is that few serious crimes impose strict liability, though offenses like statutory rape and felony murder impose strict liability for important elements.

In Lambert v. California, 355 U.S. 225, 78 S.Ct. 240 (1957), the Court went about as far in this respect as it is likely to go. *Lambert* concerned a woman who failed to register as a "convicted felon" in Los Angeles. She was convicted of a crime for her failure, and sought to defend on the ground that she was unaware of the obligation to register. The California courts held that this was no defense even if true, and the Supreme Court reversed.

The *Lambert* opinion is obscurely written, perhaps intentionally so in order not to commit the Court to much beyond reversal of the conviction. But *Lambert* can be read to stand for the proposition that it is unconstitutional to convict of a crime, and impose serious criminal punishment, for conduct committed in a context where the average citizen would have no idea that the criminal law might apply. This states a minimal condition of fairness, as it were, within which the criminal law must operate.

Note how limited this proposition is. It would not, for example, suggest that there is anything *constitutionally* wrong with the normal context in which the criminal law imposes strict liability. Consider, for example, felony murder. The armed robber who is convicted of murder because someone died during the commission of the robbery is a far cry from a person whose normally developed social conscience would not suggest that the criminal law would have something to say about given behavior. The average person knows, or cannot unfairly be assumed to know, that the law might punish armed robbery, and thus has a fair opportunity to choose not to become involved with the criminal process. The *degree* of involvement—the seriousness of the offense for which a conviction can be entered—is not a matter with which *Lambert* is concerned. *Lambert* is concerned with a person who did not have a fair opportunity not to get arrested—all Ms. Lambert did was wander around Los Angeles, entirely innocuous conduct of the sort that all of us do all the time. Robbing a bank is not innocuous. Most of us know that people get arrested for that.

Note, moreover, that *Lambert* on this reading also would not suggest that most "public welfare" or regulatory offenses were unconstitutional, even if it applied to them. A bartender who is held strictly liable for serving alcohol to a minor is in a context that warns. One can choose not to be a bartender, or can be extra careful about who gets served. Ms. Lambert had no choice not to become a criminal.

5. STATUTORY INTERPRETATION

If a criminal defendant argues about the meaning of a criminal statute and loses, it is standard practice to apply the ruling to the defendant who made the argument. What this means is that, to at least some extent, interpretations of a criminal statute that resolve an ambiguity in the meaning of the statute will result in the retroactive application of the rule adopted by the court. Is there a point at which such retroactivity is forbidden?

This was the issue in Rogers v. Tennessee, 532 U.S. 451, 121 S.Ct. 1693 (2001). The Tennessee Supreme Court held that the "year and a day rule" (see page 361) was a part of the common law of the State, but that its rationale was outmoded. It abolished the rule, and retroactively applied the abolition to a conviction of second degree murder where the victim died 15 months after the fatal event. The Supreme Court, over the dissents of the unusual coalition of Justices Stevens, Scalia, Thomas, and Breyer, upheld the conviction. It held that the common law "presupposes a measure of evolution" that can fairly be applied to criminal defendants so long as the new rules are not "unexpected and indefensible." There was "nothing" in the Tennessee Court's decision that "represented an exercise of the sort of unfair and arbitrary judicial action against which the Due Process Clause aims to protect." The Tennessee Court's decision was "a routine exercise of common law decisionmaking in which the court brought the law into conformity with reason and common sense."

C. PROPORTIONALITY

The Supreme Court has also addressed the penalties that can be imposed for criminal conduct. The most well-known decisions were rendered in the context of capital punishment, but the Court has also addressed the subject of imprisonment.

1. CAPITAL PUNISHMENT

The Court's death penalty decisions are usefully divided into two categories:

a. Required Procedures

The Supreme Court in recent years has completely revised the procedures by which capital punishment is imposed in this country. It has held that:

1) Mandatory Death Penalty Unconstitutional

It is unconstitutional for any criminal offense to *require* the imposition of the death penalty. See, e.g., Roberts v. Louisiana, 431 U.S. 633, 97 S.Ct. 1993 (1977); Woodson v. North Carolina, 428 U.S. 280, 96 S.Ct. 2978 (1976).

2) Unguided Discretion

It is unconstitutional for the death penalty to be imposed by a jury without criteria to guide the exercise of discretion. See, e.g., Godfrey v. Georgia, 446 U.S. 420, 100 S.Ct. 1759 (1980); Furman v. Georgia, 408 U.S. 238, 92 S.Ct. 2726 (1972).

3) Mitigating Factors

It is unconstitutional to limit the range of mitigating factors that the defendant can introduce as evidence in favor of a sentence other than death. Skipper v. South Carolina, 476 U.S. 1, 106 S.Ct. 1669 (1986); Eddings v. Oklahoma, 455 U.S. 104, 102 S.Ct. 869 (1982); Lockett v. Ohio, 438 U.S. 586, 98 S.Ct. 2954 (1978).

4) Heightened Need for Reliability

Close scrutiny of prosecutorial and judicial practices is warranted to insure the independence and reliability of a capital sentencing determination. See, e.g., Caldwell v. Mississippi, 472 U.S. 320, 105 S.Ct. 2633 (1985).

There is a clear tension between the second and third of these principles. The more undisciplined the mitigating factors introduced by the defendant, the more difficult it is to provide generalized criteria for the exercise of discretion. The Court has held, moreover, that the sentencer is also permitted to consider evidence in aggravation beyond a statutory list of aggravating factors. See Zant v. Stephens, 462 U.S. 862, 103 S.Ct. 2733 (1983). In effect, therefore, both aggravating and mitigating factors can be introduced beyond those designed in advance to confine the exercise of discretion. The thrust of the second principle thus seems clearly undermined.

The effective limitation seems to be (in the words of *Zant*) that the "fundamental requirement" is that predefined statutory aggravating factors "must genuinely narrow the class of persons eligible for the death penalty and must reasonably justify the imposition of a more severe sentence on the defendant compared to others. . . . " Once this limitation is met, the important principle is that of individualization of the determination—and on this issue both aggravating and mitigating factors based on the particular facts of the case can be introduced.

Beyond this, the decisions cannot be summarized briefly. The Court has indicated that each State's procedures will be examined on an individual basis, both in structure and in specific application. The key ideas are that the decision to impose the death penalty must be discretionary, it must be limited to a genuinely narrowed class of persons, the defendant must have every opportunity to offer evidence in mitigation, and the conduct of both prosecutor and judge will be closely scrutinized for behavior that undermines the independence and reliability of the sentencing determination. The Court has been sharply split on whether certain classes of defendants—the mentally ill or retarded, or persons in their teens—should be eligible for execution. See, e.g., Atkins v. Virginia,___ U.S. ___, 122 S.Ct. 2242 (2002); Penry v. Lynaugh, 492 U.S. 302, 109 S.Ct. 2934 (1989); Stanford v. Kentucky, 492 U.S. 361, 109 S. Ct. 2969 (1989); Ford v. Wainwright, 477 U.S. 399, 106 S.Ct. 2595 (1986).

The procedure now in use in most States is either the Model Penal Code procedure summarized at pages 379–80 or some reasonable variation of it. It is clear that the Model Penal Code procedure is constitutional on its face, though also clear that other procedures that address the concerns listed above are permitted. The Supreme Court has held, however, that it follows from *Apprendi* (see page 415) that an aggravating factor necessary for imposition of the death penalty cannot be found by aq sentencing judge sitting without a jury, Ring v. Arizona, ___ U.S. ___, 122 S.Ct. 2428 (2002).

b. Offenses for Which Death Penalty May Be Imposed

The Court has also held that the death penalty can be imposed for some offenses, but not others. The relevant constitutional inquiry is whether death is disproportionate to the offense.

1) Murder

The Court has held that the death penalty is *not always* disproportionate to murder. Gregg v. Georgia, 428 U.S. 153, 96 S.Ct. 2909 (1976). But the Court has held that it *might sometimes* be, and that each case must be decided on the basis of what was proved to have happened.

2) Rape

The Court has held that "a sentence of death is grossly disproportionate and excessive punishment for the crime of rape and is therefore forbidden by the eighth amendment as cruel and unusual punishment." Coker v. Georgia, 433 U.S. 584, 97 S.Ct. 2861 (1977). The Court sought to buttress its conclusion by a range of "objective factors," e.g., the history of the use of capital punishment for rape, recent legislative activity in the area, and jury willingness to impose the death penalty for rape. But "in the end," the Court concluded, "our own judgment will be brought to bear" on the issue, and the Court's judgment was that the death penalty was disproportionate for rape itself—leaving open the question of what sentence would be appropriate if the rapist kills the victim.

3) Accomplices to Murder

In Enmund v. Florida, 458 U.S. 782, 102 S.Ct. 3368 (1982), the Court held that capital punishment could *not* be imposed on an accomplice to a felony murder where there was no showing that the accomplice intended death or anticipated that deadly force would be used and where the accomplice was sitting in the getaway car some distance from the offense when other felons killed the victims. The closely divided Court engaged in the same two-step analysis relied on in *Coker*, rejecting both deterrence and retributive arguments in favor of the capital penalty.

Subsequently, the Court faced the question in Tison v. Arizona, 481 U.S. 137, 107 S.Ct. 1676 (1987), whether the death penalty was prohibited "in the intermediate case of the defendant whose participation is major and whose mental state is one of reckless indifference to the value of human life." The two defendants had supplied an arsenal of weapons to their father and another inmate, both serving sentences for murder, assisted in their escape from prison, assisted in the stopping of a car when the escape vehicle was disabled, participated in the kidnapping and robbery of the car's occupants, watched without protest while the father and the other inmate killed the occupants (a man, his wife, their two-year old son, and their 15-year old niece) with a shotgun, and assisted in further flight before their capture in a shootout with police. The Court held that "major participation in the felony committed, combined with reckless indifference to human life, is sufficient to satisfy the *Enmund* culpability requirement."

2. IMPRISONMENT

The Court has also addressed the proportionality of a sentence to imprisonment. Two cases involved "recidivist" sentences—sentences imposed on persons with a prescribed number of prior convictions.

In Rummel v. Estelle, 445 U.S. 263, 100 S.Ct. 1133 (1980), the defendant received a mandatory sentence to life imprisonment—with the possibility of parole—for a third non-violent theft offense, one occurring in 1964, one in 1969, and one in 1973. The cumulative value of the property stolen in all three thefts was $229.11. In an analysis that seemed to put an end to the argument that a prison sentence could ever be constitutionally disproportionate, the Court upheld the sentence. The vote was 5–4.

But in Solem v. Helm, 463 U.S. 277, 103 S.Ct. 3001 (1983), the Court was faced with a life sentence—*without* the possibility of parole—for a seventh non-violent felony. The most recent offense was uttering a "no account" check for $100, and the other felonies were spread over a 15-year period. The Court set the sentence aside. It looked to "objective criteria, including (i) the gravity of the offense and the harshness of the penalty; (ii) the sentences imposed on other criminals in the same jurisdiction; and (iii) the sentences imposed for commission of the same crime in other jurisdictions." The vote was again 5–4. Justice Blackmun was with both majorities, but did not write an opinion.

The Court revisited the proportionality issue in Harmelin v. Michigan, 501 U.S. 957, 111 S. Ct. 2680 (1991). The issue was whether the proportionality limitation was violated by a sentence of life imprisonment without possibility of parole for possession of 672 grams of cocaine. Justice Scalia announced the judgment of the Court: "We conclude . . . that *Solem* was simply wrong; the Eighth Amendment contains no proportionality guarantee." But he was speaking only for himself and Chief Justice Rehnquist. Joined by Justices O'Connor and Souter, Justice Kennedy voted to uphold the sentence but wrote that "stare decisis counsels our adherence to the narrow proportionality principle that has existed in our Eighth Amendment jurisprudence for 80 years." Justices White, Blackmun, Stevens, and Marshall dissented.

D. PROOF

Proof of the elements of crime was discussed from a non-constitutional perspective beginning at page 94. It may be helpful to review that discussion now. As a constitutional matter, the Supreme Court held in In re Winship, 397 U.S. 358, 90 S.Ct. 1068 (1970), that the prosecutor was required to prove "every fact necessary to constitute [a] crime" beyond a reasonable doubt. The next question is which facts are "necessary."

1. PROOF BEYOND A REASONABLE DOUBT

The line the Court seems to have drawn is that *elements* of the crime—by which the Court seems to mean the actus reus, mens rea, and any required causation—must be proved beyond a reasonable doubt, but that the State is free to place the burden of persuasion for *defenses* on either party.

The Court has held that the burden of persuasion can be placed on the defendant to prove provocation as a mitigating "affirmative defense" that reduces murder to manslaughter. Patterson v. New York, 432 U.S. 197, 97 S.Ct. 2319 (1977). And it has held that the burden of persuasion can be placed on the defendant for the insanity defense. Rivera v. Delaware, 429 U.S. 877, 97 S.Ct. 226 (1976). But it held in Mullaney v. Wilbur, 421 U.S. 684, 95 S.Ct. 1881 (1975), that Maine could not put the burden of persuasion on the defendant to establish provocation where the theory of provocation under Maine law was that it disproved "malice aforethought" and hence was offered not as a mitigating "defense" but to negate an "element" of the prosecutor's case.

The distinction between *Mullaney* and *Patterson* seems purely formal, depending on which factors the legislature chooses to call an element of the offense and which a defense. In the terminology used in this outline, the cases seem to mean that the prosecutor must prove beyond a reasonable doubt all elements of the prima facie case (see page 95) and must also disprove beyond a reasonable doubt those derivative defenses (see page 143) that are characterized by the jurisdiction involved as logically "rebutting" an element of the prosecutor's prima facie case. Thus it seems unlikely, for example, that the burden of persuasion could be put on the defendant to establish a defense of mistake of fact in a Model Penal Code jurisdiction. On the other hand, it is reasonably clear that the State may put the burden of persuasion on the defendant for all "collateral defenses" (see pages 187, 221), unless the State makes the mistake of saying that functionally they "negate" an "element" of the offense. It would seem, therefore, that legislatures have the capacity to invoke the *Winship* principle, or not, depending on how they choose to define their crimes.

This line of cases was complicated significantly by the decision in Apprendi v. New Jersey, 530 U.S. 466, 120 S. Ct. 2348 (2000). The defendant was convicted of possession of a firearm for an unlawful purpose, an offense that carried a maximum sentence of 10 years. A separate "hate crime" law provided that an "extended term" of imprisonment—up to 20 years—could be imposed if the trial judge found by a preponderance of the evidence that, in committing such a crime, the defendant acted "with a purpose to intimidate an individual or group of individuals because of race, color, gender, handicap, religion, sexual orientation or ethnicity." Based on such a finding, Apprendi was sentenced to a 12-year term for the weapons offense.

In an interesting line-up, the Court was divided 5–4. Justice Stevens wrote the opinion, joined by Justices Scalia, Souter, Thomas, and Ginsburg. The Court held that "[o]ther than the fact of a prior conviction, any fact that increases the penalty for a crime beyond the prescribed statutory maximum must be submitted to a jury, and proved beyond a reasonable doubt." Justice O'Connor's dissent, joined by Chief Justice Rehnquist and Justices Kennedy and Breyer, accused the majority of just the sort of formalism described above. The decision can't mean much, she argued, if its effect can be avoided simply by redefining the weapons offense so that it carries a 20-year maximum sentence. Alternatively, she continued, the Court might have meant to embrace a rule that "any fact (other than a prior conviction) that has the effect, *in real terms*, of increasing the maximum punishment beyond an otherwise applicable range must be submitted to a jury and proved beyond a reasonable doubt." Such a rule, she concluded, would have far reaching impact— invalidating among other things the philosophy underlying modern "guideline" sentencing schemes, under which the judge must find (under a lesser standard of proof) that specific aggravating factors existed before a sentence in the longer ranges authorized for a conviction can be imposed.

The jury is still out, so to speak, on the impact *Apprendi* ultimately will have on the allocation of factual determinations between the jury at the conviction stage and the judge at the sentencing stage. Given that most criminal convictions are the result of plea negotiations, it may be, moreover, that the most significant effect of *Apprendi* will be on the practical allocation of authority between prosecutor and judge. Some, indeed, have argued that *Apprendi* will result in a net decrease in procedural protections for defendants because of its impact on this dynamic.

Apprendi, as did *Mullaney* and *Patterson* before it, has generated a significant debate in the literature. As with many Supreme Court opinions, it will be some time to come before its full impact is understood.

In any event, when all the dust is settled, it can still be said that the State retains great flexibility in allocating the burden of persuasion in criminal cases, though increasingly it must be careful with the words it uses to accomplish its objectives. Note also that this line of cases explicitly deals only with the burden of persuasion. The cases do not affect how the burden of production is allocated.

2.   PRESUMPTIONS

In Sandstrom v. Montana, 442 U.S. 510, 99 S.Ct. 2450 (1979), the defendant was charged with "purposely or knowingly" causing a death. The jury instruction stated that the "law presumes that a person intends the ordinary consequences of his voluntary acts." The Court held this instruction unconstitutional, citing *Mullaney*'s requirement that the prosecutor must prove all "elements" of the offense beyond a reasonable doubt and noting that the "presumption" could have been interpreted by the jury as shifting the burden of persuasion to the defendant to disprove "purpose or knowledge." The Court also noted that the presumption could have been interpreted as "conclusive" by the jury, and that this would be unconstitutional because it relieved the prosecutor of the burden of proving the required "elements" beyond a reasonable doubt.

Like *Mullaney* and *Patterson, Sandstrom* seems to impose only a formal limitation. It seems to say that use of the presumption is unconstitutional if the State defines a specific intent element into the offense and then doesn't make the prosecutor prove it. Use of the presumption for "general intent" offenses is more ambiguous. Arguably if "general intent" means "negligence" in the particular jurisdiction, then all the State is doing by using the presumption is providing a definition of the term. On the other hand, the Court could decide that the presumption was somehow relieving the prosecutor of proving the general intent "element" of the offense and hold it unconstitutional.

But it seems at all events clear that the State can accomplish its objective in another way. If the offense were defined so as not to require mens rea as an "element" at all, it would apparently pass constitutional muster. Similarly, it would appear to be constitutional to eliminate mens rea as an "element" but permit the defendant to prove lack of mens rea as an affirmative defense. And it would even appear to be constitutional to define the offense so that "purpose or knowledge" was an "element" but define "purpose or knowledge" to mean "negligence" that was established whenever the natural and probable consequences of the defendant's conduct resulted in the occurrence of the actus reus of an offense. Although such a definition of "purpose or knowledge" might seem strange, it is surely no more strange than the traditional meaning of "malice aforethought" or other definitions that have been given to common law mens rea terms. See, for example, Director of Public Prosecutions v. Smith, [1960] All. E.R. 161, [1961] A.C. 290 (where "malice aforethought" was translated into a charge of "wilful murder," was re-translated into a charge that the defendant "intended to do [his victim] grievous bodily harm," and ultimately resulted in a conviction based on negligence). Finally, it is completely clear, whatever the definition of the offense, that the instruction would survive constitutional attack if the jury were explicitly told that it stated merely a "permissive inference" (see page 100).

*

PART TWO: THE DEFINITION OF CRIME

II. The Common Law

[Answers to Questions on pages 101–02]

1. ***False.*** Result elements are included only in the definition of some crimes, e.g., murder. Larceny, for example, does not include a result element.

2. ***False.*** Omissions may qualify only where there is a legal duty to act.

3. ***True.*** A specific intent does always refer to a subjective state of mind, and will always be identified with particularity in the definition of the offense.

4. ***False.*** General intent *usually* refers to a standard of ordinary negligence, as stated in the question. But it does not always do so, and the statement is therefore not invariably true.

5. ***False.*** It *might* mean this, but it could be used in conjunction with recklessness, for example, to shift the burden of persuasion, shift the burden of production, or refer to a permissive inference.

6. ***True.*** The term "dependent" intervening cause is applied to situations where some cause other than the defendant's behavior has contributed to the

result, but the result is nonetheless sufficiently foreseeable that it is fair to hold the defendant responsible for the result.

7. *False.* All measures of culpability, even strict liability, involve a combination of subjective and objective factors. No crime requires strict liability for all of its elements. In general, strict liability will only be imposed when the defendant is aware of enough of the other aspects of the offense to make it fair to impose strict liability on one element.

8. One should always begin with the definition of the offense.

9. **a.** Receiving stolen property.

 b. Receiving property.

 c. Receiving an unauthorized fee under color of office.

10. All of the actus reus, mens rea, and causation elements (if any) required by the definition of the offense.

11. Because the criminal law is about blaming and blame is normally based on bad choices that manifest themselves in behavior. And because the requirement of conduct is an important civil liberties protection. People have more control over their lives if they know that they can only be arrested for engaging in conduct that has previously been defined as criminal.

12. *D* has two arguments: (1) that no conduct satisfying the elements "burns any building" occurred—*D* set a fire, but not to the building; (2) that even if these elements are satisfied, *D*'s intent was formed *after* the act was complete—the specific intent must coincide in time with the required conduct.

The prosecutor also has two arguments: (1) that *D*'s conduct satisfies the "burns any building" elements because *D* set in motion a chain of events that resulted in a building being burned and formed the intent to defraud just as the burning of the building began; (2) that this statute is designed to prevent defrauding insurers, and establishes a duty to act where one reasonably can do so to prevent the harm from occurring. *D* failed to put out the fire in the face of this duty to act, and the resulting omission can satisfy the elements "burns any building." [The question is taken from Commonwealth v. Cali, 247 MasS. 20, 141 N.E. 510 (1923), in which—surprisingly—the latter argument prevailed and a conviction was affirmed. I say "surprisingly" because "burns any building" sounds like it ought to require affirmative conduct.]

III. The Model Penal Code

[Answers to Questions on pages 136–37]

1. *False.* "Purpose" is defined in § 2.02(2)(a). The definition provides that purpose means a conscious desire to engage in *conduct* or to cause *results*. The

defendant need only be aware that *circumstance* elements exist.

2. ***True.*** The term "situation" in §§ 2.02(2)(c) and (2)(d) builds a deliberate
ambiguity into the definitions of recklessness and negligence. The purpose
is to permit personalization of the objective standard in cases where it
seems appropriate, as for example, when the defendant has certain
physical characteristics that ought fairly to be considered in determining
capacity to conform to an objective standard of behavior. Whether a
particular characteristic of the defendant will be taken into account is a
question of law for the courts. The courts will be reluctant to personalize
the standard too much, however, since the point of both recklessness and
negligence is to measure the defendant's conduct against a societal
standard. It would undermine deterrence and remove any basis for blame
to hold every defendant to an individualized standard of guilt.

3. ***False.*** This is a tricky one, perhaps unfairly so—though there is a lesson to be
learned. Public welfare offenses could be prosecuted under § 2.05 without
mens rea. And § 213.6(1) permits certain sex offenses (those where the
victim is less than 10 years old) to be prosecuted without proving mens
rea as to that element. Thus, it is true that the Model Code permits strict
liability in a quite restricted category of cases, and that a narrow range of
sex offenses and public welfare offenses are within the restricted
category. What is false about the statement is that public welfare offenses
are prosecuted as "violations" under the Model Code, and a violation is not
a "crime." See § 1.04(5). Thus, public welfare offenses are not included
within the class of *crimes* for which strict liability is permitted under the
Model Penal Code.

4. ***True.*** This result is explicitly provided by § 1.12(2)(a).

5. ***False.*** This result is nowhere provided in § 1.12, and therefore affirmative
defenses would be covered by the provision in § 1.12(1) that the prosecutor
prove "each element" of an offense beyond a reasonable doubt. Defenses
are explicitly included in the definition of "element" in § 1.13(9).

6. ***True.*** The effect of a presumption is set forth in § 1.12(5). While this provision
does not explicitly state that the burden of production is shifted to the
defendant, it has that effect. Once the prosecutor has proved the basis for
the presumption, the case will be submitted to the jury *and* the jury will
be told that it may regard such evidence as sufficient proof of the
presumed fact. The jury need not do so, however—and if the defendant
wants it not to, then some evidence had better be offered to encourage the
jury in that direction. Thus, effectively, proof of the basis for invoking the
presumption shifts the burden of production of evidence to the defendant.

7. ***False.*** Section 1.12(5)(b) provides for precisely the contrary result: presumed
facts still must be found beyond a reasonable doubt by the jury.

8. ***False.*** It is true that the common law does not require mens rea for grading elements, but the Model Code disagrees. Grading elements are meant to be included within the definition of "element" in § 1.13(9) and, because they are elements, they can be a "material" element under § 1.13(10). They are material elements under § 1.13(10) because they relate to the harm or evil sought to be prevented by the offense. The culpability structure applies to grading elements because it applies to *all* "material elements." See § 2.02(1). Also, § 2.04(2), the effect of which is dealt with at page 175, would be unnecessary if grading elements did not require mens rea—no defense would be "otherwise afforded" if grading elements carried strict liability.

9. ***False.*** The first question is *why* the word "purpose" appears in the definition of the offense.

If it is there to provide the mens rea for an actus reus element of the offense, then the statement is true. "Purpose" will then be the mens rea for the elements appearing later in the definition so long as there is no contrary intent based on the language or structure of the offense. For example, "purpose" would apply to all of the elements of § 241.3(1)(b) because "purposely" appears at the beginning of subsection (1)(b), not because of the "with purpose to mislead" language in subsection (1). "Purposely" is in the definition of the offense provided in subsection (1)(b) in order to provide the mens rea for the actus reus element "creates." Since it is ambiguous whether it also applies to "false" and the remainder of the actus reus elements, § 2.02(4) resolves the ambiguity by providing that it applies to all of them. [Remember that if "purpose" is the mens rea level, that translates into "knowledge" for circumstance elements. See § 2.02(2)(a)(ii).] "Purposely" would *not* apply to the elements in subsection (1)(c) or (1)(d), however, because of the semi-colon at the end of subsection (1)(b). It is clear from the grammatical structure of the section that "purposely" is meant to be restricted to subsection (1)(b).

But the reason the answer is "false" is that the word "purpose" can appear in the definition of an offense for another reason, namely, to provide a motive or goal the defendant must have in addition to the mens rea for the individual actus reus elements. Section 2.02(4) has no application to such uses of the term, and the mens rea for the actus reus elements of the offense would be determined by ordinary application of the principles of § 2.02(4) and § 2.02(3) as though the motive or goal use of the word "purpose" were not present. Two examples.

One: The word "purpose" in the phrase "with purpose to mislead" in § 241.3(1) is irrelevant to the mens rea for each of the actus reus elements contained in subsections (a) through (d). The mens rea for those elements is determined by reading each subsection independently of the "with purpose to mislead" phrase. Once the mens rea for those elements has been determined, the prosecutor then must show (a) the actus reus for the subsection in question; (b) the mens rea for each of the actus reus elements; and (c) "with purpose to mislead a public servant in performing his official function."

Two: The "with purpose to hinder" phrase in § 242.3 applies to each of the subsections of the offense in the sense that the behavior covered by each of them must be undertaken with a purpose to hinder, but it does not supply a "purpose" mens rea for each of the actus reus elements contained in the subsections that follow. They would carry a mens rea of recklessness because the offense is silent as to the mens rea for them.

Finally, the second and third sentences in the question are true. Mens rea words that modify an actus reus element are rarely if ever interpreted to apply to actus reus elements that precede them in the definition of the offense. The ambiguity that § 2.02(4) resolves applies to actus reus elements that follow the use of the mens rea word.

10. ***True.*** See § 2.03(2)(a) and (3)(a). The common law "transferred intent" when the defendant shot at *A* and hit *B*. Section 2.03 of the Model Penal Code treats these cases under the rubric of causation.

11. The statute requires a concurrence in time between the conduct (starting a fire) and the intent (with purpose to defraud an insurer). Here that concurrence is lacking, and it therefore seems likely that the defendant is not guilty. The prosecutor could argue that the defendant's later omission to put out the fire should be treated as "starting" a fire, but it seems unlikely that this argument would be successful. Failure to control a fire is explicitly made a minor offense in § 220.1(3)(b). While that offense would not apply here (assuming, as is implied, that the house belonged to *D*), it seems likely that the drafters meant for § 220.1(3) to include the entire class of offenders who could be prosecuted criminally for failure to control a fire lawfully (or accidentally) started. The affirmative defense in § 220.1(1)(b), moreover, might well be applicable on these facts.

12. This is a hard question. The statute is ambiguous. Its meaning turns on how the words "knowing that he is not licensed or privileged to do so" are construed. There are four possibilities:

(1) They could designate a mental element only, one that must exist in addition to the other actus reus and mens rea elements of the offense (analogous to a common law specific intent). If they are so construed, then the defendant in effect must believe that "he is not licensed or privileged" to enter or remain, but it would not matter whether such a license or privilege actually existed. Since the remainder of the offense says nothing about mens rea, under this construction the provisions of § 2.02(3) could supply the mens rea for all actus reus elements of the offense. If that were the case, then for the petty

misdemeanor the actus reus elements (with the mens rea in parenthesis) are: *conduct:* "enters or surreptitiously remains" (recklessness); and *circumstances:* "in any building or occupied structure, or separately secured or occupied portion thereof" (recklessness). For the misdemeanor, the additional circumstance element "in a dwelling at night" (recklessness) must be added.

(2) They could designate an actus reus element that must be knowingly committed. Under this construction, the defendant must in fact not be licensed or privileged to enter or remain in the building, and must know that fact. If this construction is adopted, there remain two possibilities:

    (a) The word "knowing," since it modifies one actus reus term, should be taken to modify all of them, and the mens rea for all of the conduct and circumstance elements must be elevated to knowledge under § 2.02(4). Thus, the elements for the petty misdemeanor would require knowledge. Since it is in a separate sentence, it seems likely that the grading components for the misdemeanor, "in a dwelling at night," would still require recklessness, though it could be argued that they should require knowledge too.

    (b) The word "knowing," since it is set off by commas, could be construed to apply only to the elements within the commas. Thus, § 2.02(4) would not apply because, quoting § 2.02(4), "a contrary purpose plainly appears." If this were so, then the remaining elements could require only recklessness.

(3) But the best answer is probably that all of the elements in the first sentence of the offense require "knowledge" because of the words "to do so." Whether the "knowing" phrase is a mens rea only or contains additional actus reus elements, it is clear that "knowing" applies to the entire phrase within the commas. That means that the defendant must know "that he is not licensed or privileged *to do so.*" To do what? To do the remaining elements of the offense. The "so" that the defendant must knowingly "do" is "enter or surreptitiously remain in any building or occupied structure," etc. So in the end, probably the best answer comes from playing with the words of the statute rather than the general rules of construction provided by § 2.02. At the end of the day, it is the words in the definition of the offense that rule.

One more point. Should the words "not licensed or privileged" be construed as actus reus elements? Or is should they be read as part of a mens rea phrase that does not contain any actus reus elements? The answer is that they *ought* to be construed to contain actus reus elements for the reasons set forth at pages 285–86 above. Otherwise, the defendant's behavior would consist entirely of innocuous conduct: entering or remaining in a building. Doing so when not licensed provides better evidence of criminal behavior. It should not be sufficient simply that the defendant believed that there was no license or privilege to enter.

13. The statute contains no mens rea words, and therefore it would appear at first glance that recklessness would be the mens rea for both elements under

§ 2.02(3). But § 2.01(4) provides that "possession" can be an act *only* if the defendant "knowingly" procured the item or "was aware" of the possession long enough to have been able to terminate it. Hence the mens rea for "possession" is knowledge. And so is the mens rea for "offensive weapon," also because of § 2.01(4) (*not* because of § 2.02(4)). The knowledge under § 2.01(4) extends to the object of the possession.

PART THREE: DERIVATIVE DEFENSES

IV. The Common Law

[Answers to Questions on pages 168–70]

1. ***True.*** An involuntary act defense is limited to cases where there is no exercise of will at all. Duress is a defense available to a person who decides to commit a crime under coercive pressure from another person, but the act is still regarded by the law as voluntary. The difference is between a hard choice and no choice at all. Persons who are incapable of making any choice get an involuntary act defense. Persons who make hard choices are engaging in a voluntary act as that term is defined by the law, but may get a duress defense under limitations developed on pages 245–46.

2. ***False.*** The defendant's conduct must include a voluntary act. If it includes an *in*voluntary act, criminal liability can be based on the voluntary components of the defendant's behavior if they satisfy the actus reus of the offense.

3. ***True.*** Evidence of mental disease or defect cannot be offered to support an involuntary act defense.

4. ***False.*** The actus reus elements of a specific intent crime require general intent or impose strict liability, depending on whether they are central to criminality or grading. In neither case would a merely "honest" mistake be a defense. The mistake would have to be "honest and reasonable" if general intent were required. And of course no mistake would be a defense if strict liability were imposed.

5. ***True.*** There are some cases, like *Murdock* on page 156, where the courts have read fuzzy mens rea words to include knowledge of the criminality of behavior.

6. ***False.*** This is a tricky one. There are some cases that recognize a defense in this situation, illustrated on pages 157–58. But they do not hold that the defendant lacked mens rea. They simply say that it would be unfair to convict the defendant. The situation is thus not really a case of a "derivative" defense but a "collateral" defense. Check the Glossary in Appendix D if you don't remember what I mean by these terms.

If you answered "true" to this question on the theory that a court *could* read a fuzzy mens rea word to include a component of knowledge of the law in such a situation, then you may be right. But what you should know is that some courts have provided a defense in this situation without feeling the need to redefine mens rea to do so. One reason not to do so is to preserve the option of providing a defense in such situations for a crime that does not contain a fuzzy mens rea word on which they could hang their hat. Another is that it is hard to redefine the mens rea component of an offense so that it (a) provides a defense in situations where the defendant makes a mistake of criminal law in reliance on misleading official authority but (b) does not provide a defense in situations where the defendant makes a mistake of criminal law for other reasons. It is better to regard this potential defense as simply an exception to liability—a special collateral defense—rather than to invent an element of the offense that it can then negate. For that reason, the best answer is "false."

7. **False.** They are in specific intent offenses, but not general intent offenses. Perhaps they should be treated like mistakes of fact in all situations, but they are not.

8. **False.** Evidence of voluntary intoxication is not admissible to support an involuntary act defense.

9. Because some sex offenses that otherwise require general intent impose strict liability where the act is immoral on the facts as the defendant believed them to be, and because all general intent offenses (and specific intent offenses too, where the specific intent is not itself a grading element) impose strict liability for actus reus elements that are of grading significance only.

10. There are three rules: an honest mistake is a defense to a specific intent crime; an honest and reasonable mistake is a defense to a general intent crime; and no mistake is a defense to a strict liability crime. And there are rules about when these rules are applied, for example: the general intent rule applies to actus reus elements of specific intent crimes; no mistake is a defense unless it is relevant to a mens rea element of the crime; the ordinary general intent rule does not apply to certain sex offenses where the defendant's act was immoral on the facts as they were believed to be; strict liability generally applies to grading elements of common law crimes. But in each instance, one could eliminate the rules and hold that a mistake is a defense whenever it negates mens rea. The question then, though, would be what the mens rea for a given element would be, and of course there would have to be rules for that. Compare, for example, the approach of the Model Penal Code to these issues.

11. The statement is false. A defendant who makes a mistake as to the "nighttime" element of burglary would have committed some other crime had the facts been as imagined (at least a trespass). Thus, under the common law rule applicable to

actus reus elements of specific intent offenses, strict liability will be applied to that element. See the illustration on page 152. Hence, it does not matter how the mistake is classified. The mistake is irrelevant to any required mens rea element of the offense.

12. The mistake concerns the element "convicted felon" in what would appear to be a general intent offense. Thus, if the mistake were classified as one of fact, the defendant would be entitled to a defense if the mistake were both honest and reasonable. Whether it was reasonable would present a jury question, but there is certainly evidence of reasonable behavior here. On the other hand, if the mistake were classified as relating to the definition of the term "felon" by the criminal law, then it would not provide a defense. Mistakes as to the meaning of the criminal law are not a defense. The mistake could be analogized to a mistake of the non-criminal law, but that might do no good, since mistakes of non-criminal law often are not a defense to a general intent crime at common law anyway. Thus, the critical question is whether *D* made a mistake of fact or a mistake as to the meaning of the criminal law. How one should decide which kind of mistake it was is anybody's guess. Common sense might indicate that it is a mistake as to the meaning of the criminal law. The criminal law defines the term "felon," and we can't have convicted felons going around deciding what the criminal law means. But good policy arguments could be made for not convicting this defendant: the error was not culpable, and it could be regarded as unfair to convict *D* for making a mistake on a matter the experts couldn't even get straight.

This question is based, incidentally, on People v. Bray, 52 Cal.App.3d 494, 124 Cal.Rptr. 913 (1975), where the court held the defendant entitled to a mistake of *fact* defense, without any discussion of the possibility that the mistake may have been one of law or of the policy reasons one might advance for acquittal or conviction. *Bray* illustrates a convenient decisional technique. When the law creates two categories, one with a rule going one way and the other with a rule going the other way, there is opportunity for manipulating the outcome by forcing the case into the category that leads to a "just" resolution. This is also a litigation opportunity for inventive counsel.

13. Here is an opportunity to prepare an essay (which you might want to show to a fellow student for comment and criticism). There is legitimate debate about whether evidence of mental disease ought to be admissible to negate a specific intent component of a crime. If the specific intent is designed to identify a person with a certain character defect, then one can argue that it shouldn't matter *why* the defendant doesn't have that defect. It ought to be enough that the defendant doesn't. But there are good arguments for not admitting the evidence. See page 166.

As to intoxication, there would seem to be a lesser claim for admissibility, since the defendant might be regarded as "at fault" for drinking (or taking drugs) in the first place, and might be convicted in part for having induced the incapacitating condition. There are also strong deterrence arguments at play here—we don't want people drinking for courage, or thinking that they can get away with crime if they use drink or drugs first. Most people who have mental diseases, on the other hand, are not "at fault" in any sense for having their condition, nor (in at least most situations) can they be deterred from having their mental disease. For this reason it might be regarded as intolerable to admit evidence of voluntary intoxication but *not* admit evidence of mental disease—though that is precisely what many courts do in some situations. The question is complicated further, moreover, because some people who have mental diseases *are* at fault in some sense, for example those who use drink or drugs to an extent that they induce, as the courts sometimes say, a "settled mental illness." And some people who have mental diseases are just as subject to deterrent forces as those who do not. And both intoxication and mental illness can be faked, and present serious litigation costs and opportunities for error. And so on.

But all of this may be regarded as beside the point, since one could conclude that the same arguments of logic and fairness can be made for both the mentally ill and the intoxicated defendant. If the purpose of requiring a specific intent is to identify a defendant with a certain character deficiency, why convict a defendant who does not have that deficiency, whatever the reason?

14. Here again is a chance to write a short essay. The arguments are summarized at pages 154. The rule is generally sound and not an "outmoded relic." It is supported by prevention, social control, and deterrence considerations and by an argument derived from these considerations based on the necessities of a legal order. On the other hand, there are occasions where there should be exceptions to the rule in the name of fairness. The *Cox* case (page 158) is surely one, and the principle for which *Lambert* might be taken to stand (page 159) another.

V. The Model Penal Code

[Answers to Questions on pages 183–85]

1. ***True.*** Mistakes of fact and mistakes of non-criminal law are treated the same way by § 2.04(1). Note that § 2.04(1) covers ignorance or mistake as to a matter of "fact or law." Both can constitute a defense if they negate mens rea. Mistakes of criminal law, on the other hand, are dealt with quite differently by § 2.02(9). Such mistakes will not constitute a defense unless the statute or some provision of the Code explicitly so provides.

2. ***True.*** The voluntary part of the defendant's conduct must itself satisfy the actus reus of the offense, but so long as it does so there is no requirement that all of the defendant's conduct be voluntary.

3. ***False.*** The approach is drastically different. The common law imposes strict liability on grading elements. The Model Penal Code treats them just like other elements of crime for mens rea purposes, with the limitations provided by § 2.04(2).

4. *True.* The basic thrust of the "ignorance of the criminal law" rule is embraced by § 2.02(9). The limited exceptions based on official statements are provided by § 2.04(3)(b). The burden of persuasion is shifted by § 2.04(4). It is unclear what "reasonable" means, but that is the term used in § 2.04(3)(b). It might mean negligence as defined in § 2.02(2)(d). Or it might mean something close to ordinary negligence as used in the law of torts. The official commentary to the Model Penal Code does not speak to this issue.

5. *False.* See § 2.08(5)(c).

6. *False.* It is admissible under § 2.08(1).

7. *True.* See § 2.08(2). That provision does not in so many words say that the special rule for recklessness does not apply if the intoxication is pathological. But that's what it means. The reasoning is as follows. Section 2.08(1) says that evidence of intoxication is admissible whenever relevant to negate mens rea. Section 2.08(2) creates an exception only in the case of intoxication that is self-induced. Since pathological intoxication is not mentioned by § 2.08(2), it must therefore be covered by § 2.08(1). Hence evidence of pathological intoxication is admissible to negate mens rea whenever logically relevant. And hence the special rule of § 2.08(2) applies only to non-pathological intoxication.

There is an answer to this argument. If one reads the definition of self-induced intoxication in § 2.08(5)(b) carefully, it seems possible that pathological intoxication could be regarded as self-induced, and therefore fit literally within the language of § 2.08(2). How, then, are you supposed to know what it means? The answer is by understanding why the special exception for recklessness was made. The reasons are summarized at page 182. These reasons were rejected for "purpose" and "knowledge," as they are in many jurisdictions for specific intent crimes. But they were accepted for recklessness because of the well-settled law for general intent crimes (which the Model Code drafters thought comparable to offenses for which recklessness was the minimum culpability) and because the drafters thought there was a general moral equivalence between the act of getting drunk and the risks created by conduct once drunk. Since § 2.08(2) is based on one's fault in getting drunk, it makes sense that it be interpreted to exclude a situation where the actor is not at fault. Hence pathological intoxication ought to be excluded from the operation of § 2.08(2).

Persuaded? If not, then the answer to the question is "false." But in that case, you ought to be able to explain why the above reasoning is faulty, and ought to have some good reasons why the statute should be construed differently. The statute is not clear on its face and the available commentary by the drafters does not speak to this point.

8. ***True.*** Section 4.02(1) provides for this result for evidence of mental disease. And § 2.08(1) provides that evidence of intoxication is admissible to negate mens rea. The exception for recklessness in § 2.08(2) applies only to "self-induced" intoxication, and the definition of "self-induced" in § 2.08(5)(b) would not (or should not be read to) include an unanticipated reaction to medication. This is the same point involved in Question 7. Did you give the same answer both times?

9. The element "night" in § 221.1(2) is relevant to grading only, but grading elements carry mens rea under the Model Penal Code. The mens rea for "night," since no mens rea words in the definition otherwise apply, would be recklessness. § 2.02(3). Either a mistake of fact or a mistake of the non-criminal law could negate that mens rea. § 2.04(1). But a mistake of the criminal law could not. § 2.02(9). Since the term "night" as defined in § 221.0(2) uses the term "sunset" without defining it, presumably a mistake as to the civil law defining sunset would be treated as a mistake of the non-criminal law under § 2.04(1). Hence, which category the mistake falls in would matter, and the admissibility of the evidence would turn on its proper categorization. The statement is true.

10. This is a hard question under the Model Penal Code. The mens rea for the element "felon" would be recklessness. § 2.02(3). The case turns on whether the mistake is one of "fact or law" that negates the recklessness required for "felon" under § 2.04(1)(a), or whether it is a mistake as to the "meaning or application of the law determining the elements of an offense" under § 2.02(9). If the former, then the mistake is a defense. If the latter, it is not. The arguments for and against conviction are the same as stated in the answer to this question under the common law, page 427. Placing the mistake in either category could be defended. Can you make the arguments?

This is a good question on which to digress to make a general point about exam taking. It is very frustrating to exam readers (and to audiences to whom you will be submitting analyses as real lawyers someday) to see an answer in the form "If *A*, then *X*. But if *B*, then *Y*. I quit." What your reader wants to know under these conditions is which is more plausible, *A* or *B*? You need to follow through on such answers, in other words, to present arguments and conclusions about which as between *A* and *B* makes more sense.

To apply this point to the question under discussion, one would *begin* an answer to the question (not *end* it) by explaining why the issue is as stated above: If the mistake is one of fact or non-criminal law, it would be a defense if not recklessly made. But if it is one of criminal law, then it would not be a defense period. Strict liability in that case.

This is not the time to quit without going further to explain the rationale for why one answer might be better than the other, or why the arguments are in equilibrium, or whatever else can be said on the subject. It is the quality of your reasoning *after* you have made the "if" statements that will determine the quality of your answer—and that will translate into higher grades in law school and better job performance as a lawyer. You are not going to get very far as a beginning associate in a law firm, a junior member of a prosecutor's office, a beginner in a public interest firm, a law clerk to a judge, or whatever, if your work for your boss consists of answers in the form: "If *A*, then *X*. But if *B*, then *Y*. I quit. Now it's up to you to do the real work."

11. The jury should acquit if they believe the defendant. Knowledge is the mens rea for all of the elements of the offense, applying § 2.02(4). If, by mistake or ignorance, the defendant did not know the records were required to be kept by others for information of the government, the mistake or ignorance would be a defense under § 2.04(1)(a).

12. If the building was in fact abandoned, then the jury should acquit. The prosecutor must prove beyond a reasonable doubt that the building was not abandoned. Since elements of a defense also require mens rea under §§ 1.13(9), (10), and 2.02(1), and since the mens rea for "abandoned" would be recklessness (§ 2.02(3)), the defendant's belief that the building was abandoned would be a defense unless it was recklessly formed.

    Note that actus reus and mens rea elements in a sense work in reverse in the case of defenses:

    (1) If "abandoned" were an element of an *offense* with a mens rea of recklessness, the defendant could be convicted only if the prosecutor proved that the building was abandoned and that any belief by the defendant to the contrary was recklessly formed. From the defendant's point of view, the defense could be either that the building was *not* abandoned (the actus reus is not present) or that the defendant believed the building *not* abandoned and was not reckless in forming the belief (the mens rea is not present).

    (2) On the other hand, if "abandoned" were an element of a *defense* with a mens rea of recklessness, then the defendant could be convicted only if the prosecutor proved that the building was *not* abandoned and that any belief by the defendant to the contrary was recklessly formed. From the defendant's point of view, the defense could be that the building was abandoned (the actus reus is not present) or that the defendant believed the building abandoned and was not reckless in forming the belief (the mens rea is not present).

    This may sound confusing, but it is worth working through carefully, and perhaps trying it on some other affirmative defenses.

13. The defense is irrelevant. Section 223.0(7) defines "property of another" to include partnership property ("property in which any person other than the actor has an interest which the actor is not privileged to infringe"). Given this definition of "property of another" by the criminal law, the actus reus of the offense is

complete. The defendant took property that is the subject of theft. The defendant also had the necessary mens rea. The defendant knew that property was taken and that it was partnership property. What the defendant did not know was that the criminal law makes such conduct theft. A mistake as to the characterization of behavior by the criminal law is not a defense. The defendant's mistake was one as to the "meaning or application of the law determining the elements of an offense." § 2.02(9). Under § 2.02(9), the mistake is plainly irrelevant and would not support a defense.

14. This might be regarded as a close call. On the one hand, the Model Penal Code generally takes the position that evidence should be received for whatever its logical import. You should be able to illustrate this proposition by reference to the meaning of provisions like §§ 2.04(1), 2.08(1), and 4.02(1). The argument that the evidence would not be admissible would have to be derived from the negative implication of § 4.02(1)—since it says that evidence of "mental disease or defect" is admissible to negate mens rea, it might be read to say by negative implication that medical experts can't testify on mens rea unless they base their testimony upon diagnosis of a "mental disease or defect." The question is which is the stronger argument. You might also think about whether there are reasons why the testimony involved in the question should be admissible or inadmissible (this is something experts don't know much about, the jury would place too much credence on their guesses, and the evidence should be excluded for that reason?; or this is something experts really know about and we ought to listen for that reason?). Finally, there is the point that § 4.02(1) was put in the Model Code to overrule a long line of precedent concerning evidence of mental disease on mens rea. It was not designed, one could argue, as a limitation on the admissibility of evidence.

Note that the point of a question like this one, in any event, is not what answer you give but how well you can state the arguments on both sides.

PART FOUR: COLLATERAL DEFENSES: JUSTIFICATIONS

VI. The Common Law

[Answers to Questions on page 202–03]

1. ***True.***   This is the so-called "alter ego" rule.

2. ***True.***   Non-deadly force can be used, but deadly force cannot be used to protect *personal* property.

3. ***False.***   This is a tricky one. It is true that a police officer is permitted to use whatever force reasonably believed to be "necessary" to make an arrest. This would normally not include deadly force, because it will not be necessary to use deadly force to make an arrest—unless the defendant flees or fights back. Here the defendant fights back, but there is no

indication of the degree of force used by the defendant. The police officer would not be entitled to use deadly force against a resisting arrestee unless the arrestee used or threatened deadly force. Since we do not know that the arrestee used deadly force, the statement is not completely true.

4. *True.*   This is the way the prevailing law is usually stated. But it would be rare that deadly force was in fact "necessary" to prevent embezzlement, forgery, or tax fraud—they can be prevented by other means. Thus the prevailing law is correctly stated by the question, but it would in practice permit deadly force only where the crime to be prevented threatened violence, since only then would deadly force really be "necessary." This may be why there has been little pressure to change the law on this point.

5. *False.*   Contributory negligence by the victim would never be a defense to a crime.

6. *False.*   The existence of the emergency is a judgment which the jury would make, probably under instructions that would give the defendant a defense if any mistake were reasonably made. It is the balancing of the harms that is left to the court, and as to which a mistake costs the defendant the defense.

7. The argument against this result is that it is disproportionate to the defendant's fault. The defendant should be convicted of negligent homicide if anything. It is unfair to punish such a defendant to the same extent as a contract killer.

The argument in favor of the result is deterrence. It will encourage defendants to be extra careful in using deadly force if they know that unreasonable errors in judgment will result in a conviction for murder. And the preservation of life is a sufficiently important societal objective to justify a few disproportionate convictions. This argument is more acceptable, it should be noted, if the penalty structure for murder is flexible. If a sentence can be imposed that is comparable to the sentence for negligent homicide, then the disproportionality is substantially reduced. It is not eliminated, because the defendant still suffers the stigma of a conviction for murder. But it is reduced, and this is thus perhaps a way of having your cake and eating it too.

As to which is the better argument, take your choice and state your reasons.

8. *D* was the initial aggressor, and obviously used non-deadly force. *V* was thus privileged to respond with non-deadly force to the extent necessary to repel the attack. But *V* over-reacted and responded with deadly force. This made *V*'s attack "unlawful," and entitled *D* to respond with deadly force to the extent necessary.

At this point you need Paul Drake, who—for the uninitiated—is Perry Mason's private investigator (and if you don't know who Perry Mason is, obviously you need to watch more re-runs on TV). *D*'s initial statement "Drop the knife or I'll shoot" is plainly ok; a threat to use deadly force is not itself the use of deadly force, and plainly such a threat is permissible when you have just dodged a knife attack. But when V charged and D shot, it cannot be said without more facts whether this was justified. There are two issues:

(1) whether the circumstances were such that retreat was required, and if so whether D knew it could be accomplished with complete safety. This depends on whether retreat is required in the jurisdiction in question, and if so, on where the attack occurred (if in D's house retreat might not be required) and what avenues of retreat were open (if D was an Olympic sprinter and V a sumo wrestler with a bad throwing arm, perhaps gunplay was not needed);

(2) aside from retreat, there is the question of the necessity of shooting, a question that will involve many of the same issues. Thus, if D was an Olympic sprinter and V the hypothesized sumo wrestler, perhaps a jury would conclude it was not necessary to shoot. But if V was a knife thrower and D a third string middle guard—too small, too slow, and not tough enough—then the jury might see things the other way.

These variations, incidentally, indicate how contextual justification defenses really are, and how much room there is for careful development and presentation of evidence and for advocacy before the prosecutor, court, and jury.

VII.   The Model Penal Code

[Answers to Questions on pages 218–19]

1. ***True.***   See § 3.04(2)(a)(i). The fact that the police officer and the arrestee know (or believe) the arrest to be unlawful does not matter. The purpose of the provision is to require that the legality of the arrest be sorted out in the courts and not on the streets.

2. ***False.***   A threat to use deadly force is not itself deadly force. See § 3.11(2). Hence, there was no obligation to retreat under § 3.04(2)(b)(ii): the obligation to retreat arises under this provision only as a precondition to the actual use of deadly force. Therefore D was right that there was no obligation to retreat, and the "ignorance of the law" principle does not apply.

3. ***True.***   See § 3.05(1). One must be careful about statements like "so long as the defendant reasonably believes the stranger would be entitled to use deadly force in self defense," for they contain an inherent ambiguity. Literally taken, this belief by the defendant might be irrelevant—the defendant's *legal* conclusion about whether the stranger could rely on self defense would not matter. What the defendant must believe is a set of facts and circumstances to which the law attaches the label "self defense." A mistake as to those facts and circumstances will not negate the defense so

long as the conditions established by § 3.09(2) are satisfied. And of course if the belief is reasonable there can be no conviction under the terms of § 3.09(2) even if the defendant is mistaken. But a mistake of the criminal law as to what constitutes self defense *will* negate the defense.

Note that § 3.05(1) is very carefully (and cumbersomely) drafted to avoid this ambiguity. Because it is so cumbersome to be precise about this matter, criminal lawyers often speak in the terms quoted above and hope the listener understands what they mean. And about half the time the listener understands. On an examination, you should be precise to make sure your grader knows that you know what you are talking about.

4. *False.*   See § 3.06(3)(a), which states three situations where a request to desist need not be made. Hence, it is not true that force may "never" be used without a request to desist.

5. *False.*   The statement is true as far as it goes. While the justification defenses themselves do not require a "reasonable" belief, the net effect of § 3.09(2) is that a belief must be non-negligent before a conviction of all crimes can be excluded. So the statement that the belief must be "reasonable" is correct.

The reason the statement is false is that it is incomplete. There are four conditions to the use of deadly force to make an arrest or prevent an escape, and only three of them are satisfied here. See § 3.07(2)(b). Section 3.07(2)(b)(iii) is the one that is missing.

6. *False.*   See § 3.02(2). Recklessness in bringing about the situation will result in denial of the defense only for an offense for which recklessness or negligence is a sufficient level of culpability. Thus conviction for an offense requiring purpose or knowledge could not be obtained under the conditions stated in the question.

7. The elements of both §§ 210.3(1)(a) (manslaughter) and 210.4(1) (negligent homicide) have arguably occurred, depending on how the definitions of "recklessness" and "negligence" contained in § 2.02 are applied to this situation. For *B* to have a defense, the jury would have to be persuaded that the prevention of two points in a basketball game is a fair trade for creating a substantial risk of serious injury, that the risk of death was not substantial from such behavior, or that disregarding the risks was not a gross deviation from proper standards of behavior in that context. These are plainly jury issues, on which reasonable persons could differ.

Assuming that the elements of manslaughter or negligent homicide have occurred, the next question is whether there is any justification defense. Consent is the only possibility, and a defense might be available under § 2.11(2)(b). Given the frequency with which such behavior occurs on a basketball court these days, it is certainly true that "the conduct" is a "reasonably foreseeable hazard" of joint participation in the sport. Whether "the harm" is a "reasonably foreseeable hazard" is another matter, but given the violence of many such collisions and the vulnerability of the shooter to serious injury, it is certainly arguable that it is.

Should *B* be prosecuted? You should draw these issues out, and then make your own choice.

8. Here is an opportunity to prepare an essay, which you should show to a colleague for analysis and criticism. You probably should start by separating three kinds of mistakes: mistakes of fact (and judgment), mistakes of criminal law, and mistakes of non-criminal law. As to mistakes of fact (and judgment), the common law result is described and analyzed in Question 7 on page 202 and its answer on page 433. The Model Code, of course, provides a completely different answer in § 3.09(2), described on page 208. You should be able to draw out the differences, and make arguments both ways. As to mistakes of criminal law, they result in denial of the defense under either system. Whether this is the correct position involves the issues canvassed on page 154, which you should be able to draw out and debate. As to mistakes of non-criminal law, the Model Code plainly treats them like mistakes of fact under § 2.04(1). What the common law would do is less certain. Compare the discussion at pages 160–62. Again, you should be able to discuss what should be done in this situation.

PART FIVE: COLLATERAL DEFENSES: EXCUSES

VIII.   The Common Law

[Answers to Questions on pages 251–52]

1. *False.* The age of incapacity was seven. A child of eight was presumed to be incapable, but the presumption could be rebutted.

2. *False.* It is true that the term is not well defined. But it is clear that the "psychopath" is *not* included. That term, which is outmoded now, describes a person whose only abnormality is the repeated commission of crimes or other anti-social acts.

3. *False.* Both branches of *M'Naghten* ask cognitive questions. It is true that one could read *both M'Naghten* branches to include a volitional component, but few do this and even this would not make the statement true.

4. *False.* The tests are not alternatives but supplements to each other. Those States which use irresistible impulse use it in addition to *M'Naghten* and permit acquittal if either is satisfied.

5. *False.* The statement is a close paraphrase of the irresistible impulse test. The product test asks simply whether the crime was a product of mental disease.

6. *False.* The Supreme Court has held exactly the opposite. The Constitution does *not* require the prosecutor to shoulder the burden of persuasion on the insanity defense.

7. *True.* The two branches are substantial capacity to appreciate the criminality or wrongfulness of conduct (cognitive) and substantial capacity to conform conduct to law (volitional).

8. *False.* The term "mental disease or defect" is undefined.

9. *True.* At least that is its intent. A "false" answer could be defended on the ground that it introduces too much uncertainty into the standard. But the response would be that it introduces no more uncertainty than medical reality demands. A "false" answer could also be defended on the ground that the "substantial capacity" formula leads to a defense that is too lenient.

10. *True.* The cognitive branch comes from *M'Naghten* and the volitional branch from irresistible impulse.

11. *False.* The "nature and quality of act" branch of *M'Naghten* is omitted from the Model Penal Code test.

12. *True.* If you answered "false" because the person who asserts an involuntary intoxication defense does not have to have a "mental disease or defect," you are right. If you answered "true" because the standard against which the involuntary intoxicant is measured is the same as for the mentally diseased person, you are also right. If you answered "true" or "false" for any other reason, you better go read this section again.

13. *False.* Duress requires that another person engage in the coercion. Coercion by natural forces is not covered, and indeed is arguably an ethical gap in the law.

14. *False.* The description of the "objective" view of entrapment is correct, but the federal courts don't follow it. They subscribe to the "subjective" view.

15. Two reasons:

    (a) The "product" test is too broad, essentially asking only whether the defendant suffered from a mental disease. If there is a mental disease, it would be hard to say that *any* conduct by the defendant was caused by a part of the defendant's personality that had nothing to do with the mental disease. This problem becomes more and more exacerbated the broader the definition of "mental disease or defect." The combination of the product inquiry with a broad definition of mental disease is probably what led to the downfall of *Durham* in the District of Columbia.

(b) The "product" test does not ask the right question. The right question is whether the defendant is to be blamed for the offense. The only way the criminal law knows to get a handle on this question is to focus on relevant criteria for blame, which of course is what *M'Naghten* and irresistible impulse do. You should be able to show, briefly, how they do this and why they are therefore more consistent with the premises of the criminal law.

16. This is an essay question such as might appear on a final examination. I have used versions of it, in fact, many times. There are lots of directions in which an answer could go, and therefore it would be a good idea to try an answer and show it to a colleague for criticism.

On the affirmative side, one could argue that the "substantial" capacity idea is better than the "total incapacity" of the common law. And one could argue in favor of both a cognitive and a control inquiry, noting that two cognitive inquiries (as in *M'Naghten*) are unnecessary (see pages 236–37) and that "appreciate" is a better formula than "know" for the remaining cognitive inquiry. Moreover, one could defend the Model Code as fitting neatly into the theoretical criteria used by the criminal law for centuries to measure blame. Indeed, the reason that the Model Code caught on so well probably rested on the fact that it was solidly based on the traditions of the criminal law but at the same time better reflected modern medical reality.

On the negative side, probably the strongest argument is one against making the volitional inquiry (see page 244), although strong arguments can be made that there should be no separate insanity defense at all. Given its premises, the Model Code is pretty good, perhaps about as good as one could get. The way to attack it is to challenge its premises. A good place to start might be with the list of factors on pages 225–26. This could lead to an approach paralleling the federal test that has displaced the Model Code in many places.

IX. The Model Penal Code

[Answers to Questions on page 258]

1. ***True.*** The age of capacity is 16. See § 4.10(1)(a).

2. ***True.*** The burden is on the defendant by a preponderance for the entrapment defense. See § 2.13(2).

3. ***False.*** It follows the "excuse" rationale. See the discussion beginning at pages 247 and 255–56.

4. ***True.*** The Model Code follows the "objective" approach. See the discussion beginning at pages 248 and 257.

5. ***True.*** Section 2.13(1)(a) provides a defense where a person is misled by police officials who knowingly make false representations designed to induce the belief that conduct is not a crime.

6. Section 3.02 provides a necessity defense in cases where the defendant avoids a greater evil by committing a crime. Section 2.09 provides a duress defense where a *human agent* forces a person to commit a crime under certain defined circumstances, even though a greater harm is caused than would have occurred if the defendant had refrained from the criminal offense. There is a gap, however, if the defendant succumbs to *natural forces* and causes a greater harm than would have occurred if the defendant allowed the forces to have their natural effect, even though in all other respects the conditions of the duress defense were met.

PART SIX: PARTIES

X. The Common Law

[Answers to Questions on pages 280–82]

1. *False.* Both corporations and partnerships may be held criminally liable if the legislature so intends.

2. *True.* Vicarious liability can be imposed in other situations, but it is most often used for public welfare offenses.

3. *False.* One is indeed a principal in the first degree when a crime is committed by use of an "innocent agent." But an "innocent agent" is one coerced or duped into committing a crime, not anyone who happens to be innocent. The defendant must "cause" an innocent person to commit an offense—it is a situation where the defendant sets out to accomplish the actus reus of an offense through the use of someone else who doesn't know what is going on or is otherwise known by the defendant to be innocent. Thus, *A* is not guilty on an innocent agent theory because *A* did not "use" *P* to commit the offense.

4. *True.* If the defendant was constructively present, then the defendant is properly characterized as a principal in the second degree. Variance between allegation and proof was not fatal under the original common law rules where the charge was that the defendant was a principal in the first degree and the proof was that the defendant was a principal in the second degree.

5. *True.* One was guilty as an accessory after the fact at common law only for aiding a person who had committed a crime after the crime had been committed and (a) the person aided had in fact committed a felony; (b) the defendant knew the person aided had engaged in specified conduct and the law provided that the conduct was a felony; and (c) the defendant had a purpose to hinder detection, prosecution, conviction, or punishment of the person aided. The first person *A* aided did not commit a felony; the second also did not commit a felony; the third likewise did not commit a felony; and *A* did not know that the fourth person had committed a felony. Thus an element of the offense is missing in each case, and *A* is not guilty as an accessory after the fact in any of the cases.

Note, however, that the fourth case is ambiguously stated. If *A* knew what the fourth person did but mistakenly applied the label "misdemeanor" to what was actually a felony, then *A* would be guilty. But *A* is not guilty if *A*'s mistake was as to what the fourth person did. Compare the answer to Question 3, page 434. And see page 156 ("The Meaning of Mens Rea").

6. *False.* A husband or wife could not be guilty as an accessory *after* the fact, but could be guilty as an accessory *before* the fact.

7. *False.* It is enough if the principal knows that the defendant is trying to give aid, even if the aid is ineffective. The defendant in such a case is nonetheless "encouraging" the commission of the offense by communicating to the principal a willingness to help.

8. *True.* This would be true, for example, in those jurisdictions where it is sufficient if the principal engages in the *conduct* of an offense without the mens rea. In such a case the "offense" would not occur since the principal would lack the mens rea, but the accessory could nonetheless be convicted.

9. *True.* Some jurisdictions permit conviction of a more serious offense in any case where justified by the accessory's mens rea. The common law did so in the case of criminal homicide.

10. *False.* Traditionally, an accessory was convicted of the offense committed by the principal and was subject to the same punishment. Even though rape was defined to preclude the conviction of a husband for raping his own wife, the husband could help another commit the offense, be an accessory to that offense, and thus be convicted and punished for raping his own wife.

11. Strict liability dispenses with the mens rea. It allows the conviction of one who has committed an unlawful act without any mens rea as to one or more elements. Vicarious liability dispenses with the actus reus. It allows the conviction of one who has committed no act, premising liability on a crime committed by another person who stands in a relationship with the defendant that is itself lawful and is usually socially desirable.

12. Yes, it is a defense if one withdraws the aid and renounces the offense. Specifically, three things must be done: (a) the defendant must communicate a repudiation to the person aided; (b) the defendant must do all that is possible to render all prior aid ineffective; and (c) the defendant must do all of this before it is too late to stop the chain of events leading to the commission of the offense.

Note that recognition of this defense is arguably inconsistent with a refusal to recognize an abandonment defense for an attempt, conspiracy, or solicitation. See the answer to Question 11, page 447. After you have covered these "inchoate crimes," it would be a good exercise to prepare a short analysis of why a defense should or should not be provided in all four of these situations—accessorial liability, attempt, solicitation, and conspiracy—and whether you see any differences that justify a common law defense only in the case of the accessory.

13. The first is where the defendant is a victim of the offense, as in statutory rape. The traditional rationale for this exclusion is that the offense is designed to protect young children from themselves, and it would be inconsistent with this rationale to convict them as an accessory. The second situation is where the legislature defines as an offense conduct that necessarily has at least two parties (such as serving alcohol to a minor) but provides punishment only for one of the parties (the server in the illustration given). Here courts often infer that the legislature intended only the server to be guilty. The rationale the courts use for precluding conviction as an accessory is legislative intent. The rationale a legislature might use is less clear.

14. What the fuss is about is whether it is inconsistent with any of the justifications for punishment to convict a person as an accessory who merely knows that aid is being given to the commission of a crime. Many think—as where a person sells ordinary over-the-counter goods believing that they are probably going to be used to commit a crime—that it is unfair and disproportionate to the degree of guilt to convict one as an accessory based on knowledge alone, that such a conviction is an unwarranted interference with personal liberty and autonomy. Others think that deterrence justifies the punishment of anyone who knowingly aids the commission of a crime, and that knowledge is an adequate minimum degree of culpability in this situation. The solutions that have been developed are summarized on page 271 and will not be repeated here. The best solution may well be differential grading: to punish at the grade of the offense aided where the defendant "has a stake in the venture" (a purpose to promote or facilitate the offense) and to punish at a lesser level where the defendant knowingly facilitates the commission of the offense. This is the approach taken in those jurisdictions that have created a separate facilitation offense, which usually is limited to the provision of substantial aid to felonies or other serious offenses. These limits, plus the reduction in the grade of the offense, go a long way toward answering the criticisms.

15. Yes, because the defendant has engaged in the conduct required for accessorial liability with the required mens rea. To acquit the defendant because the principal happens to be innocent for some reason unknown to the defendant is to acquit based on a fortuity. The defendant is just as dangerous and just as blameworthy whether or not the principal is guilty. Note the relationship of this issue to several others that arise in different contexts, e.g., the problem of impossibility in attempts and how mistake should be treated when a crime would be committed on the facts as the defendant believed them to be. In both of these cases the issue, at bottom, is whether the defendant should be punished on the basis of what happened or what the defendant thought was happening. Those who believe that "what the defendant thought was happening" is the right answer in those contexts would convict the accessory in the case under discussion. Those who believe "what happened" is the

best criterion for punishment might very well acquit.

XI.   The Model Penal Code

[Answers to Questions on pages 294–95]

1. ***True.***   Under § 2.07(6)(b) any "agent" of an unincorporated association (which presumably includes a partnership) may be liable in such an instance. And a sentence to imprisonment can be imposed under § 2.07(6)(c). The term "agent" is defined in § 2.07(4)(b) to include a person authorized to act in behalf of the association *and* a "member of such association" in the case of an unincorporated association. Although this definition is not without ambiguity, it appears to include both employees and partners as "agents." The moral: read the statute carefully, including any applicable definitions.

2. ***False.***   The burden of persuasion is placed on the defendant, but the defense may not be asserted to a strict liability offense (the Model Code calls it an "absolute" liability offense, but that is the same thing). See § 2.07(5).

3. ***True.***   Sections 2.05(1) and 2.06(2)(b) contemplate the possibility of vicarious liability on natural persons, but they do not impose it. Nor does any other substantive provision. And, of course, any liability imposed on a business entity like a corporation or a partnership is necessarily vicarious, since they cannot engage in conduct themselves and are liable, if at all, for the conduct of their employees.

4. ***True.***   Accessories after the fact are not covered by § 2.06, but by the separate offenses defined in Article 242.

5. ***False.***   Membership in a conspiracy can be sufficient aid to constitute complicity, so long as one has "aided" or "agreed to aid" in the planning or commission of the offense, with a purpose to promote or facilitate its commission. But, under § 2.06(6)(c), simply abandoning the objectives of a conspiracy are not enough to constitute an effective withdrawal for purposes of liability as an accomplice.

6. ***False.***   No one, of course, can be convicted as an accomplice under the Model Penal Code simply on a showing of knowledge that aid is promoting or facilitating an offense. And if one looked at § 2.06 alone, *A* could not be guilty even if purpose to promote or facilitate were shown, because of § 2.06(6)(b). But the point of this question is that statutes must be read carefully. Those of you who did so would have noticed that § 230.1(3) would permit *A* to be convicted based on knowledge of the bigamy, not as an accomplice to anything but as one who has violated the specific crime defined by § 230.1(1).

7. *True.*   *P* can be convicted because under § 213.6(1), liability is strict on the age element when the operative age is less than 10. Thus, *P*'s mistake as to age is irrelevant and provides no defense. *A* can be an accessory to the offense, however, only by satisfying the mens rea required by § 2.06. And the mens rea for circumstance elements of the object offense under § 2.06 is knowledge, derived from the required "purpose to promote or facilitate" and § 2.02(2)(a)(ii). *A*'s mistake would negate the required knowledge, and under § 2.04(1)(a) would provide a defense. There can be no argument that § 213.6(1) applies to § 2.06, since § 213.6(1) is expressly limited to Article 213 and the mens rea for complicity under § 2.06 comes from § 2.06, not from the definition of the substantive offenses.

This result seems wrong: can you think of a reason to defend it? But it is hard, if not impossible, to construe the Model Code to come out the other way. The fact that *A* is a female is, of course, irrelevant. See § 2.06(5).

8. *False.*   The "innocent agent" case dealt with by § 2.06(2)(a) is the narrow situation where one person coerces or dupes another to commit an offense. Assuming that *A* is not liable under § 2.06(3), as is established by the previous question (whether or not *P* is guilty), it would undermine the carefully worked out provisions of § 2.06(3) to hold that *A* can be liable under § 2.06(2)(a). Finding *A* liable under § 2.06(2)(a) would not cure the anomaly revealed by the previous question, moreover, since § 2.06(2)(a) is only available when *P* is innocent of the crime. Where *P* was guilty (as in the previous question), it would be hard to say that *P* was an "innocent or irresponsible person" within the meaning of § 2.06(2)(a). Section § 2.06(2)(a) is not designed to deal with *all* cases where the principal is innocent, moreover. Cases where the accessory satisfies the mens rea for accomplice liability and where the principal is not guilty for one reason or another are fully and adequately dealt with by § 2.06(3) and § 5.01(3). Since this is so, it seems pretty clear that § 2.06(2)(a) should *not* be available for cases where the mens rea for accomplice liability is *not* satisfied. The proper interpretation of § 2.06(2)(a) is to limit it to cases where *A* knows that *P* is innocent and uses *P* to commit the offense.

9. *P* could be convicted of attempting to violate § 223.2(1). Section 5.01(1)(a) is applicable, and denies to *P* any "impossibility" defense. Since stealing property worth $25 is a petty misdemeanor under § 223.1(2)(b), the attempt would be graded by § 5.05(1) at the same level as the completed offense. Hence, under § 6.08, the maximum sentence is 30 days (assuming the "extended term" provisions of §§ 6.09 and 7.04 are inapplicable).

A has the mens rea for accomplice liability: a purpose to promote *P*'s conduct and a belief that the property belonged to another. *A* has the actus reus for accomplice liability: *A* "helped" *P* commit the offense. But since the conduct actually committed by *P* was no more than an attempt, then *A* is therefore also guilty of an attempt to violate § 223.2(1). *A* is therefore subject to the same 30 day maximum (again assuming that the extended term provisions are not applicable; if they were applicable to *A* but not *P*, *A* could of course be sentenced to a longer term than *P*).

10. This is a hard question. First, to set aside some underbrush:

> *D1* cannot be guilty of any offense relating to § 220.1(1)(a) unless a yacht is a "building or occupied structure." For a discussion of this question, see the answer to the first issue in Question 12, page 450.

> If a yacht *is* a building or occupied structure, then *D1* has the mens rea for being an accomplice to a violation of § 220.1(1)(a)—*D1* had a purpose that *D2* start a fire and a purpose that a "building or occupied structure" of another be destroyed. *D1* also committed a sufficient actus reus for accomplice liability by getting the gas and giving it to *D2*. But since *D2* did not commit the offense, did not attempt to commit it, did not engage in the actus reus of the offense, and did not engage in the actus reus of an attempt to commit it, *D1* cannot be guilty as an accomplice under § 2.06. Under § 5.01(3), however, *D1* would be guilty of an attempt to violate § 220.1(1)(a)—to paraphrase that provision, *D1* engaged in conduct designed to aid *D2* to commit a crime which would establish *D1*'s complicity under § 2.06 if the crime were committed, and *D2* neither committed nor attempted the crime.

> On the other hand, if a yacht is *not* a building or occupied structure, then *D1* is not guilty of any offense related to § 220.1(1)(a). *D1* would in this instance lack the necessary mens rea—*D1* would not have intended to promote or facilitate any conduct that violates § 220.1(1)(a), and hence *D1* could not be an accessory to any offense involving that section.

Now for the hard part: what if a yacht is not a building or occupied structure? Can *D1* be guilty of an offense related to § 220.1(2)(a)? Here again, note that any liability of *D1* would have to arise under § 5.01(3). *D2* did not engage in enough conduct to render *D1* liable under § 2.06. The analysis of *D1*'s liability under § 5.01(3) is different, moreover, depending on whether the words "places another person in danger of death or bodily injury" in § 220.1(2)(a) are classified as conduct, result, or circumstance elements:

(1) *Conduct.* Assume first that they are all a conduct element. And recall that the accessory must have a mens rea of purpose with respect to conduct elements of the object offense to be liable under § 2.06. Since *D1* was only reckless as to the existence of these elements, *D1* does not have the mens rea for accomplice liability. Thus, *D1*'s complicity under § 2.06 could not have been established had *D2* committed the offense, and *D1* therefore would not be guilty under § 5.01(3) of any offense relating to § 220.1(2)(a).

(2) *Result.* Now assume that they are all a result element. Logic would tell you that *D1* should not be liable. Recall that if the principal completes an offense containing a result element, the mens rea for the accessory is the same for

result elements as it is for the completed offense. But if the principal does not cause a required result, the mens rea for the accessory as to that element would be purpose. Here, since *D2* did not actually cause the result, *D1* cannot be an accomplice to any crime containing that result element unless a purpose to cause the result is shown.

But there is a problem with this reasoning, namely the language of the statute. Since *D2* did not commit the offense, did not engage in the actus reus of the offense, did not commit an attempt, and did not engage in an actus reus sufficient for an attempt, *D1* cannot be an accomplice under § 2.06. Any liability of *D1* would be governed by § 5.01(3). And that statute seems to say that *D1* is guilty: literally, *D1* "engage[d] in conduct designed to aid another to commit a crime which would establish his complicity under Section 2.06 if the crime were committed by such other person."

The policy of § 5.01(1), however, is not to convict persons of attempt based on recklessness as to results. If *D2* were not a cop and had attempted to start a fire, *D2* would not be guilty of an attempt under § 5.01(1)(c)—a mens rea of purpose is required for result elements. Since this is so, it is odd that *D1* seems to be liable in a similar situation under another portion of § 5.01.

How should this question be resolved? Plainly, § 5.01(3) should somehow be construed not to impose liability in this situation. Although it takes some real word twisting to do so, it is not too strained to emphasize the word "designed" and hold that § 5.01(3) requires a mens rea of purpose for all elements of the object crime, no matter what mens rea is established by § 2.06.

The soundness of such a limiting construction is reinforced, moreover, by considering what would happen if the facts of the question are changed a bit. Assume that *D2* was not a cop and actually committed the actus reus of an attempt. *D2* is not guilty of attempt under § 5.01(1)(c), since the mens rea for results must be purpose. Would *D1* be guilty as an accomplice to an attempt under § 2.06? The answer is "no" under § 2.06(4). Section 2.06(4) applies the mens rea of result elements of the object offense to accomplice liability only in the case where the result is actually caused by the principal. Section 2.06(4) was drafted this way, presumably, in order to keep § 2.06 consistent with § 5.01. And given this, it would be even more anomalous if § 5.01(3) were interpreted to permit recklessness towards results to suffice for an attempt conviction.

(3) *Circumstance.* Now assume that the elements quoted above are all a circumstance element. And recall that the accessory must have knowledge or belief as to the presence of the circumstance elements of the object offense to be liable under § 2.06. Since *D1* was only reckless, again *D1* is not guilty. A necessary precondition of liability under § 5.01(3)—an actus reus and a mens rea that would be sufficient for liability under § 2.06—is missing.

Note that this result is inconsistent with the policy of the Model Code in relation to attempts. If *D2* were not a cop and had gone far enough to commit an attempt, the required mens rea for *D2* as to circumstance elements would have been the same as for the completed offense, here recklessness. Shouldn't *D1* be held to the same standard of liability? Perhaps yes, but that is not what the Model Code does. Section 5.01(1) provides that the mens rea of the object offense applies for circumstance elements in any attempt. Section 2.06(3) provides that a mens rea of knowledge applies to the accomplice, even if the accomplice is charged with an attempt. How, then, should § 5.01(3) be interpreted? Either way the inconsistency cannot be entirely removed, and perhaps it is better in this case to take the language of the statute literally and require whatever is sufficient under § 2.06, here knowledge.

Of course the whole analysis of this issue is complicated by the fact that no one knows which category—conduct, results, or circumstances—is the right one for the elements under discussion. And it is possible that some of them fit in one category and others into another, which would change the analysis accordingly. So is *D2* guilty? Who knows, but lawyers sure can talk a long time about it. And this problem provides a nice analytical exercise to test your powers to undertake a close, technical parsing of a statute while keeping in mind the policies at stake—precisely the kind of reasoning required for many difficult legal tasks.

PART SEVEN: INCHOATE CRIMES

XII.   The Common Law

[Answers to Questions on pages 326–27]

1. *False.*   Withdrawal is not a defense to conspiracy. Withdrawal is relevant only to the duration of a conspiracy.

2. *False.*   A conviction for either offense is possible, but not both.

3. *True.*   A conviction for both the conspiracy and commission of the object offense is permissible under the common law. Where the object offense is only attempted, a conviction for the attempt, as well as the conspiracy, is permitted.

4. *False.*   Some courts would call this an "attempt to attempt" and preclude a conviction, but since an assault with intent to rape is an inchoate offense that comes very close to consummation, there is no reason in principle why one should not be convicted of an attempt to commit that offense. The ultimate question is whether sufficient actus reus and mens rea elements are proved to satisfy appropriate minimum conditions for criminal liability.

5. *False.*   "Primary" intent is a fictional, imputed intent. It is the intent to do what the defendant actually did. "Secondary" intent refers to what the defendant thought was being done. But thinking about the impossibility

issue in these terms doesn't get you very far.

6. *False.* Many jurisdictions punish solicitation only when its object is certain named offenses.

7. *True.* The trend today is towards limiting the unlawful objectives of a conspiracy to crimes, but there are still a number of laws on the books that punish agreements to achieve other "unlawful" objectives.

8. *False.* It is certainly possible for those at the end of each spoke to form a "rim" on the "wheel" by agreeing with each other to commit one or more crimes. They could all agree to contribute to a fund for paying protection money to the police, for example.

9. *True.* Conspiracy at common law requires a bilateral agreement between two competent parties. It takes two to tango.

10. *False.* Wharton's Rule precludes conviction for a conspiracy where the object of the agreement is a crime that itself requires concerted action. No rule states what the question says, and in fact it *is* possible for one who cannot be convicted of a substantive offense to be convicted of a conspiracy to commit it, as where, if *A* and *B* are both male, *A* agrees to help *B* rape *A*'s wife in a jurisdiction where a man cannot rape his own wife.

11. Abandonment is not a defense to attempt, conspiracy, or solicitation at common law. Its only significance is as a measure of the duration of a conspiracy. Conspiracy is a continuing offense that begins with the concurrence of its elements and ends with one of several events, one of which is an abandonment of the enterprise.

12. Yes, the trial judge was right. The evidence was not relevant to determine the victim's actual age, and since *A* was convicted, obviously the prosecutor was able to establish the actual age—part of the actus reus of the offense—at under 15. The only relevance of the evidence would have been as to what *A* *thought* the victim's age to be. Since the offense carries strict liability on the age element, what the defendant thought was irrelevant. Thus the evidence should have been excluded as "immaterial and irrelevant."

Of what inchoate offenses can *A* and *B* now be convicted? None. Perjury requires that the lie be "material." Since the lies *B* told were not material, *B* did not commit perjury. *A* thus solicited *B* to do something that was not a crime, and conspired with *B* to do something that was not a crime. This is a case of "true legal impossibility," and *A* is therefore guilty of neither solicitation nor conspiracy. *B* of course is not guilty of conspiracy for the same reason. *B* might be charged with attempted perjury, but that offense was not committed either. *B*'s mens rea was an intent to tell lies about the victim's age. Since the criminal law characterizes those lies as immaterial, *B* does not have the mens rea for any crime, whatever *B* thinks the criminal law says. *B* thus has a defense of "true legal impossibility" to a charge of attempt.

13. Obviously the offense of statutory rape has not occurred, since the victim was 17 and an actus reus element is missing. The prosecutor's only chance, therefore, is a charge of attempted statutory rape. This is permissible on an indictment for statutory rape, since it is a lesser included offense. The prosecutor should therefore seek an instruction on attempted statutory rape.

The case presents an issue of "legal" or "factual" impossibility. It could be either. It is "legal" impossibility because the act as completed was not a crime. It is "factual" impossibility because the crime could not be completed because of a physical characteristic—the victim's actual age—which was unknown to the defendant. The defendant's "primary" intent was to have sexual intercourse with a 17-year-old, and that's not statutory rape. The defendant's "secondary" intent was to have sexual intercourse with a 14-year-old. That is statutory rape. And thus far, analysis of the question has proceeded nowhere.

The first question in a proper analysis is whether the defendant had the mens rea for a crime, and the answer is that the defendant did: an intent to have intercourse with a 14-year-old. The second question is whether the actus reus of attempted statutory rape occurred. This question is harder. It depends, first, on what approach one takes to the actus reus for attempt. And, second, it depends on a careful analysis of why one requires an actus reus in the criminal law, and whether those values are undermined by convicting this defendant. This question therefore presents an opportunity to reason through these matters, and prepare an essay such as might be required on an examination. You might want to show it to a fellow student for criticism and debate. There is no "right" answer as an analytical matter, but only policies that should be exposed and weighed.

14. The *Pinkerton* rule imposes liability on a conspirator for crimes committed by a co-conspirator in furtherance of the conspiracy that were "reasonably foreseeable." The argument that it is unsound is that it imposes liability for negligence in a situation where the liability of the actual perpetrator of the offense may require a higher degree of culpability. It thus discriminates among the members of the conspiracy in the criteria for imposing liability. The argument for the rule would necessarily be deterrence and social control. Conspiracies, particularly those which portend violence, can be dangerous. A rule that holds all members of a conspiracy liable for violence committed to carry out its objectives maximizes the potential deterrent and social control functions of the law. The limit to offenses that are "reasonably foreseeable" builds a sufficient minimum condition of fairness into the law, so the argument would go, to justify its harsh implications. You pay your money and you take your choice.

XIII.   The Model Penal Code

[Answers to Questions on pages 354–55]

1. *False.*   Solicitation and conspiracy are crimes under §§ 5.02 and 5.03, respectively, only if their object is a crime. A violation under the Model Penal Code is not a crime. See § 1.04(5).

2. ***False.*** Strong corroboration is required under § 5.01(1)(c), but is not required if the basis for conviction is either § 5.01(1)(a) or § 5.01(1)(b)—although arguably it should be.

3. ***True.*** The requirements for abandonment to constitute a defense are rigorous, but the sections defining attempt, conspiracy, and solicitation each permit abandonment as a defense under prescribed conditions. The common law did not recognize an abandonment defense.

4. ***True.*** See § 5.05(1).

5. ***False.*** See § 1.07(1). The defendant may be *prosecuted* for both offenses, but under § 1.07(1)(b) cannot be *convicted* for both. Under the common law, the defendant could be prosecuted and convicted for both offenses.

6. ***False.*** Conspiracy under the Model Penal Code requires only a "unilateral" agreement, that is, an agreement which the defendant *thinks* is being made with another person. The Code explicitly provides, moreover, that a defense of immaturity available to one conspirator is not a defense for another. See § 5.04(1)(b).

7. ***False.*** Only one conspiracy exists if multiple agreements are made as part of the same "continuous conspiratorial relationship." See § 5.03(3).

8. ***True.*** Since the conspiracy still has unrealized criminal objectives, a separate conviction of conspiracy can be added to conviction for the five completed offenses. It would not matter (on the issue of multiple convictions) whether the separate conspiracy charge was stated as a conspiracy to commit the sixth robbery alone or as a conspiracy to commit six robberies. Its grading, however, would be judged by the penalty authorized for the sixth robbery.

9. ***True.*** The element "night" in § 221.1(2) is a circumstance element. Culpability is required for grading elements under § 2.02(1) and the definitions of "element" and "material element" in § 1.13. See pages 116–17. The culpability required for conspiracy under the Model Penal Code for circumstance elements of the object offense is knowledge, belief, or hope that the circumstances will exist when the offense is committed. Indifference as to whether they exist is not enough. The offense must be planned to occur at night.

10. ***True.*** *A*'s conduct does not constitute an abandonment under § 5.03(6), since *A* did not thwart the success of the conspiracy. There would also be no defense even if *A* begged the others not to go forward so long as they did anyway. *A* could also be convicted for the bank robbery (see page 348), but not for both the conspiracy and the bank robbery. See page 350.

11. ***False.*** *A*'s withdrawal *is* effective as a measure of the duration of the conspiracy for purposes of starting the running of the statute of limitations. See

§ 5.03(7)(c). Thus the statute started for *A* two days before it did for the others.

12. There are two issues. The first concerns *D's* potential liability under § 220.1(1)(a) and is whether the term "building or occupied structure" includes a 50-foot yacht. It is doubtful that a yacht is a "building." The term "occupied structure" is defined in § 220.1(4) to include "any structure, vehicle or place adapted for overnight accommodation of persons." A 50-foot yacht is surely adapted for overnight accommodation of persons, yet it does not sound like a "structure, vehicle, or place." This is a tough question of statutory interpretation pitting the juisdem generis principle (construe terms in a statute consistently with surrounding words) against the apparent purpose of the statute (to protect persons in sleeping places). A thorough analysis would consider § 1.02(3). If the statute does include a yacht, then *D* is guilty of a felony of the second degree. All of the remaining elements of an attempt to violate § 220.1(1)(a) are then plainly present. Clearly there can be no argument about whether *D* engaged in a substantial step that strongly corroborated the intent to burn the yacht. Spreading gasoline on someone else's yacht at night is hardly "innocent" behavior, objectively viewed. And an attempt to commit a felony of the second degree is a felony of the second degree. § 5.05(1).

Assume now, however, that *D* cannot be convicted of an attempt to violate § 220.1(1)(a) because a "yacht" is not a "building or occupied structure." Does that foreclose conviction? Not necessarily, for there is still a chance of a conviction for attempting to violate § 220.1(2)(a). A fire on a yacht that recklessly places other people in danger of death or bodily injury is a violation of that provision. Is an attempt to set a fire on a yacht, with reckless indifference to whether other people are on board, an attempt to violate this provision? The answer turns on what kind of element "places another person in danger of death or bodily injury" is construed to be. If it is a circumstance element, then the same culpability (recklessness) as is required for the object offense will suffice for the attempt. *D* is clearly reckless here, and would be guilty of a felony of the third degree if convicted under this theory. But it seems likely that the quoted phrase will be construed to state a result or a conduct element, in which case the defendant must have a purpose to cause that result or engage in that conduct in order to be guilty of an attempt. Here, *D* does not appear to have a purpose to harm the others.

13. *D1's* liability would turn on whether a yacht is an "occupied structure" as that term is used in § 220.1. If it is, *D1* is guilty of a conspiracy to violate § 220.1(1)(a), which would be graded as a felony of the second degree. It does not matter that *D2* feigned agreement; unilateral agreements suffice under the Model Penal Code. Nor does it matter that no overt act was committed, since an overt act is not required for a conspiracy to commit a felony of the second degree. See § 5.03(5). If a yacht is not an "occupied structure," then *D1* is not guilty of conspiracy. There can be no conviction under § 220.1(2)(a), since recklessness towards elements of the object offense cannot suffice for conspiracy no matter how those elements are classified and since no overt act was committed and an overt act is required for a conspiracy

to commit a felony of the third degree. See § 5.03(5).

As to whether the Model Penal Code provides the right answer in a case like this, a number of questions are raised and your response could go off in a number of quite legitimate directions. The most important are: When should an overt act be required? Is it tolerable to permit conviction of a serious crime (a second degree felony) for the mere act of agreeing in a context where one party to the agreement is feigning acquiescence? How do we know that *D1* was serious? Do we run an unacceptable risk of convicting innocent persons if we allow the evidence available here to suffice? A "substantial step strongly corroborative of intent" is required for attempt. Should that requirement apply here too? Should more "conduct" by *D1* be required before conviction of such a serious crime? There are other issues too. One is what the mens rea for conspiracy ought to be. An argument could be made that the mens rea for result (or circumstance elements) of the object offense should be sufficient for the conspiracy too. Here, for example, *D1* had a purpose to engage in behavior that created a risk of danger to other people, and was prepared to take the risk that others would be seriously hurt. Assuming sufficient conduct so that we are no longer concerned about possible innocence, why shouldn't this proof be sufficient to convict for conspiracy to violate § 220.1(2)(a)? That is not an easy question to answer, though it may be fun to speculate about.

14. Here is another opportunity to prepare an essay and ask others to evaluate it for you. Your answer should address at least three issues:

(1) "True legal impossibility" is a defense, that is, a defendant is not guilty of attempt for trying to do something believed to be a crime that is not actually a crime. This result is unanimously followed in this country, and has always been. One reason for it is that it would be hard to classify the offense for sentencing purposes if a contrary result were provided. Another is that it seems to follow from the rule of law: the legislature decides what conduct is punishable as a crime, not the citizen. On the other hand, it is arguable that a person who exhibits a willingness to break the law by doing something thought to be a crime is "dangerous" in a sense that is properly punishable.

(2) No distinction is made between "legal" and "factual" impossibility, and no defense is provided in cases where the actual facts differ from the facts as the defendant believes them to be. One reason one might give an impossibility defense is a fear that too much reliance will be placed on what the defendant thinks and not enough on what was done—that, in other words, not enough conduct will be required to corroborate inferences of intent and resolution drawn about the defendant, that the conviction will be based on thoughts alone rather than conduct. In cases prosecuted under § 5.01(1)(c), this should not be a problem, since the "substantial step" required by that provision requires strong corroboration of intent. But cases prosecuted under §§ 5.01(1)(a) and 5.01(1)(b) do not contain a similar requirement, and might be thought to run the feared risk.

(3) The Model Penal Code also contains supplementary provisions that are desirable if an impossibility defense is to be rejected. If defendants are going to be measured by the facts as they were believed to be, some account must be taken of cases where the defendant is just a harmless nut. The Model Code does this in §§ 5.05(2) and 2.12. And some have expressed concern that the impossibility defense helps to protect against overreaching by the police. The separate entrapment defense provided in § 2.13 is designed to deal with this problem.

PART EIGHT: CRIMINAL HOMICIDE

XIV. The Common Law

[Answers to Questions on pages 372–73]

1. ***False.*** The common law rule was that the child must have been born and capable of living apart from the mother. Some cases have extended this to a healthy child in the process of being born, most notably *Chavez* in California (see page 360), but the common law did not so extend the doctrine.

2. ***False.*** It might mean this, and then again it might not. In Pennsylvania, for example, it means simply an intent to kill. See page 363. The statement is therefore false.

3. ***False.*** Typically, second degree murder will consist of "all other murder." Thus, *any* felony (other than those in the first degree list) will suffice for second degree murder, unless the doctrine is constrained by some limitations. Many States have adopted this limitation for second degree murder. See, e.g., People v. Satchell, 6 Cal.3d 28, 98 Cal.Rptr. 33, 489 P.2d 1361 (1971).

4. ***False.*** The defendant would also have to show that the provocation was "legally adequate," and that the "cooling time" requirements were met.

5. ***True.*** See page 371.

6. For openers, it is clear from the statement of facts that *A* intended to kill *C* and the other person. Thus, malice aforethought is established and the jury should be told that "intent to kill" is sufficient for this purpose. The next question is whether *A* can establish some mitigation or defense. There clearly is no available defense on these facts. The only possibility is a mitigation to voluntary manslaughter on grounds of provocation. Witnessing one's spouse in the act of adultery is generally held to be "legally adequate," so the case in this respect will turn on whether *A* was in fact in the "heat of passion" (it appears that *C* and *D* were, and possibly that *A* was too) and whether it was "reasonable" or understandable for *A* to react by shooting the two of them. These are both jury issues, and may depend on the

availability of more evidence than is revealed by the facts stated in the question. For example, the fact that *A* was armed and was always checking up on *B* suggests that perhaps *A* planned to shoot anyone found with *B*. If that was indeed the case, then *A* should be guilty of murder since *A* planned the shooting and did not act in the "heat of passion." If these issues are resolved in *A's* favor, there appears to be no "cooling time" issue since *A's* reaction was immediate.

Another problem is how to treat *A's* mistake. The typical common law answer is that *A* will be considered on the facts as they were believed to be if *A's* belief was reasonable. Whether it was is a jury question, and requires more facts about how dark it was, why *A* thought *B* was in the room, how closely *B* looked like *D*, etc.

How *should* this situation be treated? Here is an opportunity to express what you think of the ordinary provocation rules, and perhaps to compare notes with a colleague. On the mistake issue, there are three options: analyze provocation on the basis of the facts as the defendant believed them to be; analyze it on the basis of the facts as the defendant *reasonably* believed them to be; and analyze it on the facts as they actually were. Clearly *A* loses on the last criterion, but that imposes strict liability and may be thought inappropriate for the same reasons that strict liability is usually criticized. You may wish to reconsider your choice between the first and second alternatives after looking at the Model Penal Code on this point. See pages 378–79.

7. Your essay can be real short. There's nothing wrong with the statement.

8. The argument in favor of the felony murder theory in general and its application to convict *A* here is deterrence. And it is minimally fair to convict *A* in this situation, one could add, because the events were reasonably foreseeable. This is not strict liability, since the defendant was culpable as to the armed robbery and at least negligent as to the death. This compromise between social control and blameworthiness, one could conclude, strikes exactly the right balance. And one might add that prosecutors also love the felony murder theory because it saves them work: they don't have to prove a culpability ingredient they otherwise would have to prove.

The argument against the felony murder theory and its application to convict *A* here is that it is unprincipled to treat one as a murderer without requiring proof of the culpability normally required for that offense. It may be that *A* is sufficiently culpable on these facts, but if so the prosecutor should be required to prove it. It is unsound, and a clear violation of important principles of individual liberty, to create doctrines that get the right folks most of the time but not all of the time. The felony murder rule is a perfect example: most armed robbers are probably sufficiently culpable to justify a murder conviction if a death occurs, particularly if, as here, they initiated a gun battle. But the doctrine is broad enough to get persons who are not sufficiently culpable, and they should not be sacrificed in the name of deterrence.

There's a lot more that could be said on both sides of this debate, but this is the general idea. It would be good practice for you to try your hand at it. This situation is a favorite on exams.

XV. The Model Penal Code

[Answers to Questions on pages 381–82]

1. **True.**   See § 210.0(1). This is the common law position.

2. **False.**   It does not punish felony murder as such, and there are plenty of felony murder cases at common law that would not be murder under § 210.2(1). It does, however, cover most of the rest of the cases that would come under "malice aforethought." "Most" is probably the right word because it is possible (but unlikely) that one could intend serious bodily injury or know that such a result is practically certain without satisfying the standard of § 210.2(1)(b).

3. **False.**   It neither rejects it nor adopts it. The word "situation" in the second sentence of § 210.3(1)(b) is deliberately ambiguous, leaving it to the courts to decide by interpretation how subjective the standard against which the defendant is to be measured should be. The defendant's mental and emotional makeup, particularly if caused by mental illness, could well be taken into account if a court were so disposed.

4. **True.**   See §§ 210.6(1)(e), 210.6(4)(b), and 210.6(4)(g).

5. The defendant would be judged on the facts as the defendant believed them to be. See the second sentence of § 210.3(1)(b).

6. Here's another favorite type of exam question. The five major differences are listed beginning on page 378. A good way to organize an answer to this question would be to recite these five differences, and explain as you go along why one might or might not favor the Model Code resolution on each. Since there are so many directions an answer could take, this is another occasion where preparing an essay and sharing it with a colleague or study group might be helpful.

Keep in mind as you think about the reasons for taking one approach or the other that the defendant is still being convicted of a serious offense. The question is whether the defendant should be treated like one who intentionally killed out of greed, spite, or for money, or whether the defendant should be placed in a different moral category—though still severely punished—because of an understandable emotional reaction to an unusual situation. From this perspective, one might well reject the rigidity of the common law in favor of the far more subjective approach of the Model Penal Code. On the other hand, the more subjectivity that is built into the law, the more opportunity for arbitrary, and perhaps discriminatory, application. One could thus favor the common law on the ground that it is likely to produce more uniform results. The tension between objective standards likely to produce uniform answers and subjective flexibility likely to produce more individualized justice is recurrent in the criminal law. It is not always obvious which is better.

PRACTICE EXAMINATION QUESTIONS

Three practice examination questions are reproduced below. These are questions I have actually used on prior examinations. In each case a suggested time is given within which you should try to write an answer. After you have done so, you may want to read Appendix C, which suggests some of the things you should have talked about.

QUESTION I
(Suggested time: 30 minutes)

This question is based on State v. Goodenow, 65 Me. 30 (1876). The situation is described in the first few sentences of the court's opinion:

> "The respondents are jointly indicted for adultery, they having cohabited as husband and wife while the female respondent was lawfully married to another man who is still alive. The only question found in the exceptions, is, whether the evidence offered and rejected should have been received. This was, that the lawful husband had married again, and that the justice of the peace who united the respondents in matrimony advised them that, on that account, they had the right to intermarry, and that they believed the statement to be true, and acted upon it in good faith."

457

The mistake made by the respondents was thus that they thought, erroneously according to Maine law, that the female-respondent's first marriage had been dissolved by her first husband's bigamous marriage to another.

Assume that the same facts arose today in Pennsylvania and that the two defendants were charged with bigamy (instead of adultery as in the original case). The Pennsylvania bigamy statute provides:

§ 4301. *Bigamy*

(a) Bigamy.—A married person is guilty of bigamy, a misdemeanor of the second degree, if he contracts or purports to contract another marriage, unless at the time of the subsequent marriage:

(1) the actor believes that the prior spouse is dead;

(2) the actor and the prior spouse have been living apart for two consecutive years throughout which the prior spouse was not known by the actor to be alive; or

(3) a court has entered a judgment purporting to terminate or annul any prior disqualifying marriage, and the actor does not know that judgment to be invalid.

(b) Other party to bigamous marriage.—A person is guilty of bigamy if he contracts or purports to contract marriage with another person knowing that the other is thereby committing bigamy.

Assume that the general provisions of the Pennsylvania statutes are in all relevant respects identical to Part I of the Model Penal Code. Would you expect a prosecution against *either* respondent in the *Goodenow* case to be successful under the Pennsylvania bigamy statute? Explain your answer carefully.

QUESTION II
(Suggested time: 60 minutes)

Hunting season in the relevant jurisdiction extends from October 1 to November 30. It is a misdemeanor to hunt at any other time.

A went hunting on September 29. Just after A got out of the car and started off into the woods, A was stopped by the game warden. The warden said: "Hey there, did you know that hunting season does not begin until October 1?" A responded: "Yes I know, but why do you ask?" The warden then said: "Don't you know what day it is today?" A responded: "Today is October 2; I always go hunting on the second day of the season." The warden then informed A of the mistake—it was actually September 29, remember—and instituted a prosecution for an attempt to hunt out of season. The court acquitted A, however, after the mistake was explained.

B went hunting on October 2 and made a kill. In casual conversation with the game warden, however, *B* let it slip that "I have a thing about hunting on September 29. I almost didn't make it today." When confronted by the warden with the fact that hunting season didn't begin until October 1, *B* responded: "Well, I guess you've got me. All I wanted to do was get a head start on the others. Does it really matter that I started a day or two early?" The warden answered that it did, and the court agreed when it convicted *B* of attempting to hunt out of season.

C also went hunting on October 2, and also made a kill. In casual conversation with the game warden, however, *C* let it slip that it was a good thing the hunting season ran from October 15 to November 30, as it had the previous year. The warden then asked: "But why, then, did you go hunting today?" *C* responded, coincidentally, in exactly the same language as *B*: "Well, I guess you've got me. All I wanted to do was get a head start on the others. Does it really matter that I started a day or so early?" Again the warden answered that it did, but this time the court disagreed and acquitted *C* of the charge of attempting to hunt out of season.

Prepare an analysis of these three situations in which you discuss whether you are surprised by the results the courts reached in each case and whether they seem consistent. How *should* the three cases have been decided? Explain your answer carefully.

QUESTION III
(Suggested time: 90 minutes)

Chevy Slyme got into a fist fight with Zephaniah Scadder outside a bar. After the fight ended, Zephaniah was handed a shotgun by a friend. Zephaniah threatened Chevy with the gun, and warned him never to return. Chevy vowed that he would, and with proper reinforcements next time.

Chevy went home, changed clothes, obtained a pistol, gave it to his good friend Montague Tigg to bring along just in case it was needed, and returned with Montague and several other friends to the scene of the fight. Zephaniah immediately jumped on Chevy as soon as he entered the bar. A furious fight then ensued, joined quickly by friends of both Chevy and Zephaniah. At least one person was stabbed.

At a crucial point in the fight, Chevy and Zephaniah had been struggling on the floor when Zephaniah managed to escape Chevy's grasp. He immediately ran in the direction of the shotgun with which he had previously threatened Chevy. Seeing this, Chevy ran for Montague, who handed him the pistol. Just as Zephaniah picked up the shotgun and turned around, Chevy fired four shots, one of which disabled Zephaniah (but did not kill him) and three of which went whizzing by Zephaniah and narrowly missed the bartender, Paul Sweedlepipe, who had taken refuge underneath the bar but had taken the precaution of arming himself in case he was threatened by the violence in his bar. When the three shots from Chevy's gun intruded upon his hiding place, Paul raised his pistol, spotted Chevy (gun in hand), and fired two shots of his own at Chevy. Paul missed Chevy, but his shots struck an innocent bystander, Seth Pecksniff, who, coward that he was, was frozen in fear at the outbreak of the fight and had been unable to get out of the bar. Seth was killed instantly.

Under police questioning, Chevy claimed that he fired because he saw that Zephaniah had gained possession of the shotgun and he feared for the lives of himself and his friends. Questioned separately, Montague stated that he gave Chevy the gun because Chevy asked him for it; he did not know, the police questioner inferred, that Zephaniah had gone for the shotgun. Paul answered in response to police questioning that he did not see Zephaniah at all, but that he thought Chevy was shooting at him and he shot back. He didn't see Seth, and regretted deeply that an innocent victim had been killed by his errant bullets.

A

You are a lawyer working for the prosecutor who must sort out this mess. You are told that your boss wants you to work *only* on the potential liability of Paul, Zephaniah, Chevy, and Montague for some form of criminal homicide. You are in a common-law jurisdiction. Your homicide statutes read as follows:

§ 1. *Murder.* All murder which shall be perpetrated by means of poison, or by lying in wait, or by any other kind of wilful, deliberate and premeditated killing, or which shall be committed in the perpetration or attempt to perpetrate any arson, rape, robbery, or burglary, shall be deemed murder in the first degree and shall be punishable as a Class A felony; and all other kinds of murder shall be deemed murder in the second degree and shall be punishable as a Class B felony.

§ 2. *Voluntary Manslaughter.* Voluntary manslaughter shall be punishable as a Class C felony.

§ 3. *Involuntary Manslaughter.* Involuntary manslaughter shall be punishable as a Class D felony.

The statutes governing attempt, conspiracy, and complicity in your jurisdiction are reproduced below:

§ 4. *Attempt.* An attempt is an act, done with intent to commit a crime, tending but failing to effect its commission. An attempt shall be punishable as an offense of the Class next below that of the offense attempted.

§ 5. *Conspiracy.* A conspiracy is a combination between two or more persons to do or accomplish a criminal or unlawful act, or to do a lawful act by criminal or unlawful means. Conspiracy is a Class E offense.

§ 6. *Accomplices.* All persons concerned in the commission of a crime, whether it be a felony or misdemeanor, and whether they directly commit the act constituting the offense, or aid and abet in its commission, or, not being present, have advised and encouraged its commission, and all persons counseling, advising, or encouraging children under the age of 14 years, lunatics or idiots to commit any crime, or who, by fraud, contrivance, or force, occasion the drunkenness of another for the purpose of causing him to commit any crime, or who by threats, menaces, command, or coercion, compel another to commit any crime, are principals in any crime so committed.

You also learn that Chevy had been convicted of the felony of stealing a bicycle four years before the incident in the bar, and had served a two-year period of probation. It is a felony in your jurisdiction for a previously convicted felon to possess a firearm.

There are no applicable precedents in your jurisdiction to give you any guidance. Prepare an analysis of *all* of the potential homicide charges that might be filed against Paul, Zephaniah, Chevy, and Montague. The prosecutor wants you to be inventive and suggestive, as well as evaluative. Obviously, you must also consider any potential defenses our four villains might assert in order to give a complete answer. And you get an extra bonus if you can identify the author and book from which these characters are taken.

B

You are now in exactly the same position, with the single exception that all of the operative statutes are taken verbatim from the Model Penal Code. Prepare a similar analysis of *all* of the potential homicide charges that could be filed against Paul, Zephaniah, Chevy, and Montague in a Model Penal Code jurisdiction. Be equally inventive, suggestive, and evaluative. And of course consider any potential defenses that might be asserted.

*

ANALYSIS OF PRACTICE EXAMINATION QUESTIONS

QUESTION I

This question is a relatively straightforward application of the basic analytical structure of mens rea under the Model Penal Code. It can easily be dealt with in 30 minutes. Note that it is a common technique on exams to give you a statute (like the Pennsylvania bigamy statute) that you never saw before and ask you to apply to it the general principles you have learned. This question asks for an application of the Model Penal Code culpability structure, but I have asked exactly the same question (you might want to try it this way) using the Pennsylvania statute and common law principles of culpability. You could then even be asked to compare the two and debate which has the better of it, as I have also done. But this question asks simply how the case should be analyzed under the Model Code.

Let's start with the female respondent (W). It is clear that if she is to have a defense to a prosecution under the Pennsylvania statute (as supplemented by Part I of the Model Penal Code), it will have to be based on her mistake as to her right to remarry. She plainly engaged in the forbidden act: she was a "married person" who "contracted another marriage." Moreover, it is clear that none of the three exceptions apply: her former husband is still alive (as far as we know) and no court has entered a judgment that purports to terminate her first marriage.

There are three ways one could characterize her mistake: (a) as a mistake of the criminal law: a mistake going to the meaning of the bigamy statute—a mistake about what kind of behavior was meant to be punished as bigamy; (b) a mistake of non-criminal law: a mistake of family law governing whether she remained married to her first husband—a legal error about her marital status; or (c) a mistake of fact: a mistake as to whether she was married—a factual error about her marital status. Under the Model Penal Code mens rea analysis, the second and third type of mistake is relevant only if it negates a required mental element of the offense (§ 2.04(1)). Moreover, it makes no difference whether the mistake is characterized as one of non-criminal law or one of fact. (This is the meaning of the "fact or law" language of § 2.04(1).) Thus the issue (if the mistake is of the second or third type) is what mens rea, if any, is required by the Pennsylvania statute.

Under § 2.02(3), recklessness is the mens rea term applicable to each actus reus element when no other provision is made. This provision plainly applies to the body of the bigamy definition in § 4301(a). The fact that other culpability terms are specified in the exceptions would not trigger § 2.02(4) and make higher culpability standards applicable to the body of the offense. Thus the issue, if the mistake is fitted into the second or third category above, is whether it negated recklessness as to an actus reus element in the body of the definition of bigamy. The relevant element would be "married person" (she thought that she was not a "married person").

The question thus would be whether she consciously ignored a substantial and unjustifiable risk that she was still married to her first husband, and if she did whether doing so was a gross deviation from the standard of conduct a law-abiding person would have observed in the defendant's situation. This could be argued either way, and would clearly be a jury question. Whether you think she was reckless or not doesn't matter. She surely was aware of the risk (she asked the JP what her status was), and it certainly was substantial (the advice was plainly wrong) and probably unjustified (there is no apparent reason why it was particularly important that she get married again; note that the substantiality and unjustifiability of the risk is measured objectively, by the risk as an observer would describe it). Whether it was a gross deviation from a proper standard of care is a point on which reasonable people could disagree.

[Note that it could be argued that the element "married person" carries strict liability. This was the common law tradition for bigamy, and remains the law in many American jurisdictions. The result is unlikely under a Model Penal Code structure, however, because of § 2.02(3) and because strict liability is so rarely imposed by the Model Code. Nonetheless, the logic of the statute could be advanced to support strict liability—the argument would be that the three "good faith" exceptions were meant to be exclusive, and that therefore no other mens rea defenses should be accepted. In a State with a tradition of strict liability, a court might ignore the thrust of the Model Code and find that strict liability governed the crucial element. Of course, if the court did so, W would have no defense of mistake and would be convicted.]

There is, finally, the possibility that the mistake could be placed in the first category described above: that it was a mistake as to the scope or meaning of the criminal law. This seems unlikely. It is not the function of the criminal law to dissolve marriages, and the mistake was as to whether the conduct of the first husband in getting remarried had that effect. If the husband's second marriage dissolved his first one, that effect would be derived from the family law, not the criminal law. It does not seem worthwhile, therefore, to explore in great detail whether a mistake of *criminal* law in this context would be a defense, *unless* one is prepared to show *why* or *how* the mistake can be construed to be one of criminal law. If by some magic it were so construed, there would of course be no defense. See § 2.02(9). The exceptions in § 2.04(3) plainly would not apply: the JP's opinion is clearly not an "official statement" of the law, and it certainly was not contained in a "judicial decision, opinion or judgment" or "an official interpretation of the public officer" charged with enforcement of the *bigamy* offense. Thus it seems clear that if *W*'s mistake is of the criminal law it will not be exculpatory; the issue in this respect is whether it should be so classified, and as argued above it seems clear that it should not be.

Finally, the question asks whether *either* respondent could be convicted, and the male respondent (*H*) must thus be talked about. His case seems easy: § 4301(b) says *H* must "know" that the other person is committing bigamy. On the face of it, *H* thought (because of the JP's advice) that *W* was not married, and that *H* was free to marry her. Hence, *H* did not "know" his marriage to be bigamous. This prosecution, in other words, involves a straightforward application of § 2.04(1): the mistake negates the mens rea of knowledge, and it does not matter whether it is a mistake of fact or of the non-criminal law. Of course, if the mistake is somehow characterized as one of the criminal law, then *H* wouldn't have a defense either.

QUESTION II

A thought the date was October 2, which is within the hunting season. The date was actually Sept. 29. *A* thus was in error as to a circumstance element of the offense, and the question is what mens rea one must have as to such an element when charged with attempt. The answer depends on the jurisdiction, but you should be aware of two possibilities. First, under the common law attempt is a specific intent offense. Translated into these facts, this means an intent to hunt on a date that falls without the hunting season. *A* did not have such an intent, and *A* would thus be acquitted under this approach. Second, one might carry forward the mens rea for the object offense as to circumstance elements, as does the Model Penal Code. The question then would be what mens rea is required for the circumstance element concerning the date in the offense of hunting out of season. If the entire Model Code structure were applied, recklessness would then be required under § 2.02(3). Or one might find in a given jurisdiction that negligence or strict liability were applied to this element. In any event, the relevance of *A*'s mistake is to negate mens rea, and since *A* was acquitted, it appears that the court required at least some level of mens rea towards the date on which the hunting occurred.

Now as to *B*. Unlike *A*, *B* had the mens rea for attempt under any approach to that question: *B* intended to hunt on September 29, and that date falls outside the hunting season. What *B* actually did, however, was lawful, since *B* in fact hunted on October

2. The question, therefore, is whether B should be allowed some kind of "impossibility" defense. Here again, you should be aware of two approaches. Under the Model Penal Code, B would be treated on the facts as they were thought to be, and B would be guilty. See § 5.01(1)(a). Under the common law, B's liability would depend on whether the mistake is classified as one of "legal" or "factual" impossibility. It could be said that the completed act was not criminal and the case therefore presents a "legal" impossibility, which gets B acquitted. Or it could be said that the crime was impossible because of some physical or factual condition unknown to the defendant, a "factual" impossibility and no defense. Who knows which it is. But the court convicted B, and so it must either have followed the Model Code approach or have classified the situation as presenting a "factual" impossibility.

Now C. C did *not* have the mens rea for any crime. C intended to hunt on October 2. That is an intent to do something that is perfectly lawful, given the dates of the hunting season. C *thought* that the hunting season started later, and thus *thought* that a crime was being committed. But surely C cannot be convicted of a crime that C made up. This is a case of "true legal impossibility," and C gets acquitted under anybody's approach.

Should you be surprised at the way the cases came out? No. All three cases could come out the way they did if the Model Penal Code applied. And they all could come out the way they did under a common law analysis too.

Are the results consistent? Sure. The first involves the policy that should govern a mistake of fact as to the existence of an element of an offense, the second whether a sufficient actus reus occurred to justify conviction for an attempt, and the third whether those who make up a crime and then try to commit it should be convicted. Different policies ought to govern each of these three situations, and it is not inconsistent to resolve different problems with different policies.

Yet there is an argument that can be made. In common sense terms, B and C look a lot alike. They both did the same thing (hunt on Oct. 2), and they both intended to hunt out of season. In terms of blameworthiness and social control, they arguably present the same situation and arguably should be treated the same way. Yet the law has never defined "intent" in the way that is meant by saying that they both "intended to hunt out of season." Normally, indeed almost invariably, the relevant mens rea for crime concerns the defendant's attitude toward the conduct, results, and circumstances of behavior. The legal characterization of these elements as or as not a crime is not generally relevant to mens rea. In this sense, the mens rea that B had was an intent to hunt on September 29. The mens rea that C had was an intent to hunt on October 2. By long tradition (and for good reason?), the law focuses on these as the relevant intents. Since B's and C's *relevant* intents are different, there seems no inconsistency in treating them differently.

How should the cases come out? Here you should discuss the various legal doctrines that will govern the outcomes in the three cases. It would be good (not only on this question, but in general as you answer examinations that call for the analysis of policy) to structure your answer in three steps: first, an analytical step to see what the issue is (accomplished above); second, a doctrinal step to see what legal doctrines are generally in use to control the issue (also accomplished above); and third, an evaluative step to see whether the doctrines make any sense (the issue now).

There are, of course, many directions one could take. In *A*'s case, one could debate whether there are any policies that suggest a higher mens rea for circumstance elements of an attempt than for the same elements in the object crime (I don't see what they might be). In *B*'s case, there is a good reason for acquittal: *B*'s conduct was entirely innocuous, objectively viewed—all *B* did was a perfectly lawful act. If *B* is to be convicted it will be without any corroboration of our guesses as to intent. This is dangerous to civil liberties, the argument would go, and the law should be structured (the Model Penal Code notwithstanding—see page) to acquit *B*. As to *C*, one can argue that *C* was just as blameworthy and dangerous (in terms of the conduct this statute is designed to prevent) as if the hunt had occurred on September 29, and that a way should be figured out to convict for that reason. But the principle that one who makes up a crime can be guilty of attempting to commit an analogous crime is one with which, if you think about it for a while, it may be difficult to live.

QUESTION III

A

Paul Sweedlepipe: Paul is the person who fired the fatal shot. Paul fired at Chevy with intent to kill, or so it appears. Since Paul missed Chevy and killed Seth, the common law would "transfer" Paul's intent from Chevy to Seth and Paul would be guilty of murder, probably first degree under the statute but at least second degree, unless a defense can be established. Self defense is of course the obvious candidate. Chevy in fact was not trying to kill Paul, and so Paul's conclusion that he had to fire in self defense was in error. But under the circumstances it is likely that a jury would conclude that Paul's mistake was honest and reasonable. It therefore appears that Paul would be able to assert self defense; all of the other elements of the defense are present. [You could elaborate on this, but probably it is a waste of time; the issue is easy, and normally you are better off struggling with the more difficult questions.] I wouldn't recommend prosecuting Paul unless we can develop more facts that make the mistake look less reasonable (or unless we have some reason to disbelieve that Paul actually shot in self defense).

Chevy Slyme: Chevy fired four shots at Zephaniah, which provoked the fatal response from Paul. It appears that Chevy meant to kill Zephaniah, and his intent can therefore be "transferred" under the common law doctrine to the person who was actually killed. Chevy thus appears to be guilty of first degree murder (or at least second), subject to two problems. The first is causation. Plainly Chevy's conduct was a "cause in fact" of Seth's death. Was it the "proximate" cause? Was Paul's conduct a "dependent" or an "independent" intervening cause of Seth's death? Some courts might hold as a matter of law that Paul's decision to return the fire was an "independent" intervening cause, but since Paul was without fault in so doing (it would appear), it is likely that many courts would not. This is likely to be a jury question, on which we would have a good chance of winning. But secondly, there is the question of whether Chevy has a justification defense, defense of himself and his buddies. Since it seems that Zephaniah was about to open fire on Chevy and his friends—he had threatened to do so before—it would appear that all of the elements of self defense and defense of another are present. The only question might be whether Chevy is regarded as the initial aggressor. But that probably wouldn't matter, since Chevy was unarmed and, as far as the facts reveal, never used deadly force against Zephaniah. Thus, Zephaniah was not privileged to go for a shotgun, and the threat of its use against Chevy was "unlawful." So it looks like we lose prosecuting Chevy for murder.

But there is another possibility. Chevy was a convicted felon, and it is a felony for Chevy to possess a firearm. Can Chevy be convicted of felony murder on the basis that he was committing that felony at the time Seth's death occurred? Certainly not first degree murder, since "possession of a firearm by a felon" is not one of the felonies listed in the statute. But second degree murder is "all other kinds of murder," which literally would include this conduct as felony murder unless there is some limitation that excludes this felony as a trigger for the doctrine. One common limitation is that the felony must be "inherently dangerous." Is this felony "inherently dangerous?" Not in the abstract, but perhaps it is in the factual context—so the case might turn on how one asks the "inherently dangerous" question, and whether, of course, this limitation is held applicable in the jurisdiction in question.

But this is still not the end of the felony murder inquiry. There are at least two other issues. The first is whether Chevy is liable for the death of a bystander caused by a bullet from another bystander's gun. This will depend on whether we are in a "proximate cause" or an "agency" jurisdiction (see page). You should explain how both of these theories work and why one or the other might be adopted in a jurisdiction with no precedents on the question. The second issue concerns self defense: assuming that Chevy's conduct otherwise constitutes felony murder, would Chevy's defense of self defense be relevant to that charge? Who knows. You would receive a lot of credit for having gotten this far in the analysis, and it probably wouldn't matter how you answered this question unless it was actually covered in your course. My guess is that most courts would hold the defense irrelevant. See, e.g., State v. Underwood, 228 Kan.294, 615 P.2d 153 (1980), the facts of which were the inspiration for this question. The issue does not arise unless the court has already decided that the underlying felony is serious enough to trigger the felony murder rule. Once that judgment is made, I think it unlikely that a court would permit a defendant to rely on self defense. Can you imagine a bank robber, for example, being able to claim self defense because a police officer used unnecessary deadly force in trying to stop the robbery?

In any event, we're not through yet. There is also the possibility of an attempted murder charge against Chevy for trying to kill Zephaniah. The elements of that offense seem clearly made out. The outcome would turn on the same self-defense issues raised in connection with charging Chevy for murdering Seth.

Zephaniah Scadder: When Zephaniah jumped on Chevy to start the brawl and later went for a shotgun, he set in motion a chain of events that caused the death of Seth in a "cause in fact" sense. Did he "proximately" cause the death, and could he be guilty of second degree murder on the theory that he was extremely reckless as to the death (remember that second degree murder is "all other kinds of murder" at common law) or manslaughter on the theory that he was reckless or negligent? Perhaps, though there were plenty of intervening causes that could be held "independent." If not, is there any way to link Zephaniah to any liability that can be imposed on Chevy? It seems unlikely that any conspiracy or accomplice theories would work, since they were fighting against each other and not working towards the same criminal objectives.

Montague Tigg: Montague would have to be liable, if at all, on either a conspiracy or accomplice theory. One argument would be that they conspired to commit a violent assault on Zephaniah and that any homicide offense of which Chevy could be convicted was a "reasonably foreseeable result" of that offense. Montague's aid (carrying the gun, giving it to Chevy without knowing that it was for self defense) could also be used to support an accomplice theory. There are several possibilities. One would be an argument that Montague was liable because a reckless or negligent (manslaughter) or extremely reckless (second degree murder) homicide was a "reasonably foreseeable result" of a crime (assault) that Montague helped Chevy commit. Another would be an argument that Montague had the mens rea for second degree murder or manslaughter and that Montague intentionally helped Chevy engage in the actus reus of a criminal homicide (an act that "caused" the death of Seth; this would raise again all of the causation questions discussed above).

[Note that this is a reasonably typical law school examination question: a fact situation that is complicated to unravel and that involves some tough issues and some easy ones. You will do better if you get reasonably quickly to the hard questions and struggle with them—but don't forget to touch the easy bases along the way just to make sure that the reader of your examination knows that you know what you're talking about. The answer given above is more cryptic in some respects than you should undertake. My objective has been only to point out some of the issues on which elaboration should be undertaken. Yours should be to expose the issues that arise from a careful analysis of the situation, to reveal that you understand the legal doctrines usually employed to resolve these issues, and to discuss (since the jurisdiction has no precedents and must choose the "best" of the available doctrines) why one might choose one answer rather than another. Moreover, as I am sure has occurred to you, there are other issues not mentioned above that could also be drawn out. The cast of characters, by the way, is from Martin Chuzzlewit, by Charles Dickens.]

B

I'll be brief on the Model Penal Code part. Basically, what you should do is try all the theories discussed above—or all that you chose to develop—under the Model Code. Thus for Paul you would want to focus on the Model Code elements of self defense, under which he would most likely get off. For Chevy, no felony murder theory could be used. He could be charged with murder (extreme recklessness), manslaughter (recklessness), or negligent homicide for Seth's death. The issues here would be whether the causation standards of § 2.03 were satisfied and whether he could rely on self defense. He could also be charged with attempting to murder Zephaniah, which again raises questions of self defense. Zephaniah could be charged with some form of criminal homicide for Seth's death, again presenting questions of causation. Montague might be liable for murder (extreme recklessness), manslaughter (recklessness), or negligent homicide on the theory that he aided Chevy to engage in conduct that caused Seth's death. It wouldn't do any good to charge a conspiracy, since the question is limited to homicide offenses and it seems clear that the two planned no homicides. Moreover, any liability of Montague for a homicide committed by Chevy would have to be based on Montague's liability as an accomplice—there is no liability for crimes committed by co-conspirators on any other theory under the Model Penal Code.

You should, of course, draw out these issues more than I have done here. On the causation questions, for example, you should show that you know what § 2.03 means and what issues would be presented in its application to Chevy's or Zephaniah's liability. These comments are not designed as "sample answers," but only are intended to point you in the right directions. And a perfectly good answer can be written that raises different issues or that deals with somewhat less than all of the issues discussed above.

APPENDIX D

GLOSSARY

[**Note:** Page references are given throughout the Glossary to places in the text where an elaboration can be found. The Glossary can therefore be used as an Index as well as for definitions of criminal law terms. Abbreviations used in the page references: c/l = common law; MPC = Model Penal Code. In addition to the definitions given here, see generally Bryan A. Garner, Ed., A Handbook of Criminal Law Terms (2000); Black's Law Dictionary (6th ed. 1990).]

A

Abandonment A term used with Inchoate Offenses to indicate that the defendant had a change of heart after the crime was committed. This was not a defense at common law. See pages 311, 318, 324. It can be a defense under the Model Penal Code under certain conditions. See pages 338, 347, 352.

Absolute Liability See Strict Liability.

Accessory A generic term used to refer to a person who is an accomplice.

Accessory After the Fact A person who rendered assistance after a crime was committed and who at common law thereby became liable for its commission. See page 275.

Accessory Before the Fact An accomplice who renders assistance before the crime is committed and is not present at the time of commission. See page 263.

Accomplice A person who assists another to commit a crime and thereby becomes punishable for it. See page 262 (c/l), 284 (MPC).

Act Some conduct by the defendant. An act is a minimal prerequisite for all crimes. See page 74 (c/l), 105 (MPC). It is also constitutionally required. See page 408.

Actus Reus A generic term referring to the conduct, results, and circumstances determined by the definition of an offense to constitute a particular crime. See page 73.

Age of Capacity The age at which one becomes capable of committing a crime. See page 224, (c/l), 254 (MPC).

Aid and Abet A description of the conduct required to make one an accomplice.

Alter Ego Rule The rule that places one in the shoes of the person being attacked when one goes to the aid of another. See page 196.

Assault With Intent An Inchoate Offense that comes closer to its object than a mere attempt. See page 311.

Attempt An Inchoate Offense that punishes a person who is trying to commit a crime. See page 301 (c/l), 331 (MPC).

B

Battered Woman Often refers to an abused woman who seeks to raise the defense of self defense for killing her husband. See page 194.

Beyond a Reasonable Doubt The standard of proof to which the prosecutor is usually held in a criminal case. See page 94. Its constitutional dimensions are considered at page 414.

Bifurcated Trial A division of the criminal trial into two parts. Some States do this with the insanity defense, considering first all issues except insanity and second the insanity defense. See page 206. Most States "bifurcate" the trial on the question of whether to impose the death penalty. See pages 380, 412.

Burden of Persuasion The obligation of the prosecutor or the defendant to persuade the jury of a given fact. The party on whom the burden of persuasion is placed will lose the case on that issue if the burden is not carried. See page 94.

Burden of Production The obligation of the prosecutor or the defendant to produce enough evidence of a given fact to justify submission of the existence of that fact to the jury. The party on whom the burden of production is placed will lose the case on that issue if the burden is not carried. See page 94.

Burden of Proof A term that refers indiscriminately to the burden of production and the burden of persuasion. This term should be avoided or carefully explained for that reason. See page 94.

Burglary See page 397.

But for Cause The threshold determination in the causation inquiry, referring to whether the result would have occurred if the defendant had not acted. Sometimes called "cause in fact." See page 91 (c/l), 128 (MPC).

C

Capital Punishment See Death Penalty.

Carnal Knowledge The common law description of the act requirement for rape. See page 386.

Cause in Fact See But for Cause.

Choice of Evils A justification defense available when a person avoids more harm than is caused by commission of an offense. See page 200 (c/l), 217 (MPC).

Circumstances The term used to refer to the external conditions described by the definition of a crime that must exist in order for the defendant to be guilty of that offense. See page 111.

Circumstantial Evidence Indirect evidence offered to prove a fact, evidence from which the jury is asked to infer that the fact exists. See page 96.

Coercion See Duress.

Cognitive Test A term sometimes used in connection with the insanity defense referring to the ability of the defendant to know certain kinds of things, specifically whether conduct was right or wrong or whether conduct was of a particular character. See page 228 (c/l), 235 (MPC).

Collateral Defense A term I made up to refer to defenses that do not rebut, and hence are collateral to, the elements of a crime which the prosecutor must establish in order to justify submission of a criminal case to the jury. It refers to defenses of justification or excuse. See pages 187, 221.

Constructive A wonderful word used by the common law to mean "let's pretend." An example is "constructive presence" used in connection with a principal in the second degree, where we pretend a person was present at the scene of a crime. See page 263.

Control Test A term sometimes used in connection with the insanity defense referring to the ability of the defendant to control behavior or to exercise will. Also called a "volitional" test. See page 232 (c/l), 237 (MPC).

Common Law Crime A term used in its technical sense to refer to crimes the definition of which was announced by the judiciary rather than the legislature. The term is sometimes used to refer as well to legislatively created crimes which are to be interpreted within the common law tradition. See page 62.

Complicity See Accomplice.

Compulsion See Duress.

Conclusive Presumption See Presumption.

Concurrent Cause A rare situation where an event is caused by two concurrent actions, either one of which would alone have caused the result. Both parties are liable in this situation. See page 91 (c/l), 128 (MPC).

Conditional Purpose A purpose to do something, conditioned on the existence of certain circumstances (as in, I'll steal the jewels if they are there). The Model Penal Code correctly states its relevance as a defense. See § 2.02(6) and page 123.

Condonation It is not a defense if the victim "condones" the offense. See page 200 (c/l), 215 (MPC).

Conduct The term used to refer to the behavior contained in the definition of a crime in which the defendant must engage in order to be guilty of that offense. See page 74.

Consent Sometimes a defense to crime. See page 200 (c/l), 215 (MPC).

Conspiracy An Inchoate Offense that punishes two or more people who agree to commit a crime. In some jurisdictions, an agreement to engage in other unlawful activity can be punished as a criminal conspiracy. See page 311 (c/l), 340 (MPC).

Contributory Negligence Contributory negligence by the victim is not a defense to crime. See page 200 (c/l), 215 (MPC).

Cooling Time A common law term used in connection with Provocation, which reduces murder to manslaughter. It refers to whether the defendant has had an opportunity to "cool down" after having been exposed to a provoking event. See page 370. The Model Penal Code does not use the term.

Corpus Delecti The actus reus of an offense.

Corrupt Motive A mens rea requirement sometimes used by the common law in a conspiracy case, meaning that the defendants had to know that what they agreed to do was a crime. See page 317. The Model Code rejects the concept. See page 346.

Corruptly A common law mens rea term of indeterminate meaning. See page 79.

Criminal Homicide See Homicide.

Criminalization A term used to refer to making given conduct a crime.

Culpability A term used to refer to the basis for holding a defendant at fault for engaging in criminal conduct. Normally "culpability" is used to refer to the mens rea required for a given crime.

D

Dangerous Proximity Test A test used to measure when one has gone beyond preparation and committed an attempt. See page 306.

Deadly Force A term used in connection with justification defenses to place limits on when life may be endangered in defense of self, others, property, etc. It means force used with a purpose to cause, or with knowledge that it will cause, death or serious bodily harm.

Death Penalty Constitutional limits on its imposition, page 411. Procedures for its imposition, page 380.

Decriminalization A term used to refer to making conduct that was a crime no longer a crime.

Defendant The person accused of crime.

Defense of Others A justification defense available when one harms or threatens another in defense of a person other than oneself. See page 195 (c/l), 212 (MPC).

Defense of Property A justification defense available when one harms or threatens another in defense of property. See page 196 (c/l), 212 (MPC).

Definition of the Offense The precise words used to describe what must happen in order for a crime to be committed, found either in a judicial definition or in a specific statute.

Degrees of Crime A term used to refer to similar conduct that is punished to a greater or a lesser extent depending on the existence of one or more factors.

Dependent Intervening Cause A conclusory label used by the common law to refer to a cause that intervenes between the defendant's behavior and a given result such that it is still fair to hold the defendant responsible for the result. See page 92.

Derivative Defense A term I made up to refer to defenses that rebut, and hence are derivative from, the elements of a crime which the prosecutor must establish in order to justify submission of a criminal case to the jury. See page 143.

Deterrence A term used to refer to the effect of the criminal law in discouraging the defendant or others from committing future crimes. The terms "social control" and "prevention" are often used as synonyms. Deterrence is one of the traditional goals of criminal punishment. See also General Deterrence; Special Deterrence; page 52.

District Attorney See Prosecutor.

Diminished Capacity A synonym for Diminished Responsibility.

Diminished Responsibility A term used to refer to the admissibility of evidence of mental disease or defect for purposes other than establishing the insanity defense. See page 165.

Domestic Authority A justification defense available when one harms or threatens a person over whom one has parental or other authority. See page 200 (c/l), 215 (MPC).

Duress A defense available when a person forced the defendant to commit a crime. See page 245 (c/l), 255 (MPC).

***Durham* Test** A test for the insanity defense named after a famous case. See pages 233–34.

E

Element of an Offense A term used by the common law to refer to each component of the actus reus, causation, and the mens rea that must be proved in order to establish that a given offense has occurred. The term is more broadly defined by the Model Penal Code in § 1.13(9) to refer to each component of the actus reus, causation, the mens rea, any grading factors, and the negative of any defense.

Embezzlement See page 394.

Enterprise One of the elements of RICO. See page 399.

Enterprise Liability Criminal liability imposed on a corporation, partnership, unincorporated association, or other artificial "person." See page 279 (c/l), 292 (MPC).

Entrapment An excuse provided in a case of overreaching police behavior that has induced an otherwise innocent person to commit a crime. See page 248 (c/l), 257 (MPC).

Excuse A defense provided because the defendant is not blameworthy for having engaged in conduct that would otherwise be a crime. The traditional excuses are Infancy, Insanity, Involuntary Intoxication, Duress, and Entrapment. See pages 191, 221.

F

Factual Impossibility A common law doctrine according to which certain reasons why an attempt cannot be committed no matter how hard the defendant tries (e.g., attempting to pick an empty pocket) is not a defense. See page 308 (c/l), 335 (MPC). The problem also can arise, but is rare, in conspiracy and solicitation. See pages 317, 323 (c/l), 347, 352, (MPC).

Fair Notice A synonym for Fair Warning.

Fair Warning A term used to refer to the idea that it is unfair to punish a defendant who did not have some basis for suspecting that given conduct would be a crime. Often it is said that the statute defining the offense must be precise enough to give "fair warning" or "fair notice." This statement is largely fictional, since one can be punished for behavior without knowing that it is a crime. What "fair warning" means is probably two things: (1) that a person with a reasonably developed social conscience would know it was wrong to engage in the proscribed behavior; and (2) that a lawyer of reasonable skill could predict from the statute and the decisions interpreting it that proposed behavior would fall within the proscription of the statute.

False Pretenses See page 394.

Felony The most serious classification of offenses (other than treason) at common law. The usual modern demarcation is an offense that carries more than one year in a penitentiary. See, e.g., § 1.04(2) of the Model Penal Code. This line is not invariable, however. Felony convictions usually carry serious collateral consequences, such as inability to vote.

Felony Murder A term used to refer to the doctrine that the defendant is guilty of murder if another person is killed while the defendant is engaged in the commission of a felony. Strict liability is imposed for the death. See 364 (c/l), 377 (MPC).

Fraud See page 397.

Fraudulently A common law mens rea term of indeterminate meaning. See page 79.

G

General Deterrence A term used to refer to the effect of the criminal law, or of a specific conviction and sentence, in discouraging people other than the defendant from committing crimes in the future. General deterrence is one of the traditional goals of punishment. See also Deterrence; Special Deterrence.

General Intent A generic term used by the common law to refer to the state of mind required for the commission of certain crimes. It applies to all common law crimes that do not require a specific intent and that do not impose strict liability. The term nearly always can be translated into some form of recklessness or negligence. See page 78. It is not used by the Model Penal Code.

Grading A term used to refer to where in the scale of severity the punishment for a given crime is placed. Example: The grading of murder is more severe than the grading of assault.

Grand Jury A group of citizens collected for the purpose of deciding whether there is enough evidence to justify filing a formal charge of crime against a given individual. The grand jury also has investigative powers. Indictment or Presentment by a grand jury is required for most federal crimes. The intervention of a grand jury is not required in many States.

Guilty But Mentally Ill A form of verdict in a case where the insanity defense is raised, meaning that the defense is rejected but the jury recommends treatment because the defendant is mentally ill. See page 242.

H

Habeas Corpus A separate civil suit filed by a person in custody against the custodian, the purpose of which is to declare the custody unconstitutional and obtain the release of the person.

Heat of Passion A term used by the common law to refer to the condition of a defendant who can assert Provocation as a basis for mitigating murder to manslaughter. See page 369.

Homicide A killing of one person by another. The term "criminal homicide" refers to all homicides punished by the criminal law. See 360 (c/l), 376 (MPC).

I

Imperfect Justification A common law term used in jurisdictions where a justification defense is lost because the defendant's behavior was unreasonable, but where the defendant's good faith belief in the existence of circumstances that would have justified the offense if true is used as a basis for mitigating a homicide from murder to manslaughter. See pages 194, 370. The concept is not used by the Model Penal Code.

Impossibility A term used in connection with Inchoate Offenses to describe a set of circumstances that make it not possible to commit the offense. It is sometimes a defense, and sometimes it isn't. See pages 307, 317, 323 (c/l), 335, 346, 352 (MPC).

Imputed Intent Sometimes used in connection with common law mens rea. It means we will pretend the defendant has a required intent, whether or not the defendant actually does—we "impute" the intent. Older courts often imposed strict liability in this manner, saying they were requiring mens rea but "imputing" the intent without asking whether the defendant actually had the mens rea.

Incapacitation A term used to refer to preventing the defendant from committing future crimes by imprisonment or some similar physical restraint. Incapacitation is one of the traditional goals of punishment.

Inchoate Crimes Attempt, Solicitation, and Conspiracy. Crimes that punish conduct preparatory to the commission of a crime. See page 301.

Independent Intervening Cause A conclusory label used by the common law to refer to a cause that intervenes between the defendant's behavior and a given result such that it is regarded as unfair to hold the defendant responsible for the result. See page 92.

Indictment A document that contains the specific charges formally accusing the defendant of a crime. The term "indictment" is used only when the formal charge is made by a grand jury at the request of a public prosecutor. See also Grand Jury; Information; Presentment.

Indispensable Element Test A test used to measure when one has gone beyond preparation and committed an attempt. See page 306.

Infancy An excuse for crime turning on the age of the defendant. See page 224 (c/l), 254 (MPC).

Information A formal charge of crime filed by the prosecutor without the intervention of a grand jury. See also Grand Jury.

Infraction A synonym for Violation.

Innocent Agent A person who is duped or coerced into committing a crime, used by the common law to describe a case where a person can be a Principal in the First Degree without committing the actus reus personally. See page 262 (c/l), 284 (MPC).

Insanity An excuse for crime in cases where the defendant was mentally ill at the time of the offense. See page 226 (c/l), 234 (MPC). See page 237 for the federal insanity defense.

Intervening Cause A common law term used to describe a cause that intervenes between the defendant's behavior and a given result. See page 92. See also Dependent Intervening Cause; Independent Intervening Cause.

Intoxication A term used by the criminal law to refer to the introduction of any substances into the body which tend to have an intoxicating effect. Specifically, both alcohol and drugs are included. On when intoxication can be a defense, see pages 163, 244 (c/l), 180, 255 (MPC).

Involuntary Act A defense available when the defendant's conduct does not include a voluntary act. See Voluntary Act.

Involuntary Intoxication Intoxication that is not voluntary, or is the result of an unanticipated or unforeseeable reaction to drink or drugs, or is so prolonged as to result in a settled mental illness. See page 244 (c/l), 255 (MPC). See also Pathological Intoxication; Voluntary Intoxication.

Involuntary Manslaughter A grade of Criminal Homicide at common law, usually consisting of reckless or negligent homicides and those committed while engaging in an unlawful act. See page 371.

Irresistible Impulse A common law test for the insanity defense. See page 231.

J

Justification A defense provided when the defendant has engaged in conduct which the criminal law does not seek to deter or prevent. The traditional justification defenses are Self Defense, Defense of Others, Defense of Property, Use of Force to Make an Arrest, Prevent an Escape, or in Crime Prevention, Use of Force pursuant to Domestic or Public Authority, Consent, and Choice of Evils. See page 187.

K

Knowledge One of the four culpability terms used by the Model Penal Code, meaning actual awareness. See page 110. Also used by the common law to mean the same thing.

L

Larceny See page 392.

Last Proximate Act A test used to measure when one has gone beyond preparation and committed an attempt. See page 305.

Legal Impossibility A common law doctrine according to which certain reasons why an attempt cannot be committed no matter how hard the defendant tries (e.g., attempting to steal one's own umbrella) provide a defense. See page

308 (c/l), page 335 (MPC). The problem also can arise, but is rare, in conspiracy and solicitation. See pages 317, 323 (c/l), 347, 352 (MPC).

Lesser Included Offense An offense of lesser gravity the elements of which are included within a more serious offense. Example: Assault is a lesser included offense to assault with intent to kill. A charge of the more serious offense will permit a conviction for any lesser included offense justified by the evidence. The Model Penal Code also provides for this result. See § 1.07(4).

M

Malice A common law mens rea term of many meanings. See page 79.

Malice Aforethought The mens rea required for murder at common law. It means neither "malice" nor "aforethought." See page 361.

Malum In Se An offense that is morally wrong. Most traditional offenses—murder, rape, assault, robbery, burglary, larceny—are malum in se.

Malum Prohibitum An offense that is not morally wrong, but that is punished in order to achieve necessary social order. Example: Going through a red light.

Manslaughter A grade of Criminal Homicide at common law, usually further divided into voluntary and involuntary manslaughter. See page 368.

Material Element A term used by the Model Penal Code to trigger its culpability requirements. See §§ 2.02(1), 1.13(10). See page 117.

Maximum Sentence A term used in two contexts: to refer to the maximum punishment that may be imposed for commission of a given crime; or the point at which the defendant must be released from prison after serving a particular sentence.

Mens Rea A generic term referring to the state of mind a defendant must have in order to commit a crime. A crime that does not require mens rea is said to be one of "strict liability." See page 76 (c/l), 109 (MPC). See also General Intent; Specific Intent; Strict Liability; and Knowledge; Negligence; Recklessness; Purpose.

Mental Disease or Defect A technical but ill-defined term used to describe a mental illness that can trigger the insanity defense. See page 226 (c/l), 235 (MPC).

Minimum Sentence A term used in numerous contexts, commonly to refer to a sentence that must be imposed for commission of a given crime or to refer to the parole eligibility date that accompanies a given maximum sentence.

Misdemeanor The least serious of the three classifications of offenses at common law (the other two: treason and felony). Today the usual demarcation is a penalty of one year or less to be served in a local jail, but this line is not universal.

Misdemeanor Manslaughter By analogy to Felony Murder, a situation where the defendant is guilty of manslaughter if a death occurs during the commission of a misdemeanor. See page 371. The Model Penal Code rejects the concept.

Mistake of Criminal Law Normally such a mistake is not a defense to crime. See page 154 (c/l), 176 (MPC).

Mistake of Fact Normally a mistake of fact is a defense if it negates a required element of mens rea. See page 147 (c/l), 172 (MPC).

Mistake of Non–Criminal Law Sometimes treated like a mistake of fact and sometimes like a mistake of criminal law. See page 159 (c/l), 180 (MPC).

M'Naghten Rules A common law test for the insanity defense, named after a famous case. See page 228.

Model Penal Code A proposed criminal code drafted by the American Law Institute and used as the basis for penal law revision and reform by both courts and legislatures. See page 63.

Motive The defendant's reason for acting. Sometimes motive matters and sometimes it doesn't. See page 83.

Murder The highest grade of Criminal Homicide at common law, divided into degrees in many jurisdictions. See page 361 (c/l), 376 (MPC).

N

Necessity See Choice of Evils.

Negligence A basis for assessing fault, turning on lack of foresight in a situation where the defendant should have foreseen. See page 79 (c/l), 114 (MPC).

Non-Deadly Force A term used in connection with justification defenses to refer to any force that is not deadly. See the definition of Deadly Force.

O

Object Offense A term frequently used to mean an offense that is the object of the defendant's attempt, solicitation, conspiracy, or complicity.

Omission An omission can be a sufficient criminal "act" under defined conditions. See page 74 (c/l), 106 (MPC).

Overt Act Sometimes a conspiracy is not a crime until an "overt act" is committed in furtherance of it. The requirement is not rigorous, however, and any old act will do. See page 312 (c/l), 341 (MPC).

P

Parole Release from prison, on conditions, prior to completion of the sentence imposed. Violation of the conditions will result in reimprisonment. The parole decision is usually made by a parole board established for that purpose. Eligibility for parole is determined in a number of ways. Commonly, it is determined either by the judge at sentencing or automatically as a statutorily stated percentage of the maximum sentence imposed.

Pathological Intoxication A term used by the Model Penal Code to mean a grossly excessive reaction to an intoxicant, considering the amount taken and assuming that the defendant does not know of a susceptibility to such a reaction. See page 181 and § 2.08(5)(c).

Pattern of Racketeering Activity One of the elements of RICO. See page 400.

Permissive Inference Permission for the finder of fact to draw an inference from one fact that another exists. The inference is "permissive" when it may, but need not be, drawn. See page 100.

Physical Proximity Test A test used to measure when one has gone beyond preparation and committed an attempt. See page 306.

***Pinkerton* Doctrine** A doctrine extending the liability of a co-conspirator beyond those offenses planned or contemplated to those that were "reasonably foreseeable." See page 321.

Possession Possession can be a sufficient criminal "act." See page 75 (c/l), 107 (MPC).

***Powell* Doctrine** The doctrine that the mens rea for conspiracy sometimes includes a "corrupt motive," that is, an intent to violate the law. See page 317.

Preponderance of the Evidence A standard of proof often used in criminal cases, usually when the burden of persuasion is shifted to the defendant on a given issue. See page 95.

Presentment A formal charge of crime filed by a grand jury on its own motion, that is, in a case where the prosecutor has not asked that an indictment be returned. See also Grand Jury; Indictment.

Presumption A confusing term of many meanings. It refers generally to evidentiary help given to a party who must prove a fact, usually permitting that party to do something less than prove the fact by the normal inferences drawn from evidence. In particular, a presumption can be "conclusive," as in Fact A is conclusively presumed from proof of Fact B. This means that proof of Fact B will establish that Fact A exists, or in effect that the proof requirement is redefined to substitute Fact B for Fact

A. It can be "rebuttable," as in Fact A will normally be assumed to exist when Fact B is proved, but the assumption can be disproved. This too can mean several things: (a) it can mean that when one party proves Fact B, the burden of persuasion to demonstrate that Fact A does not exist is shifted to the other party; (b) it can mean that when one party proves Fact B, the burden of production is shifted to the other party to produce evidence that Fact A does not exist; or (c) it can mean that when one party proves Fact B, that proof satisfies the burden of production and will justify (but not require) an inference by the jury that Fact A exists. Still a different meaning is given to the term by § 1.12(5) of the Model Penal Code. See page 98 (c/l), 134 (MPC). See also Burden of Persuasion; Burden of Production.

Presumption of Natural and Probable Consequences A confusing common law presumption, subject to all the ambiguities of meaning in the term "presumption." Basically, it refers to the fact that mens rea can be "presumed" from proof of conduct. See page 98.

Prevention See Deterrence.

Prima Facie Case The elements of a criminal case that must be proved by the prosecutor at the outset in order to justify submission of the guilt of the defendant to the jury. The prosecutor's prima facie case consists of the actus reus, the mens rea, any causation requirements, and any factors relevant to the grading of the offense charged. See page 94.

Primary Intent A fictional, imputed intent sometimes used in the common law analysis of an "impossibility" defense to an Inchoate Crime. It is the attribution of an intent to do what was done to a person who thought something else was being done. See page 308. Often contrasted to "Secondary Intent."

Principal in the First Degree The person at common law who committed the crime. See page 262.

Principal in the Second Degree An accomplice at common law who was physically or "constructively" present at the scene of the crime. See page 263.

Principle of Legality The principle that laws should be written down in advance of using them as the basis for criminal prosecution.

Probable Desistance Test A test used to measure when one has gone beyond preparation and committed an attempt. See page 307.

Probation The release of a convicted person for a prescribed time on stated conditions, usually without requiring that any imprisonment be served. Sometimes a short prison sentence must be served first, in which case it is called a "split sentence." Violation of the conditions of probation can be grounds for imprisonment.

Product Test A common law test for the insanity defense. See page 233.

Prosecutor The plaintiff in a criminal case, generally an elected official (at the state level) who is charged with representing the State in criminal matters. Sometimes called the District Attorney.

Provocation A common law doctrine having the effect of reducing murder to manslaughter. See page 369 (c/l), 378 (MPC).

Proximate Cause A common law term describing when one person can be said to have "caused" a result. See page 92.

Public Welfare Offense A minor offense, usually carrying strict liability, punished because of potential harm that might be caused to the social order by the conduct involved. The defendant is usually in a position to avoid the harm by the exercise of care. Also called a "regulatory offense." Examples: Traffic offenses, offenses relating to the purity of food and drugs, serving alcohol to a minor. See page 81. See also Violation.

Purpose One of the four culpability terms used by the Model Penal Code, meaning conscious purpose or desire. See page 109.

R

Rape See page 386.

Rape Shield Law A law limiting the admissibility of evidence concerning the sexual history of the complaining party in a rape trial. See page 392.

Rebuttable Presumption See Presumption.

Recklessness A basis for assessing fault, usually turning on the taking of a known risk. See page 78 (c/l), 112 (MPC).

Regulatory Offense See Public Welfare Offense.

Rehabilitation A term used to refer to efforts used to change the defendant's character so that future crimes will not be committed. Rehabilitation is often referred to as one of the traditional goals of punishment, though today many would suggest that punishment ought never to be imposed in order to achieve rehabilitation. Rehabilitation, the argument would be, is appropriate only within the limits of punishment justified for different reasons.

Res Gestae The facts and circumstances surrounding the commission of a crime, including those immediately before and after its commission.

Res Ipsa Loquitur Test A test used to measure when one has gone beyond preparation and committed an attempt. See page 307.

Result A consequence caused by the defendant's conduct. See page 90.

Retreat Something the defendant must sometimes do before using deadly force in self defense or defense of others. See pages 193, 195 (c/l), 212 (MPC).

Retribution Often mentioned as one of the traditional goals of punishment. The idea that people deserve to be punished for doing bad things. Retribution often operates as an important *limitation* on punishment as well, because it implies proportional punishment and punishment based on demonstrated fault. See page 52.

RICO A federal statute aimed at organized crime. See page 398.

Robbery See page 397.

S

Scienter A common law mens rea term of indeterminate meaning. It probably means "knowledge" most of the time. See page 79.

Secondary Intent Used in the analysis of impossibility situations in Inchoate Offenses by some common law courts and scholars. It is what the defendant thought was being done. See page 308. Contrast "Primary Intent."

Self Defense A justification defense available when one person harms or threatens another in defense of self. See page 191 (c/l), 211 (MPC).

Self-Induced Intoxication A term used by the Model Penal Code in lieu of "voluntary" intoxication. See page 181.

Sentence The sanction imposed following conviction for a crime, including a fine, probation, and/or imprisonment.

Social Control See Deterrence and page 52.

Solicitation An Inchoate Offense consisting of one person urging another to commit a crime. See page 322 (c/l), 351 (MPC).

Special Deterrence A term used to refer to the effect of a specific conviction and sentence in discouraging the defendant from committing crimes in the future. Special deterrence is one of the traditional goals of punishment. See also Deterrence; General Deterrence.

Specific Intent A generic term used by the common law to refer to the state of mind required for the commission of certain crimes. A "specific intent" crime requires that at the time of the offense the defendant be actually thinking or planning something specifically identified by the definition of the offense. See pages 76, 302.

Statutory Rape Sexual intercourse with an underage person. See page 390.

Strict Construction An attitude that some courts bring to the construction of criminal statutes. The idea is that criminal statutes should be narrowly construed so as not, in effect, to amount to retrospective punishment of conduct that was not a crime when committed.

Strict Liability The punishment of a crime without requiring mens rea as to one or more elements of the offense. See page 81 (c/l), 124 (MPC).

Substantial Capacity Test A term sometimes used to describe the Model Penal Code insanity test. It is not too helpful, because it does not tell you what one must have the substantial capacity to do. See page 236 for the answer.

Substantial Step The inquiry made by the Model Penal Code to determine when a person has passed beyond preparation and committed an attempt. It is an act that strongly corroborates the required intent. See page 334.

T

Theft A Model Penal Code crime consolidating many of the forms of stealing that were separately defined at common law. See page 392.

Transferred Intent A common law doctrine that punished a person who meant to harm one person but harmed another. See page 82. The Model Penal Code handles such cases in terms of causation. See page 129.

True Bill The technical name for the grand jury's action when it decides to return an indictment. A refusal to return an indictment is said to be "no true bill."

True Legal Impossibility A term used to describe a person who thinks something is a crime when it isn't, and is then prosecuted for an attempt, solicitation, or conspiracy to commit it. "True legal impossibility" is a defense in all American jurisdictions and under the Model Penal Code. See pages 307, 317, 323 (c/l), 335, 346, 352 (MPC).

V

Vagueness A constitutional doctrine requiring that criminal statutes have at least minimally clear meaning. See page 406.

Vicarious Liability The imposition of liability on one person for the conduct of another, based solely on a relationship between the two persons (such as employer and employee). See page 276 (c/l), 292 (MPC).

Violation A classification used by the Model Penal Code for public welfare offenses. A violation is not a crime. § 1.04(5). See page 124.

Volitional Test See Control Test.

Voluntary Act Every crime must include a "voluntary" act in the sense of some conduct that was the product of the defendant's will or determination. See page 143 (c/l), 172 (MPC). For consideration of the constitutional dimensions of the voluntary act requirement, see page 408.

Voluntary Intoxication The voluntary introduction of any substances into the body which the defendant knows or should know are likely to have intoxicating effects. The Model Penal Code uses the term "Self–Induced Intoxication" to refer to this idea. Evidence of voluntary or self-induced intoxication can be admitted in some circumstances but not others. See page 164 (c/l), 182 (MPC).

Voluntary Manslaughter A grade of Criminal Homicide at common law, usually consisting of conduct that would be murder but for extenuating circumstances like provocation or imperfect justification. See page 369.

W

Wanton A common law epithet often used to describe an egregious level of negligence or recklessness. See page 371.

Wharton's Rule The doctrine that forbids conviction for a conspiracy to commit a crime that itself requires more than one person to commit. See page 314 (c/l), 342 (MPC).

Wilful A common law mens rea term of indeterminate meaning. See page 79. The Model Penal Code defines it to mean "knowledge." § 2.02(8).

Wilful Blindness A term used to refer to a situation where the defendant tries to avoid knowing something that will incriminate. It is usually held in this situation that the defendant "knows" anyway. The Model Penal Code has a specific section on the point. See § 2.02(7) and page 111.

Wilful, Deliberate, and Premeditated A criterion used in many jurisdictions to separate first from second degree murder. See page 363. The Model Penal Code rejects the idea. See page 377.

Withdrawal A term used in connection with conspiracy to indicate that the defendant has had a change of heart and wants to "withdraw" from the enterprise. Withdrawal is not a defense at common law, but can affect the duration of the conspiracy and thus be of great importance. See page 321. Under the Model Penal Code, withdrawal (or abandonment) *can* be a defense, and also affects duration. See pages 347, 349. The term is also used in the context of self defense, where an initial aggressor seeks to "withdraw" from the affray. One who does so may then be eligible to assert self-defense as a defense. See page 192.

APPENDIX E

CORRELATION CHART

Criminal Law Black Letter Series	R. Boyce & R. Perkins, Criminal Law and Procedure: Cases and Materials, (8th ed., 1999)	G. Dix & M. Sharlot, Criminal Law: Cases and Materials, (5th ed., 2002)	P. Johnson & A.M. Cloud, Criminal Law: Cases, Materials and Text (7th ed., 2002)	S. Kadish & S. Schulhofer, Criminal Law and its Processes: Cases and Materials (7th ed., 2001)	W. LaFave, Modern Criminal Law: Cases, Comments and Questions (3d ed., 2001)	R. Bonnie, A. Coughlin, J. Jeffries and P. Low, Criminal Law: Cases and Materials (1997)
PERSPECTIVE		42-59		95-172	18-40	1-30
PART ONE: INTRODUCTION (General Considerations)		1-41				
PART TWO: THE DEFINITION OF CRIME	1-38	85-100; 156-366	1-84	173-312	41-253	31-215
PART THREE: DERIVATIVE DEFENSES	564-702	367-432	300-388; 572-594	35-54; 225-235; 585-602	113-253	141-148; 863-900
PART FOUR: COLLATERAL DEFENSES: JUSTIFICATIONS	805-892	753-847	389-508	749-841	491-580	325-398
PART FIVE: COLLATERAL DEFENSES: EXCUSES	703-1024	753-847	389-508	749-750; 842-950	491-580	399-418
PART SIX: PARTIES	487-509	688-752	683-726	723-729	794-899	565-632
PART SEVEN: INDHOATE CRIMES	380-474	614-687	614-726	554-584	647-793	216-267; 595-632
PART EIGHT: CRIMINAL HOMICIDE	39-154	433-539	167-299	387-516	254-377	657-862
PART NINE: OTHER CRIMES	182-189; 233-308; 441-474	571-613; 202-288	726-827	313-386; 730-748; 951-1030	581-646	268-323; 632-656
PART TEN: CONCLUSION (Constitutional Limits on Punishment for Crime)	1340-1448	60-128	52-166	493-516	99-103; 358-377	901-962

APPENDIX F

TABLE OF MODEL PENAL CODE REFERENCES